HIDDEN IN PLAIN SIGHT

Contributions of Aboriginal Peoples to Canadian Identity and Culture

Volume 1

Edited by David R. Newhouse, Cora J. Voyageur, and Dan Beavon

The history of Aboriginal people in Canada as taught in schools and depicted in the media tends to focus on Aboriginal displacement from Native lands and the social and cultural disruption that this displacement has entailed. Native people are often portrayed as passive victims of European colonization and government policy, a picture that, even when well intentioned, not only is demeaning but also does little to truly represent the role that Aboriginal peoples have played in Canadian life. *Hidden in Plain Sight* adds another dimension to the story, showing the extraordinary contributions that Aboriginal peoples have made – and continue to make – to the Canadian experience.

The volume is divided into several main sections, including Treaties, Arts and Media, Literature, Justice, Culture and Identity, Sports, and Military. Editors David R. Newhouse, Cora J. Voyageur, and Dan Beavon have brought together leading scholars and other authorities in their fields who explore and pay tribute to Aboriginal peoples' contribution to Canada's intellectual, political, economic, social, historic, and cultural landscapes. Also included are profiles of important figures such as actor Chief Dan George, artist Norval Morrisseau, author Tomson Highway, activist Anna Mae Pictou Aquash, and politician Phil Fontaine. The first of two illustrated volumes, this is a landmark work that will greatly enhance our understanding and appreciation of the heritage of Canada's Aboriginal peoples.

DAVID R. NEWHOUSE is an associate professor in the Department of Native Studies and the principal of Gzowski College at Trent University.

CORA J. VOYAGEUR is an associate professor in the Department of Sociology at the University of Calgary.

DAN BEAVON is the director of the Strategic Research and Analysis Directorate of Indian and Northern Affairs Canada.

D1430341

Hidden in Plain Sight

Contributions of Aboriginal Peoples to Canadian Identity and Culture

Edited by

DAVID R. NEWHOUSE
CORA J. VOYAGEUR
DAN BEAVON

UNIVERSITY OF TORONTO PRESS
Toronto Buffalo London

© University of Toronto Press Incorporated 2005
Toronto Buffalo London
Printed in the U.S.A.

Reprinted 2007, 2010, 2012

ISBN 0-8020-8800-7 (cloth)
ISBN 0-8020-8581-4 (paper)

Printed on acid-free paper

Library and Archives Canada Cataloguing in Publication

Hidden in plain sight : contributions of Aboriginal peoples to
    Canadian identity and culture / edited by David Newhouse, Cora
    Voyageur, Daniel Beavon.

   ISBN 0-8020-8800-7 (bound : v. 1).   ISBN 0-8020-8581-4 (pbk. : v. 1)

   1. Canada – Civilization – Indian influences.   2. Native peoples –
   Canada – Biography.   3. Native peoples – Canada – History.   4. Canada –
   Biography.   I. Newhouse, David   II. Voyageur, Cora Jane, 1956–
   III. Beavon, Daniel J.K.

   E78.C2H487 2005   971.004'97   C2005-901134-3

University of Toronto Press acknowledges the financial assistance to its publishing
program of the Canada Council and the Ontario Arts Council.

University of Toronto Press acknowledges the financial support for its publishing
activities of the Government of Canada through the Book Publishing Industry
Development Program (BPIDP).

This book is dedicated to
all those who came before
who made it possible for us to do what we do today
who believed that we can live lives of dignity and respect
who worked hard to achieve
in this new world

Contents

Preface

The most common things, like culverts, tend to be the most overlooked ... Shoulders, faces, twigs, sands, grass – they are the ordinary stuff of life. We see them and ignore them everyday. It struck me when writing the chapter on grass that if it hadn't been for this book, I might well have gone on ignoring grass my whole life. I have sat on grass, and mowed it and have picked it absentmindedly, and I have noticed it in passing when it grows too high on a neighbor's lawn. But before I sat down to write the chapter on grass, I had never really paid attention to it.

James Elkins, *How to Use Your Eyes* (New York: Routledge 2000), viii.

This text emerged from our common experience of working within universities and in the public sector, where we continually encounter notions about Indigenous peoples as highly resistant to change and where the discourse is dominated by what has come to be called the 'Indian Problem.' We take a different view. It is our hope that this book will add a new dimension to the picture of Aboriginal peoples, one that shows them to be industrious, meritorious, and accomplished. We want to help create a place of respect and dignity for Aboriginal peoples in Canada.

A few years ago I taught a third-year university class in Aboriginal governance at Trent University. The class was an exploration of the ideas that animate contemporary Aboriginal political and social collective action. In the early part of the year, I asked students to list adjectives that described Aboriginal peoples. The list we generated was filled with words depicting poverty, dispossession, anger, marginalization, and hostility, the principal traits of a community underoing great pain and suffering and struggling to maintain a way of life against great odds. Not emerging from the first round of discussion were words such as creative, innovative, persistent, artistic, assertive, or strong-willed. That same year, I conducted an informal survey of fourth-year business students and first-year Native studies students. I asked them to identify what contributions Aboriginal peoples have made to

Canada. Both groups of students had great difficulty in identifying any contribution. The most common responses involved land (mostly from Aboriginal students) and natural resources. A few identified place names, the canoe, green spirituality, and tobacco. One insightful student said that the Aboriginal peoples' contribution to Canada was, 'Canada itself, all of it, lock, stock and barrel.'

David Newhouse, Onondaga
Chair and Associate Professor, Department of Native Studies,
Trent University

In my own teaching, I have encountered the same attitude about Aboriginal peoples as described above. Colleagues in other post-secondary institutions who teach courses with Aboriginal content also echo this experience. Few students know any Aboriginal people and are entirely unaware of any contributions they have made to our country. It seems that mainstream society has little face-to-face contact with Aboriginal peoples. Most are fed a steady diet of media clips and sound bites that describe a people in conflict with society. This type of coverage does little to encourage interaction between Aboriginal peoples and mainstream society.

In one of my university courses, students must write a research paper that profiles an Aboriginal person who has made a significant contribution to Canadian society. At first, the students look terrified. They simply do not know any Aboriginal people – let alone a smart one, an accomplished one, or a famous one. Over the term, more and more notable Aboriginal individuals are included in the curriculum. The students begin to breathe a bit easier. They learn that there are many more distinguished Aboriginal Canadians than just Elijah Harper and Buffy Sainte-Marie. They also learn that there is much more to Aboriginal people and the Aboriginal community than they encounter in the media. On this note, I am proud to say that students from my undergraduate sociology of First Nations class at the University of Calgary supplied most of the profiles highlighted in this publication.

The profiles present the accomplishments of Aboriginal individuals in a wide array of sectors, including the arts, economic development, the universities, politics, the treaty process, justice, and many others. The students had difficulty condensing the accomplishments of these individuals into the 500-word limit set by the editors. Such abbreviated texts hardly begin to capture the essence of their gifted subjects.

Cora J. Voyageur, Chipewyan
Associate Professor, Department of Sociology, University of Calgary

In my own work as a public servant, I encounter the 'Indian problem' and its consequences on a daily basis. Public-policy research is dominated by an attempt to solve the problems of Aboriginal poverty, marginalization, low labour-force status, and poor health. While there is much work that needs to be done to resolve these issues, there is much more to the story of Aboriginal peoples. Indeed, concentration on the negative produces a distorted view in which Indians are portrayed as a people unable to do things for themselves or of proposing solutions to problems. Canadian society is diminished by the seemingly permanent burden represented by this view. We propose a new image of Aboriginal people – as we hope this text demonstrates.

Dan Beavon, Director
Strategic Research and Analysis Directorate
Indian and Northern Affairs Canada (INAC)

The Genesis of This Book

The chapters in this text are responses to a call for papers that we issued through a variety of networks – academic, public service, community – in the summer of 1999. We asked people to write about Aboriginal achievement and contribution to Canada. What we received surprised us. In all, there were about fifty responses to our call, many more than we could accommodate in a single volume. These papers detailed an extraordinary set of contributions ranging from the aesthetic, such as Mi'kmaq influence on early east coast furniture making, to indigenizing aspects of the Canadian justice system and what we regard as the most significant contribution of them all: the largest transfer of land from Aboriginal possession to Canada through the treaties. It is hard to argue for a more fundamental and central contribution. Without the treaties, Canada would not be Canada.

We organized the papers into the large groupings that form this volume, placing those that dealt with similar issues and contributions together. A second volume will contain those papers that we were unable to publish in this volume. We also decided that we would personalize the text by adding a series of small profiles of people we considered to have made outstanding contributions. This proved to be no easy task. We eventually chose individuals who, in our view, exemplified the achievements outlined in each section. As we prepared lists of Aboriginal people as possible candidates for these profiles, we were amazed at the level of achievement and the large number of people to choose from. We hope that those whom we were unable to profile will forgive us for leaving them out and that those who are profiled will see themselves as standing in a field also occupied by many others.

Acknowledgments

This book could not have been produced without the untiring efforts of many people. First, the book was shaped by the contributions of representatives of federal government departments and national Aboriginal organizations who served on an advisory committee and provided many of the initial ideas on how to develop this project, as well as suggestions on various topics that we might include in it. Among these individuals were Sharon Jeannotte, Pierre Beaudreau, Vivian Gray, Glen Morrison, Peter Williamson, Gail Valaskakis, Christina Delguste, Melissa Lazore, Ryan Moran, and Rebecca McPhail. Second, the initial call for papers and the selection of authors were coordinated by Maurice Obonsawin. Third, two summer students, Christine Armstrong and Valerie Green, did considerable background research and coordinated the work of the various authors. Fourth, staff within the Strategic Research and Analysis Directorate, Indian and Northern Affairs Canada (INAC), contributed substantial time and effort with respect to this project. These staff included John Clement, who contacted authors about their submissions; Paula Saunders, who worked on the initial call for papers; Cynthia Davidson, who performed the myriad administrative tasks necessary to get the manuscript into print; and, most important, Beverlee Moore, who managed the overall project and kept everyone on track. Fifth, senior bureaucrats at INAC – namely, Victoria de la Ronde and Sandra Ginnish – supported the development of this book. Finally, students from Cora Voyageur's classes at the University of Calgary prepared the short biographies of famous Aboriginal people. We are indebted to all of the individuals mentioned above for their support and assistance. Above all, however, this book could not have been produced without the thousands of Aboriginal people who have worked tirelessly, ceaselessly, and continuously over the past century to create better lives for future generations.

Contributors

Kateri Akiwenzie-Damm is an Anishinabe writer of mixed ancestry from the Chippewa of Nawash First Nation. She lives and works at Neyaashi-inigmiing, Cape Croker Reserve, on the Saugeen peninsula in southwestern Ontario. Her writing has been published in various anthologies, journals, and magazines in Canada, the United States, Aotearoa/New Zealand, Australia, and Germany and in the collection *My Heart Is a Stray Bullet*. A cd of her spoken word poetry, *Standing Ground*, with music by Indigenous collaborators as well as an anthology of erotica by Indigenous writers collected and edited by Akiwenzie-Damm, was released in March 2004. A choral music piece with lyrics by her and composed by Timothy Sullivan was first performed in October 2003 by the Bell'Arte Singers and toured in 2004. Currently, she is completing work on a collection of poetry; a collection of short stories; and various multidisciplinary and publishing projects. She guest-edited an issue of Rampike Literary and Arts magazine (an issue featuring the work of Indigenous writers); and co-edited *Skins: Contemporary Indigenous Writing*, an award-winning international anthology of fiction by Indigenous writers co-published by Kegedonce Press and the Aboriginal Australian publisher Jukurrpa Books in late 2000. She is the founder and managing editor of Kegedonce Press.

A strong advocate of Indigenous publishing and literature, Akiwenzie-Damm is a former member of the National Caucus of the WordCraft Circle of Native Writers and Storytellers and actively works with other Indigenous publishers and writers internationally to nurture, expand, and promote Indigenous publishing and writing.

Valerie Alia is professor of ethics and identity at the Leslie Silver International Faculty of Leeds Metropolitan University, senior associate of the Scott Polar Research Institute of Cambridge University, and author of *Media Ethics and Social Change*; *Un/Covering the North: News, Media, and*

Aboriginal People and the CBC 'Ideas' documentary *Nunavut: Where Names Never Die*; and co-author with Simone Bull of *Media and Ethnic Minorities*. Before moving to England in 1999, she was the inaugural Distinguished Professor of Canadian Culture at Western Washington University. She has a PhD in social and political thought from York University. Her photography has featured in exhibitions, and her poetry and essays have won prizes in Canada and the United States. Alia is listed in *Who's Who in the World* and *Canadian Who's Who*.

Jeannette C. Armstrong is from the Penticton Indian band of the Okanagan Nation. She is a graduate of the University of Victoria and founder/ executive director of the En'owkin Centre, founded in 1979 to preserve, perpetuate, and promote Okanagan knowledge education. A renowned visual artist, activist, educator, and author, she is a highly sought-after speaker and consultant who travels around the world speaking on Native issues. She was recently awarded an honorary doctorate by St Thomas University, Fredericton. She is an advocate of a healthy environment and social change, in which peace between all peoples is central, and has served as consultant to many environmental and social-justice organizations.

Morgan Baillargeon is a Metis from southwestern Ontario. For several years, he taught traditional Native art in schools in Cree and Metis communities in central and northern Alberta. Since 1992, has been the curator of Plains ethnology at the Canadian Museum of Civilization. He has curated several exhibitions at the museum, including *Legends of Our Times: Native Ranching and Rodeo Life on the Plains and Plateau*; *The New Nation – the Metis*; *Social Gatherings, Feasts, and Competitive Events*; and *Moccasins*. He has also published numerous articles on Aboriginal cowboys and is co-author (with Leslie H. Tepper and the staff of the Canadian Museum of Civilization) of *Legends of Our Times: Native Cowboy Life*. He has recently received his doctorate in the Religious Studies Department at the University of Ottawa, with a focus on Plains Cree beliefs pertaining to death and the afterlife.

Russel Lawrence Barsh has worked for First Nations on both sides of the 49th parallel since taking his law degree at Harvard in 1974. His longest and strongest links have been with the Mi'kmaq Nation in Atlantic Canada and the Samish and other Coast Salish peoples of the Seattle and Vancouver areas, but he has also represented the Oglala Sioux in disputes over sacred sites, taught on the Blood Reserve in Alberta, served as an adviser to the treaty commissioner in Saskatchewan and as legislative adviser to

American Indian tribes in Washington, D.C., and studied wildlife ecology and nutrition on Kodiak Island, Alaska, and in the Canadian Arctic. As well, he has been involved in the work of the United Nations on Indigenous peoples' rights and development, including field evaluations in developing countries. His international experience has made him more aware of the particularities of Aboriginal peoples' situation within Canada and of the particularities of Canadian political culture. He is currently the director of a Coast Salish marine-conservation program in the San Juan and Gulf Islands, and lives on Samish Island, Washington State.

Michael Cassidy was born in Victoria, British Columbia, and grew up in Toronto. After studies in political science and economics at the University of Toronto, he began his career as a journalist, working with the Canadian Press, the British Broadcasting Corporation, and the Birmingham *Post* and as Ottawa bureau chief of the *Financial Times of Canada* during the late 1960s.

Cassidy taught journalism at Carleton University in 1970–1 and then moved into politics, where he was successively a member of Ottawa City Council, MPP for Ottawa Centre, leader of the Ontario New Democratic Party, and MP and finance critic in the federal NDP caucus from 1984 to 1988.

After the 1988 election, Cassidy established himself as a consultant in public affairs and president of Ginger Group Consultants. For the past ten years he has been primarily involved with research and policy relating to Aboriginal issues, including two years of policy research with the Royal Commission on Aboriginal Peoples. He recently retired from the Treaty Policy Directorate of Indian and Northern Affairs Canada and has returned to work as a consultant.

He and his wife, Maureen, have three adult sons and two grandsons now in their teens. Formerly on the board of the Schizophrenia Society of Canada, Cassidy sings in two choirs, does carpentry at his country cabin outside Ottawa, and is active in Ottawa's First Unitarian Congregation.

Katherine Beaty Chiste is an associate professor of management at the University of Lethbridge and a former director of its Aboriginal Management Program. Her research and publication interests include constitutional law, alternative justice measures, and Aboriginal entrepreneurship. She is grateful to students in Management 3591, 'Managing Alternative Justice Systems,' for their vibrant, ongoing discussions of the issues explored in her chapter.

Jane L. Cook, former visiting professor at the McGill Institute for the Study of Canada, completed post-doctoral work investigating First Nations' furniture making as a research associate at the McCord Museum of Canadian History. Her book *Coalescence of Styles* examines immigrants in the Saint John River valley and their furniture heritage. She acknowledges the assistance of the Canadian Ethnic Studies program and the Social Sciences and Humanities Research Council of Canada in funding her initial studies.

Bryan Cummins is a cultural anthropologist whose research interests include the Native peoples of North America, the eastern Subarctic, rural Europe, land tenure and land use, ethnographic film and photography, and the anthropology of religion. He has a BA (Honours) in anthropology and history from Trent University, an MA (education) from Concordia University, and an MA and PhD from McMaster University.

Cummins is the author of *The Working Airedale* (1994); *Only God Can Own the Land: The Attawapiskat Cree, the Land and the State in the 20th Century* (1999); *Airedales – The Oorang Story* (2001); *First Nations, First Dogs – Canadian Aboriginal Ethnocynology* (2002); *Faces of the North: The Ethnographic Photography of John Honigmann* (2004); and *The Terriers of Scotland and Ireland* (2003). He is also the co-author (with John Steckley) of *Full Circle: Canada's First Nations* (2001), *Aboriginal Policing – A Canadian Perspective* (2002), and *The Ethnographic Experience* (2005).

Maria von Finckenstein is currently the curator of contemporary Inuit art at the Canadian Museum of Civilization. After studying art history in Germany and at McGill University, she began working in the area of Inuit art in 1979 when she was hired as the curator of the Inuit art collection of Indian and Northern Affairs Canada. In that capacity, she produced and collaborated on a number of travelling exhibitions. She is a frequent contributor to the *Inuit Art Quarterly* and in 1999 authored *Celebrating Inuit Art: 1948–1970*, co-published by Key Porter and the Canadian Museum of Civilization. She recently published *Nuvisavik: The Place Where We Weave* (2002), a monograph on Pangnirtung tapestries.

Bruce W. Hodgins, PhD, LLD, is an emeritus professor of history at Trent University, Peterborough, where he taught from 1965 to 1996. He has written widely on the Canadian north, on Aboriginal-settler relations in Canada, Australia, and New Zealand, on the canoe in Canadian cultures, and on Canadian federalism (including its evolving Aboriginal 'Third Order'). With Jamie Benidickson, he co-authored *The Temagami Experience* (1989) and has long been closely associated with the Teme-Augama Anishnabai land-claim negotiations. He and his wife, Carol, are northern canoe trip leaders with Wanapitei on Lake Temagami. For almost two decades, he has also been significantly involved with the Canadian Canoe Museum in Peterborough.

Cheryl Isaacs is a freelance writer currently living and working in Hamilton, Ontario. She has a particular interest in Native, minority, and literacy issues and explores these themes in her writings. She has written for government, book and magazine publishers, and non-profit ventures, and is also a long-term board member of Sacajawea, a non-profit housing organization for Native families in the Hamilton area. Through her work, Isaacs hopes to continue to make contributions to the Native community by increasing awareness of issues important to Native people across Canada.

Carol LaPrairie received her MA in criminology from the Centre of Criminology, University of Toronto, and her PhD in sociology from the University of British Columbia. She worked for the federal government for over twenty-two years both in the Department of Justice and in the Ministry of the Solicitor General. She has conducted research and published extensively in the area of Aboriginal criminal justice. During her years in government, she has been seconded by the James Bay Cree (Quebec), the Yukon Territory's Justice Department, the Ministry of the Attorney General in Nova Scotia, and Saskatchewan's Department of Justice to work on Aboriginal criminal justice issues. She was also the principal investigator for a study of Aboriginal peoples in the inner city cores of Edmonton, Regina, Toronto, and Montreal. She has worked on the evaluation of the Sentencing Reform Act and the Toronto Drug Treatment Court, and was also on secondment to the National Crime Prevention Centre in Ottawa. At present she is a consulting criminologist in Vancouver.

Gerald McMaster is deputy assistant director for cultural resources and director's special assistant for mall exhibitions for the Smithsonian Institutions's National Museum of the American Indian in Washington, D.C., where he oversees the curatorial, repatriation, and archival departments. As well, he is involved in producing the permanent exhibitions, co-editing the museum's 2004 commemorative book 'The Native Universe,' and contributing to the content development of the museum's inaugural films.

McMaster left his position as curator-in-charge of the Canadian Museum of Civilization's First Peoples Hall in 2000; before that, he was the museum's curator of contemporary Indian art, and in that capacity he produced many major exhibitions from 1981 to 2000. His awards and recognitions include the 2001 ICOM-Canada Prize for contributions to national and international museology, and selection as Canadian commissioner of the XLVI 1995 Biennale di Venezia. Originally from Saskatchewan, McMaster holds a PhD from the University of Amsterdam as well as degrees from the Institute of American Indian Arts, the Minneapolis College of Art and Design, and Carleton University.

David T. McNab is a Metis historian who has worked on Aboriginal land and treaty-rights issues for more than two decades. A graduate of Waterloo Lutheran University (Honours BA), McMaster University (MA), and the University of Lancaster, England (PhD), he is currently a professor of Native studies in the School of Arts and Letters, Atkinson Faculty of Liberal and Professional Studies, York University, and a claims adviser for Nin.Da. Waab.Jig, the Walpole Island Heritage Centre, Bkejwanong First Nations. He also teaches in the Department of Native Studies at Trent University. In addition to more than fifty articles published in scholarly journals, he has edited and published six books, including *Earth, Water, Air and Fire: Studies in Canadian Ethnohistory* (1998), *Circles of Time: Aboriginal Land Rights and Resistance in Ontario* (1999), *Blockades and Resistance: Studies in Actions of Peace and the Temagami Blockades of 1988–89* (2003), and *Walking a Tightrope: Aboriginal People and Their Representations* (2005), all published by Wilfrid Laurier University Press, with whom he is now general series co-editor of the Aboriginal Studies Series.

Marybelle Mitchell is executive director of the Inuit Art Foundation, which she established in 1987. She is also the founding editor of the *Inuit Art Quarterly*, the only periodical dedicated to the art of the Inuit, now in its twentieth year of publication. Mitchell lived in the Arctic in the mid-1960s and has worked with Inuit artists for over thirty years, ten of them as manager of arts and crafts development for the Inuit cooperatives in Nunavik. She has a PhD in sociology and is an adjunct professor in the Department of Sociology and Anthropology at Carleton University in Ottawa. She has written extensively on Inuit art, cooperatives, and northern development issues, and she is the author of *From Talking Chiefs to a Native Corporate Elite: The Birth of Class and Nationalism among Canadian Inuit*, published by McGill-Queen's University Press in 1996.

Jean-Pierre Morin holds an MA in Canadian history from the University of Ottawa. Upon graduation, he joined Indian and Northern Affairs Canada and since 2000 he has been the resident historian of the department's Treaty Policy Directorate.

David Newhouse, an Onondaga from the Six Nations of the Grand River, is associate professor of native studies and business administration at Trent University, Peterborough. He has served as chair of Trent's University's Department of Native Studies for ten years and is now principal of Gzowski College at that university.

Bryan Poirier, MA, is a PhD candidate in geography at the University of Guelph and served formerly as the education coordinator at the Canadian Canoe Museum in Peterborough, Ontario. As a canoeing instructor, guide, rescue technician, and wilderness emergency medical technician, he has spent considerable time in recent years working in the outdoors, primarily in Ontario and Quebec and most recently in the Northwest Territories. With Bruce Hodgins, he has co-instructed a community-education course at Trent University on 'The Canoe and Canoeing in Canadian Cultures.'

J. Rick Ponting is a sociology professor at the University of Calgary. Born in Welland, Ontario, he received his BA in sociology from the University of Western Ontario and his MA and PhD in sociology from Ohio State University, writing his PhD dissertation on 'Rumour Control Centres as Intermittent Organizations: A Study of a Neglected Organizational Type.' His research focuses on race relations (primarily First Nations), social issues, Alberta society, Canadian society, and public policy.

Gillian Poulter is assistant professor of Canadian history in the Department of History and Classics at Acadia University, Wolfville, Nova Scotia. Her doctoral dissertation is entitled 'Becoming Native in a Foreign Land: Visual Culture, Sport, and Spectacle in the Construction of National Identity in Montreal, 1840–1885' (York University 2000). She is currently researching the contribution of women to nation-building through the home arts.

R. Scott Sheffield was educated at the University of Victoria with a BA and an MA in history. Though his background had initially been in military history, he became interested in Aboriginal history at the MA level, when he wrote a thesis on the government policies affecting Indian recruitment, registration, and conscription during the Second World War. Moving on from this foundation, Sheffield undertook doctoral studies in the Tri-University PhD program in History at Wilfrid Laurier University. His dissertation explored English-Canadians' collective image of the 'Indian' from 1930 to 1948. It forms the basis for a manuscript, now undergoing peer review for publication, entitled 'The Red Man's on the War Path: The Image of the 'Indian' and the Second World War.' He is currently a sessional instructor at the University of Victoria and is researching dominant-society constructions of Indigenous peoples in British settler societies.

Drew Hayden Taylor is an award-winning Ojibwa playwright and writer from the Curve Lake First Nation, north of Peterborough. He is the author of thirteen books ranging in genre from short stories to humorous articles and plays. He has also written for television and directed documentaries, most recently *Redskins, Tricksters and Puppy Stew*, an exploration of Native humour. At the age of forty-two, he is waiting to be inspired by what the world will throw at him next.

Gail Guthrie Valaskakis, PhD, is director of research at the Aboriginal Healing Foundation and professor emeritus at Montreal's Concordia University, where she chaired the Department of Communications Studies and served as dean of the Faculty of Arts and Science. She is the recipient of a 2002 National Aboriginal Achievement Foundation award for media and communications.

Cora J. Voyageur is a sociology professor at the University of Calgary. She holds a PhD from the University of Alberta, where her dissertation examined Aboriginal employment and employment equity in Canada. Her research focuses on the Aboriginal experience in Canada, including leadership, employment, women's issues, and the media. She is a member of the Athabasca Chipweyan First Nation at Fort Chipweyan, Alberta.

PART ONE

SETTING THE STAGE

Introduction

John Ralston Saul, writing in *Reflections of a Siamese Twin Canada at the end of the Twentieth Century*, argues that Canada is founded upon three pillars: English, French, and Aboriginal. There has been little recognition of the third group as a pillar or as a foundational group: Canada has not yet come to terms with its Aboriginal heritage. In the history books of the last four decades, Aboriginal peoples appear at the start, and then disappear, only to pop up again like prairie gophers, as welcome as those creatures and just as much a nuisance. It is no wonder that students are unable to articulate Aboriginal contributions to Canada since the dominate idea they encounter, through schools and the media, is that Aboriginal people are a problem that needs to be solved. The third pillar, then, is seen as needing to be propped up by the other two.

We are happy to report that the results of the last two decades of work on Aboriginal history is slowly starting to find its way into Canadian history texts. There is now a general recognition that Aboriginal peoples have been present in Canada since Confederation, that the treaties were important (though they are not yet seen as central) to Canada being what it is, and that the Canadian state has treated Aboriginal peoples unfairly, with a high degree of dishonesty and ill will. We are hopeful that, as Aboriginal history becomes more prominent in overall Canadian history, the beliefs of the past can be overcome. Yet at this time we must still deal with the continuing legacy of the 'Indian Problem.'

The burning issue since the establishment of settler governments in Canada has been what to do with the Indians. Governments over the years have subscribed to different versions of the 'Indian Problem.' The problem was seen in many ways: how to persuade us to join military alliances, how to civilize us, how to assimilate us, how to eliminate us or how to have us integrate into Canada's multicultural environment. Each variation on the 'Indian Problem' has led to a particular set of actions by the state. At the dawn of the twentieth century, the prevailing view was that Indians would simply disappear. However, until they did disappear, the task became how to deal with this 'weird and waning race.' As we all know, the Indians did not disappear as predicted; the population has increased over the twentieth century. The question for us now is: What is the Indian problem as we move through the twenty-first century?

A confident, aggressive, savvy, educated, and experienced leadership has emerged in Aboriginal communities over the past three decades. This leadership is highly skilled and knows both how to push hard and how to get what it wants. Behind the leadership is an ever-growing cadre of thousands of Aboriginal professionals who have gained post-secondary credentials and workplace experience in mainstream and Aboriginal communities. These professionals are slowly moving into decision-making positions and are effecting change. Behind them are thousands of students who are currently in post-secondary educational institutions across the country. Over the next few decades, these individuals will also be moving into leadership positions. As a whole, they are well-educated, and courageous, determined to achieve a better world for themselves and for their children. Many of them see Aboriginal self-government within their grasp. They have experienced aspects of self-government in many fields, such as education, health care, economic development, social work, housing, and cultural and language programs. The members of this highly educated group have a different understanding of the world than those who came before them. They are now imbued with a sense of the fundamental condition of modern Aboriginal society; that is, they have developed a post-colonial consciousness. It is a society that understands that it has been colonized in many ways; a society that is aware of the implications of its colonization and that is choosing deliberately, consciously, and systematically to deal with that colonization; a society that is coming to terms with what has happened to it; and a society determined to overcome its colonial past. It is a society that is pulling together the knowledge and creating the wealth to effect changes in Canada and in Canadian governments' treatment of Aboriginal peoples.

Post-colonial consciousness will be the defining political and social force within Aboriginal society over the next generation. Post-colonial Indians are angry and want to dismantle the master's house – or at least renovate it to accommodate their desires more easily. This demand for change, arising out of post-colonial consciousness, brings a number of challenges for Canadians. One challenge will be finding ways to change the governing structures and institutions of Canada to accommodate Aboriginal governance. Accomplishing this will require broad public support and a will to accommodate Aboriginal aspirations.

The report of the Royal Commission on Aboriginal Peoples (RCAP) rec-ommended a major-public education effort aimed at helping Canadian cit-izens understand Aboriginal aspirations, cultures, communities, and ways of living. This is an issue that is too often neglected. We sometimes forget that this broader understanding must develop within a Canadian society that has had a hard time coming to terms with a continued Aboriginal presence, let alone a post-colonial one that is insistent upon being seen and heard. Garnering public support means changing the views that the public holds of Aboriginal peoples.

Over the years, our students have become frustrated with stories of Aboriginal pain and suffering. They tell us that they know this story; in some cases, Aboriginal students have lived it. They want to create a new story. This is the challenge before us as Aboriginal peoples, educators, pub-lic servants, and even ordinary Canadians. How do we create a new story about Aboriginal peoples – a story of talent, competence, accomplishment, and hope? This book is a story of Aboriginal contributions to Canadian society. It is a more balanced story than the story that has prevailed so far – it acknowledges success. It is part of the new story that is being written and has many parts.

Part of the story is about politics. There is a political vision of Canada that includes Aboriginal peoples as partners in Confederation, that believes that Aboriginal peoples should share in the abundance of resources of this country and be treated justly, fairly, and respectfully. This vision was set out explicitly in the report of the RCAP. The commission proposed a solution that changed the relationship between Canada and Aboriginal peoples so as to reconstitute Aboriginal Nations and their gov-ernments. It also recommended that a third order of government in Can-ada be created to enable Aboriginal peoples to govern themselves. The RCAP proposed that the process of Confederation continue until Aborigi-nal peoples are included as full and charter members of Canadian society.

A second part of the story is about Aboriginal societies. This sets the context and foundation of modern Aboriginal society as confident, aggres-sive, assertive, determined, and desirous of creating a new world. Modern Aboriginal society is creating this new world from both Aboriginal and western ideas.

A third part of the story is about history. History is the official story that we tell ourselves, about ourselves, regarding past events. Today, we con-ceive of history as consisting of many stories. In a postmodern age, the idea of one master narrative that tells the authoritative story is losing ground; one narrative simply is not complex enough to present the multitude of stories that we must now consider. The introduction to a popular 1950s television show noted that 'there are eight million stories in the naked city.' Similarly, there are millions of Aboriginals stories to add to the social and political construction of how we understand this country called Canada.

History is also the story that tells us who we are, where we came from, what we did, and why we did what we did, and sometimes, too, it tries to tell us where we are going. History defines us and makes us human. In fact, some might say that the ability to think historically, to link the past with present, and to speculate on possible futures is a fundamental characteristic of humanity.

History is also a continuing story that changes our understanding of ourselves. Our increased knowledge means that we can ask different questions about the past. Stories can change with time and with perspective. Yet we must not forget that not all stories are given equal time. Not all stories are heard and acknowledged. We cannot separate history from power. There was a time in history when only those with the ability to write could document events. It is still a fact that those who have power are able to write their version of the story and to have it accepted as 'truth.' However, the Aboriginal story is only beginning to be told. Telling it from our perspective is difficult because we do not have power to make others listen. But why should it be so difficult to extend the rafters, to use an Iroquoian term, to include these Aboriginal stories? Whose story is challenged by the inclusion of Aboriginal ones?

It seems that, at this moment in Canada's history, two intellectual projects should be of interest. The first is the 'visibility project.' This means a critical examination and rewriting of Canadian history that ensures the visibility of Aboriginal peoples. The British and French response to the presence of Aboriginal peoples is what currently defines Canada. Aboriginal participation in the formation of Canada is ignored. Without the treaty process, which transferred most of the Canadian land mass from Aboriginal control to Canadian control, Canada would not exist in its present form. In addition, the state would not possess the wealth and benefits derived from the natural resources found in that land mass. A significant portion of the history of Canada is defined by its relationship to the Aboriginal peoples within its borders. To ignore that ongoing relationship is to render Aboriginal peoples out of existence. Canada simply would not be Canada without us.

The second project is the 'tribal history project.' This means writing histories of Aboriginal communities through tribal/national/community effort. For example, despite all the scholarship, there are only a few histories of Aboriginal communities written by community members. If we view history as the way in which we come to understand ourselves through our past, then this project is critical for Aboriginal peoples. As Aboriginal peoples, we must begin to understand ourselves through histories that we create. If not, then we continue to let others define us and we remain in the same place we are now – extraneous to Canadian society and a burden for it as well.

These tribal histories already exist in every community and Aboriginal nation across the country. They are not simply the oral histories resident in the minds of a few old people and elders; rather, they are contained within the songs, dances, rituals, and ceremonies of many cultural groups. These things tell the history of a particular group and people in the same way that written histories do.

It is this second project that we think is the most important at this time and the most intellectually challenging. We ask, 'What does it mean to write a tribal/national/community history from Aboriginal perspectives?'[1] We think that this project provides an opportunity for others to see the humanity of Aboriginal peoples. In pursing it, we will portray ourselves as active agents in attempting to live in the world in which we find ourselves. We will challenge the notion that Aboriginal peoples will simply lay down and allow the steamroller of Western civilization to crush us into the ground as it moves across the land.

One of the most interesting intellectual undertakings within contemporary Aboriginal communities today is the attempt to establish a solid philosophical framework for Aboriginal societal collective action based upon ideas from traditional world-views, ways of living, and spiritualities. Can Aboriginal peoples use traditional prophecies as the interpretative framework for tribal/national/community histories? For example, the Anishnaabe prophecy of the seven fires tells us that we will almost lose our culture and languages before a revival or the eighth fire is lit. Can we interpret the events of the past century as part of the seventh fire, as part of a dark age before the renaissance and enlightenment? If so, then we can interpret all that has happened as a necessity to be endured. But is it wrong to give people hope that an eighth and final fire, promising everlasting peace, will soon arrive? How different is this Anishnaabe prophecy from the Christian teachings, which tell us that we are now in a time of waiting for the Second Coming? Or how different is this prophecy from its secular equivalent – the idea of progress? All interpretations give hope to human beings that a better world is coming, and with this hope we acquire the strength we need to get up each morning and face the day.

The RCAP laid out its conception of the history of the relationship between Aboriginal peoples and the newcomers as having four distinct evolutionary phases: (1) separate worlds; (2) contact and cooperation; (3) displacement and assimilation; and (4) negotiation and renewal. Is this how we see our shared history on this continent? Do we all agree that we are in the negotiation and renewal phase? Some might argue that we are still in the assimilation and displacement phase. Yet, despite this debate, we must ask ourselves whether the RCAP's interpretative framework holds. Does anything come after the negotiation and renewal phase? Will it be, as the RCAP implies, sweetness, light, and a better world?

Olive Dickason, a Metis scholar, and winner of the National Aboriginal Achievement Award, writes in her seminal text, *Canada's First Nations:A History of Founding Peoples from Earliest Times*, that the themes of persistence of identity and the adaptability of Aboriginal peoples are the keys to understanding Aboriginal history. We admit that we like that interpretative framework. It resonates within us just as it probably resonates within most Aboriginal peoples. Is this the story that we will come to tell ourselves? That we are people of persistence, adaptability, and strength who have survived much and who are forging a new life for ourselves in a much changed land? It certainly is a story very different from the one found in Canadian history texts. Yet, even so, we think that by embracing this story we are falling into the trap of looking for only one narrative that makes sense of it all. Surely, we want complexity in our history rather than just a simple story? We, too, need to stop and remind ourselves that we live in a pluralistic world – even within Aboriginal communities. A traditional Anishnaabe person might write a history that is very different from one written by a Metis scholar or a Mohawk lawyer.

As mentioned earlier, history consists of the stories that we tell ourselves about past events. But what happens when a story is incorrectly told, or when a story is missing altogether? When significant parts are missing, then the story is incomplete and understanding is skewed. If the story is incorrectly told, then our understanding of ourselves is erroneous. However, if there is no story at all, then humanity is denied. We do have opportunities and, we believe, responsibilities to fill in omitted story segments, to correct the stories that are inaccurate, and to include missing stories. In doing so, we acknowledge the humanity of Aboriginal peoples.

This book is an attempt to add to the story of Canada by making visible Aboriginal contributions to Canada in a wide variety of areas. We have entitled the collection *Hidden in Plain Sight* because what these commentators have written about has been in front of us all along. Canadian society has simply been unable or unwilling to see it.

We also recognize that there is a continuing debate within the broader Aboriginal communities about Canada and its relationship with Aboriginal peoples. Some Aboriginal peoples see themselves as part of Canada. For example, recall the Inuit who, on the occasion of the establishment of

Nunavut, who referred to themselves as 'Mothers and Fathers of Confederation.' Similarly, Chief Joseph Gosnell, upon the ratification of the Nisga'a Treaty on 13 April 2000, proclaimed: 'I am proud to be a Canadian and a Nisga'a.' However, there are some Aboriginal peoples who do not consider themselves Canadian citizens. They see Canada as having illegally established itself as a country, on their land, and believe that the state has ignored the legitimacy of First Nations territory. They claim that Canada committed the illegal act of annexation and absorption by taking their ancestors into the new country of Canada. Finally, there are also those Aboriginal peoples who are ambivalent about being Canadian; for many, their daily lives are filled with acts of mere survival. We hope that this book will, in some way, help to improve the lives of all.

We see our book as contributing to a broader awareness of Aboriginal peoples. We focus on contributions, while recognizing that the problems of marginalization and poverty continue to exist and must be addressed. Helping Canadians to see Aboriginal peoples as contributing members of Canadian society may, we hope, make it easier to address some of other problems faced by Aboriginal peoples today. If mainstream society begins to understand that Aboriginal peoples have made and continue to make significant contributions to Canada, this will assist in breaking down the barriers between us and illustrating that we all have similar concerns, that we all want happy, healthy, and productive communities.

We hope to show that Aboriginal peoples have made remarkable contributions, ranging from the treaties, military service, and justice through to arts, media, literature, education, sports, and culture. Behind these contributions are outstanding people who have pushed the boundaries of their communities and of Canada itself. They have demonstrated extraordinary leadership and deserve to be recognized.

Within the book, we have divided the contributions into eight categories and profiled some twenty-five individuals. As noted in the Preface, selecting individuals has been difficult because the list of possible candidates is so large. A quick check of the National Aboriginal Achievement Foundation (NAAF) list of award nominees for each year yielded several thousand names. In making our selection, we have chosen those who have had, we believe, an effect upon the public consciousness of Canada: Chief Dan George, Harold Cardinal, Billy Diamond, Norval Morriseau, Jeannette Armstrong, Alwyn Morris, Douglas Cardinal, and Tommy Prince – to name a few.

As editors, we were surprised at the range of contributions and the interconnectedness of the topics. Who would have thought that Mikmaq quill artists would have an effect on seventeenth-century furniture making, or that Inuit were involved in dog breeding, or that Indian cowboys played an important role in Canadian rodeos? We also became more aware of the cental role of treaties and treaty makers in Canadian political history. In our view, Canada simply would not be what it is today without historical treaties. That is why we chose to start this volume with this topic. Similarly, David McNab's article on his fur-trade family illustrates the complex, interwoven social nature of Canada and the constant interaction between Aboriginal peoples and newcomers. In fact, it is a story of how individuals from these two groups met, married, had children, and tried to make the best of their lives. Russell Barsh, for his part, shows how Aboriginal peoples have served as a conscience for Canadian society by reminding citizens of the need to pursue social justice continually. Even today, the Canadian criminal justice system continues to evolve and incorporate into it many of the ideas on justice long held by Aboriginal peoples.

In the twenty-seven-year period between the White Paper on Indian Policy in 1969 and the release of RCAP Report in 1996, Canada moved from an official government policy of termination and assimilation to a reluctant acceptance of the inherent right of self government. Section 35(1) of the Constitution Act, 1982 recognizes and affirms Aboriginal and treaty rights in Canada. These rights are given to Metis, Inuit (formerly called Eskimo), and Status Indians. There is a broadly supported and well-functioning set of political organizations and associations whose goal it is to advance Aboriginal interests. A number of court cases such as *Calder, Sparrow, Guerin*, and *Marshall* have resulted in a well-tested foundation of jurisprudence which gives legal strength to Aboriginal and treaty rights and the special relationship between Canada and Aboriginal peoples.

In the arts, the Woodland School of Aboriginal Art based upon the work and techniques of Norval Morriseau, developed new forms of carving, painting, and pottery. There is now a recognized and celebrated genre of Canadian Aboriginal art which includes a wide variety of expression, including. Inuit stone carving, Iroquoian soapstone, Haida masks, Mi'kmaq baskets, Ojibwa quills, and postmodern Aboriginal expressionism, represented by artists like Carl Beam and Jane Ash Poitras.

There is also an expansion of Aboriginal music beyond Winston Wuttanee and Buffy Sainte Marie. We have now Kashtin, Red Power, 7th Fire, and Robbie Robertson. *Aboriginal Voices Magazine* used to publish the top ten albums in Indian country music. Aboriginal production companies have appeared on the music scene and are thriving. The Genie Awards have created a special category for Aboriginal music.

There is also an abundance of writers. Thomson Highway, Jeannette Armstrong, Drew Hayden Taylor, Gregory Shofield, and Maria Campbell, to cite but a few, have made a name for themselves in mainstream society. In fact, there is sufficient Aboriginal literature to fill several university-level courses which are gaining popularity on campuses across the nation.

Aboriginal people have been involved in television and radio productions. The Canadian Broadcasting Corporation (CBC) launched two regular series featuring Aboriginal peoples: 'North of 60' and 'The Rez.' CBC radio launched, to popular acclaim, the 'Dead Dog Cafe.' For a brief period in the 1980s, CBC radio also had a weekly public affairs show on Aboriginal issues. And, in September 1999, with the approval of the Canadian Radio-television and Telecommunications Commission (CRTC), the new Aboriginal Peoples Television Network was launched into most cable viewers' homes across Canada.

The National Aboriginal Achievement Foundation, formerly the Canadian Native Arts Foundation, gives out awards every year to Aboriginal people from across Canada who have made outstanding contributions to society. This award has been given to Aboriginal artists, performers, entrepreneurs, athletes, academics, and others. It has no difficulty in finding nominees. Choosing winners from such an accomplished group of individuals is a daunting task for the judges.

In the area of health and healing, we have seen the emergence of a widespread healing movement that affects just about every Aboriginal person in Canada as well as the establishment of Aboriginal health centres in many locations across the country. In 2001 the Canadian Institute of Health Research (CIHR) awarded $12 million to research teams to develop four research centres to study Aboriginal health in Canada.

In education, there is now one Aboriginal university and seventeen Aboriginally controlled, post-secondary institutes in Canada. The last federally run Indian residential school was closed in 1985. All public schools on Indian reserves are now under Indian control. In urban centres, there are Aboriginal survival schools that seek to retain Aboriginal culture and keep Aboriginal languages alive in the educational setting.

There are also now an increasing number of Aboriginal people choosing academic careers and working as teachers and as professors in post-secondary sectors. There has been a great increase in the number of Aboriginal people attending post-secondary institutions in Canada. There are also more than 30,000 Status Indian students in post-secondary education institutions – up from 160 in the early 1970s. These students are now studying in a vast array of academic disciplines including medicine, law, education, social work and the natural and social sciences.

In large urban centres, there is an extraordinary array of service and cultural organizations serving the ever-increasing urban Aboriginal population. There are now almost 130 Aboriginal Friendship Centres located across the country to aid Aboriginal people as they make the transition from the rural to the urban environment. More than half of the Aboriginal population (and approximately 40 per cent of Registered Indians) now lives in urban centres. Canadian cities like Winnipeg, Vancouver, and Edmonton have larger Aboriginal populations than the largest Indian reserves.

We have come a long way in three decades. There is now a solid foundation of hard-won legal rights, locally controlled institutions, and pride, alongside a renewed sense of capacity and responsibility and a strong desire to maintain and enhance Aboriginal identities. These changes affect the writing of Aboriginal history. Until recently, Aboriginal peoples have been portrayed in the historical literature in a way that almost completely ignores the role of human agency. We reacted against government policy. We rarely pursued our own interests. We acted mostly in self-defence or in response to the reactions of others. Even when Canadians write about the last twenty-five years, we are written out of the central part of the play and are mere bit players. Only seldom are we seen as human beings attempting to build our communities.

Several years ago, the CBC radio show *As It Happens* featured a member of Parliament who talked about the reasons he had sponsored a private member's bill that overturned the conviction of the Metis leader, Louis Riel, and had him declared a Father of Manitoba and a Father of Confederation. A professor who taught Canadian history at the University of Toronto was also asked to comment. While presenting his case, the MP was quite rudely rebuffed by the professor, who said that the whole idea was silly, even imbecilic, and that the MP's efforts would not make a bit of difference. He argued that Louis Riel was indeed insane and that it was not good form to honour someone who had killed so many people in a rebellion against the Canadian state. The professor seemed oblivious to the fact that we honour many people who have killed thousands of people all the time.

The interview ended in a shouting match between the two, with the *As It Happens* moderator saying at one point: 'You cannot understand each other if you keep talking all at once.' What was striking about this exchange was the absolute refusal of the professor even to consider what clearly is an alternative thesis – his open hostility to another point of view.

While a debate about Louis Riel can be highly emotional, what is important to note is the unwillingness of many to accept alternative theses and interpretations of history. The official history is indeed hard to challenge. The story of Canada is incomplete, perhaps immorally so, unless we also include the history of Aboriginal contributions. This book provides one attempt to document Aboriginal contributions to Canada. In the process, we hope that it can help to foster a new Canada: one that includes a place of dignity and respect for Aboriginal peoples.

Like the blades of grass mentioned in the opening quotation of the preface, Aboriginal peoples in Canada are often overlooked but ever-present. Just as the presence of grass can enhance the beauty of a landscape, so too can the presence of Aboriginal peoples and a recognition of our accomplishments help complete the Canadian societal landscape. Harvey A. McCue puts it well when he writes that, 'As a nation, we have yet to embrace fully the importance of an Aboriginal past, an Aboriginal history, if you will, to a national history. Nor have we embraced the importance of this history as a source of knowledge and possible instruction for survival on this great land. We humbly suggest that the time for such an embrace is overdue. We humbly suggest that our history as a nation is incomplete without it. We humbly suggest that our identity as Canadians, our presence marked as it is and has been for eons by this vast and magnificent geography demands nothing less.'[2]

Notes

1 We use the term tribal/national/community to reflect the complexities surrounding the entity about which we are writing. Some groups use community, some use nation, still others use tribe.
2 Harvey A. McCue, 'Native Culture and the Recording of History,' in *Place of History: Commemorating Canada's Past, Proceedings of the National Symposium Held on the Occasion of the 75th Anniversary of the Historic Sites and Monuments Board of Canada* (Ottawa: Royal Society of Canada 1997), 96.

Profile of Chief Dan George (1899–1981)

Squamish, Actor, and Tribal Leader

Chief Dan George is the only Aboriginal actor in Canadian history with the right to use the title 'Chief.' Coming from a family boasting six generations of chiefs,[1] he upheld this tradition by serving as leader of the Squamish First Nation of Burrard Inlet from 1951 to 1963 and retained the honorary title after his term ended.[2] In fact, he ventured into professional acting only after serving as chief, making his screen debut at the age of sixty-five as Ol' Antoine in CBC-TV's 'Caribou Country' series.[3]

Born in a small Salish village (now North Vancouver), Chief Dan George, then known as Geswanouth Slahoot, did not consider acting until late in life. As a boy, he attended a missionary school where he first adopted the name 'Dan George' because the missionaries required him to take on a white man's name while attending the school.[4] He quit school, however, so that he could work as a lumberjack and longshoreman, which he did for twenty-three years before suffering a serious accident.[5] During that time, he married his wife, Amy, with whom he stayed together for fifty-four years until her death in 1971. They had six children (Robert, Leonard, Marie, Ann, Irene, and Rose), thirty-four grandchildren, and twenty-two great-grandchildren.[6]

Generations of the George family have also been canoe carvers and champion canoe builders, and Dan George was no exception, building his first war canoe in 1963.[7] He once joked that '[his] greatest achievement came when [he] was thirty-five years old ... [he] took [his] canoe and started training. Every day for weeks and months, ten miles up and down the inlet. And that summer [he] cleaned up every race on the West Coast. And that, to [him], [was] the greatest achievement of [his] life.'[8]

His Hollywood film career was launched with his role as Old Lodge Skins in *Little Big Man*. The role, which made him famous, won him an Academy Award nomination for best supporting actor and paired him with screen legend Dustin Hoffman, who actually asked Chief Dan George's permission to call him 'Grandfather' while working on the film.[9] The role also

Chief Dan George. Courtesy of the George family.

won him a New York Film Critics Award for best actor,[10] and the film itself was revolutionary in its portrayal of Native Americans as victims of massacres rather than the ruthless killers so often portrayed by Hollywood.[11] Chief Dan George also starred in other critically acclaimed films, such as *The Outlaw Josey Wales, Dan Candy's Law* (also known as *Alien Thunder*), and *Harry and Tonto*.[12] To this day, he remains the first of only two Native Americans ever to be nominated for an Academy Award.[13]

Although Chief Dan George passed away more than twenty years ago, he still lives on in the memories of many as a North American icon who helped change forever the image of Native North Americans in the eyes of the media. Whether through his movies, his books (*My Heart Soars* and *My Spirit Soars*),[14] or his rich heritage, Chief Dan George touched the lives of many, Aboriginal and non-Aboriginal alike.

'Be proud of every drop of Indian blood in your body. It ties you to the land. Children like you represent the best of both worlds, be wise enough to learn the best of both worlds, white and red.'[15] – Chief Dan George.

CHRISTINE ARMSTRONG

Notes

1 Richard A. Payne, *Rick and Jim's Real Reel Indians* (Fort Collins, Colo.: Blue Sky Graphics 1994), 29.
2 'Chief Dan George,' in *Aboriginal People Profiles: Actors* (cited 18 July 2002). Available from www.ainc-inac.gc.ca/ks/english/3022_e.html.
3 Hilda Mortimer with Chief Dan George, *You Call Me Chief: Impressions of the Life of Chief Dan George* (Toronto: Doubleday Canada 1981), 19.
4 Payne, *Rick and Jim's Real Reel Indians*, 29.
5 Ibid.
6 Ibid.
7 Mortimer, *You Call Me Chief*, 177.
8 Ibid., 179.
9 Payne, *Rick and Jim's Real Reel Indians*, 29.
10 *Aboriginal People Profiles: Actors.*
11 Mortimer, *You Call Me Chief*, 45.
12 Ibid.
13 Payne, *Rick and Jim's Real Reel Indians*, 31.
14 Ibid., 29.
15 Ibid., 30.

PART TWO

TREATIES

Treaties and the Evolution of Canada

JEAN-PIERRE MORIN

The treaties the crown has signed with Aboriginal peoples since the eighteenth century have permitted the evolution of Canada as we know it. In fact, much of Canada's land mass is covered by treaties. It would be fair to say that, without the long history of treaty making, Canada probably would not have the geographic borders it has today. This treaty-making process, which has evolved over more than three hundred years, has its origins in the early diplomatic relationship that developed between European settlers and Aboriginal peoples. Their early agreements were cooperative ones, negotiated with both parties' interests in mind and dealing primarily with their protection and well-being. As the two parties made economic and military alliances, Canada began to take form. These diplomatic proceedings were the first steps in a long process that has led to today's comprehensive land-claims agreements between the crown and Aboriginal groups.

Prior to contact, European colonial powers and the Aboriginal peoples of North America both had long traditions of diplomacy and treaty relations which had evolved over the centuries. While these different traditions tended to have common goals of peaceful relations, trade, and military alliances, their protocols and diplomatic trappings were so strikingly different as to be nearly incomparable. The diplomatic protocols and undertakings between Europeans and Aboriginal peoples were hammered on the forge of relations in North America into a new treaty-making dynamic that adopted and adapted aspects of each culture. The scope of this achievement is apparent when one considers the distance the two systems had to move to create a shifting middle ground, rife with competing interests, where diplomatic discussions could take place. The European system was centralized, hierarchical, and secular. The Aboriginal system, on the other hand, maintained elements of the sacred, allowed everyone a voice in negotiations, and incorporated reciprocal and highly formalized procedures. Both systems moved beyond symbolism and protocol, however, into the realms of hard, realistic bargaining (Jones 1988, 185).

Within Aboriginal North America, as within Europe itself, diplomatic practices between various nations differed in style, as opposed to substance. Of these practices, the best understood are those of the Aboriginal groups in the northeast and the Mississippi and Hudson Bay drainage basins. These groups developed protocols and procedures that became the focal points of their diplomatic meetings and established the significance and validity of their negotiations. All centred their activities around a sacred object that represented their commitment to the diplomatic process. For the Iroquoian and Algonkian peoples of the Great Lakes drainage basin, this sacred object was the wampum or covenant belt. In the Mississippi and Hudson Bay drainage basins, the calumet, or peace pipe, was the focal point of all diplomatic negotiations. Before diplomatic meetings could officially begin, the parties had to show their commitment to the process, and recognize its sacredness, through the exchange of wampum belts or by smoking the peace pipe. In Aboriginal diplomatic traditions, this ceremony signified that treaties were more than agreements between two groups. They were 'sacred obligations for all involved and their violation ran the risk of divine displeasure' (Jones 1988, 186).

Sacredness had been an aspect of diplomacy in Europe as well, but by the sixteenth century it had been displaced by the humanism of the Renaissance. The humanist movement widened the separation between the worlds of church and state. European diplomacy was based on hierarchy and the centralized authority of the monarch and was conducted between organized states. European states undertook diplomacy and treaty making with pomp and circumstance, thereby recognizing the equality of the monarchs who were parties to the negotiations through their diplomats. This diplomacy was largely temporal, often with time limits attached to treaties and agreements, and had none of the sacred elements that underlay North American Aboriginal diplomacy. Whereas Aboriginal people feared divine retribution for treaty violations in North America, it was the fear of military retribution that prevented parties from breaking their treaties in Europe.

These fundamental differences forced the two groups to adapt and modify their practices and protocols into a single framework that they both understood and accepted because it incorporated aspects from their respective systems. This framework, which continued to evolve over the next three hundred years as relations developed and changed, enabled the disparate Aboriginal and European groups to work on goals of mutual interest. Both groups adopted practices and protocols from each other in order to facilitate the process. Dorothy V. Jones describes 'this new diplomacy [as] ... neither Indian or European. It was a complex mix that changed over time according to changing power relationships' (Jones 1988, 185). Aboriginal peoples were quick to recognize some of the protocols that Europeans expected from diplomatic negotiations. For example, they noted the importance that Europeans attached to Christianity. The significance of their own rituals in negotiations, and the sacredness they attached to this process, encouraged their belief that participating in the rituals of Christianity would improve and strengthen alliances with the Europeans (Dickason 1984, 253).

The French colonial authority also quickly realized the value of adopting local protocols, especially in light of their relatively weak position in relation to the British colonies. The use of the wampum belt in both diplomacy and trade became a standard practice early in the French period, as did the use of figurative speaking. The French developed a general policy for diplomacy in North America which can be described as a reciprocal relationship of friendship with their Huron, Algonquin, Montagnais, Maliseet, and Mi'kmaq allies (Dickason 1984, 245). This relationship did not, however, entail the making of many treaties.

South of the St Lawrence River valley, the British undertook a different approach to ensuring strong ties with their allies. They were also quick to adopt the use of the wampum belt, recognizing its importance to their main Aboriginal allies, the Iroquois Confederacy. Through this protocol, British officials established a series of agreements and treaties that addressed military alliances, trade, and, later, land cessions (Jones 1988, 188).

This diplomatic framework had two main goals. For the Europeans, the purpose was at first mainly economic, but, as colonial conflicts evolved, military alliances became more predominant. For Aboriginal peoples, on the other hand, the framework was largely a military relationship (Jones 1988, 197).

Economically, the European establishment of trade alliances with North America's Aboriginal population made some commercial success possible for expensive European colonial projects. With the assistance of Aboriginal hunters in the fur trade, exports of furs to Europe generated huge profits for relatively small expenditure. As colonial expansion continued and European conflicts spread to North America, both French and British colonial and military authorities began to depend heavily upon their new Aboriginal allies for help in defending their colonies and in offensive attacks on their enemies. From the very first diplomatic meetings, Aboriginal peoples had regarded these treaties as military agreements, rather than economic ones. Through these treaties, the various Aboriginal groups gained strong military allies with powerful technologies that could be used in campaigns against their traditional enemies.

The various colonial authorities held different views of Aboriginal land title. For the French and Spanish, the act of discovery and a symbolic taking of the land were sufficient to accord the territorial rights of the land to the discovering state. France affirmed its territorial right of discovery by the raising of crosses, at first along the coast and later in the interior, and by the presentation of the coat of arms of France. Based on this view, French colonial officials never attempted to negotiate land cessions from their Aboriginal allies. The French also believed that they received these lands in exchange for their efforts at converting the Aboriginal population to Christianity. Furthermore, the populations of France's North American possessions were too small to lead to much encroachment on Aboriginal lands. British and Dutch attitudes differed insofar as they recognized, at least symbolically, Aboriginal peoples' right to the lands they occupied. In order to ensure peaceful conditions and to provide land for their colonies, the British and the Dutch therefore made agreements with the Aboriginal inhabitants through which lands were exchanged for goods and alliances (Dickason 1984, 132).

France undertook the first colonial expeditions within the territory that is now part of Canada. Although the first European exploration of the Gulf of St Lawrence took place in the mid-1500s, settlements were not established until the beginning of the next century. The first French colonial settlement was in the Annapolis valley in southern Nova Scotia. Although the settlement of Port Royal had a rough start it did establish important contact and alliances with the Aboriginal peoples of the Maritimes. Long accustomed to the presence of Basque whalers and French fishermen along the Atlantic coast, the Mi'kmaq and Maliseet were willing to participate in the fur trade and fishery with the French settlers. At the same time, the small size of the French settlement and its initial difficulties resulted in the settlers being heavily dependent on the Aboriginal population of the region. The food and goods supplied by the Mi'kmaq and the Maliseet assured the early survival of Port Royal and other settlements in Acadia. The general French policy of reciprocity with Aboriginal people, and the presence of missionaries throughout the Maritimes, allowed France to establish not only a trade alliance with the Mi'kmaq and Maliseet but also an important military alliance that was useful for the defence of Acadia (Dickason 1992, 109). The Mi'kmaq and Maliseet also benefited from this alliance. The French forces, with their European weapons, provided much assistance in Aboriginal conflicts. This alliance would continue even offer the loss of Acadia to the British in 1713.

Shortly after the establishment of the Port Royal settlement, French colonial efforts were directed towards the interior with the founding of the Quebec settlement in 1608 and the arrival of the first settlers in New France. As a result of a series of explorations of the interior, the land mass of New France gradually extended down the St Lawrence River, through the Great Lakes region, west to the Red River, and south to the Mississippi Delta. Throughout this period of exploration, France expanded not only its territory but also its influence with the fur-trading Aboriginal peoples, increasing the number of its Aboriginal allies in the process. Settlement did not extend throughout this entire territory, however; it was concentrated along the St Lawrence River and in the Mississippi Delta. The French confirmed alliances with the Algonquin, Montagnais, and Huron, not through treaties but rather through their participation in battles against the Iroquois Confederacy. This initial participation set the stage for future French military action in Aboriginal conflicts, alongside their allies. Lasting until the end of the French period, this military alliance also fostered a strong trade alliance, led by the Huron, and made Quebec one of the most important centres of the fur trade (Dickason 1992, 122). The French contribution to battles against the Iroquois would, however, have long-term consequences.

The Iroquois Confederacy, also known as the Five Nations, was the traditional enemy of the Huron, Algonquin, Montagnais, and Abenaki living in what is now Maine and Massachusetts. Because of France's alliance with these groups, and the inability of the Iroquois to access French trade, the Five Nations initiated trade and alliances with the Dutch merchants along the Hudson River and with the British in New England (Dickason 1992, 130). With new armaments, the Iroquois set out to disrupt Huron control of the fur trade. These efforts persisted until 1701 when France, its Aboriginal allies, and the Iroquois signed a treaty at Montreal known as the Great Peace. Although this treaty brought nearly forty-five years of prosperity and growth to New France, it did not change the traditional colonial alliances. Through treaties and agreements such as the Covenant Chain, the Iroquois and the British formed a military alliance that would last well into the nineteenth century. This alliance greatly assisted Great Britain's colonial wars against the French and helped the Iroquois to control much of the fur trade.

For most of this period, North America's two colonial powers waged almost constant warfare against each other on the continent. Both France and Britain used their Aboriginal allies in numerous campaigns in Acadia, the St Lawrence valley, and the Mississippi valley. Aboriginal warriors proved to be essential components for both armies, and in some cases were indispensable, especially for the smaller French forces.

Events in Europe then brought about major change in the New World. The Treaty of Utrecht in 1713 ceded the mainland of Acadia to Great Britain, leaving Île Royal (Cape Breton Island) and Île Saint-Jean (Prince Edward Island) as the sole French possessions in the area. As Great Britain began to organize and exert its authority over its colony of Nova Scotia, it had to contend not only with the remaining French colonists but also with France's Aboriginal allies in the region. Fearing further cooperation between Aboriginal peoples and the French, and continued harassment of British settlers, the colonial authority undertook the negotiation of a series of treaties with the Mi'kmaq and Maliseet. Through these treaties, made from 1725 to 1779, peace and friendship were assured between the colony and the Aboriginal population. The Mi'kmaq and Maliseet benefited from better trade conditions and the assurance that their religious practices would be undisturbed (Daugherty 1983a, 65).

It is important to note that these treaties did not in fact ensure peaceful relations. Because of the Mi'kmaq's and Maliseet's lasting alliances with the French, and French encouragement, these two Aboriginal groups often violated their treaties with the British. This was especially the case during the Seven Years' War, when the Mi'kmaq and Maliseet openly sided with France. After the treaty violations, the various parties drafted and agreed upon new treaties, as was the case with the 1760 treaty, which coincided with the end of French military activities in North America.

Royal Proclamation of 1763 to the War of 1812

The end of the Seven Years' War in 1763 brought about major changes not only in colonial settlement but also in the diplomatic relations between Aboriginal groups and the British colonial authority. Throughout this final colonial conflict, the French military had relied heavily upon its Aboriginal allies. French and British Aboriginal allies also had their own stake in this battle. These conflicts pitted traditional Aboriginal enemies against one another, and, through the alliances that they had made with either France or Britain, the various groups could receive the necessary military support. With the war increasingly favouring Britain and its Iroquois allies, France began to lose some of its traditional allies in the New World. As the French lost their two most important settlements, Quebec and Montreal, France's long-standing alliance with the Algonquin, Montagnais, Huron, Mi'kmaq, Abenaki, and Maliseet came to an end. In both the Maritimes and the St Lawrence valley, Great Britain made peace treaties in 1760 with France's allies, who shifted their allegiances to the British crown.

Subsequent to the signing of the 1763 Treaty of Paris, which formally transferred the colony of New France to Great Britain, a British Royal Proclamation was issued officially announcing Great Britain's authority over the French colony. In this proclamation, the British authority formally recognized Aboriginal peoples' title to the land they occupied and established an 'Indian Territory' to the west of the existing colonies (Cottam 1997, 8). This land was to be protected from settlement until a proper surrender of the Aboriginal title to the land had been made. In order to control this process, Aboriginal peoples could surrender their title only to a representative of the crown in a public meeting. Although the general policy of land surrenders was then a British practice, its inclusion in the Royal Proclamation, and the establishment of protocols for obtaining land surrenders, aimed to control and regulate the expansion of settlement into the 'Indian territory.' Since new lands were needed for settlement, British officials arranged land surrenders throughout the western part of the Province of Quebec, soon to become the new colony of Upper Canada (Ontario).

The Aboriginal peoples' role as military allies of Great Britain was also affected by the Treaty of Paris and the Royal Proclamation. Although there was no longer any military threat in North America between 1763 and 1776, British authorities continued to give presents to their allies in order to ensure good relations. As the American colonists began their fight for independence from Great Britain in 1776, Aboriginal peoples played a defensive role alongside British forces in the St Lawrence and Ohio valleys and across the frontier. Great Britain's concession of American independence in 1783 created a new defensive role for its Aboriginal allies north of Lake Erie, Lake Ontario, and the St Lawrence River. The British presence south of the Great Lakes, however, continued for a decade. Through a series of fortifications in the Great Lakes region and the Ohio valley, British military authorities wished to create a type of 'Indian buffer zone' between the expanding American state and its remaining colonies of Upper and Lower Canada (the eastern part of the old Province of Quebec), as well as maintain military alliances with the region's Aboriginal population (Cottam 1997, 8). Aboriginal peoples in the Ohio and Mississippi valleys, however, felt betrayed by the British and feared American reprisals. In order to maintain their loyalty to Britain and counteract feelings of betrayal, the British continued to give Aboriginal groups in American territory their annual presents of armaments, ammunition, and other goods. The end of the American War of Independence brought about a period of massive migration as inhabitants of the former American colonies loyal to the British crown relocated to other British territories in North America. Some

Aboriginal allies living in American territory also emigrated, most notably a significant portion of the Iroquois Confederacy; these Iroquois settled in Upper Canada near the Bay of Quinte and along the Grand River.

Between 1763 and 1812, and especially after the arrival of the Loyalists in the 1780s, British authority was extended down the St Lawrence River and into the territory between the Great Lakes. In the first decades after the surrender of these lands, the relatively slow settlement had little impact upon the Aboriginal population, mainly composed of Mississauga, who were not severely dislocated (Surtees 1984, 9). In 1812 Upper Canada's population was approximately 75,000, scattered across a large territory in settlements close to the shorelines of major rivers and lakes.

Until Jay's Treaty of 1796, the British maintained military posts throughout the Michigan peninsula and in the old northwest (Leslie 1979, 6). These posts preserved crucial contact between the British and their allies and facilitated the distribution of presents. After the British abandoned these posts, American Aboriginal groups continued to receive presents but were required to travel to Upper Canada to do so. This practice proved to be beneficial to Britain's interests since thousands of Aboriginal warriors fought alongside the British in opposition to American forces during the War of 1812.

The signing of the Treaty of Ghent in 1815 marked the beginning of a new period of British-Aboriginal relations. The treaty was the reinstatement of the pre-war status quo, including a return to pre-war boundaries and the removal of all foreign troops from British and American territories. Since the War of 1812 was the final colonial conflict involving Great Britain in North America, the end of the war also signified the end of a traditional role for Aboriginal peoples. By terminating all hostilities with the United States of America, Great Britain also eliminated the need for a military alliance with its Aboriginal allies.

In order to manage more effectively the numerous complicated treaties and alliances that it had with its Aboriginal allies, Great Britain had established the Indian Department in 1755. This body alleviated some of the problems caused by the lack of central control and worked to establish a more general and uniform policy in regard to the crown's Aboriginal allies, instead of the patchwork of policies influenced by local circumstances (Leslie and Maguire 1979, 3). Under the guidance of Sir William Johnson, who quickly learned and used Aboriginal diplomatic protocols, the Indian Department strengthened its alliances throughout a period of heavy warfare. Until the War of 1812, the Indian Department's main goal was to maintain and strengthen these military alliances, and, as a consequence, it was controlled by the military authorities in British North America. As the importance of the alliances diminished and the costs increased, military control of the Indian Department came into question. This issue was resolved by the department's transfer to civil authority in 1795; however, after the War of 1812, it reverted back to military control, an arrangement that lasted until 1830.

Shift in European Priorities

After the War of 1812, increased settlement and American treaties with Aboriginal peoples south of the Great Lakes further reduced Aboriginal peoples' military role. Simultaneously, the rapidly increasing rate of settlement created new pressures on the lands occupied by the Mississauga and other Aboriginal groups. As more and more lands were surrendered and agricultural settlements spread across Upper Canada, Aboriginal bands were increasingly displaced from their traditional lands. The system of presents, an important part of diplomacy and military alliances, was now becoming a burden to the British authority, which also had to contend with the arrival of large numbers of American Aboriginal peoples fleeing the U.S. policy of forced relocation. As a result, present giving was abandoned in 1855, which brought an end to the once dominant and long-standing military alliance between the European powers and Aboriginal peoples.

When the Indian Department was returned to civil authority in 1830, it underwent major changes, both in its structure and in its policies. Influenced by the growing humanitarian and evangelical movements in Great Britain, the department's policies shifted towards the promotion of 'civilization and Christianization' of Aboriginal peoples. The new approach, which envisioned a transformation of Aboriginal peoples into a sedentary and Christian agricultural people (Leslie and Maguire 1979, 16), would dominate Indian policy for the next century. In the immediate term, however, the Department came under close scrutiny and criticism as a number of commissions examined its administration throughout the 1840s and 1850s. These commissions were critical of the lack of cohesion in policy and the increasing alienation of traditional Aboriginal lands. Between 1830 and 1867, several pieces of colonial legislation were passed in an attempt to protect Aboriginal lands and to increase the rate of Aboriginal assimilation into colonial society. Meanwhile, through a series of efforts to reduce the administrative cost of its colonial empire, the imperial government transferred control of the Indian Department to the Province of Canada in 1860. Renamed the Department of Indian Affairs, this revamped administration shifted its emphasis from the 'protection of self-governing Aboriginal agricultural communities to their complete assimilation' (Cottam 1997, 13).

The new emphasis on the 'civilization and christianization' of Aboriginal peoples directly affected the treaty and diplomatic relations between the crown and Aboriginal peoples. As the process of land surrenders continued throughout Upper Canada, there were attempts to link these new policies with the surrenders. One example was a project involving Manitoulin Island in Lake Huron. Spearheaded by Lieutenant Governor Sir Francis Bond Head in the 1830s, this project involved the surrender of various lands around Georgian Bay. Aboriginal groups in the area were encouraged to relocate to Manitoulin Island, which, through the 1836 Manitoulin Island Treaty, would be entirely reserved for them (Surtees 1986a, 14). Because of Manitoulin Island's relative isolation from European settlers, colonial officials believed that its Aboriginal inhabitants would be able to adapt gradually to agriculture and Christianity. Yet, despite some early success, this 'Indian Homeland' was eventually judged to be a failure, with only a few thousand Aboriginal people relocating to the island over the course of twenty-five years.

Initially, settlement had been the driving impetus for land surrenders in Upper Canada. By the mid-1800s, however, the agricultural lands of the southern part of the colony were largely occupied, and the discovery of rich deposits of minerals and metals in the lands along the northern shores of Lake Superior and Lake Huron led to the creation of a new kind of treaty. In 1850, responding to Aboriginal demands, William B. Robinson negotiated two treaties with the Aboriginal inhabitants of the area: the Robinson-Superior and Robinson-Huron Treaties (Surtees 1986b, 24). These treaties differed remarkably from the simple land surrenders in the south. While the early land surrenders, with their one-time payments, created few lasting responsibilities for the government, the Robinson Treaties established permanent government obligations to the Aboriginal signatories. Supplemental to a one-time lump sum payment, Aboriginal people also received an annuity of $4 per person and reserve lands in return for the surrender of their traditional lands. In addition, they maintained their right to hunt and fish on unoccupied land. These two treaties would become the model for the Numbered Treaties of the prairies in the late nineteenth century (see Plate 1 in colour section).

On North America's west coast, quite a different relationship developed between European settlers and the region's Aboriginal inhabitants. For nearly fifty years, settlement there had been overshadowed by the commercial aspirations of the Hudson's Bay Company (HBC). Holding a trade monopoly for the entire British half of the Oregon territory, the HBC was content to restrict its diplomatic dealings with the west coast Aboriginal peoples strictly to commercial matters relating to the fur trade. Following the relocation of the HBC primary post to Vancouver Island and a new mandate to establish a colony, James Douglas, the HBC's chief factor and, after 1854, colonial governor, undertook the signing of fourteen treaties with various Coast Salish communities on Vancouver Island between 1850 and 1854 (Madill 1981, 31). These treaties surrendered land required for settlement around various HBC posts, exchanged for lump-sum cash payments and goods along with recognition of the Aboriginals' continued right to hunt and fish. Treaty making was curtailed in the 1860s because of British Colombia's reluctance to recognize Aboriginal peoples' land title, which was in sharp contrast to the practice in all other British colonial jurisdictions. This denial of Aboriginal land title persisted even after British Colombia joined Confederation and was contrary to the new Dominion's recognition of this title in other parts of Canada.

Confederation and the Numbered Treaties

The creation of the Dominion of Canada in 1867 marked another watershed in the crown's relationship with Aboriginal peoples. Section 91(24) of the British North America Act established that the Parliament of Canada held legislative authority over 'Indians and Lands reserved for Indians,' making Aboriginal affairs the responsibility of the federal government (Constitution Act, 1867). For Aboriginal people, this was an important change from their relationship with colonial authorities. With the creation of the federal Department of Indian Affairs, one administrative body became responsible for the administration of most Aboriginal issues. (Prior to Confederation, the colonial Indian Department dealt with these issues as an extension of British colonial authority.) Through the federal Department of Indian Affairs, a branch of the Department of the Interior, the Dominion of Canada could develop national policies that would affect all Aboriginal peoples while also setting local policies in a national context. The consolidation of these various policies into a single act became one of the department's first concerns, a goal that achieved between 1868 and 1876 under the terms of the Indian Act (Leslie and Maguire 1979, 52). The Indian Act affected many aspects of Aboriginal peoples' lives, determining such things as membership and the internal governance of bands. Through a series of modifications and amendments, the Indian Act would come to control and influence nearly all aspects of daily life for Aboriginal peoples in Canada.

Although the Department of Indian Affairs was a new administrative body, it retained much of its colonial structure and ideology. The department was divided between officials in Ottawa and agents in the field. In

Ottawa, it was headed by a deputy superintendent General, who reported to the minister of the interior, and was staffed by a few clerks and other officials who planned policy. Scattered across the country, Indian agents were to implement these policies, many of which were incongruous with circumstances in the field. This structure would lead to serious administrative problems. In terms of ideology, the new Department of Indian Affairs adopted policies similar to those of the colonial Indian Department. Strengthened by Victorian humanitarianism and the growing evangelical movement, the department developed policies with the specific goal of 'civilizing' Aboriginal people.

With this ideology in mind, the federal crown undertook to establish a new treaty relationship with the Aboriginal people in the west. Since 1670, the HBC had had an exclusive monopoly over trade and commerce in all lands where the waters drained towards Hudson Bay, making the territory of what was then known as Rupert's Land virtually its private domain. In 1869, after nearly two hundred years of control, the HBC sold its title to Rupert's Land to the Dominion of Canada. Through this transfer, Canada gained full control of all resources in the now renamed North-West Territories and was also able to open a fertile region to settlement and agriculture. The transfer of Rupert's Land caused considerable animosity among the territories' Aboriginal and Metis population, who saw the sale as a surrender of their traditional lands without their consent or consultation. This animosity would have long-standing repercussions for future treaty negotiations.

For the Metis population concentrated in the Red River colony, situated at the site of present-day Winnipeg, resentment of Canada turned into an open revolt which led to the creation of a provisional government headed by Louis Riel in 1869. The crisis was resolved only by the creation of the province of Manitoba the following year. After that event, the need for clear title to the land became a major concern for the crown.

By the 1870s, the Aboriginal peoples of the prairies were in an increasingly precarious position. Intensified hunting in both the Canadian west and the American west had significantly reduced the number of migrating Plains buffalo (Milloy 1988, 104). This decrease in the buffalo population had a profound impact upon the traditional way of life of the Plains Cree, Assiniboine, Ojibwa, and the Blackfoot. Aboriginal hunters ignored traditional boundaries as they followed the few remaining buffalo, and wars erupted between the tribes who vied for control of a vanishing resource (Milloy 1988, 114–15). Less than fifteen years after the transfer of Rupert's Land to Canada, the buffalo were all but extinct in the North-West Territories. Weakened by famine, starvation and war, the nomadic peoples of the prairies came to negotiate with the crown.

After Confederation, the new Dominion of Canada envisioned a radical expansion of its boundaries. The valuable resources that lay west of Lake Superior had long been coveted by European settlers and colonial administrators. The 1869 purchase of the HBC's Charter permitted Canada to push westward into new and unsettled territory, but question of aboriginal land title throughout the North-West Territories had to be resolved both to enable coordinated settlement and to ensure Canadian sovereignty over an immense region (Daugherty 1983b, 3). Fear of American expansion across the 49th parallel was ever-present, especially in light of the rapid settlement south of the border. Witnessing events in the American territories, the Canadian government also wanted to avoid the kind of costly Indian wars that had occurred throughout Montana and the Dakotas.

With these considerations in mind, Canada decided to make treaties with the Aboriginal peoples of the prairies. As noted earlier, diplomatic protocols in the North-West differed from those in the Great Lakes basin. Here, the calumet or peace pipe signified the sacredness of the meetings. Smoked before discussions and negotiations could begin, the pipe was the focus of an essential ceremony for all treaty meetings. The crown also changed its protocols. Taking a page from the negotiations for the 1850 Robinson Treaties, the government decided that treaty negotiations for large tracts of land were to be undertaken with many bands assembled in one or two locations. Also like the Robinson Treaties, these treaties would be more than simple land surrenders. In addition to one-time, lump-sum payments, treaty signatories would receive annuities, specific amounts of reserve lands, recognition of a continued right to hunt and fish on unoccupied crown lands, schools, agricultural implements, cattle, and ammunition. Between 1871 and 1921, the crown signed eleven treaties, known as the Numbered Treaties, with the Aboriginal peoples of the prairies, the Mackenzie River region, and northern Ontario. Through them, the crown secured the title for nearly half of the Canadian land mass, secured its jurisdiction north of the border, opened the west for settlement, and connected British Columbia to the rest of the country (Carter 1999, 119).

While these treaties provided wealth and prosperity for the Dominion of Canada, the same cannot be said of the treaties' Aboriginal signatories. When the buffalo herds vanished in the early 1880s, bands became nearly entirely dependent upon government rations for survival. As reserves were surveyed, a once nomadic people had to adapt to a new life as sedentary agriculturalists. Without the benefit of proper teaching and implements, and constrained as they were by the restrictive terms of the Indian Act and the policies of the Department of Indian affairs, Aboriginal peoples found this adaptation nearly impossible (Carter 1990, 108). Furthermore, differences in interpretation of the treaties were becoming apparent. While the government largely viewed the treaties as binding legal contracts ceding land in exchange for specific benefits, Aboriginal signatories saw them as something much more. Today, their attitude is encapsulated in the words of Treaty 4 Saulteaux elder Danny Musqua who says that, treaties are 'a covenant with Her Majesty's government, and a covenant is not just a relationship between people, it's a relationship between three parties, the Crown, First Nations and the Creator' (Cardinal and Hildebrandt 2000, 32). In this perspective, ceremonies surrounding treaty making created duties and obligations for both the Aboriginal signatories and the government. As Saskatchewan elders have stated, when promises and agreements are made with the Creator, they are 'irrevocable and inviolable' (Cardinal and Hildebrandt 2000, 7).

For the government of the Dominion of Canada, as we have seen, one of the main goals of the Numbered Treaties was to secure the cession of Aboriginal title to the North-West Territories. As stipulated in the Rupert's Land and North-Western Territory Enactment of 1870, the government agreed to settle any Aboriginal claims to the land in the North-West Territories prior to settlement. In the eyes of the government, the Numbered Treaties were land transactions; for Aboriginal peoples, they were not. According to Aboriginal leaders and the oral traditions of Treaty 4 and Treaty 6 elders, the treaties were agreements to share the land with the government, and only to the depth of a plow (Cardinal and Hildebrandt 2000, 36). John Leonard Taylor states that 'the elders do not believe that the Indians surrendered the subsurface rights. They believe that their ancestors understood the treaty as providing for a limited surrender or sharing of territorial rights' (Taylor 1999, 43). Treaty 7 elders uniformly maintain that there was no surrender or sharing of land in Treaty 7; the treaty's purpose was to establish peace in the area, stop intertribal warfare, and end disruptions caused by alcohol (Hickey, Lighting, and Lee 1999, 105).

The Victorian humanitarian ideology of 'civilizing' Aboriginal people dominated all aspects of Aboriginal affairs. Missionaries, teachers, and Indian agents all believed that the plight of these people could only improve if they adopted a more 'European' way of life. They saw the Aboriginal way of life as incompatible with 'modern' society, and believed that only by abandoning it would Aboriginal people be able to enter fully into Canadian society. The government attempted to develop policies that would give Aboriginal people the means necessary to make this transition. These policies continued well into the 1940s, further isolating Aboriginal communities on their reserves in the government's attempt to assimilate them into Canadian society (Leslie and Maguire 1979, 89). It was generally believed that, over time, Aboriginal people would disappear completely, absorbed into the general population. But, in the end, things did not work out this way. Although Aboriginal languages were largely lost, Christianity replaced many traditional religions, and poverty was widespread throughout Aboriginal communities, Aboriginal identity endured. The government's desire to transform Aboriginal people into white prairie farmers had been a failure.

The evolution of Canada is closely tied to its relationship with its Aboriginal inhabitants. Diplomatic relations led to alliances which benefited both European and Aboriginal signatories. This diplomacy facilitated the early settlement of the Maritimes, the St Lawrence valley, and the Great Lakes basin. Through treaties that assured both military and economic cooperation, settlements flourished and developed. As colonial wars raged throughout North America, Aboriginal military strength played an important role in battles between European powers striving for colonial conquest. The end of conflicts, and the move towards increased settlement, also changed the diplomatic relationship between the crown and Aboriginal peoples. The crown no longer saw its once powerful allies as assisting, but rather as an obstacle to, settlement and development. Aboriginal land title needed to be surrendered ahead of settlement so as to minimize any conflicts between settlers and Aboriginal peoples. Throughout the Great Lakes region and into the Prairies, as the land was surrendered, settlement followed.

To examine the evolution of the treaty process in Canada is also to reflect on the historical evolution and shaping of Canada. The continuing discussion and debate on the historic treaty relationship, and the modern negotiations of that relationship through the comprehensive land-claims process, continue to exert a formative influence on Canada and its future direction.

Bibliography

Canada. Constitution Act, 1867, Para. 91 (24), 30 and 31 Victoria, c.3.

Cardinal, H., and W. Hildebrandt. 2000. *Treaty Elders of Saskatchewan*. Calgary: University of Calgary Press.

Carter, Sarah. 1999. *Aboriginal People and Colonizers of Western Canada to 1900*. Toronto: University of Toronto Press.

– 1990. *Lost Harvests: Prairie Indian Reserve Farmers and Government Policy.* Montreal and Kingston: McGill-Queen's University Press.

Cottam, Barry. 1997. *Aboriginal Peoples and Archives: A Brief History of Aboriginal and European Relations in Canada*. Ottawa: National Archives of Canada.

– 1984. *The Myth of the Savage.* Edmonton: University of Alberta Press.

Daugherty, Wayne E. 1983a. *Maritime Indian Treaties in Historical Perspective.* Ottawa: Department of Indian Affairs and Northern Development.

– 1983b. *Treaty Research Report: Treaty One and Treaty Two.* Ottawa: Department of Indian Affairs and Northern Development.

Dickason, Olive Patricia. 1992. *Canada's First Nations.* Toronto: McClelland and Stewart.

Hickey, Lynn, Richard L. Lightning, and Gordon Lee. 1999. 'T.A.R.R. Interview with Elders Program.' In Richard T. Price, ed., *The Spirit of the Alberta Indian Treaties.* Edmonton: University of Alberta Press.

Jones, Dorothy V. 1988. 'British Colonial Indian Treaties.' In *Handbook of North American Indians*, vol. 4, *Indian-White Relations.* Washington: Smithsonian Institution.

Leslie, John. 1979. *The Treaty of Amity, Commerce and Navigation, 1794–1796: The Jay Treaty.* Ottawa: Department of Indian Affairs and Northern Development.

Leslie, John, and Ron Maguire. 1979. *The Historical Development of the Indian Act.* Ottawa: Department of Indian Affairs and Northern Development.

Madill, Dennis. 1981. *British Columbia Indian Treaties in Historical Perspective.* Ottawa: Department of Indian Affairs and Northern Development.

Milloy, John S. 1988. *The Plains Cree: Trade, Diplomacy and War, 1790 to 1870.* Winnipeg: University of Manitoba Press.

Surtees, Robert J. 1984. *Indian Land Surrenders in Ontario, 1863–1867.* Ottawa: Department of Indian Affairs and Northern Development.

– 1986a. *Treaty Research Report: The Manitoulin Island Treaties.* Ottawa: Department of Indian Affairs and Northern Development.

– 1986b. *Treaty Research Report: The Robinson Treaties.* Ottawa: Indian Affairs and Northern Development.

Taylor, John Leonard. 1999. 'Two Views on the Meaning of Treaties 6 and 7.' In Richard T. Price, ed., *The Spirit of the Alberta Indian Treaties.* Edmonton: University of Alberta Press.

Profile of Harold Cardinal (1945–)

Cree, Author, Activist, Academic, and Politician

Harold Cardinal is widely admired for his persistence and dedication in creating opportunities for positive change for First Nations communities in Canada. His passion for seeking equality for First Nations peoples has led him to wear many vocational hats, including those of author, politician, activist, scholar, professor, entrepreneur and treaty-rights consultant.

Harold Cardinal was born on 27 January 1945 to Frank and Agnes (Cunningham) Cardinal in High Prairie, Alberta. He was raised, along with his seventeen siblings, on the Sucker Creek Reserve in northern Alberta.[1] After completing high school in Edmonton in 1965, he moved to Ottawa, where he studied sociology at St Patrick's College.[2] Cardinal first dabbled in politics as a student. He was the associate secretary for Indian affairs for the Canadian Union of Students in 1967 and was elected president the following year.[3]

After returning to Alberta in 1968, Cardinal was elected president of the Indian Association of Alberta (IAA), the youngest person ever to hold this post. He remained the IAA president for nine controversial years,[4] and during this time he initiated many programs and policies to benefit Indians. In 1969 he wrote The *Unjust Society: The Tragedy of Canada's Indians*, a stinging criticism of the reigning Liberal government's Indian policies.[5] In 1969 the federal Liberals drafted the *Statement of the Government of Canada on Indian Policy* (also known as the White Paper), which proposed sweeping changes to the relationship between the federal government and Canada's treaty Indians.[6] As IAA president, he helped write an Aboriginal response, *Citizens Plus* (also known as the Red Paper), the following year. For a short period in 1977, Cardinal was regional director general of Indian Affairs – the first Indian to hold this position.[7]

After writing his second book, *The Rebirth of Canada's Indians* (1977), Cardinal became a director of an oil and gas company and a treaty-rights and land-claims consultant with northern Alberta Indian bands.[8] During this

Harold Cardinal. Courtesy of Windspeaker, Canada's National Aboriginal News Source.

hiatus from public life, he also served as the chief of the Sucker Creek Band and the vice-chief for the Western Region of the Assembly of First Nations.[9]

Cardinal also returned to school. He obtained a Bachelor of Law degree at the University of Saskatchewan and a Master of Law degree from Harvard University (his thesis dealt with the underlying principles of Treaty 8). He received an honorary doctorate from the University of Alberta in 2000 and currently is pursuing a PhD at the University of British Columbia.[10]

Harold Cardinal continues to work towards his lifetime goal of parity and justice for Native Canadians. In the fall of 2000 he ran unsuccessfully as a federal Liberal candidate in the Athabasca region.[11] The following year, he received a Lifetime Achievement Award from the National Aboriginal Achievement Foundation for his association with the *Red Paper* and his book, *Unjust Society: The Tragedy of Canada's Indians.*[12] The NAAF declared that his 'very presence helped Canadians at large opt for pluralism and tolerance during a very crucial time. He is a true Aboriginal – and a national treasure.'[13]

CATHERINE CLENNET

Notes

1 'Harold Cardinal,' *Biographical Dictionary of Indians of the Americas* (Newport Beach, Calif.: American Indian Publishers 1991), 114.
2 Bruce E. Johansen and Donald A. Grinde, Jr., ed., 'Harold Cardinal,' *Encyclopaedia of Native American Biography: 600 Life Stories of Important People, from Powhatan to Wilma Mankiller* (New York: Henry Holt 1997), 77.
3 University of Alberta, 'Harold Cardinal,' *Contemporary Canadian Biographies* (1997). CPI.Q Database. P.1 http:/web4.infotrac.galegroup. com/ itw/ i_L9746468&dyn=16_ar_fmt?sw_aep=edmo698.
4 Ruth Rosenburg, 'Harold Cardinal.' In Sharon Malinowski, ed., *Notable Native Americans* (New York: Gale Research 1995), 69.
5 Bob Bettson, 'Cardinal Again Cast in Leading Role,' Calgary Herald, 10 Nov. 1983, D1.
6 Bettson, 'Cardinal Again Cast in Leading Role,' D1.
7 University of Alberta, *Contemporary Canadian Biographies*, 1.
8 Rosenburg, 'Harold Cardinal,' 70.
9 'Harold Cardinal.' In Elizabeth Lumley, ed., *Who's Who in Canada*, vol. 35 (Toronto: University of Toronto Press 2000), 77.
10 University of Alberta, 'Harold Cardinal,' *Folio* (1999), http://www.ualberta. ca/ FOLIO/9899/06.18/04.htm.
11 Tina Kennedy, '"Liberal Loss Not All Bad" Cardinal,' *South Peace News* (2000), http://www.southpeacenews.com/electon2000/story3.html.
12 *Aboriginal Achievement Foundation, 2001 Recipients*, National Aboriginal Achievement Foundation 25 Nov. 2001, http://www.naaf.ca/rec2001.html#4.
13 Ibid.

Treaties and Aboriginal-Government Relations, 1945–2000

MICHAEL CASSIDY

Aboriginal peoples were almost invisible members of Canadian society from the end of the War of 1812 until the era of reconstruction following the Second World War. During that long period, they were held back by disease and poverty at a time when millions of settlers from the British Isles and continental Europe were pouring into Canada to find land and opportunity and build new lives. Even though treaty making continued during these years, its primary purpose was to win access to fertile farmlands and to resources for the growing non-Aboriginal population. New treaties continued to be signed in the prairies and northern Canada, but they were largely ignored as the federal government imposed control over every aspect of Aboriginal life. The government did so through successive versions of the Indian Act, aided by missionaries anxious to save souls and by settlers eager to take over Aboriginal lands that were apparently unused. In this era, Aboriginal peoples went from being active allies and trading partners to becoming wards of the state.

As late as the 1969 White Paper, the federal government remained wedded to the policy, which had begun at Confederation, of assimilating Indians into mainstream Canadian society. In the White Paper, it sought to disown the crown's historic treaties with Indians rather than to implement them. The White Paper ignored to Aboriginal peoples' pleas for recognition of their unique status as the original inhabitants of Canada. Government officials and politicians did not subcribe to the Aboriginal concept of a treaty relationship based on sharing the land, as it had been understood by Indians at the time of treaty making. Since Indian reserves were mostly located far from the areas of settlement, few non-Aboriginal Canadians knew or cared about the desperate conditions that marked the daily lives of most Indians and Metis in Canada.

This chapter starts from the perspective of the historic treaties between Indians and the crown and the comprehensive claims agreements that are the modern-day equivalent of those treaties. Historically, treaties are the means by which different societies or nations seek to regulate their relations. Treaty agreements between Indians and the crown were the major vehicle used to arrange the peaceful settlement of Canada by newcomers, primarily from Europe, over two-hundred-year-period from 1725 to the 1920s (RCAP 1996).

Prior to the Second World War, the situation of Aboriginal people, especially Status Indians living on reserves, was compounded by restrictions that hindered efforts to improve their conditions at almost every turn. From 1927 until 1951, Indians were prevented from accessing legal counsel to undertake action in defence of their treaty and other rights. They were also hampered in efforts to form organizations that could advance their rights. Band council funds were subject to government control and could not be used for Indian organizations. Indians on reserves suffered from desperate poverty, inadequate housing, and almost total unemployment. In addition, development of Indian leadership was held back by the control Indian agents exercised over reserves and by abysmal levels of Indian education.

After the Depression of the 1930s and the Second World War, the search for accommodation between Aboriginal and non-Aboriginal peoples in Canada broadened into a range of relationships and agreements that have continued to evolve to this day. The story of Aboriginal-government relations during the post-war period played out in the courts, in Parliament and the legislatures, in constitutional conferences and referendums, at negotiating tables, in dramatic appeals to public opinion, and, at times, in direct confrontations between Aboriginal peoples and the agents of government.

Aboriginal peoples are now emerging from decades of neglect and marginalization, gradually creating a distinctive place for themselves in Canadian society. The assertion of their Aboriginal identity and the distinctive mechanisms being developed to accommodate that identity are in turn becoming an important element in Canada's own identity as a generous, tolerant, and diverse society.

Two events – the Second World War, and the federal government's 1969 White Paper – were initial turning points in the reassertion of Aboriginal identity over the past half-century. Even though they were not subject to conscription, Aboriginal peoples had volunteered for service in the First World War in large numbers. They signed up just as willingly to take part in the Second World War and distinguished themselves in battle. During their war service, many Aboriginal soldiers came into contact with non-Aboriginal Canadians on an equal basis for the first time in their lives. On their return home, however, these soldiers were denied many of the benefits for land, housing, education, and other services that non-Aboriginal veterans received (RCAP 1996).

The resentment that this provoked was one of the factors that prompted the resurgence of Aboriginal peoples in Canada over the past half-century. This resurgence was not unique to Canada. Beginning with the independence of India, the period after the war saw a movement of decolonization and national independence that touched almost every corner of the world. The 1948 United Nations Declaration on Human Rights set a standard for honouring human rights that Canada, as a leading proponent, could not ignore in its treatment of Aboriginal peoples at home. Many of the constraints on Aboriginal peoples in Canada were uncomfortably close to the racism and persecution of minorities found in Nazi Germany. As Canadian society changed after the war, non-Aboriginal Canadians began to be aware for the first time, through the media, of the reality of conditions in Canada's Native communities.

After the Second World War, Aboriginal people continued to face determined efforts by the federal government to maintain a policy of assimilation designed to end Indian status and identity, do away with treaties and the special relationship of Indians with the crown, and turn them into just another ethnic group in the multicultural fabric of Canada. A primary reason for this policy's failure has been the determined efforts of Indians and other Aboriginal peoples to maintain the special status they hold as descendants of the original inhabitants of Canada. These efforts have been reinforced by the rapid growth in Canada's Aboriginal population over the past half-century, their increasing presence in urban areas, the dramatic increase in Aboriginal students at Canadian colleges and universities, and the leadership of the courts in enlarging the definition of Aboriginal and treaty rights. The federal and provincial governments, for their part, have tended to respond to the pressure of Aboriginal activism, court rulings, and public opinion rather than lead in the move to expand Aboriginal rights. This pressure is likely to continue, however, and to result in further recognition of Aboriginal rights and of the important place of Aboriginal people in Canadian society.

Three examples illustrate just how successfully Aboriginal people have moved out of the shadows and onto centre stage in Canadian society over the past half-century. One is the transformation of their role in government deliberations. Before 1951, Indians were forbidden to hire lawyers to appear in defence of their rights by virtue of the Indian Act. By the 1980s, Indian and other Aboriginal leaders were active participants in the constitutional process and even engaged in direct and public negotiations with provincial premiers and the prime minister over Aboriginal rights.

A second example is the extraordinary change in the settlements of Indian land claims and treaties that governments now conclude with First Nations[1] compared with the historic treaties signed prior to the 1920s. In their written form, these treaties generally provided yearly annuities of $5 per head for Indians and their families, with no allowance made for inflation. Although they contained promises concerning health and education, the treaties left Indians with reserves that were a fraction of the land that they surrendered. The contrast in recent land-claims settlements is striking. In addition to large transfers of land to the Aboriginal signatories, payments by governments amounted to $196 million in the 1999 Nisga'a Treaty, $1.15 billion in the 1993 Nunavut agreement, and $3.5 billion in the new James Bay and Northern Quebec Agreement signed in 2001 between Quebec and the Aboriginal peoples of northern Quebec.

The third example is symbolic. The embassy that Canada opened in Washington in 1989 is a symbol of this country's relationship with our closest neighbour, largest trading partner, and most powerful ally. The centrepiece of this stunning new building is *The Spirit of Haida Gwaii*, a monumental sculpture by an Aboriginal artist, the late Bill Reid of Vancouver. By choice, Canada has given its new embassy in Washington an Aboriginal face.

As noted earlier, treaties embody the relationship between different societies. Although treaties are normally concluded between sovereign nations, Aboriginal treaties in Canada have been judged to be unique, *sui generis* agreements that help define the domestic relationship between Aboriginal peoples and the Crown but lack the international standing of conventional treaties.

The development of the treaty relationship in Canada can be viewed from two perspectives: that of the slow but continuing evolution of Aboriginal and treaty rights, expressed in legislation, litigation, government policies, and claims agreements; and the underlying change in the relationship that these events reflected. The Royal Commission on Aboriginal Peoples described the first century of Confederation as a period of 'displacement and assimilation,' while it termed the last half-century a time of 'negotiation and renewal.' Step by step, it can be said that Aboriginal peoples and governments are together creating a contemporary version of the more equal relationship that existed when settlers coming to the New World first encountered Indians.

The progress of the past half-century has not come easily, nor is it anywhere near complete. Many Aboriginal people still live in poverty and in dysfunctional communities where unemployment and alcoholism are widespread. A number of issues relating to treaties are still unresolved or in dispute. However, few people could have dreamed fifty years ago that Aboriginal leaders would soon be sitting at the same table with the leaders of Canada's governments, that treaty and Aboriginal rights would be entrenched in the Canadian constitution, and that the federal government would have agreed, at least in principle, that Aboriginal peoples have an inherent right to self-government (Canada 1995).

1945–69: Laying the Foundation

Two significant developments during the first part of the post-war period were the return of Aboriginal war veterans to their communities, discussed above, and the parliamentary hearings of a special joint committee on the Indian Act in 1946–48. The policy development that followed the parliamentary hearings culminated in the 1951 Indian Act.

The special joint committee was only the third parliamentary committee to consider Aboriginal affairs since Confederation. At first it was reluctant to hear the views of Indians directly, but in time it opened its doors to a substantial number of Aboriginal witnesses and briefs. The focus of its consultations was to review and update the Indian Act, which had not been substantially revised since the first years of Confederation.

This committee gave Indians the first opportunity they had ever received to speak directly to parliamentarians and to be exposed to the parliamentary system. Its hearings brought to public attention the economic disparities between Aboriginal peoples and other groups of citizens; Aboriginal peoples' limited access to education; and the degree of power that government exercised over Aboriginal affairs, especially for Indians on reserves.

Indians appearing before the committee stressed the need for historic treaty rights to be respected and for outstanding Indian treaty and land claims to be honoured. They emphasized the need for self-government and for Indian control of Indian education. But, while winning sympathy from some committee members, they did not win support. In its report, the committee endorsed the continuation of the government policy of assimilation. It proposed a package that included increased power for band councils and improved health and welfare services but that would maintain the governing role of the federal Indian Affairs Branch and its successors for another generation (Canada 1948).

When the Indian Act was brought to Parliament for revision in 1951, the government of the day gave its proposals to a hand-picked group of nineteen First Nations representatives for review. As the government had intended, they found little to criticize (Johnson 1984).[2] The new act did not differ radically from its predecessor, although it did remove the ban on potlatches and other Native ceremonies and restored the right of Indian bands to engage lawyers to advance their issues. The joint committee's recommendations to establish an Indian claims commission and to give Indians the vote were ignored. It took another decade before Indians finally won the right to vote without giving up their Indian status.

1969–82: Indians Assert Their Rights

Prior to 1969, INAC had embarked on another round of consultations in preparation for a second comprehensive review of Indian policy. This review was sparked in part by the post-war movement for decolonization around the world and the influence of the U.S. civil-rights movement. Publication in 1966 of the *Hawthorn Report*, prepared by a group of non-Aboriginal academics from the University of British Columbia, had helped demonstrate that the old Indian policies were not working, even after the Indian Act changes of 1951. This report also introduced the concept that Indians could have special rights because of their status as Canada's original inhabitants, making them 'citizens plus.'

One of the major conclusions of the consultation meetings with Indians across Canada prior to 1969 (DIAND 1969) was that Indian treaty and Aboriginal rights should be reinstated and written into both the Indian Act and the constitution. These consultations might have had positive results had they been heeded. However, the policy process was taken over by officials in the Privy Council Office who put Prime Minister Pierre Elliot Trudeau's commitment to equality and his concerns regarding Quebec ahead of the special concerns of Aboriginal peoples.

The resulting *Statement of the Government of Canada on Indian Policy*[3] (Canada 1969) – commonly known as the 1969 White Paper – represented the final effort of federal officials and of non-Aboriginal society to impose a policy of assimilation drawn from the old practices of Canadian Indian policy.

Starting from a stated belief in equality, the White Paper proposed to eliminate discrimination against Indians by abolishing Indian status and giving the provinces responsibility for the delivery of government services to Indians. Indians would therefore be treated like other ethnic minorities, rather than as original peoples of Canada with special rights. 'Once Indian lands are securely within Indian control,' the White Paper stated, 'the anomaly of treaties between groups within society and the government of that society will require that these treaties be reviewed to see how they can be equitably ended.' As for the potential claims of Aboriginal peoples for some of the territory taken from them without treaties in eastern Canada, British Columbia, and the north, the White Paper concluded that these claims 'are so general and undefined that it is not realistic to think of them as specific claims capable of remedy.' It saw a policy to treat Indians equally with other Canadians as the only possible resolution.

Indians had no advance warning of this new direction in government policy. They felt betrayed by the White Paper and reacted swiftly and negatively (Weaver 1981). Indian reaction crystallized around the Indian Association of Alberta's 'Red Paper,' entitled *Citizens Plus* (IAA 1970), which once again set out Indian demands for recognition, the honouring of treaties and other lawful obligations, creation of an Indian Claims Commission in consultation with Indians, and an end to the federal government's paternalistic policies. Faced with unbending opposition from Indians, the federal government withdrew its White Paper a year after it was issued (NIB 1970). Indians remained suspicious, however, that the government was still following the policies set out in the White Paper despite its withdrawal of their formal expression.

This period saw further significant developments that had a strong impact on future relations between governments and Aboriginal peoples. One was the establishment of the National Indian Brotherhood (NIB) (now the Assembly of First Nations), the first permanent national organization for Status Indians. It was followed soon after by the formation of the Metis Council of Canada and of the Native Council of Canada (now the Congress of Aboriginal Peoples), representing Metis, off-reserve, and non-status Indians.

Even as the federal government pressed for assimilation on one hand, it began to provide funding for national Aboriginal organizations on the other and to consult with them on Aboriginal issues. This support enabled Aboriginal organizations to become more active players on the national stage. It also helped to build Indian support for the NIB and its efforts to present a united Indian view on important issues of federal policy at the national level.

At the local level, Indian bands began to acquire more practical autonomy with the government's decision to withdraw Indian agents from reserves in 1969. Three years later, the NIB began a campaign of 'Indian Education for Indian Children' which quickly received a positive response. This campaign started the process of transferring substantial responsibilities for the delivery of education and other programs from non-Aboriginal governments to First Nations. The process has evolved to the point where today more than 80 per cent of the program spending by INAC is administered by First Nations rather than delivered by government.

A new element in Canadian politics that affected Aboriginal peoples was the emergence of constitutional issues. These issues first arose with Quebec's Quiet Revolution in the 1960s and became a national priority with the election of the Parti Québécois on a separatist platform in 1976. This change of power in Quebec, which had traditionally taken moderately independent positions within Confederation, set in motion a process of constitutional change that ultimately led to the 1982 Constitutional Accord and patriation of the Canadian constitution.

Although the NIB participated in constitutional discussions in the late 1970s, Aboriginal peoples were excluded from the negotiations that led to the agreement with the provinces for an amending formula and for the terms of a proposed Charter of Rights and Freedoms. However, a last-ditch campaign by Aboriginal groups was successful in adding Section 35 (2) to the 1982 Constitution Act. This gave constitutional protection for the first time to the 'existing Aboriginal and treaty rights of the Aboriginal peoples of Canada.'

That provision was of particular significance for two reasons. First, it closed off the right of provincial or federal governments to pass legislation that unilaterally extinguished long-standing Aboriginal or treaty rights, a power that had been based on the supremacy of legislatures over executive agreements of government such as treaties. Secondly, the 1982 amendment has served as a springboard for the expanding interpretation of Aboriginal and treaty rights that has occurred over the past two decades through court rulings and through agreements with Aboriginal peoples.

1973–Present: The Courts Step In

While Aboriginal organizations were struggling to establish themselves and to gain recognition in the political and constitutional arena, they were fighting battles of equal significance in the courts. The Supreme Court's *Calder* decision of 1973[4] was a major landmark in a succession of court rulings that have profoundly affected Aboriginal rights and the place of Aboriginal peoples in Canadian society today.

In *Calder* the Supreme Court dealt with a century-old issue, the effort of the Nisga'a of northern British Columbia to have their right to traditional Nisga'a territory recognized and to enter into a treaty relationship with the federal and British Columbia governments. The *Calder* case was rejected in the British Columbia courts but eventually referred to the Supreme Court of Canada. Even at this level the case was rejected, but on a technicality. The importance of *Calder* was that, for the first time, a majority of Supreme Court judges recognized that Aboriginal title over unceded lands could possibly have survived the assertion of sovereignty by the crown and the creation of overlapping federal and provincial jurisdictions in British Columbia.

The recognition by Supreme Court justices that some form of Aboriginal title could exist over lands that had never been ceded or surrendered was enough to persuade the federal government of a need to act. Months after the *Calder* decision, the federal government established a policy to address comprehensive claims over unceded lands from Aboriginal organizations and bands (Canada 1973).[5] At the same time, the government established a process to address specific claims from Treaty First Nations arising out of unfulfilled treaty or other promises.[6]

Calder was one of a number of landmark decisions in which the Supreme Court gradually established a legal framework for the recognition and interpretation of Aboriginal and treaty rights. In *Baker Lake* (1980) the Supreme Court set out principles for the identification and interpretation of Aboriginal title, including the concepts of continuous use and of exclusive use. In *Guerin* (1984), the court established the concept that a trust-like relationship had been established between the crown and Aboriginal peoples; from this it concluded that the federal government had a 'fiduciary' or trust-like duty to act in the best interest of First Nations for which it was responsible. In *Simon* (1985) the judges recognized the validity of a 1752 Maritime peace and friendship treaty and ruled that Indian treaties should be given a 'fair, large and liberal interpretation.' In *Sparrow* (1990) the Supreme Court drew on the 1982 Constitution Act to establish rules designed to restrict any infringement of Aboriginal and treaty rights by governments to a minimum. These rules required that any infringement be based on a valid legislative objective and occur only after consultation. The *Badger* ruling of 1995 set down principles that recognized the unequal results that would occur if historic treaties were interpreted solely on the basis of British legal practice. 'Any ambiguity in the treaty will be resolved in favour of the Indians,' the court stated, and 'treaties should be interpreted in a way that maintains the integrity of the Crown, particularly the Crown's fiduciary obligation toward Aboriginal peoples.'

Finally, in *Delgamuukw* (1997), its most far-reaching decision to date, the Supreme Court accepted that Aboriginal oral history and testimony from elders could be used in cases involving Aboriginal land claims. This decision enlarged and clarified the definition of Aboriginal title from what had been previously understood, and recognized that this title could extend over large areas of traditional lands. The court's decision allowed First Nations a wide range of options in using lands to which their Aboriginal title applied, including access to mineral rights, and effectively placed their rights on these lands ahead of those of the crown. The exercise of these rights, however, required negotiation of modern treaties in order to determine the boundaries of Aboriginal lands. The implications of this decision for future land-claims negotiations are still being explored.

Through these and other cases, the Supreme Court took an increasingly liberal interpretation of Aboriginal rights. It did so, moreover, while restricting the ability of governments to infringe on Aboriginal rights without justification and without searching out the least destructive alternative policies.

Lower court decisions have also played a part in the continuing development of jurisprudence recognizing a wide range of Aboriginal rights. In 1971 Native people in the James Bay region of northern Quebec learned through the media that the Quebec government was planning a huge hydro-electric power development in their region, primarily to support electricity exports to the United States. The Cree, Naskapi, and Inuit in the region had never signed treaties or surrendered land rights, and they had not been consulted about Quebec's plans or informed in advance.

Even as construction began, the Cree went to court and were successful in winning an injunction to put the James Bay power development on hold. Their victory was very soon overturned on appeal, but it had a long-term effect in that it led to Quebec's decision in 1975 to sign the first modern treaty or comprehensive claims agreement in Canada, the James Bay and Northern Quebec Agreement.

This agreement allowed Quebec's power project to proceed, but at a significant price: the province undertook to provide the three Aboriginal groups with more than $230 million in compensation and as funding for economic and community development. In addition, more than 160,000 square kilometres of territory in northern Quebec were placed under full or partial Aboriginal control.

The implementation of the James Bay Agreement has been a subject of controversy virtually since it was first concluded. This controversy may have been resolved, however, with Quebec's signing of a second agreement with Aboriginal peoples in northern Quebec late in 2001.[7] The new agreement allowed for further hydro-electric development in exchange for payments valued at $3.5 billion over fifty years and important new commitments relating to jobs, land, and co-management of resources in the region.

Another avenue for restoring Aboriginal rights has been through international tribunals. In 1981 the United Nations Commission on Human Rights responded to the appeal of an Indian woman, Sandra Lovelace, with a ruling that Canada's practice under the Indian Act of removing status from Indian women marrying non-Indians was discriminatory. Even though it had no legal force, the commission's ruling was an important breakthrough. The federal government responded with legislation in 1985 (Bill C-31) that ended the discrimination and allowed Status Indian women married to non-Indian men to retain their Indian status, or to regain it. To date, more than 100,000 Indian women and their descendants have regained Indian status under Bill C-31, a major addition to the Status Indian population of Canada.

The 1980s and 1990s

The recognition of Aboriginal and treaty rights in the 1982 Constitutional Accord was only one of the remarkable steps in the acknowledgment of Aboriginal rights that began in the 1980s. Following the 1982 accord, first ministers and Aboriginal leaders held four special constitutional conferences on Aboriginal issues. The focus of these discussions was recognition of an Aboriginal right to self-government, a concept that had recently been recommended in a strong report by a parliamentary committee headed by MP Keith Penner (Canada 1983).

The major conflict at these conferences was between the federal government position that the right of First Nations self-government should be a right delegated from the crown, and the First Nations' contention that self-government was an inherent right that flowed from their historic occupation of Canadian territory (Behiels n.d.). The conferences failed to resolve this conflict, but, as it turned out, the federal government would change its stand within a decade. In 1995 it accepted the inherent right of self-government as a matter of policy, though on a somewhat restricted basis (Canada 1995), and began negotiations with First Nations in many parts of Canada to implement Aboriginal self-government alongside existing federal and provincial jurisdictions.

The 1980s saw the conclusion of the first comprehensive claim in the Northwest Territories, with the Inuit of Inuvialuit in the most northern part of the NWT, and the signing of an umbrella agreement in the 1990s that, in time, would lead to eight comprehensive claims settlements in the Yukon. At this time, the foundations were also laid for the creation of the new Inuit-controlled territory of Nunavut, covering one-fifth of the land mass of Canada. As part of the establishment of Nunavut, Canada undertook to pay the Inuit $1.15 billion in compensation as well as giving them direct control over 18 per cent of the area of the new territory. As the largest group in the Nunavut electorate, the Inuit were also poised to control the public government that would take office in 1999.

The failure of the Meech Lake Accord of 1987[8] demonstrated the growing influence of Aboriginal peoples. The accord was an agreement by Ottawa and the provinces that responded to Quebec's constitutional demands and its opposition to the 1982 constitution. The omission of Aboriginal concerns from the accord proved to be its Achillies heel; Meech was lost in the end through opposition in the Manitoba legislature led by an Aboriginal MLA, Elijah Harper.

A subsequent effort to repair the damage left by the loss of the Meech Lake Accord resulted in the Charlottetown Accord, a comprehensive agreement that this time promised to address the constitutional concerns of First Nations as well as those of Quebec (Canada 1991, 1992). The accord promised recognition of the inherent Aboriginal right of self-government within Canada, along with recognition of Aboriginal governments as one of the three orders of government in Canada. It also included a guarantee of Aboriginal representation in the Senate. The Charlottetown Accord would have been another landmark in the evolution of Aboriginal rights in Canada, but Canadians had grown weary of their country's incessant constitutional debates. Although it was supported by the federal government and all of the provinces, the accord failed to win majority support in a national referendum in 1992 – even in First Nations communities.

At the start of the 1990s, a two-hundred-year disagreement over Mohawk rights to lands at Oka, a short distance from Montreal, led first to a Native barricade and the death of a Quebec provincial police constable, and then to a seventy-nine-day confrontation between the Mohawk and the federal and Quebec governments. This conflict was the catalyst for the federal government's creation of the Royal Commission on Aboriginal Peoples, which had been promised at the time of the Meech Lake Accord. One of the most comprehensive and costly royal commissions in Canadian history, the RCAP made more than four hundred recommendations and focused public attention on Aboriginal rights and concerns as never before (RCAP 1996).

In place of the assimilation policies that Canadian governments had pursued for more than a century, the RCAP called for a renewed relationship between Canada and Aboriginal peoples, including recognition of the right to Aboriginal self-determination and implementation of historic treaties in a way that reflects their spirit and intent. Its proposals, based on a twenty-year agenda, elicited a positive response from the federal government. In *Gathering Strength: Canada's Aboriginal Action Plan* (1997), the government accepted the principles of mutual respect, mutual recognition, mutual responsibility, and sharing on which the royal commission had based its report. *Gathering Strength* promised renewal and a new partnership with Aboriginal peoples; apologized for the harm done to Aboriginal people in a *Statement of Reconciliation*; and addressed past grievances such as the treatment of Aboriginal children in residential schools and the continuing gap between the living standards of Aboriginal peoples and those of most Canadians.

One of the most significant elements of *Gathering Strength* was the policy it enunciated with respect to treaties: 'The Government of Canada affirms that treaties, both historic and modern, will continue to be a key basis for the future relationship ... In moving forward, the federal government believes that treaties, and the relationship they represent, can guide the way to a shared future. The continuing treaty relationship provides a context of mutual rights and responsibilities which will ensure that Aboriginal and non-Aboriginal people can together enjoy the benefits of this great land' (Canada 1997: 17).

The 1990s also saw the creation of a treaty process in British Columbia, a province where settlement had proceeded for over a century without any treaties or agreements with First Nations. From its entry into Confederation in 1871, the British Columbia government had refused to acknowledge that Aboriginal peoples in the province had any treaty rights or other claims over traditional lands. By the 1980s, when Aboriginal peoples exceeded 3 per cent of the province's population, First Nations reserves accounted for only 0.4 per cent of the territory in British Columbia that had once been in Aboriginal hands.

In 1991 the province reversed its policy and agreed to join Canada and British Columbia First Nations in a comprehensive treaty process. The recognition that Aboriginal rights might exist and needed to be addressed was a significant step forward, as was the formation of a British Columbia Treaty Commission which still serves as a neutral body to monitor and assist the treaty process. By 2000, close to fifty British Columbia First Nations were engaged in treaty negotiations. The process proved to be much slower and less productive than originally hoped. Although it ran into added difficulty with a change in government in Victoria in 2001, the process had become a testing ground of international significance for the recognition of Aboriginal rights.

In an equally significant but separate process, the Nisga'a of northern British Columbia were able to conclude a treaty with Canada that recognized their right to self-government and to land. The treaty provided for Nisga'a control of more than 2,000 square kilometres of territory plus $196 million in compensation for lost lands. This was the first comprehensive claim to be settled south of the Northwest Territories since the James Bay agreements of the 1970s.

In 1995, the federal government addressed one of the key issues that had been highlighted during the royal commission hearings with a formal policy statement recognizing the inherent Aboriginal right of self government.[9] So far this has proved to be more of a victory in principle than in practice; the federal policy's requirement that Aboriginal self-government powers be coordinated with those of other government jurisdictions has inhibited progress in most self-government negotiations.

Saskatchewan was the setting for another breakthrough in the early 1990s when First Nations in the province and the federal government negotiated a $450-million settlement for treaty land entitlement (TLE). This settlement was to compensate for illegal losses of reserve lands and the fact that many First Nations had not received the amount of land to which they were entitled in their historic treaties. As part of this TLE process, Saskatchewan also saw the creation of a neutral treaty body, the Office of the Treaty Commissioner (OTC). This office has evolved and taken responsibility for exploratory talks involving the federal government and First Nations concerning the current significance of historic treaties in Saskatchewan. The OTC's 1998 report, *Treaties As a Bridge to the Future*, is the most comprehensive joint statement on the treaty relationship ever made by Canada and a group of First Nations.

Further confirmation of the increasing legal and political recognition of Aboriginal rights came in the Supreme Court *Marshall* decision of 1999. In this decision, the court concluded that peace and friendship treaties made between the Mi'kmaq and the British in 1760–1 gave the Mi'kmaq a treaty right to share in the Atlantic commercial fishery. This recognition quickly led the federal government first to promise an $800-million program to assist First Nations to enter the fishery and exercise this right, and then to launch comprehensive negotiations with the Mi'kmaq and Maliseet over treaty and Aboriginal rights. These included rights to land, an issue that was never addressed in the historic Maritime peace and friendship treaties.

Conclusion

This chapter has sought to show how Aboriginal peoples have asserted their identity within Canada over the past half-century and, in the process, have become an important element in the country's identity as a diverse and tolerant society. Many of the mechanisms that have been employed in this process are unique to Canada, as are the relationships that are gradually developing between Aboriginal peoples and the wider society.

Issues of Aboriginal rights have emerged from the shadows in Canada, particularly in the past generation. At times they dominate the front pages, as during the Oka crisis and in the debate in British Columbia over the province's 2002 referendum on the B.C. treaty process. With the support of the courts and public opinion, Aboriginal peoples have been successful in re-establishing an important place in Canadian society and in the constitution for their treaty and Aboriginal rights. They have been consistent in their goals; as early as the parliamentary hearings in the 1940s, First Nations were advancing an agenda that included treaty rights, land claims, self-government, and economic development.

Although many reports have tended to favour Aboriginal claims, governments have often ignored or rejected Aboriginal demands until some outside event – a court decision or a conflict such as Oka, for example – moves them to accept the policy they had previously rejected. Examples include the First Nations lobby to entrench Aboriginal and treaty rights in the 1982 constitution after provincial opposition led to those rights being removed. Another prime example is the federal government's adoption of a land-claims policy after the *Calder* decision in 1973 first raised the possibility that Aboriginal title to traditional lands had not been extinguished.

Today, both historic and modern treaties are acknowledged in Canada, even though all their implications have not been explored. Although the federal government tends to be a reluctant partner, the process of treaty making now under way points to a future in which constitutionally protected treaties or equivalent agreements are in place with Aboriginal peoples in almost every corner of Canada. The progress of self-government is less assured, but the future may also see large numbers of Aboriginal communities, regional bodies, or nations governing their internal affairs independently of the provincial and federal governments. First Nations have used international fora to press their case for greater recognition but have generally accepted that their powers should be exercised within Canada, not separately from it (Cairns 2000).

These developments make Canada almost unique among settler nations. The closest parallel may be the ongoing revival of the Treaty of Waitangi as the basis for the relationship between Maori and the non-Indigenous population of New Zealand. The melding of European and Aboriginal traditions of treaty making has been a major factor in permitting the orderly settlement of Canada by newcomers. The Canadian concept of peace, order, and good government is reflected in the practice and traditions of treaty making that began with the Royal Proclamation of 1763.[10]

The post-war period has seen a striking expansion of the relationship between Aboriginal peoples and governments in Canada. Innumerable agreements have been concluded which, while less comprehensive than treaties, have increased the autonomy of Aboriginal communities and given them greater control over their own affairs. These include control of education, band administration, health services, and co-management of resources.

Court rulings that placed more power in the hands of First Nations have led to a reassessment of the treaty relationship between Aboriginal peoples and the other peoples of Canada. The relationship can no longer be seen as a one-sided concession of rights by the Aboriginal signatories. Canada is a nation rich in resources, and it is becoming clearer every year that the development of many resources requires a partnership with First Nations and respect for their treaty or Aboriginal rights.

Aboriginal peoples contend that they originally intended to share their lands with the newcomers from abroad, not to give them away. These intentions were forgotten for almost two centuries as the settlers multiplied and Aboriginal peoples seemed to fade from sight. Recent developments such as the Nisga'a Treaty, the creation of Nunavut, and the second James Bay Agreement indicate that the original treaty model is being revived. Court decisions are contributing to that revival by providing a clearer and stronger understanding of Aboriginal and treaty rights.

It is too soon to reach a final conclusion on a process that is still ongoing. There is no question, however, that the treaty relationship, the recognition of Aboriginal rights by governments and the courts, and the assertion of these rights by Aboriginal peoples have, in the past half-century, become distinctive elements in Canada's identity.

Appendix

Summary of Aboriginal Relations with Government, 1945–2002.

Date	Event	Comment
1939–45	Aboriginal soldiers in Second World War	Aboriginal soldiers were treated as equals in war but excluded from many veterans' benefits when war ended.
1946–7	Special joint committee of Parliament on Indian Act	First opportunity for Indians to participate in parliamentary deliberations. Committee listened carefully but ignored Indian proposals and favoured continued policies of assimilation.
1948	North American Indian Brotherhood established	First major national Indian organization; continued to operate until 1960s.
1951	Revision of Indian Act	Basic structure of federal stewardship and control of status Indians preserved; petty restrictions on Indians removed, and right of bands and Indians to hire lawyers and to file claims for past grievances restored.
1960	Indians win right to vote	Indians were previously excluded from voting unless they were enfranchised and gave up Indian status.
1966	Hawthorn Report	First major study of the social, educational, and economic situation of the Indians of Canada documented failures of the Indian Act and need to improve Indian education and to strengthen band councils and Indian government. No reference made to treaties.
1967	Indians at Expo '67	Indian pavilion attracted millions of visitors, gave

		many Canadians their first exposure to Aboriginal history and culture.
1969	White Paper on Indian Policy	White Paper ignored concerns raised by Indians in prior consultations and proposed renewed policy of assimilation based on abolishing Indian status, abandoning Indian treaties, and transferring delivery of services to Indians to the provinces.
1969	Indian agents withdrawn from reserves	Regional offices of Indian Affairs took over the administration of matters relating to First Nations in place of the Indian agents, who had been primary instruments of direct federal control over Indian bands.
1970	White Paper withdrawn	Strong resistance from Indians, including Alberta Indians' 'Red Paper,' persuaded federal government to withdraw the 1969 White Paper.
1971	Formation of National Indian Brotherhood	Indian response to the 1969 White Paper led to formation of the NIB to represent Indian concerns at the national level on a continuing basis.
1973	Beginnings of Indian control of Indian education	Federal government responds to NIB campaign, begins to transfer control of Indian schooling on reserves to Indian bands.
1973	*Calder* decision opens door to creation of federal policies to recognize specific and comprehensive claims	Although Nisga'a case rejected, Supreme Court's decision found that Aboriginal title over unceded lands may have survived the assertion of sovereignty by the crown.
1975	First comprehensive claims agreement concluded with Indians of James Bay and northern Quebec	Quebec plans to develop hydro-electric potential in northern Quebec lead to first 'modern treaty' with Cree and Naskapi Indians, including promise of $234 million in compensation over twenty years and full or partial Indian control over more than 160,000 square kilometres of land.
1975–2000	24 comprehensive-claims agreements settled or in negotiation	After James Bay agreement, twelve comprehensive claims settled in Yukon and Northwest Territories. Ten more claims are in negotiation, mainly in southern Canada. Nisga'a Agreement (2000) was first treaty to include both land claims and self-government provisions.
1975	Canada embarks on process of constitutional change	Election of Parti Québécois government in Quebec sets off process of constitutional change through federal consultations with the provinces. Native people are excluded.
1981–2	Constitutional recognition of Indians, Metis, and Inuit and protection	Despite exclusion from earlier negotiations, Aboriginal peoples win amendments to the 1982 constitutional package to provide recognition and protection

	of existing Aboriginal and treaty rights	of their rights. Meaning of 'existing' rights not defined.
1982–5	Constitutional conferences on Aboriginal rights	Following the 1982 constitution, Aboriginal leaders met with First Ministers at four conferences to discuss the Aboriginal right to self-government. The conferences broke down because of disagreement over the inherent Aboriginal right of self-government.
1983	Report of the special committee on Indian self-government in Canada (Penner Report)	The committee proposed that Indian self-government be recognized in the constitution as a third order of government in Canada. Initially ignored, its proposals were largely accepted with the federal recognition of the inherent right of self-government in 1995.
1984	Rights of Indian women recognized in Bill C-31	Bill C-31 ended discrimination that had deprived Indian women marrying non-Aboriginals of their Indian status and led to a substantial increase in First Nations population as women and children regained status.
1980–90	*Guerin, Baker Lake, Van der Peet* decisions	In landmark decisions the Supreme Court set out principles for identification of Aboriginal title and established the concept of the federal government's fiduciary duty to act in the best interest of First Nations.
1987–90	Meech Lake Accord defeated	Meech Lake proposed recognition of Quebec as a 'distinct society' but made no specific reference to Aboriginal concerns. It failed to achieve unanimous provincial endorsement within the required deadline of three years when Aboriginal MLA Elijah Harper blocked adoption by the Manitoba Legislature.
1990	Oka dispute flares into violence	The seventy-nine-day confrontation at Oka between Mohawk and the federal and Quebec governments highlighted Aboriginal concerns and was a major reason for the establishment of the Royal Commission on Aboriginal Peoples.
1991–6	Royal Commission on Aboriginal Peoples	The RCAP set out a twenty-nine-year agenda for the creation of a new relationship between Canada and Aboriginal peoples, based on the historic treaty principles of mutual recognition, respect, and sharing. The report led to creation of an Aboriginal Healing Foundation and increased spending on economic development, but many of its proposals were shelved.
1992	Treaty land entitlement in Saskatchewan	Under this $450 million settlement, twenty-five Saskatchewan First Nations received funding to acquire some 1.5 million acres of land they were entitled to receive under historic treaties signed with the crown prior to 1906.

1992–present	British Columbia Treaty Commission and treaty process established	In 2002 negotiations were under way with forty-nine First Nations in B.C. on lands that were never ceded or surrendered to the crown. Most had reached the stage of negotiation on agreements-in-principle, but none had reached final agreement.
1995	Canada recognizes inherent right of self-government as a s. 35 constitutional right	Federal recognition was hedged with restrictions requiring that negotiated arrangements accompany the establishment of Aboriginal self-government.
1996–present	Exploratory talks on treaties launched in Saskatchewan	First exploratory talks on treaty issues between Canada and First Nations held under auspices of Office of the Treaty Commissioner in Saskatchewan. Results include a joint statement on treaty issues, *Treaties As a Bridge to the Future*, published in 1998.
1998	*Gathering Strength* – federal response to RCAP report	Canada's response promised a new partnership between Aboriginal people and other Canadians; Aboriginal governments that would reflect their communities' needs and values; and action to address outstanding grievances such as the abuse suffered by Aboriginal children at residential schools.
1998	Nisga'a Final Agreement	Canada, British Columbia, and the Nisga'a Nation sign the Nisga'a Final Agreement, the first treaty in B.C. in more than a century. The treaty took effect in 2000.
1999	*Marshall* decision leads to new focus on Aboriginal and treaty rights in the Maritimes.	In response to the Supreme Court ruling, the federal government moved to give First Nations access to commercial fishing rights in the Atlantic and to negotiate land, treaty, and Aboriginal rights issues not included in the historic Maritime treaties.
1999	New territory of Nunavut in Canada's eastern Arctic	The Nunavut settlement gave Inuit 350,000 sq. km. of territory along with more than $1 billion in compensation and effective control of one-fifth of Canada's land mass.
2001	New James Bay Agreement in Quebec	Quebec and the James Bay Cree enter a $3.5-billion agreement that gives the Cree greater control of development in northern Quebec in return for allowing more hydro-electric power development in their region.
2002	Land Claims and Treaty Negotiations	Aboriginal claims or treaty negotiations under way in almost all parts of Canada where Aboriginal land and other rights not already resolved.

Notes

1 'First Nations' is the term now commonly used in Canada to refer to Indians, particularly those with status recognized under the Indian Act, as well as to Indian bands or communities and to Indians in general. This is the origin for the title taken when the National Indian Brotherhood was reorganized as the Assembly of First Nations in the early 1980s.

2 Canada, '1951 Indian Act: Summary of a Conference with Representative Indians,' 28 Feb.–3 March 1951. Summary of government report regarding consultation with selected Indian representatives prior to 1951 Indian Act.

3 See n.2.

4 For citations of court cases, see the list following the notes.

5 The comprehensive-claims policy was reviewed and updated in the *Task Force to Review Comprehensive Claims Policy: Living Treaties, Lasting Agreements* (Ottawa: Department of Indian Affairs and Northern Development 1985).

6 Canada's policy on specific claims was revised and set out more fully in Department of Indian Affairs and Northern Development, *Outstanding Business: A Native Claims Policy* (Ottawa: Minister of Supply and Services Canada, 1982).

7 Government of Quebec, 'Historic Agreement Between Québec and the Crees,' 7 Feb 2002. Includes background information. www.mce.gouv.qc.ca/w/html/w2057002.html.

8 Canada, 'Meech Lake Accord,' Ottawa, June 1997. www.uni.ca/meech.html.

9 Canada. *Federal Policy Guide, Aboriginal Self Government* (Ottawa 1995).

10 Royal Proclamation of 1763. The Royal Proclamation set out a process that required Indian consent and agreement with the crown before settlement could take place on Indian lands. The principles of the proclamation continue to be reflected in Indian treaties and similar agreements, and it is now considered to be a part of Canada's constitution. www.bloorstreet.com/200block/rp1763.htm#2.

Bibliography

(Some documents listed below may be accessed via the Internet where indicated or at the Department of Indian Affairs and Northern Development Library, 10 Wellington Street, Hull, Quebec.)

Printed Primary and Secondary Sources

Aronson, Stephen, and Ronald C. Maguire. 1994. *Federal Treaty Policy Study.* Ottawa: Royal Commission on Aboriginal Peoples.

Behiels, Michael. n.d. 'In Quest of the Holy Grail: The AFN Campaign to Entrench the Inherent Right to Self-Government.' Ottawa: Department of History, University of Ottawa.

Borrows, John. 2000–2. 'Delgamuukw and Treaties: An Overview.' Vancouver: Assembly of First Nations, Delgamuukw Gisday'wa National Process. www.delgamuukw.org.

British Columbia Treaty Commission (BCTC). 2002. *Treaty Handbook*. Vancouver: The BCTC. www.bctreaty.net/education/trbk-introduction.

Cairns, Alan. 2000. *Citizens Plus: Aboriginal People and the Canadian State.* Vancouver: University of British Columbia Press.

Canada. 1995. *Aboriginal Self-Government: The Government of Canada's Approach to Implementation of the Inherent Right and the Negotiation of Self-Government.* Ottawa: Minister of Public Works and Government Services Canada.

– 1992. 'Consensus Report on the Constitution.' Charlottetown. www.uni.ca/charlottetown.

– 1997. *Gathering Strength: Canada's Aboriginal Action Plan.* Ottawa: Minister of Public Works and Government Services Canada.

– 1948. House of Commons. *Report, Special Joint Committee on the Indian Act.* Ottawa: Queen's Printer (June).

– 1983. House of Commons. *Report, Special Committee on Indian Self-Government.* ('The Penner Report'). Ottawa: Queen's Printer (20 Oct.).

– 1973. House of Commons. *Statement on Claims of Indian and Inuit People.* House of Commons Debates (8 Aug.).

– 1991. 'Shaping Canada's Future Together.' Ottawa. www.cnfs.queensu.ca/documents/CanadasFutureTogether.pdf.

– 1969. *Statement of the Government of Canada on Indian Policy.* Ottawa: Queen's Printer. (Also known as the 1969 White Paper.)

Cardinal, Harold. 1969. *The Unjust Society.* Edmonton: M.G. Hurtig.

Christie, Gordon. 2000–2. 'Delgamuukw and Modern Treaties.' Vancouver: Assembly of First Nations, Delgamuukw Gisday'wa National Process. www.delgamuukw.org.

Department of Indian Affairs and Northern Development. 1997. *First Nations in Canada.* Ottawa: Minister of Public Works and Government Services Canada.

– 1969. *Résumé of Reports of the Indian Act Consultation Minutes* (March).

Dickason, Olive. 2001. *Canada's First Nations: A History of Founding Peoples.* Toronto: McClelland and Stewart. Especially chapters 23, 26, 27, and Epilogue.

Elliott, David W. 1997. *Law and Aboriginal Peoples in Canada.* 3rd ed. North York, Ont.: York University Captus Press.

Fleras, Augie. 2000. 'The Politics of Jurisdiction: Pathway or Predicament.' In David Long and Olive Dickason, ed., *Visions of the Heart: Canadian Aboriginal Issues.* 2nd ed. Toronto: Harcourt Canada.

Frideres, James S., and René Gadacz. 2001. *Aboriginal Peoples in Canada: Contemporary Conflicts.* Toronto: Prentice-Hall. Especially chapter 8.

Hall, Anthony. 2000. 'Indian Treaties.' In *Canadian Encyclopedia.* Toronto: McClelland and Stewart.

Hawthorn, H.B., ed. 1967. *A Survey of the Contemporary Indians of Canada* ('Hawthorn Report'). Ottawa: Indian Affairs Branch, Government of Canada.

Hurley, James Ross. 1994. 'The Canadian Constitutional Debate: From the Death of the Meech Lake Accord of 1987 to the 1992 Referendum.' New Zealand Conference. Government of Canada, Privy Council Office. www.pco-bcp.gc.ca/aia/default.asp?Language=E&Page=consfile&Sub=Theconstitutionaldebate.

Indian Association of Alberta (IAA). 1970. *Citizens Plus.* Edmonton: IAA.

Johnson, Ian. 1984. *The 1951 Indian Act Consultation Process.* Ottawa: Treaties and Historical Research Centre, Department of Indian Affairs and Northern Development.

Joyce, David. 1998. 'A Basic Philosophical Response to the Infamous White Paper.' *Indigenous Thought* (winter). www.sifc.edu/Indian%20Studies/Indigenous Thought/winter98/white.htm.

Lajoie, Andrée. 2001. 'What Constitutional Law Doesn't Want to Hear About. History.' In *Speaking Truth to Power: A Treaty Forum.* Ottawa: Law Commission of Canada.

Leslie, John.1993. 'A Historical Survey of Indian Government Relations, 1940–1970.' Paper prepared for the Royal Commission Liaison Office. Ottawa: Department of Indian Affairs and Northern Development.

– 'Presentation on Aboriginal History to the Present.' House of Commons Standing Committee on Aboriginal Affairs, 12 March, Meeting no. 43. www.parl.gc.ca/InfoComDoc/37/1/AANR/Meetings/Evidence/aanrev43-e.htm.

Macklem, Patrick, and Roger Townshend. 1992. 'Resorting to Court: Can the Judiciary Deliver Justice for First Nations?' In Diane Engelstad and John Bird, ed., *Nation to Nation: Aboriginal Sovereignty and the Future of Canada.* Concord, Ont.: Anansi Press.

McCue, Harvey. 1997. 'The Modern Age, 1945–80.' In Edward S. Rogers and Donald B. Smith, ed., *Aboriginal Ontario: Historical Perspectives on the First Nations.* Toronto: Dundurn Press.

McNeill, Kent. 1998. 'Defining Aboriginal Title in the 90's: Has the Supreme Court Finally Got it Right?' Twelfth Annual Robarts Lecture. Toronto: York University.

– 2000. 'The Post-Delgamuukw Nature and Content of Aboriginal Title.' Toronto: Osgoode Hall Law School.

Miller, J.R. 2000. *Skyscrapers Hide the Heavens.* 3rd ed. Toronto: University of Toronto Press.

National Indian Brotherhood (NIB).1972. *Indian Control of Indian Education.* Ottawa: NIB (December).

– 1970. Transcript of Meeting with Cabinet, 4 June 1970. Ottawa, NIB, and Department of Indian Affairs and Northern Development.

Office of the Treaty Commissioner (OTC). 1998. *Statement of Treaty Issues: Treaties as a Bridge to the Future.* Saskatoon: Office of the Treaty Commissioner (October).

Ponting, Rick, and Cora Voyageur. 1998. 'A Hundred Points of Light.' Calgary: Department of Sociology, University of Calgary. ponting@acs.ucalgary.ca.

Royal Commission on Aboriginal Peoples (RCAP). 1996. *Report.* Ottawa: Minister of Supply and Services Canada.

Task Force on National Unity. 1978. *Report*. Ottawa: The Task Force.

Tully, James. 2001. 'Reconsidering the British Columbia Treaty Process.' In *Speaking Truth to Power: A Treaty Forum*. Ottawa: Law Commission of Canada.

United Nations. 1948. *Universal Declaration of Human Rights*.

Weaver, Sally. 1986. 'Indian Policy in the New Conservative Government.' University of Waterloo.

– 1981. *Making Canadian Indian Policy: The Hidden Agenda, 1968–70*. Toronto: University of Toronto Press.

Jurisprudence

Baker Lake v. Minister of Indian Affairs and Northern Development, [1980] 1 F.C. 5l8.

Calder v. Attorney-General of B.C., [1973] S.C.R. 313.

Delgamuukw v. British Columbia, [1997] 3 S.C.R. 1010.

Guerin v. The Queen, [1984] 2 S.C.R. 335.

R. v. Badger, [1996] 1 S.C.R. 771.

R. v. Marshall, [1999] 3 S.C.R. 456.

R. v. Marshall, [1999] 3 S.C.R.. 533, Motion for Rehearing and Stay.

R. v. Sparrow, [1990] 1 S.C.R. 1075.

Simon v. The Queen, [1985] 2 S.C.R. 387.

Profile of Albert ('Billy') Diamond (1949–)

Cree, Politician, and Businessman

Billy Diamond is a man admired not only by the Aboriginal peoples but also by those in the political and business communities. Lubicon Chief Bernard Ominayak says, '... At enormous personal cost Billy Diamond prevailed, winning recognition for the rights of his people and serving as an inspiration to other aboriginal peoples still struggling to achieve recognition and rights.'[1] Diamond's business savvy and negotiation skills have made him someone who cannot be ignored. He has been called the 'Lee Iacocca of the North.'[2]

Billy Diamond was born to Hilda and Malcolm Diamond on 17 May 1949 in a tent on a trapping line near Waskaganish, Quebec.[3] As a child, he and his siblings worked with their father on their trapline. On his eighth birthday he was sent to Moose Factory, Ontario, to attend an Indian residential school.

At his father's request, Diamond returned to Waskaganish to work for his people after receiving his high school diploma. In 1969, as an employee of Indian and Northern Affairs Canada, he established the Band Management Program for the Waskaganish band and became its first administrator. He was elected chief of Waskaganish at the age if twenty-one.[4] Two years later, in 1972, he was elected regional chief.

Billy Diamond has been involved in politics and business for most of his adult life. He was a founding member of the Grand Council of the Crees of Quebec[5] and served as its grand chief from 1974 to 1984.[6] When hydro-electric development threatened the Crees' homeland in the James Bay area, Diamond negotiated on behalf of the Quebec Cree.[7] The agreement he negotiated with the Quebec government gave the Quebec Cree greater political control over their homeland and led to the signing of the James Bay and Northern Quebec Agreement (1975) – Canada's first modern land-claim settlement. In 1978 he became chairman of the Cree Regional Authority, the organization established to oversee the implementation of the James Bay

Billy Diamond. Courtesy of Terry Lusty, photographer.

Agreement. He also served as chairman of the James Bay Cree School Board and helped establish the Cree Board of Health and Social Services. He has participated in the Working Group on Indigenous Peoples and other international committees, representing the Cree and Native Americans all around the world. In the early 1980s, he negotiated with the federal government on behalf of the Assembly of First Nations to include section 35(1), the clause that recognizes and affirms existing Aboriginal and treaty rights, in the Canadian constitution.[8]

Diamond's energies are not confined to the political sphere. He is also active in business matters. He was president of Air Creebec Inc. and has held executive positions in companies such as Cree Yamaha Motors and Servinor Food Wholesales.[9] In 1997 Diamond received the National Aboriginal

Achievement Award for business and commerce. Later that year, he received an honorary doctorate of laws degree from Carleton University.

Still active in the political and business sphere, Billy Diamond is happily married to wife, Elizabeth.

ALAN CHO

Notes

1 Roy MacGregor, *Chief: The Fearless Vision of Billy Diamond* (Markham, Ont.: Penguin Books 1990), prologue.
2 John Hayes, 'Chief Albert "Billy" Diamond: Grand Chief an Inspiration to the Young,' *Windspeaker*, 9 March 1997). 9.
3 Formerly known as Rupert's House.
4 Bennett McCardle, 'Billy Diamond,' *Canadian Encyclopedia, 2000 World Edition* (Toronto: McClelland and Stewart 2000).
5 An organization dedicated to the advancement of Cree interests in Quebec.
6 McCardle, 'Billy Diamond.'
7 Ibid.
8 Hayes, 'Chief Albert "Billy" Diamond,' 9.
9 McCardle, 'Billy Diamond.'

PART THREE

ARTS AND MEDIA

The Art of Survival

MARIA VON FINCKENSTEIN

Art made by the Inuit – citizens of the far north – has a unique place in Canadian art history. Any comparisons to other mainstream Canadian arts are doomed to fail because the origins of Inuit art are utterly different.

To begin with, until recently, all Inuit artists and artisans were entirely self-taught. They were not products of art schools or academies. They never took classes in life drawing or design. They grew up in a hunting and gathering milieu rather than in industrialized society. In addition, they did not view themselves as artists. Most of the people discussed in this chapter experienced throughout their adult years a nomadic lifestyle in which there was no word for 'art' and no separate occupation defined as 'artist.' Men were hunters, trained as such from a young age. Women processed the skins of the animals their hunter-husbands killed, transforming them into highly efficient clothing, tents, and water craft such as boats and kayaks.

During the 1950s and 1960s, when these nomadic hunters and their families abandoned their centuries-old lifestyle, they carried their ancient skills with them into life in modern settlements. Consider the following examples.

Jessie Oonark was fifty-two years old, a widow with eight children, when she was rescued in 1958 by a Royal Canadian Air Force plane and brought to the Baker Lake settlement (now in Nunavut). Until then, she had sewn all the clothing necessary for the family and had helped supplement the family's diet of caribou meat by catching birds, picking berries, and jigging for fish – unusual training for a person destined to become a world-renowned artist.

When she first came to Baker Lake, she tried to feed her family by taking a job as the janitor for the small Anglican church run by the local missionary. This new career was short-lived. The Northern Services officer, charged with building an arts and crafts program, soon discovered Oonark's keen sense of design, obvious in the beautiful, traditional garments she produced for sale. He gave her a sketchbook, which she filled with strong, bold designs illustrating aspects of the only life she knew: life on the barren tundra where caribou provided all the necessities of life, that is, the food, shelter, and transportation necessary to find new hunting grounds.

After that, things happened quickly. Encouraged by a succession of arts and crafts officers, Oonark continued to draw and to sew parkas, kamiks (skin boots), and small appliqué wall hangings. By the time a printmaking program began in Baker Lake, Oonark was already a recognized talent among the Inuit. In this new environment, their lives were controlled by the Anglican Church, the Hudson's Bay Company trading post, the Royal Canadian Mounted Police (RCMP), and the federal day school. Gone were the days when the weather, the seasons, and the biannual migration of caribou determined every aspect of life.

The first collection of prints in 1970 included nine images by Oonark. One of her images, *Woman*, was chosen for the cover of the catalogue for that year's annual print collection issued by the Baker Lake print shop. From the creation of her sewing and appliqué wall hangings, Oonark had learned to think in shapes and colours. The figure is divided into geometric shapes, highlighting the essential features of the traditional woman's parka among the Caribou Inuit. In the same year, the Canadian Museum of Civilization in Ottawa organized a show for Oonark, along with sculptor John Pangnark, in which fifty of Oonark's drawings were featured.

Until 1979, Oonark worked exclusively as an artist, drawing when she was not sewing one of her wall hangings. A favourite device she used was the symmetrical composition that gave her images a highly formal, sacerdotal quality, which can be perceived even in the small hanging in which four birds clothed in human parkas are facing each other in a timeless pose, seemingly acting as guardians to the central figure. Some of her wall hangings were too large ever to be fully unfolded in the small house that served as her 'studio.'

One of the highlights of Oonark's career was a trip in 1976 to New York City, where she autographed the cover of the portfolio of a limited edition of prints she had designed to accompany a United Nations stamp. By then, she had been admitted to the Royal Canadian Academy of Arts.

In the safety of her warm house, Oonark had a chance to exorcize some of the painful memories of the last four years of camp life where, after her husband died in 1954, she and her family had existed on the edge of starvation. Having left behind poverty, deprivation, and a humiliating dependency on the charity of her relatives, she could recreate the joyful aspects of life on the land. More frightening aspects of evil spirits and powerful shamans were encoded in enigmatic images she was not willing to explain.

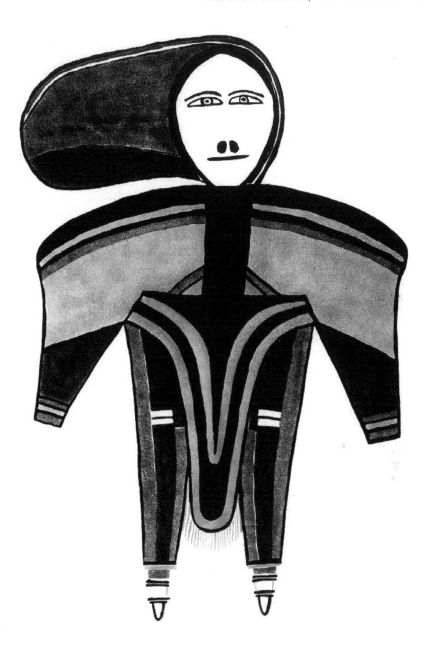

Woman, 1970, by Jessie Oonark and Thomas Nectoralik Manik. Copyright by permission of the Public Trustee for Nunavut, estate of Jessie Oonark. Courtesy of the Inuit Art Foundation.

In 1986, a year after her death, the Winnipeg Art Gallery organized a solo exhibition of her work. Few Canadian artists receive such an honour, among the Inuit almost none.

John Tiktak came from the same region as Oonark, the Keewatin, also called the Barren Lands. Born in 1916, he was forty-two years of age when he gave up his life as a hunter. He has left behind an autobiography that best sums up his early years: In it he recounts:

> I was born in 1916, at 'Kareak,' a small temporary or nomad camp, located not far from Whale Cove, where my father, an experienced hunter, initiated me during my childhood in the art of hunting for caribou.
>
> Then we moved permanently to Eskimo Point. There I became an adult, and with very little experience of life, I got married. (Grenier 1969)

Tiktak's wife was Antaga, an excellent seamstress, with whom he had four children. In 1958 he moved to Rankin Inlet (now in Nunavut) where he applied to work at the newly opened nickel mine. As he said, 'the good Lord granted my wish.' He worked there for four years until his leg was crushed when a load of timbers fell on him. Because he was unable to hunt or to work in the mine, he turned to carving. In his words: 'I have always given myself to the work of carving stone, ever since I was young, and have made small sculptures representing Eskimo faces of persons which I sold to visitors or strangers as souvenirs of Rankin Inlet' (Grenier 1969). Carving became a full-time rather than an occasional occupation.

Tiktak stuck to his representation of faces as well as single figures, often a mother carrying her child. Indeed, he was very attached to his own mother. When she died, he went to visit Bob Williamson, his anthropologist friend, and said simply: 'I have come to weep with you' (Williamson 1965, 12). And so he did. We do not know whether Tiktak's love for his mother inspired these carvings. Until the end, he claimed that he worked without premeditation, taking the stone and allowing the shape inherent in it to emerge.

His figures, single and multiple, are among the finest that have been created during the fifty-year span of contemporary Inuit art. When they are successful – and not all of them are – they have breathtaking simplicity and purity of form. He reduces the figures to sensuously rounded forms, often with arms flowing out of hips. Mother and children seem to be organic units. It is impossible to tell where one ends and the other begins, symbolizing an interdependent if not symbiotic relationship. Tiktak described himself disparagingly as a bad carver. His stylization of form and its resulting sophistication – so attractive to the southern audience – was a sign of inadequacy

Mother and Child ca. 1962, by John Tiktak. Copyright by permission of Marie Tiktak. Courtesy of the Inuit Art Foundation.

both in his own and those of his fellow carvers' eyes. (Inuit admire technically accomplished, detailed, realistic carvings.) The Inuit art historian George Swinton sums up what art lovers admire about his work: 'Tiktak is preeminently an image maker. A producer of thoughts and ideas rather than of actions and events; a maker of form rather than subject matter' (Swinton 1970).

Tiktak, elected to the Royal Canadian Academy of Arts in 1973, experienced the rare honour of having a one-man show in Winnipeg as early as 1970. He died in 1981.

Pitseolak Ashoona is another example of an Inuit for whom art making became a way of surviving with dignity and of escaping the ignominious fate of having to rely on charity from the state or from relatives. Born on Nottingham Island, off Baffin Island, Pitseolak Ashoona was married to a prosperous hunter at a young age and became a widow when she was around forty years old. She had seventeen children, of whom only six survived. She describes her married days looking after a large family: 'In the old days I was never done with the sewing. There were the tents and the kayaks, and there were all the clothes which were made from different skins – seal, caribou and walrus. From skins we also made cups for drinking and buckets for carrying water' (Eber 1971). When her husband, Ashoona, died, Pitseolak was still carrying her youngest son, Ottochie, on her back. 'For a long time after Ashoona died we were very sad. Sometimes I thought I would lose my mind. Whenever a dog team came to the camp, Ottochie would go and look for his father. He thought he would find him ... After Ashoona died we were very poor and sometimes we would be out of oil for the kudlik. Things were given to us by other people ... we were very poor and often we were hungry. We were poor until Sowmik (James Houston) and the government houses came' (Eber 1971).

James Houston, the Northern Services officer for Cape Dorset (now in Nunavut), was setting up a printmaking program in 1957. For this he needed drawings. 'We heard that Sowmik told the people to draw anything, in any shape, and to put a head and a face on it.' This bizarre instruction was vague enough to allow Pitseolak to give her imagination free reign. She says in a matter-of-fact way: 'Jim Houston told me to draw the old ways and I've been drawing the old ways and the monsters ever since' (Eber 1971).

Thus, as a widow, after scraping a living for herself and her large family by sewing parkas, Pitseolak began her astonishing career as a graphic artist. By the time she died in 1983, she had created several thousand drawings, all depicting the old camp life and 'monsters.' Her drawing style was distinctive from the beginning. Far from stiff, as might be expected from somebody who had never drawn before, her line was fluid and lively. A sense of joy pervades her images. The line shows vigour, freshness, and an astonishing assurance. From graphite pencil, she moved to felt-pen and coloured pencil. While her drawings are kept in archives, many of her images have been translated into prints by Cape Dorset printmakers. In *The Shaman's Wife*, printmakers have chosen a particularly dramatic image that depicts a woman with a tattooed face and a bird as a spirit helper. Equally wonderful is the *Caribou at Play*, which illustrates the sense of motion and energy that is such a characteristic of her work.

Pitseolak was showered with honours during her lifetime, including a visit with Jean Chrétien, then minister of Indian affairs, when she came to Ottawa in 1971 to sign her autobiography, *Pictures Out of My Life*. A listing of all the exhibitions of her work is pages long. Pitseolak received the Order of Canada in 1977.

In Nunavik, once known as Arctic Quebec, *Davidialuk Alasua Amittu*, from Puvirnituq, experienced a dramatic reversal of fortune because of art making. His early beginnings were particularly harsh and painful. In the 1930s, after a relatively happy childhood steeped in tradition, he experienced hunger and deprivation when he was in his twenties. Johnny Pov, a fellow artist also from Puvirnituq, describes his circumstances: 'As Davidialuk was growing up he was poor because he was a descendant of poor people. That is the custom of the Eskimos. Even when he was a grown man he had neither dogs and komatik nor kayak and he used to walk around looking for food from other people ... For about five or six years there was great hunger. The people in Davidialuk's group, and others, had to get clothing from their neighbours' (Myers 1977).

When he moved to Puvirnituq in 1951, at the age of thirty-seven, his life changed dramatically. He started carving as a way of making an income and, for the first time in his life, experienced success and relative security. His art, depicting the many stories he had heard during his life on the land, was appreciated and celebrated among the collectors in southern Canada who had started to collect after the first sale ever of Inuit art in 1948. Davidialuk's style – expressive and immediate, with spontaneous, quick scratches, rather than carefully controlled lines, that detail hair and facial features as well as fur or bird's feathers – stood out and attracted attention. He became one of the most successful artists in his community and received the recognition and status that had eluded him as a hunter.

Davidialuk never developed a formula, a recurrent theme or a motif that has sometimes trapped other Inuit artists. His repertoire of scenes and images is enormous. Apart from a prolific outpouring of sculptures, he also started to draw, eventually becoming a printmaker. As customary in Puvirnituq, he would take a stone slab home and chisel an image directly onto

Shaman's Wife, 1980, by Pitseolak Ashoona and Pee Mikkigaq. Courtesy of the Inuit Art Foundation.

Caribou at Play, 1980, by Pitseolak Ashoona and Simigak Simeonie. Courtesy of the Inuit Art Foundation.

the printing surface, giving his prints the spontaneity and immediacy of drawings.

Survival is a theme in any of Davidialuk's work. Says Ian Lindsay, one of the first collectors of Davidialuk's work: 'Pre-eminently, his themes dwell on survival: of man in conflict with man; man in conflict with animal; man in conflict with nature; woman's despair with the loss of her mate; and awe of the supernatural. Little of the tranquil is considered – nature and man never rest' (Myers 1977). The sculpture *Puungittuq killing Quviqsalualuk* is one such depiction of conflict. The story of a son killing his father, who was considered dangerous by the members of his camp, demonstrates the drama and intensity so characteristic of much of Davidialuk's works. *Nauyavinaaluk Killing* tells the tragic story of a man visiting a relative's camp and proceeding to kill that man's wife and baby. The woman's expression and her fruitless attempt to protect herself with her woman's knife is storytelling at its most powerful.

Nauyavinaaluk Killing, 1960, by Davidialuk Alasua Amittu. Copyright permission of Aisa Amittu. Courtesy of the Inuit Art Foundation.

Davidialuk died in 1976, leaving behind an amazing legacy. Fully conscious that his culture was doomed to be absorbed by modern technological society, he made an effort to collect stories passed down through oral history and to document them in sculpture, drawings, prints, and recordings. To this day, he is considered a giant among the Nunavik storytellers of the last fifty years.

For some Inuit artists, art making has been a matter of emotional survival as well as economic independence. This applies to the younger generation born during the 1940s. They are in some ways the lost generation, caught in cultural upheaval, neither comfortable in the old culture nor yet part of the new. Some have chosen to become traditionalists, emphasizing the importance of Inuit culture in their art as well as in their lives.

Lypa Pitsiulak from Oopinivik, an outpost camp near Pangnirtung on Baffin Island (now in Nunavut), is part of this group. He is the son of Mark Pitsiulak, the camp leader of Illutalik, one of the winter camps along the Cumberland Sound that were abandoned during the 1960s. Lypa lived in Pangnirtung for ten years as a sculptor and printmaker, becoming the manager of the Community Print Shop in 1975. Although successful as an artist and manager, he decided to move his family – his wife, Annie, is also an artist – to the outpost camp Oopinivik, where he lives to this day. This is documented in the film *Lypa* produced by the National Film Board of Canada. Lypa Pitsiulak's sculptures often depict spirit creatures. Although they seem to be from the realm of the imagination, they are very real to him. He has stated: 'I have seen a "kalopalik" [a sea monster that is assumed to snatch children], a human creature that lives in the water, and I have also seen spirits more than once. I have heard them myself when they have made noises. My mother, too, has seen these human creatures. The water has its own dogs, its own birds, as well as different kinds of animals' (Driscoll 1983). He has also noted: 'However, I am not the only one who has seen these creatures. They will still be seen in the future because we live in a hard way in the Arctic. That's why I do these accurate drawings of the creatures that live on the land. They are accurate because these creatures really exist' (Driscoll 1983).

Lypa also tries to hold onto the heritage of his ancestors by illustrating the myths that have been passed down through oral history. He says: 'I do drawings that follow the very old Inuit way of life' (Driscoll 1983). In the tapestry *Blind Man's Anger*, he chose an episode from the epic myth of the blind boy and the loon. He illustrates the moment when the blind boy has regained his sight and realizes that he has been betrayed by his stepmother. In anger, he chops off one leg of the precious bearskin that has been stretched onto a frame to dry.

Taleelayo, 1980, by Lypa Pitsiulak, Canadian Museum of Civilization. Courtesy of Indian and Northern Affairs Canada.

Lypa Pitsiulak is typical of his generation in that he makes his living by working in several areas. Besides hunting and fishing, he draws both for the Pangnirtung Community Print Shop as well as for the Pangnirtung Tapestry Studio. Lately, he has become involved in taking young offenders onto the land to teach them traditional skills as part of their rehabilitation. He always carves. His work can be found in numerous public and private collections. Over the years he has had a number of solo exhibitions at commercial galleries. His print *Disguised Archer* was reproduced as a twelve cent postage stamp in 1977.

Another member of the generation between two cultures, *Nick Sikkuark*, from the central Arctic, has had life experiences that are very different from those of Lypa Pitsiulak. At the age of twelve, he was taken into the care of the Oblate missionaries in Gjoa Haven. In 1961, at the age of nineteen, he was sent to Winnipeg and later to Ottawa to study for the ministry. However, in 1965, he discontinued his studies and returned to Kitikmeot where he had grown up. For the next ten years he moved around, working mainly as a carpenter and serving as a Roman Catholic catechist.

Blind Man's Anger, 1990/1, by Lypa Pitsiulak. Canadian Museum of Civilization image number: S2001–4771.

In 1976, says Sikkuark, 'when the building [he was working on] was finished, I had no job so I decided to carve to earn money' (Mitchell 1991, 16). He found that he liked carving better than carpentry. 'I began carving steadily and even when I was called to work at building houses, I would refuse' (Kunnuk 1997, 12). He continues: 'I really enjoy the process of carving. I have a variety of materials to choose from in the Arctic: soapstone, whalebone, ivory tusk, caribou antler, I even use some of the small bones of seals and the skulls of caribou' (Kunnuk 1997, 12–13).

The central Arctic is known for a particular carving tradition that had been introduced by Karoo Ashevak, who died in 1974. Ashevak used weathered whalebone in new and highly original ways. Rather than taking one solid piece of bone as material for a sculpture, he tended to assemble works out of various pieces taken from different parts of the whale, inserting whale baleen to indicate eyes and grotesquely formed mouths.

Building on this tradition, Nick Sikkuark carried it beyond Karoo Ashevak's innovations. Not limiting himself to whale bone, he added fur, antler, skulls, and bones of land animals and other found objects from the tundra.

These scurrilous, droll creations have spawned a new tradition in carving in the Kitikmeot – his style is imitated by many others.

Sikkuark, also a graphic artist, has written and illustrated a series of five booklets published by the Education Department of the government of the Northwest Territories. Some of his carvings seem to be three-dimensional representations of these stories. To make the story more explicit, he often gives them long titles. *Skinny Man with Bags of Tools Being Pulled by a Lemming* reveals the humour often contained in his work. The artist himself considers that it would be useful to have a written story accompanying his carvings, but 'the co-op managers generally don't bother with that' (Kunnuk 1997, 12–13).

Whether droll and humorous or sinister, all of Sikkuark's carvings appear to be steeped in Inuit culture and folklore. The years spent studying to become a Catholic priest are not reflected in any of his work. When asked for the sources of inspiration for his creations, he claimed that he draws from stories for some and others come 'just from imagination' (Mitchell 1991, 16). In addition, he tries to show 'how Inuit life was a long time ago' (Mitchell 1991, 16).

It may be surprising to some that Nick Sikkuark is an author as well as a sculptor, a carpenter, and a Catholic catechist. In the mixed northern economy, this is not unusual. Drawing from different sources of income is part of daily survival in Canada's north.

David Ruben Piqtoukun, from Paulatuk in the western Arctic, is part of a group referred to as 'Urban Inuit Artists.' Rediscovery of his Inuit heritage through his art has been, for him, a matter of emotional survival in the struggle between two worlds.

David Ruben was born in 1950 into a large family, being one of fifteen children. They lived a nomadic life along the Arctic coast north of the Mackenzie River Delta. Tragically, at the age of five, he was sent to Roman Catholic residential schools in Aklavik and later in Inuvik.

The move to residential school was the beginning of his alienation from his cultural roots. He learned to speak English but lost his ability to speak Inuktitut. After finishing high school, he left the Arctic determined to see the world. He worked on oil rigs and did roofing, construction, and drywalling, but nothing seemed to satisfy him. In 1971 he reconnected with his brother, Abe Anghik, who had studied art in Alaska. Inspired by Abe to start carving, he soon made it clear that he had found his calling.

Art making became for him more than a means of earning a living; it developed into a way of expressing thoughts and feelings through stone. As he explained in an interview in 1994: 'I became more aware of not just carving for the market, but searching inside me and making statements'

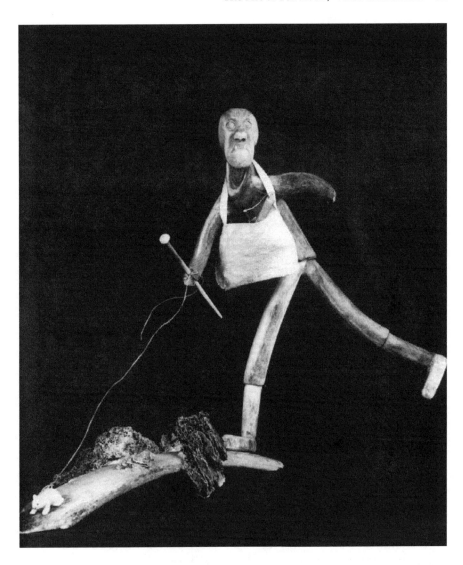

Skinny Man with Bag of Tools Being Pulled by a Lemming, 1980–2, by Nick Sikkuark. Courtesy of the artist and Indian and Northern Affairs Canada.

(Ayre 1994, 20). Thus, in the sculpture *The Carver Who Found a Stone*, he expresses the satisfaction any carver would feel on finding a stone that can be carved to earn money and that allows him to form images from his imagination (Seidelman 1981, 376). The lip plugs are an indication that the carver is attached to the old times when people wore labrets. Carving themes from the old times was Piqtoukun's ambition from the start. As early as 1979, he wrote in an exhibition catalogue: 'Our legends and mythologies have been passed on through the songs and carvings for centuries but recently our traditional lifestyle has been influenced greatly by the Western cultures. Despite this sudden integration of opposing lifestyles, we will continue to exist through our art forms, and there will always be a variety of stone with which to shape our Inuit thoughts' (Inuit Gallery 1979).

Heroes in ancient myths often have to leave their villages to travel and go through adventures only to return eventually and impart whatever they have learned to their original community. In a similar fashion, David Ruben returns to the north periodically to give workshops and to encourage carvers to be true to themselves. He said in a recent interview: 'Words of wisdom from me: Don't accommodate the market. Do it because you believe it.' In more wistful note, he continued: 'A lot of artists in the North never really developed. They were good at one object and kept doing it. They never really developed their skills' (Ayre 1994, 22). He is referring to gifted Inuit artists who have developed a successful formula and are unwilling to depart from it.

Ruben has enjoyed a satisfying career as an artist since 1972. Making his home outside Toronto, he is in great demand for lectures, carving demonstrations, commissions, and festivals. The Winnipeg Art Gallery organized a solo show of his work in 1996 entitled *Between Two Worlds*. In this extraordinary exhibition, Ruben explored his personal experiences in navigating between two cultures. Created as a series between 1995 and 1996, some of these works are highly abstract, devoid of any visual or thematic reference to Inuit culture. In *Tradition Lost*, four shapes are carved out of soapstone, 'like waves that die out and leave no trace something important is being lost. Our minds were hard like stone – solid, in touch with nature and ready for any challenge. Now they have been bent out of shape, made useless in the new society' (Piqtoukun 1996).

With one difference, Ruben's work can easily be recognized as coming out of the tradition of contemporary Inuit sculpture. Unlike carvers in the north, he is not limited to using local stones but works mainly with Brazilian soapstone, which he favours because of its rich texture. He worked with jade for two years – one of the hardest materials – which taught him 'patience,

The Carver Who Found a Stone, 1981, by David Ruben Piqtoukun. Copyright permission of the artist. Canadian Museum of Civilization. Image no. T2002–142.

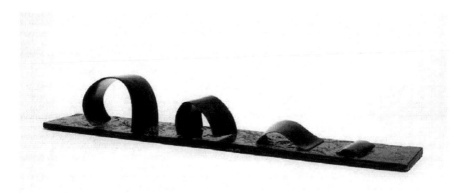

Tradition Lost, 1996, by David Ruben Piqtoukun. Copyright permission of the artist. Courtesy of the Winnipeg Art Gallery. Photograph by Ernest Mayer, the Winnipeg Art Gallery.

competence, determination' (Ayre 1994, 20). This is reflected in the flawless execution of his pieces, which often include complicated inserts of materials for eyes, claws, and teeth.

All of these artists cover a spectrum in terms of life experiences and how they have reacted to them. Of the younger generation, Lypa Pitsiulak and David Ruben Piqtoukun are on opposite ends of this spectrum, both having returned to their cultural roots in an attempt to come to grips with the overwhelming cultural change they have been caught up in. Lypa has responded by retreating to an outpost camp where he lives as his ancestors did. David lives in urban Canada but often returns to Paulatuk to go hunting and fishing and to listen to the stories of his elders. Both gain strength and a sense of identity from their culture.

Over centuries, the Inuit perfected the art of physical survival in one of the world's harshest environments. In recent times, survival has been determined by economic rather than physical means. Art making has become an important source of income in the cash economy in which the Inuit have been involved since the 1950s. Equally, as the lives of the artists discussed here illustrate, it has been a way to survive emotionally. Many artists talk about how therapeutic it is for them to become immersed in their art. Pitseolak noted: 'I am happy doing the drawings. After my husband died I was very alone and unwanted; making drawings is what has made me happiest since he died. I am going to keep on doing them until they tell me to stop. If no one tells me to stop, I shall make them as long as I am well. If I can, I'll make them even after I am dead' (Eber 1971). And, at the end of her life, Oonark said: 'Drawing was a release from everything in the world' (Blodgett and Bouchard 1987, 24).

There is another layer of survival – on the cultural level. Inuit culture is going to survive in peoples' minds through the great outpouring of images in stone, on paper, and on textiles during the last fifty years. Artists like Pitseolak Ashoona or Davidialuk have made a lasting contribution by preserving Inuit culture through thousands of images. Inuit culture is going to stay alive in memory, not through the musty reports by anthropologists and missionaries buried in archives, but as seen through the eyes of the Inuit themselves, the observant eyes of hunter-gatherers turned into artists.

In the process they have created works of beauty and great meaning for other Canadians to enjoy and for future generations of Inuit to take pride in.

Bibliography

Ayre, J. 1994. 'David Ruben Piqtoukun.' *Inuit Art Quarterly* 9, no.3.

Blodgett, J., and Bouchard, M. 1987. *Jessie Oonark: A Retrospective*. Winnipeg: Winnipeg Art Gallery.

Driscoll, B., ed. 1983. *Baffin Island*. Winnipeg: Winnipeg Art Gallery.

Eber, D. 1971. *Pictures out of My Life*. Toronto: Oxford University Press.

Grenier, C. 1969. 'Autobiography of Tiktak.' Ottawa: Indian and Northern Affairs Canada Archives.

Inuit Gallery. 1979. *Sculpture of the Inuit Masterwork Exhibitors of the Canadian Arctic*. Vancouver: Inuit Gallery.

Kunnuk, S. 1997. 'Nick Sikkuark: I Love the Carvings Themselves.' *Inuit Art Quarterly* 12, no.3: 12–15.

Mitchell, M. 1991. 'Seven Artists in Ottawa' *Inuit Art Quarterly* 6, no.3: 6–12.

Myers, M., ed. 1977. *Davidialuk 1977*. Montreal: La Fédération des Coopératives du Nouveau-Québec.

Piqtoukun, David Ruben. 1996. *Notes in Exhibition Catalogue for Between Two Worlds: Sculpture by David Ruben Piqtoukun*. Winnipeg: Winnipeg Art Gallery.

Seidelman, H. 1981. 'David Ruben Piqtoukun.' *Arts and Culture of the North* 5, no.4: 375–7.

Swinton, G. 1970. *Tiktak: Sculptor from Rankin Inlet, N.W.T.* Winnipeg: University of Manitoba Press.

Williamson, R. 1965. 'The Spirit of Keewatin.' *The Beaver* 296 (summer): 5–12.

Profile of Norval Morrisseau, (1932–)

Ojibwa, Artist, and Storyteller

Norval Morrisseau has been described as the most accomplished painter in Canadian history and, within Aboriginal society, itself, it has been said that his magical paintings have helped re-create Ojibwa culture.[1] Well known in both Germany and France, he was the first to paint the ancient myths and legends of the Eastern Woodlands. He was also the first artist to 'break the sacred Shaman taboo by depicting legends that were previously handed down orally.'[2] Some have called Morrisseau 'the Father of Ojibwa Art.'[3]

'Copper Thunderbird,' his traditional name, was born on 13 March 1931 on Sandy Lake Reserve, near Thunder Bay, Ontario. He is the eldest of seven boys. Norval was raised by his grandfather, Moses 'Potan' Nanakonagos, a sixth generation Ojibwa-speaking shaman. His grandfather inspired and influenced Norval throughout his life.[4]

As a young boy, Norval would draw on rocks or damp sand; his first attempts at painting were on birchbark, brown paper, and cardboard using ink, pastels, and crayons.[5] He contracted tuberculosis at age nineteen and was sent to a Fort William (now Thunder Bay) sanatorium.[6] There he met his future wife, Harriet Kakegamic. The couple would have six children before their marriage ended in divorce.[7]

At the sanatorium, Morrisseau came into contact with Dr Joseph Weinstein, who encouraged him to pursue his talent. In 1962 Morrisseau walked into the Pollack Gallery, an establishment owned by artist and teacher Jack Pollack, and offered to sell his paintings on birchbark for five dollars.[8] Instead of purchasing the paintings, Pollock offered to exhibit them. The show was a great success, with all of the paintings selling the first day and earning Morrisseau more than $3,000.[9] From this point forward, Morrisseau experienced tremendous artistic success.[10] Between 1963 and 1993, Morrisseau's work was displayed in twenty-two group exhibitions, and it has also been shown in twenty-five solo exhibitions between 1962 and

Norval Morrisseau. Courtesy of Terry Lusty, photographer.

2001.[11] His personal life, however, has been plagued by health and alcohol-related problems that sometimes had him living on the street.[12] Fortunately, he always manages to return to painting.

Throughout his lifetime, Norval Morrisseau has received many awards and honours. In 1970 he was appointed a member of the Royal Canadian Academy of Arts. In 1978 he received the Order of Canada. He was awarded an honorary doctorate from McMaster University in Hamilton, Ontario, in 1980. Morrisseau was appointed grand shaman of the Ojibwa in Thunder Bay, Ontario, in 1986.[13] The Assembly of First Nations awarded him an eagle feather, the highest First Nations' honour, at a chiefs' conference in 1995.[14]

Today, Norval Morrisseau, now suffering from Parkinson's disease, lives in British Columbia.

AMANDA SELLAR

Notes

1 Donald C. Robinson, *Norval Morrisseau* (Toronto: Key Porter Books 1997), 123.
2 www.kinsmanrobinson.com/html/morrisseau.html#Biography.
3 'Norval Morrisseau,' *Morrisseau Artwork in Canada House Gallery* (2002). wysiyg:29/http://www.canadahouse.com/dynamic/artists/Mor risseauNorval_public.htm.
4 Bruce E. Johansen and Donald A. Grinde, Jr, ed., 'Norval Morrisseau,' *Encyclopaedia of Native American Biography: 600 Life Stories of Important People, from Powhatan to Wilma Mankiller* (New York: Henry Holt and Company 1997), 257.
5 www.canadahouse.com/dynamics/artists/MorrisseauNorval_pu blic.htm.
6 Alice Glibb, 'Norval Morrisseau.' In Sharon Malinowski, ed., *Notable Native Americans* (New York: Gale Research 1995), 277.
7 Ibid.
8 Johansen and Grinde, Jr, 'Norval Morrisseau,' 258.
9 Ian MacLeod and Jacquie Miller, 'Norval Morrisseau,' Ottawa Citizen, 1 July 1996.
10 www.southam.com/nmc/ohcanada/snapshots/morrisseau.html.
11 www.canadahouse.com/dynamics/artists/MorrisseauNorval_pu blic.htm.
12 Glibb, 'Norval Morrisseau,' 278.
13 Kinsman Robinson Galleries, 'Norval Morrisseau' (2002). http://www. kinsmanrobinson.com/html/ morriseau.html.
14 Robinson, *Norval Morrisseau*, 123–4.

Connecting the Artists with the Art

MARYBELLE MITCHELL

Few in number and geographically isolated, the Inuit have been perhaps the least visible of Canada's minorities. Prior to the twentieth century, they had been encountered by explorers, whalers, missionaries, traders, and the Royal Canadian Mounted Police, but it took the Canadian Guild of Crafts, a small, non-profit handicraft organization based in Montreal, to bring them definitively to national attention. In 1948 Canadian Inuit established an indelible presence in the national consciousness by means of simple stone carvings that excited art professionals and amateurs alike. Fifty years later, art made by the Inuit has become the most popular Canadian art export. Along with beavers and totem poles, it serves as an icon of Canadian nationalism. The Inuit have contributed other items of their material culture to the Western world – the kayak, the parka, and, more recently, the ubiquitous inuksuk – but nothing has had as global an impact as their soapstone sculpture and, to a lesser extent, original prints.

Sought after by tourists and collectors, the *art* has been better known than the *artists*. With the advent of Inuit-owned village cooperatives in the 1960s, the Inuit began playing a role in promoting their own art. But, given their isolation and unilingualism, their perceptions were, of necessity, mediated mainly by non-Native organizers and promoters. Feeling their way, these putative spokespersons – civil servants, dealers, co-op personnel, and others – enthusiastically took up the challenge of bridging two cultural worlds and of finding a commercial niche for a new commodity that defied established categories.

These early efforts to 'explain' Inuit art succeeded in establishing it as a desirable item for which people were prepared to pay high prices. But the downside of the promotional rhetoric that surrounded Inuit productions in those early days is that it created a bedrock of mythology that is hard to dislodge. A history of Inuit art emerged which, though colourful, was sometimes more fantasy than fact. Predictably, these fanciful stories began to pale as the north and its artists became better known to the outside world, and as the artists began to speak for themselves.

One of the things Inuit artists tell us is that they would not make art if they could not sell it, a message that non-Inuit resist, steeped as they are in the Western tradition of 'art for art's sake.' By the 1970s, the making of art, especially stone sculpture, had become the largest single source of income for most adult Inuit, an important component of a mixed economy encompassing subsistence hunting, welfare, and some full-time but mostly casual labour. Unemployment is still rampant in the Canadian Arctic, where people hunt for food and scramble for the cash they need to buy gas and equipment and other necessities sold in co-ops and stores.

Art may sometimes be dismissed in Western societies as a marginal activity, but it has never been that for the Inuit. When the market for wild fur declined, carving took over from hunting as the measure of worth in Inuit society, replacing hunting as a means of survival. For most of Canada's 45,000 Inuit living in 56 isolated villages scattered across the far north, making art remains the surest way to earn the cash needed to survive.

Apart from its economic importance to impoverished Arctic villages, art is considered by people like Bill Nasogaluak of the western Arctic to be an important cultural identifier for the generations to come. As he says, we all know what Van Gogh did, but we do not know who the mayor of his city was at that time (Olson 2002).

The cottage-industry production of art is also one of the few expressive outlets available to Inuit. We are only now hearing from the northern artists about the many levels of meaning that making art has for them; it is a way to survive, to support one's family, to express feelings, to document a way of life and cultural disruption, and to communicate to the outside world (most art is made for export). It was to facilitate these aspirations that, in 1985, the Inuit Art Foundation was established. In a nutshell, the mandate of the Inuit Art Foundation – now governed by Inuit artists – is to empower Inuit.

Making the Artists Visible

By the late 1970s, Inuit artists had begun attending their exhibitions in the south in increasing numbers and researchers were occasionally making their way north. Nevertheless, the Inuit voice has been conspicuously lacking in the discourse surrounding Inuit art. Perhaps because they do not have an academic art tradition and lacked a written language until the late nineteenth century – let alone concepts that parallel those in the Western argot – it appeared that the Inuit were relatively inarticulate about what they do. Efforts were made to involve artists in conferences and exhibitions, but these were not venues in which they could shine – and so it was that the task of interpreting and handling Inuit art remained largely in the domain of outsiders.

That has changed in the fifteen years since the Ottawa-based Inuit Art Foundation was established. Dedicated to serving the needs of Inuit artists, the foundation began operations with the launching of the *Inuit Art Quarterly*, a modest newsletter that has since grown to become a professional periodical. For non-Inuit, the magazine is an invaluable research and teaching tool; for the Inuit, it is a place in which to advance their ideas and to learn about art being made by their colleagues across the Arctic. Artists from Tuktoyaktuk to Nain are talking to each other and sharing solutions to problems. They may meet at Inuit Art Foundation events, but the main way they get to know each other is through the *Inuit Art Quarterly*.

Within a few years of its inception, the Inuit Art Foundation had expanded its programs to include professional-development services for artists and the promotion of their work. The foundation's operating philosophy is that the artists must play a key role in managing their own affairs and in solving their own problems. This begins with making them visible. The foundation makes it possible for artists from across the Canadian Arctic to meet with each other and to participate in the wider art community. To come together from all parts of Arctic Canada was a new experience for them. Until the foundation organized cross-cultural opportunities for Inuit artists, they rarely had the opportunity to connect with each other, let alone other Canadians.

In 1992, for example, five Inuit joined with five southern Canadian artists for a month-long intercultural symposium at the Ottawa School of Art. The idea was to encourage the artists to push beyond existing boundaries in their artistic thinking and work. Cultural differences were at first front and centre, but it was not long before the similarities between north and south became apparent. Both Inuit and non-Inuit participants reported that the experience sparked an artistic revitalization. As one Inuit artist said, 'it frees your mind to approach your art in a more creative way in your own environment.'

The foundation has also sent artists to the Vermont Carving Studio in the United States to work side by side with artists from all over the world. Although they were there as students, the Inuit, in recognition of their highly developed stone-carving skills, were soon hired to provide some instructional sessions.

Although the Inuit Art Foundation will, upon request, organize community workshops, the more typical scenario is for a group of artists from different communities to assemble at the foundation's Ottawa headquarters. There, they not only work together (in rented studio space at the Ottawa School of Art) but also have the opportunity to connect with art institutions, marketing agencies, and other artists, the natural allies of the Inuit as they try to assert themselves. Besides having much in common with Western artists, the Inuit are part of a global movement of Aboriginal peoples asserting their right to take control over the content and direction of their artwork and, furthermore, to have a voice in how it is represented to the public.

Similarly, the *Inuit Art Quarterly* has taken as its mission the promotion of the artist's voice, making it possible for the Inuit to contribute to a revitalized Inuit art history in which their perspective has its rightful place. It was difficult at first to find Inuit who could write about art, but a beginning was made in interviews in which artists are invited to speak candidly about how and what they do, as well as their hopes and plans.

Inuit isolation from mainstream society, coupled with their natural reticence, made it easy for outsiders to stake claims of ownership over the art. But, as many artists say, the Inuit have to learn to speak out. 'Inuit are very silent people, but it is time to say and do something,' said Leah Inutiq (Mitchell 1990, 97). Her sentiments were echoed by the late artist Charlie Kogvik: 'When we come up against something we don't agree with, our way has always been to walk away. We have to stay and let them, the people we disagree with, get in our shoes' (Mitchell 1993, 4).

Speaking Out

The Inuit are becoming more outspoken about the inequality of their relationship with southern Canadians, but, still, they could never be considered aggressive. Witnesses in the remarkable 1995 video, *In the Reign of Twilight*, talked about their disadvantaged economic situation, the skills they have lost, the carving up of their land, and the imposition of real and metaphorical boundaries. But, with one exception, they talked about these things in a typically non-confrontational way.

A growing number of Inuit *are*, however, speaking out, and the interesting thing is that it is not just younger people who are publicly critical. Objecting to being treated as if he had nothing of consequence to say at a 1992 symposium on Inuit art, elder Iyola Kingwatsiak of Cape Dorset complained: 'I enjoyed being there, but the problem was that we sat there like pieces of art in a showcase display. The non-Inuit at the conference spoke as much as they pleased about their own lives and how they lived like

Inuit. But they never gave us a chance to speak or asked us questions about our work. The white people dominated as usual. They think they are the experts and know everything about Inuit. This goes on all the time. I myself felt that the white people should be asking us Inuit what we think ...' (Goo-Doyle 1992, 28).

Only three years later, Inuit at an exhibition presentation in Baker Lake rejected an agenda devised by critics and curators, insisting instead on discussing topics of interest to them, such as artists' fees. Artist William Noah raised 'the issue of curatorial control and noted that, in many cases, the works valued by southern communities are not the works most admired by Inuit artists and their communities' (Butler 1995, 31).

The political climate in Canada is now more conducive to accommodating cultural diversity, and there are promising signs that the boundaries of Western museum practice will be expanded in innovative ways. The vestiges of colonialism are being challenged daily by artists and academics and the discipline of art history has undergone a transformation from within that makes it possible to go beyond merely *consulting* with Aboriginal peoples to *collaborating* with them, that is, sharing power and authority. Incorporating artists' commentary into catalogue texts is one thing; allowing them to select objects for an exhibition or to display them in unorthodox ways is yet another.

Isumavut: The Artistic Expression of Nine Cape Dorset Women, an exhibition organized by the Canadian Museum of Civilization in 1995, was a big first step towards a cross-cultural model of collaboration. Seven Inuit women, whose work was included in the exhibit, worked with the museum curator for over a year to discuss and, in some cases, retitle their work. Although they did not decide which works would be included, the artists influenced the thinking behind the exhibition, and hence the presentation of the works. They wrote lengthy essays for the accompanying book and captions for their artwork. The result made for an unusually satisfying aesthetic experience of a body of Inuit art. Non-Aboriginals learned a lot about these Inuit women artists and what they do and think and why they use the images they do, information that 'we have heard very little of before' (Berlo 1995, 32).

The museum's path-breaking collaborative effort was followed by *Threads of the Land*, another exhibition in which Inuit women participated. This time, they were involved even at the conceptual stage. Indeed, the curators gave Pauktutiit, the Inuit Women's Organization, a veto over the very idea of doing such an exhibition. Others are following suit. The Winnipeg Art Gallery worked closely with artists for its 1999 Kitikmeot show, and the following year, in a collaboration between the Baker Lake Heritage

Centre and the Art Gallery of Ontario, *An Inuit Perspective: Baker Lake Sculpture* was co-curated by an art historian and the artists represented.

Taking Their Place

By the turn of the millennium, there were Inuit able to write knowledgeably about their art, some of them graduates of the Inuit Art Foundation's cultural-industries training program. This innovative six-month program – a combination of seminars, field trips, and practicums – is designed to promote the development of an Inuit cultural leadership that will begin to influence interpretation of Inuit art and culture. Until the Inuit Art Foundation came on the scene, the Inuit did not write about their art or fill any of the many arts-related jobs in museums and public and private galleries. Although still under-represented, Inuit are now, for the first time, publishing articles, participating meaningfully in symposia, and curating exhibitions. Their professional involvement of Inuit has been the missing link to a full appreciation of this art form. As for the artists, with the support of the Inuit Art Foundation, they have become more visible in the world art community, carving out a new space, and many, aware that communication is a two-way street, are communicating more directly with each other and with their audiences.

We do not often think of what we are learning from the Inuit, but Canadian artist Jack Butler considers that his experience working in the north 'had a deep effect upon [his] world view and [his] understanding of the purposes of art and the ways of artmaking' (Butler 1987, 7–9). The Inuit have not had much opportunity to exert their influence, although that is changing now that they are being invited to teach in community colleges and to serve as artists-in-residence at mainstream art schools and institutions.

The Inuit Art Foundation can lay claim to having developed inter-community and north-south networks that are overcoming the isolation of Inuit artists and making more resources available to them. Although still weak, links have also been made to the network that serves artists in southern Canada. Collaboration with southern-based art institutions has resulted in Inuit regularly attending festivals, conferences, and exhibitions around the globe. A few have served or are serving as interns at national arts institutions, and they have forged connections with universities and with the Canada Council for the Arts. The artists/directors comprising the Inuit Art Foundation's board play a prominent role in the foundation's bi-annual cultural festivals – *Qaggiqs* – where they interact with audiences who are eager to hear directly from artists.

Although funding does not enable it to meet the demand for its services, the Inuit Art Foundation has succeeded in bringing the Inuit into an entirely different relationship with other Canadians. It is fair to say that it has made unprecedented strides in bringing to life what was merely an exotic commodity. There is growing international recognition of the contribution Inuit art/artists make to the Canadian economy and reputation. The connection has been formed and a new model for bridging the gap between Indigenous peoples and the rest of the Canadian population has been established. More than that, it is a model that is being studied with interest by Aboriginal peoples in Russia and elsewhere.

Bibliography

Berlo, Janet Catherine. 1995. 'An Exhibition, a Book and an Exaggerated Reaction.' *Inuit Art Quarterly* 10, no.1 (spring): 26–36.

Butler, K.J. (Jack). 1987. 'How the Time I Spent with the Inuit Influenced My Work as an Artist.' *Inuit Art Quarterly* 1, no.3 (summer): 7–9.

Butler, Sheila. 1995. 'Baker Lake Revisited.' *C Magazine*, 45 (spring): 22–33.

Goo-Doyle, Ovilu. 1992. 'Iyola Kingwatsiak on Being Patronized.' *Inuit Art Quarterly* 7, no. 2 (spring): 28–9.

In the Reign of Twilight, 1995. Writer and dir. Kevin McMahon, TV Ontario, videocassette.

Mitchell, Marybelle. 1993. 'Getting in Their Shoes.' *Inuit Art Quarterly* 8, no. 3 (fall): 3–4.

– 1990. 'Trying to Present the Inuit World to the non-Inuit World.' *Inuit Art Quarterly* 5, no. 4 (fall/winter): 90–3.

Olson, Michael. 2002. 'Bill Nasogaluak, Masterful Apprentice.' *Inuit Art Quarterly* 17, no. 1 (spring): 35.

Profile of Daphne Odjig (1919–)

Odawa, Artist, Muralist

A highly regarded artist, Daphne Odjig gained celebrity for portraying the life of Native Canadians and for incorporating her own thoughts, beliefs, and experiences into her work. She describes herself as a 'strong-willed woman who believed in herself and her abilities and managed to survive through times when artists really were a struggling breed.'[1] When she began painting, most Aboriginal artists had their work relegated to ethnographic displays or museums; only a few received art gallery displays.[2]

Daphne Odjig was born on the Wikwemikong Reserve, Manitoulin Island, Ontario, in 1919.[3] Her father, Dominic, of Odawa-Potawatomi ancestry, and her mother, Joyce, an English warbride, served as her mentors. The stories her grandfather told her as a child about how her ancestors lived would figure significantly in her later artistic pursuits.[4]

At age eighteen and as a Grade 8 dropout, Odjig left the reserve and moved to Toronto where her artistic fire was lit.[5] Odjig met and married Paul Sommerville at the end of the Second World War. The couple moved to Coquitlam, British Columbia, where they raised two sons and ran a strawberry farm. After her husband was killed in an automobile accident in 1960, Odjig began sketching to help pass the lonely nights after her husband's death.[6] She later remarried and moved to Manitoba, where creating art became a full-time endeavour.

She had her first public showing in Port Arthur, Ontario, in 1967.[7] In the early 1970s, Odjig set up a craft shop in Winnipeg, where she and her second husband, Chester Beavon, produced a series of Nanabush storybooks.[8] At this time, she formed a short-lived, but important, alliance with other Aboriginal artists: Jackson Beardy, Alex Janvier, and Norval Morrisseau.[9]

Her artwork includes the *Jerusalem Series: The Indian in Transition* and many other pieces,[10] and it has been exhibited in New York, Los Angeles, Amsterdam, Tokyo, and Lahr, Germany.[11] In addition, Odjig is the subject of two books, *A Paintbrush in My Hand*, by Mary Southcott and Rosamond

Daphne Odjig. Courtesy of Windspeaker, Canada's National Aboriginal News Source.

Vanderburgh (1992), and one she co-authored with Bob Boyer in 2000 and entitled *Odjig: The Art of Daphne Odjig 1966–2000*, published by Key Porter.

Daphne Odjig has won several awards for her many artistic achievements. In addition to winning a National Aboriginal Achievement Award in 1998, Odjig has also received the Manitoba Arts Council Bursary, the Canada Silver Jubilee Medal, appointment to the Order of Canada, election to the Royal Canadian Academy of Arts and the ceremonial eagle feather from her home community of Wikwemikong.[12]

In the early 1970s, Odjig and her husband moved back to British Columbia and now reside in Penticton.[13]

RENEE VARDY

Notes

1 Terry Lusty, 'Daphne Odjig's Hand an Extension of the Soul,' *Windspeaker* 13 (1995): 8.

2 Ibid.
3 'Daphne Odjig.' In Elizabeth Lumley, ed., *Who's Who in Canada*, 35 (Toronto: University of Toronto Press 2000), 952.
4 Ibid.
5 'Canada Post to Issue Christmas Stamp of Daphne Odjig Painting Genesis,' *Canadian Press Newswire*, 6 June 2001.
6 Ibid.
7 Lusty, 'Daphne Odjig's Hand an Extension of the Soul,' 8.
8 Ibid.
9 Rosamond M. Vanderburgh, 'Daphne Odjig,' *Canadian Encyclopaedia: 2000 Edition* (Toronto: Historica Foundation of Canada 2000), 1.
10 Lusty, 'Daphne Odjig's Hand an Extension of the Soul,' 8.
11 Ibid.
12 Alison Kydd, 'Dance Yourself across Yugoslavia, Odjig Recommends,' *Windspeaker* 16 (1995): 13.
13 'Canada Post to Issue Christmas Stamp.'

Nunavut Territory: Communications and Political Development in the Canadian North

GAIL GUTHRIE VALASKAKIS

Speaking in the House of Commons in 1936, Mackenzie King remarked about Canada that 'if some countries have too much history, we have too much geography' (Colombo 1974, 306). Today, our ongoing constitutional debates, our anxiety over the possible separation of Quebec, and our struggle over Aboriginal rights and land claims suggest that we may have too little *shared* history. However, geography continues to be a critical factor in Canada's historical formation, including the unfolding history of Inuit self-determination and communication technologies in the far north. Canada is the second-largest country in the world and its population is only 30 million people. Living along an extended border in the shadow of the United States, Canada owes a great deal to the technologies that have linked us together as a nation: historically, the transcontinental railroad, and more recently a system of domestic satellites that extends to the new Territory of Nunavut.

Nunavut – which means 'our land' in Inuktitut, the Inuit language – is the result of a land-claims settlement that recognizes the rights and self-determination of Aboriginal nations whose land was never subjected to treaty or surrendered. Signed in 1993, this land-claims settlement is a treaty that allocates more than two million square kilometres in the eastern Arctic and $1.14 billion dollars over fourteen years to Inuit in the Baffin, Keewatin, and central Arctic regions of the far north. An extension of the land-claims settlement carved Nunavut out of the Northwest Territories, creating a new territory that represents one-fifth of the land mass of Canada.

On 1 April 1999 Nunavut became the first addition to the political landscape of Canada since Newfoundland joined Confederation in 1949. With a population of about 22,000 living in twenty-eight communities, the 17,500 Inuit (56 per cent under the age of twenty-five) in Nunavut hold title to 355,842 square kilometres of land, an area almost the size of California. This agreement establishes the Inuit – who constitute 85 per cent of the territory's population – as the largest landholders in North America. The Inuit also share royalties and responsibilities for renewable resources throughout Nunavut, where they govern with administrative autonomy.

Like the creation of Nunavut, the elections for the new government that took place on 15 February 1999, were ground-breaking events for the north and unusual by Canadian political standards. The election process was more communal than adversarial. There were no political parties. Competing candidates flew together, sharing costs, to reach the smaller communities in Keewatin, Baffin, and the Central arctic. In one community, candidates gave up campaigning altogether to join search teams for hunters who did not return when expected. Ten thousand votes were cast, representing an 88 per cent turnout, nearly twice the level of participation in the last Northwest Territories election. The election results, like the structure of the Nunavut government, were a mixture of the traditional and the new. Nineteen members were elected to the Legislative Assembly, including thirteen Inuit and five non-Inuit; there were eighteen men and one woman. The gender imbalance of the elected government was surprising because, in a unique plebiscite held in 1997 in preparation for the Nunavut elections, only a small majority of voters – 57 per cent – rejected a government regulation requiring gender parity. Given the considerable political experience of several legislators, the election of a young, inexperienced Inuit lawyer as premier of the Legislative Assembly was equally surprising. The new government includes a single-tier territorial justice system, a decentralized administrative structure with departmental headquarters in eleven communities, and a civil service that will eventually be 80 per cent Inuit. With the establishment of a government framework and substantial federal transfer payments, the Arctic has entered a new political era.

As Nunavut was being launched, a second pivotal event occurred in the north that received less public attention. In mid-February 1999 the Canadian Radio-television and Telecommunications Commission (CRTC) granted a national network licence to Television Northern Canada (TVNC), a dedicated satellite distribution system that has broadcast Native programming across the north since 1991. This consortium of government, university, and Aboriginal producers formed a national network to broadcast the Aboriginal Peoples Television Network (APTN). The APTN was approved by the CRTC in September 1999. Now all cable companies with 2,000 or more subscribers carry the network on a mandatory basis, reaching over seven million households across Canada. Canadians in both the north and the south can watch a full schedule of Aboriginal television broadcasts, which will eventually be broadcast in fifteen Aboriginal languages, as well as English or French. Linked to the formation of Nunavut, this first national Aboriginal television network in North America marks three decades of social and political change in the far north.

The Inuit have long recognized communications as a basic requirement for their cultural, social and political development. Their interest in media reflects the significant role that communications can play in supporting Inuit identity, culture, and institutional formation. In interwoven developments, Nunavut and APTN represent a dynamic movement towards Inuit self-determination and Indigenous peoples' control over land, governance, and social institutions. The roots of this Inuit empowerment reach back to the late 1960s, when two government initiatives – one political, the other technological – set in motion a process of interaction between dominant and marginalized peoples that no one predicted.

The Legacy of 1969

In 1969 Jean Chrétien, then minister of Indian affairs, issued the *Statement of the Government of Canada on Indian Policy*, called the White Paper, which called for the abolition of the Indian Act and the elimination of the special status of Aboriginal peoples entrenched in this legislation, including the entitlement of Indian reserves. In an ironic turn of events, this White Paper, on which proposed the absorption of Aboriginal peoples into common Canadian citizenship, generated a new political process that fostered Aboriginal self-determination. The Inuit were not directly covered by the White Paper; however, as with other Aboriginal peoples across Canada, their political response led to the establishment of provincial and territorial organizations. The development of representative Aboriginal organizations reflected the participation of Aboriginal groups within a political system that values oppositional debate and advocacy.

Among Aboriginal peoples, denunciation of the White Paper was led by the National Indian Brotherhood of Canada, later renamed the Assembly of First Nations. In a paper that became known as the Red Paper, this organization described First Nations status as 'Citizens Plus.' By 1971, when the Inuit formed a national organization called the Inuit Tapirisat of Canada (which is now called Inuit Tapiriit Kanatami), the government's White Paper had been withdrawn, leaving a legacy of Aboriginal political participation and action. In the early 1970s, Inuit formed new organizations in northern Quebec, Labrador, and Keewatin. In 1977 the Inuit Circumpolar Conference was established.

At the same time, Aboriginal rights and land claims were gaining momentum in Canadian federal courts and at negotiation tables. In an effort to communicate with their own people, regional assemblies of First Nations moved quickly to establish communication units or societies. In 1968 the Alberta Native Communications Society (ANCS) was funded as a pilot project. ANCS became a model for provincial Aboriginal organizations as they transformed their communications branches into separate units or supported the development of independent, regional communications societies. In 1974 the federal government established the Native Communications Program to provide funding for Native Communication Societies in both southern and northern Canada.

The legal basis for Inuit land claims emerged in 1973, when the Supreme Court of Canada ruled that the Nisga'a in British Columbia had a claim to Aboriginal title. The decision was not an undisputed victory, but the government of Canada began to negotiate land claims with Aboriginal peoples who had never signed treaties. In 1975, the same year that the first fully elected Northwest Territories Council took office (with an Aboriginal majority), the first modern Canadian treaties were negotiated in Quebec. The James Bay and Northern Quebec Agreement was signed with the Cree, the Inuit, and the Naskapi (later followed, in 1978, by the Northeastern Quebec Agreement). The implementation process took until 1991, when the Cree-Naskapi Act was passed by Parliament, replacing the Indian Act for these First Nations. What became known as the James Bay Treaty also paved the way for subsequent land-claims agreements with the Inuvialuit in the western Arctic in 1984, the eastern Arctic Inuit and other Aboriginal nations in Nunavut in 1993, and the Nisga'a in British Columbia in 1999.

In retrospect, the 1970s and 1980s represented a stunning shift in control from southerners, outsiders, or non-Natives to Aboriginal peoples themselves. The response to the 1969 *White Paper* had activated a process that, through the organization and actions of Aboriginal peoples, pressured all levels of government to recognize Aboriginal status and rights. However, something else occurred in 1969 that was critical to the process of Aboriginal self-determination and land claims.

In the late 1960s, northern settlements were connected by high-frequency radio-telephone, a service that was tentative and undependable, and operated primarily to communicate between missions, trading posts, and police stations. Few Inuit spoke English and fewer southern Canadians living in the north spoke Inuktitut. Short-wave radio was a cultural lifeline for southerners, but it carried only occasional Inuktitut news. For the most part, Inuit were excluded from radio broadcasting, continuing a pattern of non-Native control that was deeply embedded in the interaction patterns between Inuit and non-Natives that frame the social history of the north.

In 1969 Parliament passed the TeleSat Canada Bill, which proposed the first domestic geostationary satellite system in the world as a vision for the future development of the far north. The Anik satellite system was an important response to the great distance and sparse population of the north, but satellites were a mixed blessing for Aboriginal northerners, who were not consulted during the discussions about the media that the satellite would distribute. The reaction of Aboriginal peoples led to the formation both of Native Communication Societies and of a broad Aboriginal movement that eventually would break the pattern of non-Native political control established by whalers, missionaries, traders, police, and other representatives of southern institutions who went north during the 1800s and early 1900s.

Technology and Social Change: Historical Trends

For decades, the relationship between the Inuit and the non-Native northerners was defined and cemented through technology and the conditions of its access and transfer from a dominant to a marginalized people. Historically, technology was provided by non-Natives on a limited basis, in exchange for Aboriginal services. The earliest and most continuous form of interaction between the Inuit and newcomers took the form of trading. As Canadian traders, missionaries, and police moved north, technology was traded for goods, skills, and information. This relationship created clear patterns of cultural and social change in Inuit communities.

Three major trends are important to the role that communications technologies play in the history of Inuit social and political change. First, non-Natives gained overriding authority through mere possession of technology and control over its distribution. In the eastern Arctic, the authority that metal knives, guns, and wooden boats conferred upon all non-Natives was reinforced by European navigational skills, the impact of the English language, the Christian religion, and a seemingly endless supply of trade goods.

Second, through the directed transfer of technology, non-Natives initiated new criteria for leadership in Inuit society. Whalers and traders who were motivated by economic enterprise required supplies and services from the Inuit. Some Inuit became contact agents, that is, leaders, designated by non-Natives, who directed Aboriginal activity that served the needs of the economic and social agencies that moved north. Inuit became 'whaling bosses,' intermediaries between the non-Native captain and the Inuit hunters, guides, and workers who were required for the whale hunt. They were rewarded for their efforts with technology – guns, ammunition, boats – that, in turn, secured their positions of status in Inuit communities. Those Inuit with wooden boats could decide where and when to travel and those with guns were able to provide more food for their families. Leadership began to shift towards people with access to technology and authority. Social and cultural change was not extensive during the seasonal activity of whalers during the late 1880s, but Inuit contact agents were engaged by all non-Native institutions that moved into the north in the early 1900s.

Missionaries produced 'lay readers' or 'catechists,' Inuit who assisted ministers or themselves propagated the faith. Fur traders named both camp and district 'trading bosses' who organized Inuit trapping and trading on a local level. Eventually, some Inuit families remained in the employ of traders as 'post servants.' As missionaries and traders were joined by the police, settlements began to develop in the Arctic. The Royal Canadian Mounted Police (RCMP) engaged Inuit guides and hunters or providers, later designated as special constables.

With the formation of small northern settlements, the role of contact agent led to new activities and functions that demanded new language and interaction skills. These skills were acquired, used, and diffused through families who established 'the forerunners of new groups for Eskimo society' (Vallee 1967). With the development of trading posts and Christian missions, 'People of the Land' could be distinguished from 'People of the Whites' (Vallee 1967), Inuit contact agents who adopted Euro-Canadian languages and customs through their association with non-Native traders, missionaries, or police. With several institutions operating in the north, Inuit were absorbed into a new, pluralistic society that distinguished between those who were contact agents and those who were not and established leadership based on non-Native criteria. This development 'was instrumental in eroding or eliminating the process of local decision making, except in those matters well outside the white man's interest' (Phillips 1967, 80). At the same time, pluralism began to undermine the consensual basis of Inuit social action rooted in extended families and camps.

A third aspect of new technology affected oral tradition in the contact period. Beginning with the explorer Martin Frobisher in the 1500s, non-Natives traded goods for certain information. This exchange of information for trade goods was formalized as non-Native institutions moved north. As new technologies became essential to Inuit lifestyle, information developed into a commodity used to control credit, trading, residence, and movement. The control of Inuit behaviour grew more explicit as the police joined the missionaries and traders in establishing southern social order in the north. Shared information, which had played a role in integrating Inuit society, began to be partially redefined as a commodity when access to the Arctic increased. The Inuit found it more difficult to withhold information from researchers and government services who joined the missionaries, traders, and police. At the same time, the Inuit became literate in their own language, but not in English or French. However, Inuktitut literacy actually restricted their access to southern information and reinforced the development of two separate, non-complementary communication systems, one within the Inuit community, and the other within the non-Native community.

Missionaries introduced syllabic and Roman orthography systems for writing northern Aboriginal languages in the late 1800s. By 1910, probably 99 per cent of Inuit in the eastern Arctic were literate in Inuktitut (Graburn 1979, 204). However, three different orthographies in southern Canada, and six across the greater north, were developed by missionaries. The diversity of writing systems maintained dialect differences and regionalization among Inuit whose languages are basically similar. Because Inuit in the eastern Arctic did not become functionally literate in English until the 1970s, written information did not allow Inuit to adapt their own social structure to accommodate the economic and political institutions that outsiders brought north, or to participate in the development of northern enterprise and services. Before 1972, only nine secular books and four periodicals were published in Inuktitut. At the same time, Inuit oral tradition seemed to lose much of its legitimacy and function in Inuit society as Inuit cultural information became marginalized and information between Inuit and non-Natives passed through contact agents or community 'go-betweens.' Diamond Jenness writes that oral tradition in the form of 'professional' storytelling was no longer evident by 1924 (Jenness 1965, 179).

As a result of historical-interaction patterns, technology and communication during the first half of the twentieth century contributed to Inuit economic and political dependency and acculturation within a model that can best be described as 'cultural replacement.' Oral information continued to express Inuit culture and community; however, Inuit society was modified and marginalized by the development of new technologies and writing techniques. Because syllabic literacy was limited largely to Christian communication, Inuit wrote no historical or territorial documents, no community policies, no codes of social behaviour. In Harold Innis's terminology, non-Natives established an English-language 'monopoly of knowledge' (Innis 1950, 179) as they moved southern institutions to the north, absorbing Inuit into extensions of economic enterprise. Non-Native authority defined public process in northern communities. Non-Native control of public information and new technologies excluded Inuit from participating in the cultural and social changes fundamental to broader Inuit adaptation and development. In 1972, when the Anik satellite system was established in part to bring southern information to the north, one observer, R.G. Mayes, wrote: 'Most of the important sources of messages are not native to the Arctic, and ... most messages flow into the region from outside ... the political and social position of the senders determines their authority ... and decision-makers of the most important channels of information are almost exclusively white, and located outside the Arctic' (Mayes 1972, 84).

During the next three decades, the Inuit would become active participants in the social and cultural development of their communities and their territory. Their initiatives reflect an increasing awareness of the role media can play in reinforcing cultural values, economic change, and political control.

The Introduction of Northern Media

Radio entered the far north in the late 1920s, just as airplanes assured easy access to the Arctic. Reception was often poor but, by the early 1930s, Hudson's Bay Company trading posts, missions, and RCMP posts were equipped with high-frequency radios. Small radio networks emerged that communicated the directives of southern headquarters, and the authority of local traders, missionaries, and police diminished. The role that radio played in the development of the RCMP illustrates the relationship between early communications networks and the increasing marginalization of the Inuit. In 1927 three radio stations were established in the eastern Arctic, to which RCMP constables were attached in an advisory capacity. For the following three years, RCMP annual reports included a discussion of 'wireless and radio telegraph communication' within the section entitled 'Control of the North.' In 1934, after he had toured the Arctic posts by airplane, the RCMP commissioner centralized the control of Arctic detachments 'for greater administrative convenience' (Kelly and Kelly 1973, 171). Until that time, the headquarters of the MacKenzie and Western Arctic posts were in Edmonton, detachments on the west side of Hudson Bay reported to Winnipeg, and the eastern Arctic posts were under the jurisdiction of Montreal. With increased access by air and communication by radio, all the Arctic detachments were now integrated into 'G Division,' which issued directives from headquarters in Ottawa. During the same period, Inuit communication was limited largely to personal interactions. The first Inuktitut radio program was broadcast in 1960, two years after the formation of the Canadian Broadcast Corporation (CBC) Northern Service. In 1972 most Inuit did not speak English and only 17 per cent of CBC short-wave service to the north was broadcast in the Inuit language (Mayes 1972, 93).

Northern television initially extended southern service to the north, following the pattern established by radio broadcasting. The delayed transmission of videotapes of CBC programming began in the western Arctic in 1967, but this 'Frontier Package' television contained no Aboriginal-language programming. In 1973 the Anik satellite system introduced compelling new media to the north 'by parachuting telephone, radio and live television simultaneously into a region that is culturally different from that of the producers of both the technology hardware and software' (Roth 1982, 3).

From the perspective of social interaction, the historical experience of the eastern Arctic Inuit suggests that Jurgen Habermas's concept of a 'public sphere' (Seidman 1989), reflecting a network of social relations and institutions that engage in rational discussions which critique the exercise of political authority, was neither an Inuit nor a colonial tradition. With the development of the Anik satellite system, however, the Inuit began acting upon their determination to gain access to media in the north to advance both cultural and political development. In the 1970s new regional and national Inuit organizations lobbied for inter-community communication links and against the 'cultural assault' (Kuptana 1982, 5) of southern satellite television, which posed a threat to the language, cultural values, and the leadership of their older people (*The Northerners* 1974). The Inuit mounted political pressure to gain access to radio and television 'to strengthen the social, cultural, and linguistic fabric of Inuit life' (Inuit Broadcasting Corporation 1982, ii).

The Development of Inuit Broadcasting

In the mid-1970s, the CBC made repeated efforts to provide television service to Aboriginal communities in the North, but no provision was made for Indigenous-language programming. Responding to the repeated protests of Aboriginal northerners, the Department of Secretary of State supported the first of twenty-one Native Communication Societies, thirteen of which were located in the north. As a result of this federal program and a series of satellite experiments, Aboriginal people themselves – through their communications training and production, their presentations to regulatory bodies and their persistent lobbying – established Aboriginal-language broadcasting across the north.

The opportunity to work with media that fostered the growth of an Inuit public sphere arose through small-scale communications projects and satellite-access experiments that Canada sponsored in the late 1970s. The most important of these with respect to Inuit broadcasting were the Nalaakvik and the Inukshuk interactive satellite projects, which provided media technology, experience, and expertise to Inuit in northern Quebec, Labrador, and the Northwest Territories between 1974 and 1981. Inuit in northern Quebec used the Hermes satellite to establish an eight-community interactive radio network. An Anik B satellite experiment followed, providing interactive television broadcasts in northern Quebec, Labrador, and the Baffin, Keewatin, and central Arctic regions of the Northwest Territories. These projects established training and regional production facilities for Inuit broadcasting. By the time the Inuit Broadcasting Corporation (IBC) was formed in the summer of 1981, the Inuit had gained considerable experience, expertise, and credibility in Inuktitut television broadcasting. This first Aboriginal television network provided 'a means of cultural expression through drama, documentary, current affairs, news, entertainment and the arts ... in the context that is most comfortable for us: an Inuit system that can link the old and the new Inuit' (Kuptana 1982, v–vi). At the same time, regulatory bodies began to recognize the relationship between broadcasting and cultural and linguistic rights, particularly with respect to Aboriginal peoples.

In 1980 the CRTC issued a report asserting that the federal government has a responsibility to assure broadcasting that supports Aboriginal languages and cultures. What became known as the 'Therrian Report' (CRTC 1980) contains five principles calling for the widespread participation of northern Aboriginal peoples in all aspects of media programming, distribution and regulatory practice on the basis of 'fair access' and 'consultation' (Government of Canada 1983, 2). In 1993, a year after an Inuit plebiscite approved the creation of Nunavut, the CRTC passed the Northern Broadcasting Policy, which recognized the communications needs of Aboriginal northerners and established the Northern Native Broadcast Access Program, which provided $13.4 million a year to fund the production of regional Aboriginal radio and television through the Native Communication Societies located in the Canadian north. In 1990, when Canada was absorbed in the 'Oka Crisis' over Mohawk land issues, a new Native Broadcasting Policy was passed. At the same time, the Native Communications Program was closed, which eliminated financial support for Aboriginal media in southern Canada. Over the next three years, the Inuit agreed on the boundaries of territorial division and ratified an agreement with the Canadian Parliament that established the new northern territory. By 1993, when the Nunavut Implementation Commission was established, Aboriginal television was available across the north through the dedicated satellite channel of Television Northern Canada. In 1999, as we have seen, broadcast television reflecting Aboriginal perspectives and realities became available across Canada.

The Future

The formation of Nunavut represents profound changes in the far north over the last thirty years, but the future is challenging. The transfer of programs administering culture, public housing, and health care will not be complete until 2009. Working out the roles of citizenship and the new institutions of governance will take much longer. Remapping the Northwest Territories cannot remove the economic marginality of the Arctic or erase the issues of low education, high unemployment, high suicide, and drugs, alcohol, and domestic abuse. With more control over their lives, the Inuit are addressing these issues. They are adapting southern political processes and institutional structures to reflect Inuit traditions, including media.

There is, of course, no 'cause and effect' relationship between media and the political development of the far north. Broadcasting cannot be isolated from other variables related to socio-cultural or political change. Because we actually construct who we are in our identification with the written and visual images and cultural narratives that dominate our ways of seeing and representing our world (Hall 1989, 68–81), the stories that the Inuit tell through media are more than a window on their identity, culture, and community. From this perspective, culture involves the shared practices and experiences that we construct and express in our social relations and communications. Identity is formed not in internal conceptions of the self but in the adoption of changing representations and narratives that express the cultural, social, and political realities we experience. As George Gerbner once said, 'If you write a nation's stories, you needn't worry about who makes its laws. Movies, videos and TV today tell most of the stories to most of the people most of the time' (Gerbner 1990).

This short chapter cannot detail the persistence of oral tradition or the ways in which the Inuit media reflect and reinforce narratives and representations that build Aboriginal identity, community, and empowerment. However, the increasing importance of the Inuit media is suggested in Kate Madden's analysis of IBC television programming, in which she suggests that the news program 'Qagik' (which means 'coming together') reflects the Inuit values of cooperation and consensus building in its approach to production and content. The non-linear programming format of 'Qagik' more closely resembles the oral-communication patterns of Inuit social formation, which can contribute to the exchange of cultural and political information among Inuit. Kate Madden writes: 'Qagik demonstrates that IBC has managed to put together a news/current events show which espouses Inuit values. Its definition, organization and structure promote the Inuit value of personal autonomy through sharing information in cooperative, non-combative, consensus-building ways. It does not copy US/ Southern Canadian conventions. If anything, it sets those conventions on their ear in the sense that the convention in Qagik seems to be allowing the organic to develop' (Madden 1990, 18).

Like the transcontinental railroad of an earlier era, communications technologies and the cultural industries they spawn continue to shape the Canadian experience. For Aboriginal peoples, the experience of media has too often been one of exclusion, stereotypical inclusion, or appropriation. However, if the images and narratives of mainstream media have contributed to a generational gap between those Inuit who speak English or French and those who do not, today the Inuit recognize that, as Robin Ridington writes, 'electronic media may be used either to suppress the genuine experience and discourse of people in an oral culture or to document and share it' (Ridington 1990, 256). Sharing their own images and narratives with each other and with Canadians the Inuit are building the cultural and linguistic basis for an increasingly active partnership in the political landscape of Canada.

On 1 April 1999 the ceremonial signing of the land-claims agreement that created Nunavut was broadcast across the north on the newly established Aboriginal Peoples Television Network. A reporter for the Toronto *Globe and Mail* described the celebration that followed as a blend of tradition and technology.

Jose Kusugak, who later became president of Inuit Tapiriit Kanatami, spoke at the ceremony about the symbolism of creating the new Territory of Nunavut during the season of Easter, a time of rebirth. Though the intertwined developments of the APTN and Nunavut, Inuit have built upon old traditions and new technologies to change their political lives, social institutions, and civic roles.

Bibliography

Brody, Hugh. 1975. *The People's Land: Eskimos and Whites in the Eastern Arctic*. Harmondsworth, U.K.: Penguin.

Canadian Radio-television Telecommunications Commission (CRTC). 1980. 'The 1980's: A Decade of Diversity: Broadcasting Satellites and Pay-TV.' In *Report of the Committee on Extension of Service to Northern and Remote Communities*. Ottawa: Canadian Government Printing House.

Colombo, John Robert. 1974. *Columbo's Canadian Quotations*. Edmonton: Hurtig.

Gerbner, George. 1990. *The Gazette*. Montreal.

Government of Canada. 1983. 'The Northern Broadcasting Policy.' News release. Ottawa.

Graburn, Nelson H.H. 1979. *Eskimos without Igloos*. Boston: Little, Brown.

Hall, Stuart. 1989. 'Cultural Identity and Cinematic Representation.' *Framework* 36.

Innis, Harold Adams. 1950. *Empire and Communications*. Toronto: University of Toronto Press.

Inuit Broadcasting Corporation, August 1982.

Jenness, Diamond. 1965. *Eskimo Administration, III Labrador*. Montreal: Arctic Institute of North America Technical Paper, no. 16.

Kelly, N., and W. Kelly. 1973. *The Royal Canadian Mounted Police: A Century of History*. Edmonton: Hurtig.

Kuptana, Rosemarie. 1982. Brief to the CRTC. Ottawa: Inuit Broadcasting Corporation (30 Nov.).

Madden, Kate. 1990. 'The Inuit Broadcasting Corporation: Developing Video to Sustain Cultural Integrity.' Paper Presented at the Annual Meeting of the International Communication Association. Dublin.

Mayes, R. Greg. 1972. *Mass Communication and Eskimo Adaptation in the Canadian Arctic*. MA thesis. Montreal: McGill University.

The Northerners. 1974. Taqramiut/Les Septentroinaux. LaMacaza, Que.: Northern Quebec Inuit Association.

Phillips, R.A.J. 1967. *Canada's North*. Toronto: Macmillan.

Ridington, Robin. 1990. *Little Bit Know Something: Stories in a Language of Anthropology*. Vancouver: Douglas and McIntyre.

Roth, Lorna. 1982. *The Role of Canadian Projects and Inuit Participation in the Formation of a Communication Policy for the North*. MA thesis. Montreal: McGill University.

Seidman, Steven, ed. 1989. *Jurgen Habermas on Society and Politics*. Boston: Beacon Press.

Vallee, F.G. 1967. *Kabloona and Eskimo in the Central Keewatin*. Ottawa: St Paul University.

Profile of Kenojuak Ashevak (1927–)

Inuk, Artist

One of the most widely recognized Inuit artists today is a woman named Kenojuak Ashevak.[1] She has produced drawings, paintings, and sculptures for more than forty years.

Kenojuak Ashevak was born at the Ikerrasak campsite on southern Baffin Island in 1927.[2] Moving was a way of life for Inuit, and Ashevak's family relocated regularly to find food. When Ashevak was three years old, her father, Ushuakjuk, was killed in a dispute with nearby residents.[3] Ashevak loved her father dearly and was devastated by his death. Ashevak's widowed mother then moved her family to Cape Dorset to live with Ashevak's grandmother.[4] There, Ashevak learned the skills all Inuit women needed to keep a home and raise a family. She had a close relationship with her grandmother and so, when her mother decided to move away, Ashevak stayed behind.[5] She married Johnniebo in 1946. The newly formed family moved constantly and would eventually have ten children.[6]

Around 1956, artist James Houston noticed her talent when she was sewing designs on sealskins. He encouraged her to draw.[7] Both Ashevak and her husband began to draw and carve to satisfy an emerging market. Art provided a means for the Inuit to gain financial security.[8]

Kenojuak Ashevak has received many honours for her work. In 1962 the National Film Board produced the film *Kenojuak* about her and her husband, Johnniebo, in Cape Dorset.[9] In recognition of her contributions to Inuit art, Ashevak was appointed to the Order of Canada in 1967.[10] The federal government asked Ashevak and her husband to carve a wall mural for the Canadian Pavilion at the 1970 Expo in Japan.[11] That same year, her print *The Enchanted Owl* was featured on a Canadian postage stamp.[12] Again in 1980, her 1961 print *Return of the Sun* was featured on another stamp.[13]

Her other accomplishments include election to the Royal Canadian Academy of Arts in 1974.[14] She was made a companion of the Order of Canada in 1982 and received an honorary doctorate from Queen's University in 1991 and an honorary doctorate of laws from the University of Toronto in

Kenojuak Ashevak. Courtesy of John Reeves, photographer.

1992.[15] Most recently, she designed the April coin for Canada's Millennium Coin Series.[16]

Ashevak prefers carving to any other art form but that process has become more difficult for her as she advances in years. Now, she spends more of her time drawing and painting. A widow since 1972, Ashevak lives with her children in Cape Dorset.

JENNIFER SINGH

Notes

1 Jean Blodgett, *Kenojuak* (Toronto: Mintmark Press 1985).
2 'Kenojuak Ashevak,' *Who's Who of American Women* (New Jersey: Reed Publishing 1993), 15.

3 Blodgett, *Kenojuak*, 8.
4 Ibid., 9–10.
5 *Who's Who of American Women*, 15.
6 Ibid.
7 Ibid.
8 Blodgett, *Kenojuak*, 23.
9 Gale Group, 'Kenojuak Ashevak,' *Biography Resource Center, 2001*. http://www.nativepubs/Apps/bios/0414AshevakKenojuak.asp?pic=no.
10 *Who's Who of American Women*, 15.
11 Elizabeth Lumley, ed., *Canadian Who's Who*, (Toronto: University of Toronto Press 2000), 39.
12 Blodgett, *Kenojuak*, 28.
13 *Who's Who of American Women*, 15.
14 Jean Blodgett, 'Kenojuak Ashevak,' *Canadian Encyclopedia 2000 World Edition* (Toronto: McClelland and Stewart, 2000).
15 Lumley, ed., *Canadian Who's Who*, 39.
16 Ibid.

Natives and Newcomers in the New World: Maritime Furniture and the Interaction of Cultures

JANE L. COOK

In the eighteenth and nineteenth centuries, Maritime Canada was a meeting ground for many peoples, Native and newcomer alike.[1] Native lifestyles and how these manifested themselves in the world of arts and crafts intrigued those visitors to the New World who were fascinated by different cultures. Products alien to Western culture were sought after as visitors shipped home representations of the exotic and the novel. Yet items also remained in the New World, as Native craftspeople sold merchandise in regional centres to newcomer artisans who packaged them for resale. Thus, while recent historical research focuses on First Nations as 'souvenir cultures' (Phillips 1998), producers of wares sent to Europe and outside British North America, the effects of these wares on the Canadian colonies were also marked. At the same time, First Nations experimented making furniture for their own consumption. This post-contact phenomenon of exchange and adaptation indicates that cultural interaction affected the worlds of both Natives and newcomers. The result for Canadian domestic materialism in the Victorian era was the reshaping of cultural worlds as changing technologies, the adoption of imported materials, and the alteration of traditional designs wove together the worlds of maker, vendor, and buyer.

The objects left to us from Maritime societies, when combined with documentary and oral records, give insights into actual contact and exchange experiences between Native and newcomer. In order to understand this interaction, of an adoption here and a rejection there that prove a certain blending of cultures, it is necessary to focus on the material evidence. However, furniture is not the first thing that springs to mind. The stereotypical image of Native Canada is shaped by depictions of canoes, snowshoes and, however erroneously, wigwams (Cook in Robinson, forthcoming). Even when pushing beyond stereotypes, we readily cling to images of those tangibles used to overcome hardships in centuries past – winters made survivable by indigenous corn crops and bark tea as food and medicine, for instance. The study of furniture does not sit well with our constructed image of First Nations, peoples whom we generally do not imagine living in permanent, well-furnished Victorian domestic residences. And if we do think about furniture, we think about sophisticated and stylish non-Native products. Reality is a different story.

Over the nineteenth century, technology in the furniture world moved away from items made by sedentary master craftspersons towards mass production of wares made by itinerant untrained workers. Processed metals (such as wrought iron) and woods (papier mâché) became fashionable. With trade and reciprocity, geographical boundaries were not restricted to imperial nations and their colonies; trade was pursued throughout the Americas and with other European nations.

The production of early First Nations furniture in eastern Canada thus straddles changing eras – from contact to exchange, from natural to processed materials, from individual to mass production, from a consolidation to an expansion of markets. Native peoples produced furniture and their parts through an adaptation of their traditional productions to new formats; birch baskets become birch seat panels. The closest we come to mass production of indigenous-made wares are the sets of six chair-seat panels, all the same size, used in dining room furniture. Old Eastern Woodlands designs, such as the reverse-curve-motif, were retained as imported new materials, such as aniline dyes, were adopted. In a way, the First Nations experimented with technology just as the technology itself evolved. Old ways met new and a reassessment was in order. It might be argued that First Nations rejected Western-style technological development while at the same time providing inspiration for experimentation, something that had been lost in the machine era. In effect, the First Nations' work provided a link with nature, a link with the past, a link with the vitality inherent in skilled design and individual production. And, all the while, Native peoples accommodated the new.

The manufacture of furniture also offered some form of assurance that Natives were integrating into non-Native economic structures or, at least, were accommodating themselves to a cash as well as a barter economy. Economic interaction, of course, meant some form of assimilation, as Native peoples altered traditional production techniques in the process of acclimatizing to newcomer trade practices. In addition, in a post-Confederation era, the nascent Canada sought to distinguish itself from Britain. Cultural pursuits provided less controversial avenues towards asserting national independence than those focusing on economic and political issues.

Naturally, the types of furniture that were made and their longevity varies from coast to coast. But, in all parts of the country, both Native artistic skill and cultural interaction were in evidence. Thus, while Northwest Coast art is often seen as synonymous with Emily Carr paintings of the totem poles set in forested seafront landscapes, we might also recall the lavishly carved chief's chairs and those large bent-wood cedar chests that stored precious materials and potlatch gifts. French and Native styles are embedded in the canted-back chairs of the Métis, seen at the Glenbow Alberta Institute. Miniature quilled dolls' furniture made by the Ojibwa are stored in Royal Ontario Museum collections. Chests-of-drawers made in Quebec are ornamented by reverse-curve motifs, so deftly described by the Woodlands anthropologist Frank G. Speck.[2] Iroquois ceramic designs featuring chevron patterns are reproduced along the top edges of armoires in French Canada. Bent-wood furniture made from local saplings are sold at the roadside by Maliseet vendors in New Brunswick. Caribou horn is used for door pulls on a Labrador cupboard. Spanning the eighteenth and nineteenth centuries, these wares embody the spirit and sagacity of peoples interacting across the country. Thus, examples of nineteenth-century furniture stand as testaments, not only to First Nations' skills, but also to the interaction with those who acquired the final products.

Mi'kmaq Furniture Making

We now turn to one of the furniture wares produced by a Maritime First Nation, namely, the Mi'kmaq.[3] Skilled Mi'kmaq produced porcupine-quilled panels that found their way into Canadian, European, and Native-made furniture. They collected the birchbark, twigs, spruce root, sweet grass and porcupine quills that became the ingredients for panels embedded into hardwood receptacles – furnishings in the form of tables, chairs, babies' cradles, screens, journal caddies, and boxes. They also made their own tools, including crooked knives, to process the local and imported materials, and experimented with new methods of manufacture. The furniture decorations illustrated here are all attributed to the Mi'kmaq and, while appearing in collections around the world, were primarily made during the Victorian era in Nova Scotia.

Attributing woven panels to First Nations' craftspersons is relatively straightforward, but the manufacturers of the furniture items usually were not Natives but newcomers. This is not to say that Natives did not make furniture, but examples of them are rare and, as with newcomer furniture, a specific maker is difficult to identify. To complicate matters further, it is known that female newcomers turned their hand to making 'Native trifles' (that is, quillworking) and were taught classes in such in both Halifax and Saint John.

Table 1. Existing state of panels in furniture collections

Incomplete	Incomplete	Complete	Complete
Unfinished panel	Finished panel not inserted in furniture frame, e.g., Figure 1	Finished panel partially covers furniture frame, e.g., Figure 2	Finished panel totally covers furniture frame, e.g., Figure 3

Two Types of Quillwork: Incomplete and Complete

From my study, I have developed two general categories of quillwork designed for furniture – consisting of either incomplete or complete panels (Table 1). First to be considered are the birch panels that were never actually finished, as well as panels completed but never incorporated in furnishings (Figure 1). These Native products are technically 'incomplete' and now exist primarily as study pieces in museum collections in immigrant homelands. Multiple copies (that is, pairs of similar or dissimilar pattern) and sets of panels (for example, seats in dining room chairs or a seat with matching back in a single chair) also exist. Additionally, panels are incorporated in completed furniture forms such as chair seats and backs (Figure 2), table tops and their shelves, piano stool seats, dressing screens, and so on. In this category, the furniture may be dated later than the panels – essentially the panels were stored until a maker was commissioned. The last category is also a completed furniture form. Here generic panels are not sold separately but quillwork is custom-fit across a prepared ground (for example, the cradle in Figure 3).

These categories can be further subdivided according to furniture style and design, form and use, and whether a Native or a newcomer made the item. Furniture is dated according to style and materials. The former includes Victorian high style as well as experimental designs. In terms of material, dye colours are stronger and have a greater range in the post-aniline period. Forms of quilled furniture vary, since panels were sold separately and thus might be inserted into any conceivable frame. Thus, we find quilled deck chairs from salmon fishing lodges in New Brunswick.[4] Different chair forms indicate different limits to experimentation. By this I mean that furniture makers who received panels, be they at home or abroad, might find the restrictions to their imaginations lifted. A chair might be hastily thrown together with materials not really designed to last, as in the deck chair. Or the exotic panel might meet with an exotic chair design – for example, a heart-shaped back placed in an unusual support frame.

Victorian chair makers were familiar with oval or balloon-shaped backs,

Figure 1. Porcupine quill seat panel, decorated with 'gogwîts' or eight-pointed stars. H–52. From the Permanent Collection of the Canadian Guild of Crafts, Montreal, Quebec.

and so developing a heart-shaped frame was different but not overly challenging. The top or crest of the chair back dips into the heart's 'cleavage' while the side posts of the reshaped balloon-back are pinched, or hipped, below the bulging heart. In addition, the crest-rail design looks as though it has been based on an ox yoke. Yet it is neither a balloon nor a yoke-back but is something new. Added embellishments include carved detailing on the top of the chair crest. These personal touches further indicate the innovation of the unknown maker. The base of the chair is more traditional, with standardized machine-turned posts below the seat.

The earliest furniture panels appear in the 1840s. A temporary resident of the province commented that a Mi'kmaq woman had boasted to him that she had 'very handsome chair bottoms of birchbark, ornamented with dyed porcupine quills' (Alexander 1849). An early reference to 'Native curiosities' in the form of furniture is found in the catalogue of the 1851

Figure 2. Side chair. Gift of Dr James B. Richardson. Carnegie Museum of Natural History.

Figure 3. Mi'kmaq Cradle. Photo by Steve Welsh. Courtesy of the DesBrisay Museum Collection, Bridgewater, Nova Scotia.

Great Exhibition in London. Representing Nova Scotia was 'an Indian dress, cradle, chairs, seats, mats, cigar cases, and other Indian work ... [and an] Indian fan, reticule, hood, purse and moccasins' (*Colonies and Dependencies* 1851, 970). From extant furniture styles, it appears that quillwork was popular until 1900.

Panel Characteristics

A variety of basic materials are used in assorted combinations for the construction of quilled panels. Every panel is shaped from two birchbark sheets, one of which is decorated on its front with porcupine quills, with the other acting as a backing. The surface remains unquilled for a border of one-half inch (or a little over a centimetre). Small brad or nail holes may be seen in this edging area, evidence that the artisan nailed the panel in place. Oftentimes this border is hidden underneath a hand-wrapped sweet-grass edging or there is split spruce root applied in a haphazard running stitch, both of which help attach the backing. The backing itself is attached using natural or dyed root (blue or red). This second panel, of identical shape to the front, covers the free ends of the protruding woven quills and reinforces its strength, thus promoting the longevity and integrity of the finely decorated product.

The shapes of the panels vary. Specific geometric panel shapes fit specific objects: circles are used in stands and on some round chair seats, large rectangles grace table tops, Norman-arched panels are used in chair backs, and both T-back slipper chairs and balloon-back Victorian chairs have panels that fit snugly to supporting side rails. More unusual are heart-shaped chair back panels. Four heart-shaped panels are known – the first two in Montreal collections (the McCord Museum of Canadian History and the Canadian Guild of Crafts), another in the Indianermuseum, Zürich, Switzerland. The last heart-backed chair surfaced in an e-Bay auction in April 2002, selling to a Toronto buyer for around US$1,000. No example of X-shaped panels has been found; technical difficulties likely prevented their construction.

Panel decorations are rarely identical. Most commonplace are 'full-field' covered panels; quills cover the entire centre of the panel, leaving no birch-bark exposed. Decorations are geometric in design – featuring crosses, stepped lines, circles and triangles, or variations upon these themes. The patterns themselves embody traditional images – for example, eight-pointed stars (known as 'gogwits'). While these designs probably embody spiritual significance, much of their traditional meaning is lost to the modern-day viewer, both Native and newcomer. The geometric rendition of living organisms was not part of newcomer artistic traditions; they preferred anthropomorphic figures and more realistic representations of flora and fauna. Yet certain other designs hold significance for both Native and newcomer, namely, crosses representing spirituality and swastikas representing prosperity and good fortune.[5] Other panel decorations are 'partial-field' covered. Here the birch backing is clearly visible since the quilled decorations are spaced out. Natural figures predominate, such as flowers, stems, and leaves. Examples of these are found in western Canadian collections and probably are not Mi'kmaq in origin.

Division of Labour Evident

In *Letters from Nova Scotia*, published in London in the 1820s, Captain William Moorsom related that 'the Squaws sit for hours a day, in their smoky wigwams, making baskets, or ornamental trifles, generally a sort of Mosaic work, in moose hair or quills of the Nova Scotian porcupine, stained of various colours, and worked upon a shell of birch bark' (Moorsom 1830, 113).

Thus we see a division of labour. Contrary to newcomer traditions, it was not the male artisan who built goods that he then marketed in his own store. Instead, the Native female deftly applied her skills in both the manufacture *and* the sale of these wares. In essence, she acted as an entrepreneur selling directly on the street or down by the water's edge in newcomer neighbourhoods. A local resident noted that 'their canoes are often seen crossing from a camp opposite to Halifax, with articles to dispose of ... [while] at length their goods are exposed on the bank' (Murray 1839, 215). Native men did participate, naturally. But reference to men is usually linked to their work in providing raw materials – that is, their collecting of birchbark, their preparation of spruce root, and their hunting of porcupines. The women processed the raw materials that the men provided by skinning and cleaning the animals, boiling and dyeing quills, and shaping and piercing birchbark panels in various designs of their own invention. In addition, there are references to men selling wares, but it was the women who were known for their understanding of the negotiation process.[6] The Mi'kmaq, one writer reported, 'are disposed to drive a pretty hard bargain, especially the females, on whom that task usually devolves' (Murray 1839, 73). Alternatively, dealers resold wares acquired directly from the Mi'kmaq; for example, the F. Stemshorn company of Halifax dealt in quilled panelling (Whitehead 1978, 163). Usually, however, Native women set the price, sold the wares, and brought the money back home. A visitor to the New World noted the division in labour in other provinces: 'The women occupy themselves in gardening, attending the cattle, and manufacturing various articles of Indian dress, and ornaments in leather, worked with porcupine's quills and the hair of the moose deer, richly coloured; and in birch and basket-work, of fanciful forms and devices. These they sell to visitors, generally at a handsome price, while some are sent to the shops at Quebec, where they find a ready sale among strangers visiting the City, and where they may be seen in great variety' (Buckingham 1843, 288–9).[7]

Marketing and Distributing the Furniture

Records of shipments of Native-made panels abroad are extant, as are notices of merchandise sold in English ports. Alexander Monro wrote in 1855 that 'the ingenuity of the native tribes, in manufacturing fancy boxes and other articles of this bark, ornamented with coloured porcupine quills and strips of various kinds of roots, is well known; and they generally command a market in Europe as well as in America' (Monro 1855, 99).[8] In other words, their products were sold in local, national, and international venues.

However, because a guaranteed and constant supply of quality wares could not be achieved, Native and non-Native cultures clashed. Native artisans made articles when the fancy struck, whether because materials were available seasonally, barter for other supplies had become essential, or family and friends cajoled them. One potential customer lamented that 'they cannot be depended upon for making or procuring any article to order. They produce and bring their commodities to market when it suits their own convenience' (Murray 1839, 73). Principles of salesmanship differed between maker and buyer that proved frustrating to the latter. Quilled panels were sold along with a diverse quantity of other wares – from brooms through to baskets and dresses. It is unlikely that quill panels were the only items made for sale by individuals, and the buyer might not always find what he or she wanted. A way to acquire specific work was to commission dependable quillworkers.

The Mi'kmaq rarely made furniture frames, but examples of these do exist. They took traditional materials and methods and produced objects in new formats – making furniture for personal use.

Examples of Native-made Furniture

We look now at a custom-made cradle with quills covering its exterior contours, and a couple of panelled chairs. One of the chairs was made by professional English chairmakers; a local Mi'kmaq made the other. These items display an interaction of cultures in design and manufacture in both Native and newcomer traditions. In all instances, the furnishings depended on the innovative and experimental abilities of their makers.

The cradle is shown in Figure 3. Ruth Whitehead of the Nova Scotia Museum has written about the maker of the cradle's quillwork, Christianne Morris, who was appointed quillworker to Queen Victoria (Whitehead 1977, 1–14). The queen recognized Christianne by awarding her land on the North-West Arm of Halifax harbour. The illustrated cradle is a copy of the one presented to Edward, Prince of Wales, and is currently in the collections of the DesBrisay Museum in Bridgewater, Nova Scotia. It is believed to have been copied in 1868 for the son of Reuben Rhuland in Nova Scotia. Mrs Rhuland's brother, Alexander Strum, made the wooden frame. The frame was the mount for the custom-shaped panels that, tradition says, took Christianne a year to quill. The patterns incorporate a variety of Native and non-Native motifs from geometric forms, including gogwits and partial reverse-curves, to rounded animalistic forms of moose as well as the swastika. The south shore of Nova Scotia was home to German immigrants and other newcomers who often incorporated the swastika into artistic motifs. Both quillwork and cradle frame are sophisticated, embodying a blend of cultural traditions in presentation. Perhaps this cultural confrontation is best illustrated in the formal image of a Mi'kmaq woman taken by Joseph S. Rogers (Figure 4).[9] Here she has donned a traditional Mi'kmaq woman's cap while also wearing a European-style paisley scarf and taffeta dress.

In addition to the blending of styles in the above cradle and portrait, the two chairs illustrate a coming to terms with different cultures. The British chair (Figure 5) is from the shop of Goff and Gully in Exeter, Devon, England. Nova Scotia Museum records date the chair to 1889. Goff and Gully took over the business of J. Kingden and Sons around 1880 and went out of business in 1890 (Whitehead 1982, 55). The chair's only Mi'kmaq feature is a single quilled panel, used as a splat (or vertical central board), in the back of the chair. Usually, back panels match seat panels, in contrast to this instance, where there is fragile silken brocade upholstery on the padded seat. While not commonly considered a durable seat covering, it was fashionable among European high society in the late nineteenth century. Ruth Whitehead points out that the quills are dyed black, green, and gold on a white field, matching the paint colours that highlight portions of the chair. It is unlikely that a chair would be painted this way without having this particular splat fitted; it is integrated into the chair through the use of matching colours. The maker acknowledged that aesthetic cultures can be amalgamated through the complementing of certain features. In other words, the chair maker had endeavoured to adopt nuances of Native devices in the completed chair. There are two scenarios to consider. In all likelihood this customized chair results from a client commission, rather than the chair maker acquiring a panel in the hope that an intrigued customer might purchase it. It should be noted that unknown parties shipped out quilled panels individually and in sets from Halifax for independent sale, just as visitors to the colonies sent mementos back home to named recipients.

Experimentation is also evident in some incongruous chair features. The scrolled intaglio carvings flanking the more formal floral design at the top of the chair crest suggest design exploration. With respect to construction, the proportions of the chair seem out-of-kilter; the seat-to-back ratio is unusual. The counterpoint of fine spindles, or turned pieces at the base of the back, seem to contradict the strength of the back posts or even to match the spacing of spindles in the skirt below the seat. The sophisticated floral carving of a golden-stippled ground contrasts with the geometric quill-

Figure 4. Micmac Woman in European Dress. Nova Scotia Archives and Records Management.

Figure 5. English-made chair with Mi'kmaq quilled back panel. History Collection, Nova Scotia Museum, Halifax.

work directly below. The inner posts flanking the splat, while thinner versions of the side posts, also seem incompatible. Yet, without them, the width of the back of the seat would look visually compromised. The firm, bulbous nature of the splat also seems incompatible with the more delicate and fussy Victorian detailing. It is as if the maker is struggling to blend in the quillwork while endeavouring to create a central showcase in the chair back. A marriage of cultures did not always succeed.

The other chair (Figure 6), which I attribute to Nova Scotian Indigenous manufacture, presents other features that are also slightly discomforting to the Western eye. The chair has a huge back that seems to overwhelm the seat. The seat itself is flat and does not cater in any way to comfort; the seat is not saddled and its edges display harsh lines. The rounded shape to the back is made by cumbersomely adding wooden strips in strange places. Nova Scotia Museum records state that this chair is made from birch stained to resemble mahogany, yet the heavy weight of the piece is baffling. Using birch for the entire chair is not associated with newcomer ways of manufacture. Chair posts and slats spanning chair backs are made from white and black birch, but these were not favoured materials even though they were easy to turn (Monro 1855, 98–9). A close look at the construction of the chair shows a certain lack of professionalism. The joint of seat to back is fraught with tension as the seat protrudes behind the back and, most unusually, widens out to the rear. The bases of the back posts both narrow at the seat juncture, where we would expect greater support.

The panel in the back seems peculiar also in that an elongated smaller central panel inset appears in the larger overall quillwork. Yet the pattern does not blend because the geometric lines do not precisely align. Perhaps this smaller panel was inserted to replace worn quills in the larger piece, but the technique of insertion and colouration of the quills suggest similar age. The intaglio carving in the crest rail depict what I call the 'hissing snake with quiver and arrow' motif, the significance of which is perplexing and the description of which may even prove incorrect. However, similar Native-style patterning is seen on other chairs – namely the in-cutting of small designs, whether as rising suns, triangles with dots inside, or scrolled frond-like lines with dotted ends. In addition, the sectioning of the legs is not well executed. Lines are etched into the stock to form rings, rather than shaping bulbous turnings. Other parlour chairs made by Europeans have elaborately turned posts and feet. Such fashionable posts are not cut in such an informal manner but are assertively turned into balls, barrels, and sausage shapes.

In the case of these two chairs, both Native and newcomer faced difficulties in producing items that are both aesthetically pleasing and techni-

Figure 6. Mi'kmaq-made chair with quilled seat and back panels. History Collection, Nova Scotia Museum, Halifax.

cally sophisticated.[10] The marriage invokes innovation, but the parts do not complement each other – in fact, they tend to conflict visually. Perhaps there was a lack of understanding on the part of the English chair maker, who was unfamiliar with the techniques and world-view associated with the culture of the splat's maker. The Native-made chair, conversely, features back and seat panels as focal points and the chair as receptacle has secondary importance. The large back is reminiscent of chief's chairs. However, dealing with its size and shape was difficult for the maker. Two world-views met with different results. The skills in the Native chair are emphasized in the quillwork; the English chair focuses on elaborate Victorian decoration. Both makers sought to incorporate 'the other' in an attempt to blend cultures.

Materials Used in Native Furniture-making

This brings us to a consideration of the parts of the chair and how they indicate Native or newcomer traditions. Materials familiar to newcomers included turned wood, textiles such as silk and velvet, and chemical aniline dyes. Unfamiliar were the birchbark panels woven with the dyed quills of the eastern Canadian porcupine (*Erithizon dorsatum*), and the flora that provided natural earth-tone colouration schemes.

The change in the source of quill colour indicates the influence of imported dyes in varying both the spectrum and the diversity of colours used. This helps us date certain panels. Bolder-coloured and multicoloured panels result from using aniline dyes; vivid purple quills suggest manufacture in the late 1850s, at the earliest. Aniline, while originally a derivative of indigo, also refers to a synthetic construct ($C_6H_5NH_2$-phenylamine) now used as chemical oil in dye, drug, and plastics manufacture. Developed in 1826, it was introduced from Europe in the 1860s as a potential replacement for domestic dyes derived from flowering plants and trees. Acid green had been developed in 1835 and Sir William Henry Perkin's bright purple came to light in 1856 (Garfield 2001, 6). Additionally, imported crêpe papers used in womens' crafts provided yellow, green, and red dyes when soaked. In fact, anything that was not colourfast could have some amount of tincture extracted, and so imported blankets and materials provided further dyes. One observer, Patrick Campbell, referring to small pieces of cloth, stated that the Mi'kmaq used 'every colour they can find. These they scrape down as small as they can, and boil separately in kettles, till the dye is extracted from the wool' (Campbell 1937, 61).

Traditionally in the New World, pale yellow might be extracted from wild sunflowers, coneflowers, goldthread, roots of the black willow, fox moss, and swamp plants (Waldner McGrath 1977). Across Atlantic Canada, the colour red might be derived from buffalo berry, squaw currant, tamarack and elder bark, spruce cones and sumac berries. A red-gold tone is taken from bloodroot (*Mohawk, Micmac, Maliseet* 1985, 12–13). Black is extracted from chocolate-coloured stone, wild grapes, or black spruce bark. Lichen and moss produce brown, blueberries produce purple, and larkspur produce paler shades of purple. Moosewood might be boiled to provide a green shade (MacLaren 1974, 167–77).[11] Mordant binders that act as fixatives and ingredients that prevent fading (including currants and gooseberries) are boiled with the quills, while dock root makes the colours brighter and stronger. Quill interiors might be hollowed in order to enhance their ability to accept dyes.[12] It is difficult to identify colour source, but quilled panels in earth tones are associated with greater age (that is, they are early nineteenth century rather than later) and reflect their natural versus synthetic nature (*Quillwork* 199–).

Another European material employed in furniture making is velvet. Several examples of tables and chairs exist that have a dull brown velvet edging. At this time, the traditional centres of velvet production included Utrecht in the Netherlands and Genoa in Italy (*Hutchison's Educational Encyclopedia* 1999). Technological advances enabled an additional second 'pile' warp to be placed over a base warp-and-weft woven fabric. The pile warp is rich and dense in thread, woven into the ground fabric and then piled over metal wires in loops; the result was a material resembling corduroy. When the wires are removed from the pile warp, knives fixed to the wire-ends cut through the piled loops of the corduroy to form plush tufts. Velvet seats and table trim grace examples of quilled furniture in the Nova Scotia Museum collection.

A Native alternative to velvet edging on chair seats is the use of sweetgrass wrapping, a technique in favour in the 1880s. Moose hair is used in chair decoration, but it was more difficult to acquire the raw material, took greater time to finish, and might prove more expensive for the consumer. Examples of furnishing decorations of this nature were made by the Huron in Lorette (Quebec), under the direction of newcomer proselytizers; moose-hair chair decoration has not been found in Nova Scotia.[13]

Clearly, the availability of panels and exchange of techniques made it possible for newcomers to make panels and Natives to make furniture. Perhaps their joint productions indicate the first exploration in a blending of cultures that resulted in the creation of the first identifiably Canadian furniture form.

A note might be made here regarding indigenous tools. Imported tools augmented the traditional, but there is little in the record to say who owned what and from where it came. However, Natives did follow technological developments. For example, a crooked knife was used to work the ash required for box and basket making, and in 1915 Montréaler David Ross McCord purchased what was touted as the 'first machine' used by the Abenaki to plane ash strips. Made in 1819 by John Monatack, this type of machine was used until the end of the nineteenth century (McCord 1915).

Cultural Modification Seen in Furniture-making

Initially, adaptation and acculturation, whereby contact between different groups leads to cultural modification, is more readily seen than an actual process of assimilation in which there is a gradual adoption of customs and attitudes in the prevailing culture. Olive Patricia Dickason points out that Natives adopted materials first, then techniques, accompanied by the beginning of change in concepts and traditions, as Natives moved to non-Native practices.[14] By the 1960s, plants endemic to Nova Scotia, providing dyes and mordant used in colouring and fixing quills, were joined by synthetic oil products such as aniline dyes. Spruce root wrapping was augmented by the introduction of fashionable European velvets and silk brocades. Geometric patterns featuring traditional Mi'kmaq motifs were augmented by images of flora and fauna favoured by the newcomer culture. Certainly, it is towards the mid-nineteenth century that we see the consistent creation of furniture panels for the eastern non-Native market. By the end of the century, First Nations were experimenting with complete furniture forms (that is, frames as well as panels) of their own.

   In a Victorian society in technical upheaval, the products of First Nations rooted newcomer to place and encouraged an increasingly impersonal business to pause and reconsider the benefits of individual experimentation. Permutations in who made the furniture, panel and frame, gave limitless possibilities to the development of a Canadian form. The activities of Mi'kmaq craftspeople and entrepreneurs led to the production of what might be termed our first Canadian furniture. First Nations working with newcomers in the creation of products integrated old with new in a world of exchange.

Notes

1 The years in question (1840s to late 1890s) span a period in which Canada began to take shape – the colonies of Lower and Upper Canada, New Brunswick, and Nova Scotia becoming, after 1867, the new country of Canada.

2 Frank G. Speck, *The Double-Curve Motive in Northeastern Algonkian Art* (Ottawa: Canadian Department of Mines, Geological Survey, memoir 42, no.1, Anthropological Series 1914).

3 At contact there were seven Mi'kmaq districts: Breton/Wunama'kik; Pictou/ P.E.I./Epekwitk; the Eastern Shore/Eskikewa'kik; the South Shore/Spekne'katik; the Annapolis valley/Kespukwitk; Cumberland County and southern New Brunswick/Sitnikt; and northern New Brunswick, Gaspé/Kespek.

4 This, in turn, raises the question of whether or not the Maliseet of the St John River valley produced wares similar to those of the Mi'kmaq. While chairs are found in provincial collections and were used in the province, there is no documentation giving an insight into Maliseet manufactures of this nature. I would presume that, should examples of Maliseet quilled panels be found, that these would be of a much more sophisticated and detailed nature, with perhaps the use of smaller quills and a more painstaking attention to detail. There were also fewer Maliseet in New Brunswick than Mi'kmaq – Captain Levinge estimated half the number (that is, 500 people). See R.G.A. Levinge, *Echoes from the Backwoods; or, Scenes from Transatlantic Life*, vol.1 (London: J. and D.A. Darling 1849) 101. This might explain why there are no extant examples, but; since bent-wood furniture does exist, perhaps it indicates a greater propensity to build alternative goods.

5 A former curator of the Nova Scotia Museum, George MacLaren, suggests that the pre-existence of crosses in Native life favoured proselytization. George MacLaren, 'The Arts of the Micmac of Nova Scotia,' *Nova Scotia Historical Quarterly* 4, no.2 (1974): 169. The swastika is a newcomer symbol for well-being and good luck or prosperity and good fortune. Following Hitler's expropriation of it (in order to foster prosperity in the Germany of the 1930s), of course, it became symbolic of Nazi anti-Semitism (just as the Confederate Flag now symbolizes White Power). Symbols change connotations according to the memory of the populace in contact with it.

6 Henry David Thoreau tells a story of a Native man selling baskets house to house. He comments that the basket maker did not see it as his concern to develop a market for it – it should sell itself since everyone should automatically want it. *Walden or, Life in the Woods* and *On the Duty of Civil Disobedience* (New York: Signet Classic/New American Library 1960), 17–18.

7 This is a commentary on the Huron of Lorette.

8 Ruth Whitehead points out that other colonial destinations for Mi'kmaq work included the British West Indies. It is likely that any vessel leaving the port of Halifax might carry such exotic wares for sale in a foreign market. An example of trade with England includes that between the Indian Bazaar of Saint John and Ira Cornwall of Liverpool. See J.R. Hamilton, *Saint John and the Province of New Brunswick: A Handbook for Travellers, Tourists and Businessmen* (Saint John: J. and A. McMillan 1884).

9 Dr Whitehead wonders if this is Miss Morris. Consult the Mi'kmaq Portraits

Collection database, Nova Scotia Museum. www.museum.gov.ns.ca/mikmaq/index.htm.

10 This is not to say that examples of sophisticated wares do not exist – both Native and newcomer produced a variety of wares using different skill levels.

11 Whitehead, *Micmac Quillwork*, 66–71.

12 Hollowed-out quills are also good because they deter insect infestation by reducing a potential food source.

13 A recent exhibition of moose-decorated chair back, seat, and arm rests of 'Micmac' origin proved to be made by Huron girls from Lorette, Quebec. Canadian Guild of Crafts, 'Works from Permanent Collection of Amerindian Art,' 5 April 2002 – 25 May 2002.

14 Consult Olive Patricia Dickason, *Indian Art in Canada* (Ottawa: Department of Indian Affairs and Northern Development 1977).

Bibliography

Alexander, James Edward. 1849. *L'Acadie, or, Seven Years' Explorations in British America*. Vol. 2. London: Henry Colburn.

Buckingham, James S. 1843. *Canada, Nova Scotia, New Brunswick and the Other British Provinces in North America with a Plan of National Colonization*. London: Fisher, Son.

Campbell, Patrick. 1937. *Travels in the Interior Inhabited Parts of British North America in the Years 1791 and 1792*. Edited with an introduction by H.H. Langton. Vol. 23. Reprint. Toronto: Champlain Society Publications.

Colonies and Dependencies. 1851. *Section IV. British Possessions in America. Great Exhibition of the Works of Industry of All Nations, 1851*. Official descriptive and illustrated catalogue by authority of the Royal Commission in three volumes. Vol. 2. London: Spicer Brothers.

Cook, Jane L. Forthcoming. 'From Iconography to Eye Con: Variations on Teepee Image in Canadian Postcards.' In M. Robinson and N. Morgan, eds., *Cultures through the Past: Essays on Tourism and Postcards*. Clevedon, U.K.: Channel View Publications.

Dickason, Olive Patricia. 1977. *Indian Art in Canada*. Ottawa: Department of Indian Affairs and Northern Development.

Garfield, Simon. 2001. *Mauve: How One Man Invented a Colour That Changed the World*. London: Faber and Faber.

Hamilton, J.R. 1884. *Saint John and the Province of New Brunswick: A Handbook for Travellers, Tourists and Businessmen*. Saint John, N.B.: J. and A. McMillan.

Hutchison's Educational Encyclopedia. 1999. Oxford, U.K.: Helicon Publishing.

Levinge, R.G.A. 1849. *Echoes from the Backwoods; or, Scenes from Transatlantic Life*. Vol. 1. London: J. and A. Darling.

MacLaren, George. 1974. 'The Arts of the Micmac of Nova Scotia.' *Nova Scotia Historical Quarterly* 4, no. 2: 167–77.

McCord, David Ross. 1915. Handwritten note dated 9 Dec. Record 2660. McCord Museum of Canadian History.

Mohawk, Micmac, Maliseet and other Indian Souvenir Art from Victorian Canada. 1985. London: Canada House Cultural Centre.

Monro, Alexander. 1855. *New Brunswick: With a Brief Outline of Nova Scotia, and Prince Edward Island ... Intended to Convey Useful Information, as Well to Their Inhabitants, as to Emigrants, Strangers, and Travellers, and for the Use of Schools.* Halifax: Richard Nugent.

Moorsom, Captain W.S. 1830. *Letters from Nova Scotia; Comprising Sketches of a Young Country.* London: Henry Colburn and Richard Bentley.

Murray, Hugh. 1839. *An Historical and Descriptive Account of British America: Comprehending Canada, Upper and Lower, Nova Scotia, New Brunswick, Newfoundland, Prince Edward Island, the Bermudas and the Fur Countries ...* Edinburgh: Olive and Boyd.

Phillips, Ruth B. 1998. *Trading Identities: The Souvenir in North American Art from the Northeast, 1700–1900.* Montreal and Kingston: McGill-Queen's University Press.

Quillwork from Canada's Northwest Territories. 199–. Yellowknife: Government of the Northwest Territories.

Speck, Frank G. 1914. *The Double-Curve Motive in Northeastern Algonkian Art.* Ottawa: Canadian Department of Mines, Geological Survey, memoir 42, no.1. Anthropological Series.

Thoreau, Henry David. 1960. *Walden or, Life in the Woods* and *On the Duty of Civil Disobedience.* New York: Signet Classic New American Library.

Waldner McGrath, Judy. 1977. *Dyes from Lichens and Plants.* Toronto: Von Nostrand Reinhold.

Whitehead, Ruth Holmes. 1977. 'Christina Morris: Micmac Artist and Artist's Model.' *Material History Bulletin* 3 (Spring): 1–14.

– 1978. 'Micmac Porcupine Quillwork: 1750–1950.' In Richard J. Preston, ed., Papers from the 4th Annual Congress, Mercury Series, Canadian Ethnology Service Paper no.40. Ottawa: National Museum of Man.

– 1982. *Micmac Quillwork.* Halifax: Nova Scotia Museum.

Profile of Robert Charles Davidson (1946–)

Haida, Artist, and Teacher

Robert Davidson's ability to express his Haida heritage as a master carver of totem poles and masks and through printmaking, painting, and jewellery has contributed to the survival of his tradition and culture, thus making him a significant figure in Canada's Aboriginal community. His concern for Haida cultural traditions caused him to take steps to revive it and make it important to the Haida community.

Robert Davidson was born in Hydaburg, Alaska, on 4 November 1946 to Claude and Vivian Davidson.[1] A year later he moved to Old Massett on Haida Gwaii (Queen Charlotte Islands).[2] As a child, Davidson gained a great deal of knowledge about his ancestors and the Haida way of life from his parents, grandparents, and uncles.[3]

Davidson comes from a long line of craftspeople. He is the great-grandson of the renowned Haida carver Charles Edenshaw.[4] Both his grandfather, Robert Davidson, Sr, and his father, Claude, were accomplished and respected carvers in the community who encouraged him to continue the family's artistic tradition. He carved his first totem pole – a miniature – at the age of thirteen.[5]

He remained in Old Massett until 1965 when he moved to Vancouver to pursue secondary education at Point Grey Secondary School. During his first year in Vancouver, Davidson publicly demonstrated his carving techniques for the first time at Eaton's department store.[6] Soon after, Davidson began an eighteen-month apprenticeship with the late Bill Reid.[7] In 1968 he gave a course on Northwest Coast Indian art at the newly formed school for Indian artists at the 'Ksan Indian village near Hazelton, British Columbia.[8]

Returning to Old Massett as an adult, Davidson witnessed the Haida culture disappearing all around him. Deeply saddened by what he saw, yet also determined to do something about it, he embarked on a mission to revive the culture and heritage of his people. In 1969 he carved a great totem pole for the village that was raised with the traditional ceremonies,

Robert Charles Davidson. Courtesy of Ulli Stelzer.

including a potlatch.[9] As well, to promote his people's cultural traditions and ideas, Davidson organized a feast to celebrate life in Old Masset in 1980. That same year, with his brother Reg (also an accomplished artist), Davidson formed the Rainbow Creek Dancers, a dance group whose primary activity is to perform traditional and contemporary Haida songs and dances.[10]

As Davidson's reputation as an artist and craftsperson spread, he was chosen to represent Canada in numerous events. In 1972 he presented a ten-foot totem pole to the city of Montreal. In 1984 he carved *The Three Watchmen*, a three-pole commission for the Maclean-Hunter building at College Park in Toronto.[11] He was also commissioned by the Catholic Church of Vancouver to make a killer whale talking stick for presentation to Pope John Paul II during his papal visit to Vancouver.[12] He produced four works for PepsiCo: a large bronze frog and three totem poles entitled *Three Variations on Killer Whale Myths*, installed at PepsiCo's International Sculpture Park in New York. He also reproduced a watercolour painting as the Expo '86 poster in Vancouver.[13]

Robert Davidson has received many prestigious awards, including the Order of British Columbia, a National Aboriginal Achievement Award, and three honorary doctorates. In March 1997 the governor general of Canada awarded him the Order of Canada. That same month, the Royal Canadian Mint released a twenty-two-carat gold coin of his masterpiece painting, *Raven Bringing Light to the World*. Robert Davidson continues to preserve the identity of his people through his artwork. His value to Native American culture is not only as an artist but as a teacher and visionary.

DOMENYK LEACH

Notes

1 Barbara Hager, 'Robert Davidson,' *Honour Song: A Tribute* (Vancouver: Raincoast Books 1996), 1–9.
2 Hilary Stewart, *Robert Davidson: Haida Printmaker* (Vancouver: Douglas and McIntyre 1979), 11.
3 Robert Davidson and Ulli Steltzer, *Eagle Transforming* (Vancouver: Douglas and McIntyre 1994), 16.
4 Carol Sheehan, 'Robert Charles Davidson,' *Canadian Encyclopedia 2000 World Edition* (Toronto: McClelland and Stewart 2000).
5 Stewart, *Robert Davidson*, 15.
6 Ibid., 20.
7 Ian M. Thom, *Robert Davidson: Eagle of the Dawn* (Vancouver: Douglas and

McIntyre, 1993), 16. www.douglasreynoldsgallery.com/artists/davidson.htm. 27 Nov. 2001.

8 Thom, *Robert Davidson*, 16.

9 Stewart, *Robert Davidson*, 22.

10 Davidson and Steltzer, *Eagle Transforming*, 160.

11 Ibid., 75.

12 Ibid., 80.

13 Ibid.

Contributions to Canadian Art by Aboriginal Contemporary Artists

GERALD MCMASTER

In the last fifty years, Aboriginal peoples have made tremendous strides in rebuilding their cultural identities through language, music, dance, and visual art. Because of the historic ruptures faced by all Aboriginal communities, it is little wonder that so many Aboriginal people distrust outsiders. Yet, paradoxically, it seems, Aboriginal people's are, more than ever, open to expressing their identities, often through the arts. These expressions are directed not only outward to non-Indians but also, and more important, to Indigenous peoples themselves. With access to new media and practices that balance tradition, Aboriginal artists are now defining the forefront of a new modernity.

Who are these Aboriginal contemporary artists? Why should we concern ourselves with them? And, what if anything, have they contributed to this country?

Unconventional, somewhat non-traditional, and sometimes controversial, Aboriginal contemporary artists continue to be strongly committed to expressing their identity. They fall into gaps between well-defined spaces – for example, between tradition/modern, city/reserve, art/craft, and so on – and they are more likely to move on the peripheries of Native and non-Native communities. The Metis artist Edward Poitras once called this loose and unconventional group the 'new tribe.'[1]

Aboriginal contemporary artists see their work as contemporary, not as an anachronistic or essentialist phenomenon of the past that belonged to their ancestors. There are many conceptual differences that distinguish Aboriginal contemporary artists' works from the traditional historical works we see most often in anthropology museums. The earlier artists produced works that were closely related to, and constituted within, band/tribal cultures and languages. Today, artists create works, for the most part, for any and all publics. In the case of tribal art, the dialogue was always internal; in Aboriginal contemporary art, the dialogue moves outward into the aesthetic, political, moral, and didactic realms.

For the Aboriginal contemporary artist, *identity* has always been an important issue, for it is one of *survival*. Yet, as identity becomes increasingly objectified and globalized, it is paramount that we recognize the diversity and complexity that exist within all cultures, especially in a country like Canada. We have only to look within our own country to find that fifty-three distinct Aboriginal languages are spoken. This diversity is little understood, which often makes it easier for mainstream Canada to universalize us as *Indians* or *other*. This universal *othering* results in the homogenizing of identities at the expense of local cultures. Identity can also take us beyond local culture and into all segments of society.

Few people outside the cultural field of art realize that it is a contested space constantly being negotiated by all sorts of individuals and groups, to such an extent that it is often referred to as a 'site of struggle.' At one time, it was essentially a space where the younger artists displaced their elders for recognition; now it is Aboriginal people, women, and others who are struggling for space and recognition. Generally, these struggles are about uneven power relations. For example: What do we have to do to shift the mainstream's focus on art as a universal ideology to one that is Canadian, one that has its roots and identity in Canada? Canadian institutions of art can no longer continue looking in other directions – Europe, for example – and pretend that art in those places is more than it is. I recall Ojibwa artist Carl Beam saying to an audience of Aboriginal artists in a half-joking, half-serious way that the Canadian mainstream was not as fast or as deep as everyone thought; he said, 'It's more like a muddle puddle, or a tiny creek at best. It may look like a mile deep, but it is only up to your knees.' The field of art continues to be a contested space, and it does not get any easier to make the argument that because you are an artist or Aboriginal, you should automatically be included in all the big shows, or that your work should be collected by the big institutions. Artists such as Beam, Poitras, and many others have worked hard to attain their status. No doubt much younger and talented Aboriginal contemporary artists will someday displace them too.

Aboriginal contemporary artists have had the double bind of recognition and practice, both in and outside the mainstream; and as they continue seeking recognition in art's mainstream, they are also re-examining other centres of activity. They are coming to the realization that some of these old centres once marginal to others are now the new cultural centres. These places, once thought of as prisons, are Indian reserves. While many Aboriginal artists live and work on reserves, they are more likely artists who create works for tribal use, or for the tourist and craft market. Artists such as these create works often associated with traditional forms of expression that could be described as necessary for cultural survival. For the contemporary artist, on the other hand, negotiating with the constant play of crossing borders – centre/margin/centre – is a strategic practice, where they must always be willing to accept new experiences, new ideas, and new languages.

When we think of Aboriginal art as an expression and representation of cultures, cultures irrevocably changed, we should think in terms of *survival* and *survivance*. Native American author Gerald Vizenor has defined these two terms: survival, he argues, is more reactionary, while *survivance* is much more about condition, with a much wider breadth of understanding a bigger picture. In Canada, in the context of Aboriginal peoples' history, cultural *survivance* is little understood. For example, several generations of Aboriginal people who suffered from the paralysing effects of government control, as signified in the Indian Act, must have felt that change would inevitably come, that it would be a younger and newer generation who would bring about a cultural revolution. From the third quarter of the nineteenth to the mid-twentieth century, Aboriginal peoples' *survivance* is a story of sadness and loss. It was only after the Second World War that Native political organizations drew attention to cultural practices through efforts to encourage positive self-awareness; yet everywhere in mainstream society, Aboriginal peoples continued to exist on its margins.

Finally, a note on this chapter's focus. Although much of the following gives a context for Aboriginal artists in Canada, I have made some references to Aboriginal artists in the United States.

The Roots of Aboriginal Contemporary Art

As noted above, following the Second World War, Native organizations increasingly focused on cultural practices, although Aboriginal peoples continued to exist on the margins of mainstream society. Depending on the perspective, isolation was both a scourge and a godsend. Banishment onto reserves was disastrous for the continuity of a traditional way of life, and any change and development were arduous; yet, ironically, segregation actually helped maintain cultural traditions like language and some spiritual practices. Meanwhile, the traditional arts waned and, over the first half of the twentieth century, shifted from production to meet band/tribal needs to production for a growing external market (McMaster 1993, 93–120).

Change began slowly. In 1950 the Royal Commission on National Development in the Arts, Letters and Sciences (McMaster 1993)[2] tabled a report on the state of national culture. Sixteen briefs and presentations were submitted to the commission on the state of Native art and craft. However, the report made no major recommendations on the subject, and the commission was content to shift the responsibility elsewhere in the government.

The commission barely examined the situation of Aboriginal cultures as a whole, because they were viewed more as an economic than an aesthetic concern. Aboriginal artists were not yet part of this picture, since they were still thought of as tribal artists, rather than fitting the mainstream notion of the individual artist. It was, however, during this period that the federal government was considering extending religious and cultural freedom to Aboriginal peoples by revising the Indian Act.

Despite the lack of support from the federal government and the art world, other institutions did step in to encourage positive change. Two British Columbia institutions, for example, took up the challenge. In 1949–50 the University of British Columbia Museum of Anthropology (MOA) commissioned two Kwakwaka'wakw carvers, Mungo Martin[3] (c. 1881–1962) and Ellen Neel (1916–66), to restore a number of 'totem'[4] poles at the museum. This project heralded the beginning of active museum involvement in the promotion of Northwest Coast art by practising artists, and not just the acquisition of historic art. Martin worked at the MOA until 1951.[5] A long-renowned master carver, he spent the next ten years as carver-in-residence at the British Columbia Provincial Museum (BCPM, now the Royal British Columbia Museum). This responsibility entitled him to teach traditional carving techniques to several generations of Kwakwaka'wakw carvers, notably Henry Hunt (his son-in-law), Tony Hunt (his grandson), and Douglas Cranmer (his step-grandson). In 1957 the MOA commissioned two young artists, Haida Bill Reid and Kwakwaka'wakw Douglas Cranmer, to carve six poles and a memorial figure for the institution. Reid worked at the museum for three and half years and eventually became one of Canada's best-known Aboriginal artists, while Cranmer eventually moved over to, and began working with, the BCPM in Victoria.[6]

Across the country, rave reviews had greeted a young Ojibwa artist in his first commercial exhibition. His name was Norval Morrisseau and the show at the Pollock Gallery, a commercial gallery in Toronto, in 1962 was a decisive event that changed the way people were to look at Aboriginal art and artists for years to come. Ruth Phillips has argued that Morrisseau's non-Aboriginal audiences (conditioned by European notions of 'primitivism,' and witnessing Native art appropriated by Canadian nationalism) saw in him fresh 'pagan' qualities (1993, 244). He was seriously censured by his tribal elders, however, for representing and commodifying sacred images.[7] In reaction to the sad realities of Aboriginal life, Morrisseau's controversial cultural strategy – breaking with tradition to salvage Ojibwa beliefs[8] – constructed a vision for the future, and for himself, artistically. Morrisseau was motivated by his despair in seeing the younger generation losing its ties with traditional Ojibwa culture. He saw the elders dying and

Mungo Martin carving totem poles at the University of British Columbia, 1949.
University Archives, University of British Columbia Library, 1.1/9769-3.

Bill Reid and Douglas Cranmer carving a totem pole. University Archives, University of British Columbia Library, 3.1/1280. Courtesy of Douglas Cranmer.

Mishipashoo, by Norval Morrisseau, 1960. Permission granted by artist. Courtesy of the Canadian Museum of Civilization, artist Norval Morrisseau, catalogue no. III-G-1103, image no. 80-5744.

young children being removed from the reserves to be educated in white schools. Morrisseau became the conduit for cultural transfer, positioning himself as a new communicator or 'image-maker.' In Mungo Martin's case, the tradition for cultural transfer was guaranteed because he had learned from his elder, Willie Seaweed; in Morrisseau's case we see a kind of post-reservation act, where tradition is transformed into a new strategy. Both strategies maintain a self-conscious link with the past and intentionally oppose repeated efforts by governments and other state-sanctioned institutions to sever Native people from their roots and traditions. Many artists have followed Morrisseau's lead.

In the 1960s, Aboriginal artists such as Daphne Odjig, Alex Janvier, Tom Hill, Noel Wuttunee, Gerald Tailfeathers, Carl Ray, and Jackson Beardy/

played important roles in spearheading the Native cultural revolution. Their emergence was buoyed by their convictions about personal identity, and also by their dexterity in adapting to both the traditional and the modern world.

The most significant cultural event of the late 1960s for many Native peoples was Expo 67, hosted in Montreal, which celebrated the centennial year of Canadian Confederation. For the first time, Indian artists and politicians came together from across Canada to assert their Native identity.[9] The Indians of Canada Pavilion was their venue. It was a vital moment for Canada, because it wanted to be seen, in the eyes of the world, as a successful developed country, as well as one that acknowledged Indians as equals and distinct members of society. Native artists such as Norval Morrisseau, Carl Ray, Alex Janvier, Tony Hunt,[10] George Clutesi, Noel Wuttunee, and Tom Hill received commissions to paint murals and panels on the façade of the pavilion (Brydon 1993). They responded with enthusiasm and confidence, and their artistic expression came to be seen as modern and sophisticated, speaking out to an international community about who they were, where they came from, and where they were going. After Expo 67 closed, Native people continued to run the Indians of Canada Pavilion, with exhibits on art and culture, some of which were highly critical of the federal government, the pavilion's sponsor.

Back on the west coast, the Vancouver Art Gallery (VAG) also celebrated the centennial by presenting *Arts of the Raven*, an exhibition many regarded as the turning point in the appreciation of Northwest Coast art. The exhibition presented these works as fine art, not as ethnographic or curio art. The VAG enlisted Bill Reid to help organize the exhibition, which proved to be a decisive catalyst for artistic activity on the Northwest Coast. Peter Macnair (1980) writes that, in the three years following *Arts of the Raven*, several dozen young Native artists would gain ascendancy in the art world (85). Many of them gathered in northern British Columbia, near Hazelton, at an artists' training program called the Kitanmaax School of Northwest Coast Indian Art. The place was called 'Ksan. It had opened in the mid-1950s, as a product of local initiative and federal funding, and its objective was to revive interest in Nisga'a (Tsimshian) art and culture and train graduates for the future. A section of the reconstructed village of 'Ksan was opened for tourists in 1970, complete with a craft museum and an interpretation and cultural centre (MacDonald 1972). One artist who taught at 'Ksan was Robert Davidson (Haida). In the summer of 1969, Davidson carved and raised a new pole, in his village of Masset, the first to go up on the Queen Charlotte Islands tribal grounds since 1884. The ceremonial raising of the pole heralded the rebirth of Haida culture as a whole. Macnair notes that 'like many of his peers, Davidson has sought to contribute monumental works to his village to remind people that aspects of the ancient culture still live' (Macnair 1980, 90). Several years later, Davidson was to construct a building in honour of his great-grandfather, Charles Edenshaw.

Northwest Coast artists responded to this rebirth. Many of them searched deep within themselves and their communities for the elusive artistic tradition, because they needed a sculptural language to manifest itself. Martine Reid describes this new art as 'a signifier in search of meaning ... Clearly, though, it is an art in gestation, soon to emerge in a different context, with new cultural significance. The process is not a decline into non-authenticity or an ascent into rediscovery, but a transformation and another metamorphosis in a long history of change' (1993, 76).

In 1970 a group of Aboriginal artists living in Winnipeg, some of whom had met at Expo 67, realized that once the interest generated by the Indians of Canada Pavilion abated, questions would remain about their future as artists. They formed a group and called themselves the Indian Group of Seven; they were Jackson Beardy, Joseph Sanchez, Carl Ray, Alex Janvier, Eddie Cobiness, Roy Thomas, Daphne Odjig, and, later, Norval Morrisseau (Martin 1992, 28). The Indian Group of Seven lasted until 1976. Three of the seven had their first gallery showing at the Winnipeg Art Gallery (WAG) in 1972, in an exhibition which was titled *Treaty Numbers 23, 287, and 1171: Three Indian Painters of the Prairies* and which included the work of Jackson Beardy, Alex Janvier, and Daphne Odjig. Although the exhibition was intended to display the works by these three Native artists in a critical aesthetic context, its title suggested otherwise. For them, the exhibition at the WAG became a political space within which their voices could be heard. Janvier, the more radical thinker of the three, had been signing his work using his treaty number – *287* – for ten years, protesting the impersonal viewpoint of the Department of Indian Affairs, which saw Aboriginal people solely as treaty numbers. Hence the name of the exhibition. Unlike 'Ksan, which was interested in reviving artistic and cultural traditions, this group focused on finding new markets for their work; but without institutional backing, they never had the same clout. Odjig opened a print shop and quickly became popular; Beardy continued working but never received great artistic acclaim.

In the late 1960s, the world was changing, yet, for Aboriginal Canadians, change seemed unhurried. Still, the combined efforts of Aboriginal organizations to stop the federal government from abolishing their rights were gradually producing results; and, in the early 1970s cultural centres were springing up across the country. In the meantime, a bombshell exploded in the United States.

Seven Ravens, by Robert Davidson. Courtesy of the Canadian Museum of Civilization, artist Robert Davidson, catalogue no. VII-B-1833, image nos. S94-13482 & S94-13483.

The occupation of Wounded Knee, South Dakota, by several hundred Native Americans in the late winter of 1973, was a defining moment for Aboriginal peoples across North America. For the first time in modern-day relations between Aboriginal and non-Aboriginal peoples, the international media focused its attention on Native issues. Aboriginal artists in the United States, inspired previously by the revolutionary fervour of the occupation of Alcatraz Island in 1969 and the 'Trail of Broken Treaties' and subsequent occupation of the Bureau of Indian Affairs building in Washington, D.C., in November 1972 used the Wounded Knee conflict as detonation for their art making. Despite this energy, there was little artistic reaction in Canada to political issues.

In the following year, Tom Hill (Seneca) prophetically announced that, 'in the future, art will probably manifest the political struggle more, especially as Indians become more vocal in their demands to be treated fairly' (Hickman 1975, 20). Impatient for change, Hill organized *Indian Art '74* at the Royal Ontario Museum in Toronto, an exhibition many regard as a landmark in the development of Aboriginal contemporary arts. He gathered a wide range of individual and tribal expressions and redefined 'Indian art' in economic, cultural, and political terms: economic, because the opportunity for artists to sell their works opened a new market; cultural, in that artists originating from different cultural groups across the country now had a chance to express themselves as such; and political, since, by virtue of all the artists coming together as a singular artistic voice, they realized that a space had now opened up for them. The new artist proved to be highly eclectic, borrowing styles from many sources: Native and non-Native, traditional and contemporary. Their intention was to try to incorporate themselves into the mainstream, instead of merely slipping by or getting tossed out. Collectively, they became a new kind of post-reservation artist. Ruth Phillips describes this artist as one who does not replicate 'ancient forms known only by traditionalists, but one who has transformed [the visual forms] into new kinds of art in order to explore their meanings in the context of the modern world. This "appropriation" is legitimate for these artists because it is a means of preserving knowledge for future generations and of uniting the self divided between two worlds' (Phillips 1993, 251). As well, it was a way to insert themselves into new discourses that included the art market and collections, and thus make the shift from craft to art.

With the federal government's relinquishment of its assimilation policies in 1951 and the rising tide of political, historical, and cultural consciousness in the 1960s, the 1970s seemed the right time for Aboriginal artists to begin organizing themselves. The First National Native Artists

Symposium was held in October 1978, on Manitoulin Island, with subsequent gatherings in Regina (1979), Hazelton (1982),[11] Lethbridge (1987), and Halifax (1993). Artists exchanged ideas on identity, traditional and contemporary artistic practices, centre/periphery, Native/non-Native art, art/craft, museum/gallery, and access to government funding. The conferences attracted the curious and the engaged. Government and arts council representatives, curators, anthropologists, sociologists, elders, and commercial gallery owners[12] helped create a forum for greater articulation regarding issues of post-reservation definitions of art, and of what it means to be an artist and Aboriginal. Rather than arriving at clear conclusions, the conferences resulted instead in individual affirmations of identity and conviction, which served to strengthen Aboriginal arts in all fields.

By the late 1970s and early 1980s, the international economic downturn that had affected the country was having an impact on Aboriginal artists. Some whose fortunes had risen quickly disappeared almost as fast; others managed to transcend the constraints of recessionary times[13] by concentrating on experimental work and participating in a growing number of exhibitions. It was a decade of solidarity which saw the emergence of newer and younger artists, as well as persuasive and articulate voices who produced important scholarly writing on Native, women's, and environmental issues and subsequently strengthened the resolve of visual and expressive artists. In 1982 Aboriginal Canadian and American artists gathered together in an exhibition called *New Work by a New Generation* at Regina's Norman Mackenzie Art Gallery.[14] It focused on the artist as individualist, yet as the curator, Robert Houle, explains: 'Each artist is invariably and intimately involved in recording personal experiences determined by tribal culture. This leaves the artist to create works of art traditionally inspired, but expressed through modern concepts and techniques. To deny the legitimacy of this inspirational source would be like refusing the Renaissance its Greco-Roman heritage; and to treat the validity of this creative process with deliberate reserve is sanctimonious' (1982, 2).

This statement concerned a theme of self-emancipation from an established tradition – that all Native artists drew their subjects only from myths and legends.[15] Several artists moved beyond this notion and began showing works based on political issues and ideas. Artists such as Clifford Maracle, Robert Houle, Carl Beam, and Edward Poitras built on Janvier's political interests as expressed in his work, and found new ways of expressing the political moment. Their works were no longer conceived as primarily vehicles for Aboriginal cultural expression; they were also making audiences aware of the complex realities of Aboriginal life.

Aboriginal Contemporary Artists at the End of the Twentieth Century

In the 1990s there was a notable shift in Aboriginal contemporary artists' attitudes as they seemed to become more detached from the quagmire of political issues. They no longer felt disenfranchised; rather, they were comforted in knowing that their subjectivity was more complex than previously understood; they realized they were different, as was everyone else. They supported the postmodern position that celebrated plurality and reinforced the observation that Western art was in effect just another *other* in a theatre of *others*. Furthermore, the notion of centre/periphery took on new meaning as Aboriginal contemporary artists started to realize that their reference points were their communities, their reserves, their homes. Such realizations underlay discourses of identity where artists now examine definitions of self as being critical to understanding their everyday realities.

Hence, appreciative audiences of Aboriginal contemporary art may find individual artists more thought-provoking than artists who reflect traditional conventions. Names like Houser, Scholder, Morrisseau, Pudlo Pudlat, Quick-to-see Smith, Poitras, Reid, Tasseor, Howe, Davidson, and Piqtoukin resonate within us because they explore the human condition of the present. These artists are making new audiences aware of their personal perspectives.

Aboriginal contemporary art is made up of a vast number of artists living in both Canada and the United States, who participate within the dynamic mainstream art scene. As participants in the global community, they are intensely aware of the current conditions and circumstances that affect us all; in their everyday lives they are often driven to reflect and engage with a directness not always evident in traditional art. Through their works, both individually and collectively, Aboriginal artists are effective communicators. James Luna's *The Artifact Piece* (1987) at the San Diego Museum of Man wrested the stereotype – that Aboriginal identities existed only in the past – away from ethnographic museums. In addition, Aboriginal communities have recently been benefiting from artists' projects like Rebecca Belmore's cross-Canada tour of *Ayum-ee-aawach Oomam-mowan: Speaking to their Mother* (1991), in which she used a large wooden megaphone designed for people to speak directly to Mother Earth. In 1992 three major art exhibitions, *Indigena*,[16] *Land Spirit Power*,[17] and *Submuloc*,[18] brought attention to Aboriginal issues. Bill Reid's installation of *The Black Canoe* (1993) at the Canadian Embassy in Washington, D.C., for instance, helped to give Canada a new identity, one that was now inclusive. Hachivi Edgar Heap of Birds's national tour of the *16 Song/Issues of Personal Assessment and Indigenous Renewal* (1996) became a collaboration with Australian

Bearings and Demeanours, 1990, by Eric Robertson. Copyright permission from artist. Photograph by Harry Foster. Courtesy of Indian and Northern Affairs Canada.

Spirit of Haida Gwaii, 1991, by Bill Reid, Canadian Embassy, Washington, D.C. Courtesy of Ulli Steltzer.

Aboriginal artists. The message of each of these projects is to give a voice back to Aboriginal peoples, a strategically powerful tool. The artists have helped their audiences understand how to move into the larger world with an Aboriginal sensibility, across a millennial divide, and into the twenty-first century.

Aboriginal contemporary art, by its very nature, is work being done today, for today, and about today. Artists borrow from everywhere. They look at ancient images, forms, and techniques, with an understanding that what their ancestors had to say continues to have meaning for them, and for us all, in the present. None of them wishes us to believe they are located in some mythic past; instead, they understand their realities as energetic practices of today, which offer them an unparalleled range within which to express themselves. They will, however, continue to tap into the past to try to make sense of this complex world. These complexities are as true of reservation communities as they are of urban areas, and contemporary Aboriginal art reflects this. The recent exhibition *Reservation X* (1998), for example, examined issues of community and identity. Artists find themselves driven to social and political lives beyond their artistic identities. In Canada, Art

Thompson led a massive group of former boarding school students into the courts seeking restitution, while Earl Muldoe and Neil Sterritt led the Nisga'a people through history-making land-claims negotiations. Meanwhile, in the United States, Colorado jeweller Ben Night Horse Campbell was elected state senator.

The world of Aboriginal art is further complicated by our co-existence with many diverse ethnic and tribal identities, particularly in urban centres. San Francisco's *Salad Bar*, which included Teresa Harlan and Hulleah Tsinhnahjinnie, was an art collective whose name metaphorically reflected the mix of equal but differing identities. This pointed to the reality of living in an international community, whose members bring with them new ideas and experiences. Coming in contact with multicultural conditions activates new relationships, which are then reflected in ourselves and in the art.

Artists realize that traditional spaces within which they produce and exhibit have now gone well beyond the walls of the art gallery or similar institutions, to artist-run centres, community houses, cultural centres, restaurants, private homes, or anywhere outdoors. They continue to exhibit in the craft-market place – such as the Santa Fe Indian Market – in small booths, where vast numbers of people can come; they realize the power these centres have as places of commerce. There continue to be numerous market-type centres and fairs in cities throughout the world, where artists and galleries converge to exhibit and examine recent works. The art world's most critical audiences, professional and popular, often frequent these sites.

Aboriginal contemporary artists interpret the conditions of their times. Richard Ray Whitman's series *Street Chiefs* is an example of displaced and landless Aboriginal people struggling with urban life, a facet other than the fictional and romantic ones normally accorded Indian people. Jeffrey Thomas's *Exploring Metropolis* examines urban sociality where the mix of tribal identities is both persistent and contradictory; for him, Buffalo, New York, contains some of the bleakest spaces of urban life.

Above all, contemporary artists realize that an important reality today is knowing, understanding and accessing new technologies. A prime example of the depth to which artists can go in combining new technologies with Aboriginal traditional knowledge is Melanie Printup's website at www.albany.net/~printup/. Similarly, there was Edward Poitras's *JAW-REZ* website, which once had a home at the Banff Centre for the Arts (in Banff, Alberta). Also, Hachivi Edgar Heap of Birds's *In Our Language* (1982), a public project on the Spectacolour Lightboard in Times Square, used new communicative strategies in public places. These Aboriginal contemporary artists communicate with vast audiences using high-tech media; the latter are a perfect medium – the choice of a specific technology, for the articulation of a specific idea, grants a specific expression. In this regard, the computer has become a powerful tool and venue.

This reality contrasts with the generally held stereotype that Aboriginal peoples exist only in the past, and are not part of the modern world. The gulf between that reality and the perceived stereotype lies, again, within the shifting sense of identity. Maintaining a strong connection with the past can be somewhat strenuous in that, while keeping up with the rest of society, one must struggle to hold true to tradition, which is the source of subject-hood. This is a fundamental concern faced by many Aboriginal contemporary artists. Often inspired by visual traditions, they readily express themselves in contemporary media and yet strive to maintain their Aboriginal principles and philosophies. Some artists have maintained their particular responsibilities in carrying familial and tribal identities forward into the future. Generally, however, they find, negotiate, and express their responsibilities in different ways: Nora Naranjo-Morse continues a family tradition of working with clay, whether by creating ceramic sculptures or building her own home; Dempsey Bob carves masks for both the art market and local ceremonial use; Dorothy Grant designs clothing (she calls it 'Feast-wear') based on family crests which can be worn at important functions or as upscale everyday clothing.

Until the end of the twentieth century, the National Gallery of Canada gave little regard to Aboriginal contemporary art as a Canadian phenomenon, like Quebec's Automatism, for example. An exception was Inuit art, which, given its more cohesive role in the art market, was more consistent with the Gallery's views of a discursive entity. But the Gallery tended to view Aboriginal or First Nations artists – apart from Northwest Coast or Woodlands-style art – as individualist, and it therefore collected their works as creations by Canadian artists who happened to be Aboriginal. During the late 1980s and early 1990s, however, the Gallery began holding shows of Aboriginal contemporary art; and more recently, it has begun to integrate Aboriginal historical works into its Canadian galleries, positioning objects as equivalent to traditional and historic Canadian art. This development is a remarkable turnaround for the Gallery, which for a long time, did not consider Aboriginal art to be art. For the Gallery, art is an expression by a known individual who creates outside a cultural context, devoid of ethnicity, a person not slavishly tied to tradition. With new and expanded articulations, intellectually and artistically, Aboriginal contemporary and historic art does have strong aesthetic traditions that should be regarded as an important aspect of the Canadian art historical landscape.

There is much to celebrate about the quality and diversity of artistic production, but one area of Aboriginal contemporary art and art history that needs academic attention is the level of related criticism and artistic discourse. There is a shortage of in-depth critical texts. On the surface it would seem that artists reject scrutiny by critics – yet such critical analysis is an integral part of the discourse. It is true that we are more apt to read descriptive rather than critical reviews, and that some critics may hesitate to critique contemporary Indian art for fear of being misinterpreted. As a result, few comprehensive critical texts of Aboriginal contemporary art have been written in the last thirty years. Nonetheless, we are now seeing some critical texts, like the recent *St. James Guide to Native North American Artists* (1998); critical surveys of American and Canadian contemporary art, such as *Indianische Kunst im 20. Jahrhundert* (1985) and *Zeitgenössische Kunst der Indianer und Eskimo in Kanada* (1988), edited by Gerhard Hoffmann, which appear only in German; and Lucy Lippard's 1990 book, *Mixed Blessings: New Art in a Multicultural America*, which is important for its comprehensiveness and timeliness in profiling a number of Aboriginal contemporary artists (but few Canadians). Beyond these are a number of fine monographs on individual and group artists. However, these texts tend to be short on context, perhaps because of time constraints or the relative importance of the artist. Finally, there is Lawrence Abbott's *I Stand at the Center of the Good: Interviews with Contemporary Native American Artists* (1994), which contains several interviews but no critical text; sadly, there is only one colour plate per artist.

Conclusion

As late as the 1970s, Aboriginal artists were, for the most part, still finding themselves exhibiting in anthropology museums, but they soon grasped that the world was opening up to them when their audiences, national and international, began increasing. These audiences included a small but powerful critical group of collectors and connoisseurs who appreciated specific aesthetic and artistic viewpoints. They tended to look at how works fit within their collections, acquiring pieces based on quality, and how the works connected to particular themes. The influence of these collectors continues to be great; members of the general public, that is, non-Natives, account for the largest group purchasing Indian art. This public's appreciation is not based on an informed understanding; these purchasers are more interested in owning something that is produced by an Indian artist. Nonetheless, there are those artists who are marginalized from such well-defined circles and who prefer to live and work outside accepted spaces. Where do these Aboriginal contemporary artists practise today? What is their relation to their community?

Aboriginal artists, like all Aboriginal people, live in highly contestable spaces – spaces that continually collide and mix, spaces they will forever negotiate. The artist, however, sees these spaces – and their negotiation – as stimulation, finding themselves living or practising both in, and between, many communities. Consequently, they use art as a means of persistence and identity. Though we are often quick to think of polar opposites, like reserve and urban spaces, these artists are nomads between the two. Within and without these traditional centres, they will find other centres for themselves. This has always been their reality. As a game of perception, artists constantly search for a periphery, knowing that being just beyond will bring out the trickster in them, either as a form of inspiration, a radical expression, or a practice. Meanwhile, some artists may luxuriate in the knowledge that they are the centre, until, of course, they are displaced by some other artist. Though centres and peripheries are imaginary, constructed, loose, mobile, and ever-changing, they help us understand the nature of artistic practice. To this end, artists perceive the centres of production, or the markets, as being out of their reach in the larger cities. In reaction, some artists have re-examined their practice, seeing it not as production but as strategy. Consequently, they have become consciously aware of the idea of centre and have influenced how the centre is perceived, shifting our perspective at the same time. They now help us to understand that centres include culture, language, or family, for example. These new centres of reference have come to include the reservation (both urban and rural) and are now a new and renewable source of infinite inspiration.

The new tribe is not so much warrior-like, because that position is not creative, as mischievously energetic, clever, and self-willed. Its members emerge out of tribal and non-tribal spaces, departing on a quest like an ancient rite of passage, in search of inspirational adventures and experiences, people who will open new doors, places where they can meet others with like dispositions and with whom they can share stories and secrets, and where they can demand to be taken seriously.

Aboriginal art, in all its diversity, articulations, and representations of tribal realities, has always been a part of Canada. As a country, Canada has long used various representations of Aboriginal people, or certain works of art, to signify a Canadian identity that is tied to the land and its people. Indeed, two of the most significant markers of Canadian identity are a (totem) pole from one of the west coast tribes and an Inuit inukshuk. Another enduring symbol has been the image of a Blackfoot chief in full regalia standing alongside a Royal Canadian Mounted Police officer, in his or her red serge, the pair symbolizing peace and friendship. As well, Aboriginal people, especially from the prairie provinces of Saskatchewan and Alberta, have been the subjects of non-Aboriginal artists, photographers, and writers, from Paul Kane to Edward Curtis and Hugh Dempsey. In a contemporary context, the works of Aboriginal artists such as Norval Morrisseau, Bill Reid, Carl Beam, and Edward Poitras have contributed to our national heritage. Their contributions, and those of others, are what will make this country strong, vibrant, and confident in the future.

Notes

1 For further reading on this concept, see 'The New Tribe: Critical Perspectives and Practices in Aboriginal Contemporary Art,' PhD thesis, University of Amsterdam, School for Cultural Analysis, Theory and Interpretation, 1999.
2 The 1950 Royal Commission's report gave birth to the Canada Council, whose responsibility was – and still is – to encourage the development of the arts and to support artistic activity in Canada.
3 Mungo Martin, who had learned from master carver Willie Seaweed (c. 1873–1967), has been called the 'slender thread' by members of the U'mista Cultural Society of Alert Bay, British Columbia, because he was an important link with earlier traditional masters. Both Seaweed and Martin had trained under the traditional apprenticeship system and contributed to the development of the southern Kwakwaka'wakw style, now practised most notably by the Hunt family carvers. Both carved model poles not only for sale to the non-Native public but for potlatches as well.
4 The preferred term is simply 'poles,' since not all poles refer to family, clan, or personal totems. The word 'totem' is from another cultural group altogether, who are the Algonquian speakers. The term refers to 'relations': family, clan, the entire cosmos; for example, in Cree the word *ni-totemuk* means 'my relations.'
5 Martin died in 1962. He was posthumously honoured by the Canada Council in 1964.
6 Until this day the RBCM continues to work with Kwakwaka'wakw artists while MOA works with Haida artists. This curious fact can be seen in the types of exhibitions each institution holds.
7 See Valda Blundell and Ruth Phillips, 'If it's Shamark, is its ham? A examination of media responses to woodland school, art, *anthropologica*, N.S., 25, no.1 (1983): 117–32; and Elizabeth McLuhan and Tom Hill, *Norval Morrisseau and the emergence of the image makers* (Toronto: Art Gallery of Ontario 1984).
8 See McLuhan and Hill, *Norval Morrisseau*, 70. Were Reid, Cranmer, and the Hunts in a similar predicament? The artists on the Northwest Coast come from very different visual traditions, where individual rights to possession of clan symbols exist. Also, Northwest Coast artists did not experience that same long-term interruption or disruption of cultural practices as did other Aboriginal peoples, particularly in the east. The right to express one's clan symbols pub-

licly and for profit is different from claiming ownership of stories or narratives of a people or drawing on a visual tradition that is seen as the property of spiritual leaders. In a conversation with George Longfish, in April 1992, he offered an updated interpretation of such a dilemma: 'owning cultural information,' he says, is, basically, understanding certain information and making one's own choices and decisions.

9   The NIC, through the Centennial Commission, provided sponsorship for Native organizational meetings, Pow wows, and other cultural activities beginning in December 1964. The Centennial Indian Advisory Committee Celebrations subcommittee had taken control of these cultural events by March 1965. Each national pavilion at Expo 67 was represented by a commissioner general. Andrew Delisle (Kahnawake) was appointed commissioner general to reflect the independent status of Indian people.

10   Tony Hunt and his father, Henry, were commissioned to carve a pole which still stands at the Expo site on Île-Notre-Dame.

11   At the Third National Native Artists Symposium in Hazelton, a special lobby group for the artists was created not only to organize future symposia but to press for changes in the way national cultural agencies and institutions represented contemporary Native art. As a result, the Society of Canadian Artists of Native Ancestry (SCANA) was born, its membership consisting mainly of professional artists. Since its inception, it has worked closely with the Indian Art Centre at the Department of Indian Affairs and Northern Development, providing input into the development of the centre's programs as well as organizational structure. SCANA provided collaborative support for the Canadian Museum of Civilization's 1992 exhibition, *Indigena: Perspectives of Indigenous Peoples on Five Hundred Years.*

12   During each session, tensions heated up through passionate discussions that somehow carried over to the next gathering. Each gathering had its own character and atmosphere, giving everyone a chance to be heard, to experience the local environment, to see the traditions of the people, and to meet artists, curators, dealers, and others in the field of Native art.

13   Also during the mid-1980s, at a time when Aboriginal cultures across Canada became increasingly mobilized, when cultural centres and artists' cooperatives proved their worth, when media and other forms of Native communications provided news and information about the Native community both locally and to an international audience, major sources of government funding were severed. Indeed, many important Indian newspapers ceased to exist, as well as the Canadian Broadcasting Corporation's popular weekly radio program, *Our Native Land.* There is bitter irony in the fact governments, which helped create these strategies to assist in overcoming the devastating effects of assimilation, withdrew their critically needed support of Aboriginal telecommunications and thus hurt the Aboriginal community. Henceforth, the 'low-tech' moccasin telegraph, or word-of-mouth, as it were, became the major means of communication.

14 This project was jointly organized by the Mackenzie and the Saskatchewan Indian Federated College during the World Assembly of First Nations in Regina in 1982.

15 This stereotype was particularly aimed at the works done by Norval Morrisseau and the great many artists he influenced, sometimes called the 'Woodland School.' Houle, himself, once referred to them as the 'Woodpecker School.'

16 See the exhibition catalogue *Indigena: Contemporary Native Perspectives*, in which artists and writers responded to the Columbus Quincentennary in 1992.

17 See Diana Nemiroff, Robert Houle, and Charlotte Townsend-Gault, *Land Spirit Power: First Nations at the National Gallery of Canada*. Held in 1992, celebrating Canada's 125th birthday, this was the first major international exhibition of Aboriginal contemporary art held at the National Gallery.

18 *Submuloc* was a Native American art campaign to 'decelebrate' the Columbus Quincentennary through an exhibition of works critiquing aspects of European culture. 'Submuloc' spells Columbus backwards.

Bibliography

Abbott, Lawrence, ed. 1994. *I Stand in the Center of the Good: Interviews with Contemporary Native American Artists*. Lincoln: University of Nebraska Press.

Blundell, Valda, and Ruth Phillips. 1980 'If It's Shamanic, Is It Sham? An Examination of Media Responses to Woodland School Art.' *Anthropologica*, N.S., 25, no.1: 117–32.

Brydon, Sherry. 1993. 'The Indians of Canada Pavilion.' *American Indian Art Magazine*, 19.

Hickman, James. 1975. 'The Quiet Birth of the New Indian Art.' *Imperial Oil Review*, 59, no.2, issue 323.

– ed. 1988. *Im Schatten der Sonne: Zeitgenössische Kunst der Indianer und Eskimos in Kanada*. Stuttgart, Germany, and Ottawa: Edition Cantz and Canadian Museum of Civilization.

Hoffmann, Gerhard, ed. 1985. *Indianische Kunst im 20. Jahrhundert*. München, Germany: Prestel-Verlag.

Houle, Robert. 1982. *New Work by a New Generation*. Exhibition catalogue. Regina: Sask. Norman Mackenzie Art Gallery.

Lippard, Lucy. 1990. *Mixed Blessings: New Art in a Multicultural America*. New York: Pantheon.

MacDonald, George. 1972. *'Ksan, Breath of Our Grandfathers*. Ottawa: National Museum of Man.

Macnair, Peter L., Alan L. Hoover, and Kevin Neary. 1980. *The Legacy: Continuing Traditions of Canadian Northwest Coast Indian Art*. Victoria: British Columbia Provincial Museum.

Matuz, Roger, ed. 1998. *St. James Guide to Native North American Artists*. New York: St. James Press.

McLuhan, Elizabeth, and Tom Hill. 1984. *Norval Morrisseau and the Emergence of the Image Makers.* Toronto: Art Gallery of Ontario.

– 1996. *Jeffrey Thomas: Portraits from the Dancing Grounds.* Ottawa: Ottawa Art Gallery.

– 1998. 'Living on Reservation X.' In Gerald McMaster, *Reservation X: The Power of Place in Aboriginal Contemporary Art.* Hull, Quebec: Canadian Museum of Civilization and Goose Lane Editions.

McMaster, Gerald. 1993. 'Tenuous Lines of Descent: Indian Art and Craft of the Reservation Period.' In *In the Shadow of the Sun: Perspectives on Contemporary Native Art.* Quebec: Canadian Museum of Civilization.

McMaster, Gerald, and Lee-Ann Martin. 1992. *Indigena: Contemporary Native Perspectives.* Vancouver: Douglas and McIntyre and Canadian Museum of Civilization.

Nemiroff, Diana, Robert Houle, and Charlotte Townsend-Gault, ed. 1992. *Land Spirit Power: First Nations at the National Gallery of Canada.* Ottawa: National Gallery of Canada.

Phillips, Ruth. 1993. 'Messages from the Past: Oral Traditions and Contemporary Woodlands Art.' In *In the Shadow of the Sun: Perspectives on Contemporary Native Art.* Hull, Quebec: Canadian Museum of Civilization.

Reid, Martine. 1993. 'In Search of Things Past, Remembered, Retraced and Reinvented.' In *In the Shadow of the Sun: Perspectives on Contemporary Native Art.* Hull, Quebec: Canadian Museum of Civilization.

Profile of Allen Sapp (1928–)

Cree, Artist

The Plains Cree artist Allen Sapp, is world-renowned. A forerunner of the 'New Native Arts,'[1] he works in the realist tradition, painting simple and vivid scenes from his childhood and portraying the texture of reserve life in the 1940s and 1950s.

Born on the Red Pheasant Reserve near Battleford, Saskatchewan, on 2 January 1928, Allen was a sickly child and was raised by his grandmother, Maggie Soonias. She nicknamed him 'Kiskaytum,' meaning 'he perceives it' in the Cree language.[2] She encouraged him to draw after he first expressed an interest at about age five, and profoundly influenced his subsequent artistic career. He sold his first piece of art to his teacher for a nickel.[3]

In 1960 Sapp and his wife, Mary Whitford, moved from the reserve to the nearby town of North Battleford, Saskatchewan.[4] There he sold or bartered his artwork to townspeople.[5] Selling his work without a permit brought him a warning from a North Battleford police officer who immediately purchased one of his paintings for $35.[6]

A local doctor, Allen Gonor, recognized his talent and became his friend, adviser, and patron.[7] Gonor introduced Sapp to University of Saskatchewan art professor Wynona Mulcaster.[8] During weekly lessons, she offered instruction and guidance that helped him hone his talents. Mulcaster's garden was the venue for Sapp's first art show – at which all of his paintings sold.[9] His next exhibition, at the Mendel Art Gallery in Saskatoon, Saskatchewan, drew more than 13,000 people. By 1969, Sapp was beginning to gain international recognition. His art is now displayed and sold in galleries around the world.[10]

Sapp's talent has been widely recognized over the years. In 1975 he was elected to the Royal Canadian Academy of Arts, which represents a cross-section of Canada's most distinguished artists.[11] Election to membership in this prestigious group is an acknowledgment of the quality and value of Sapp's work 'by one of the most demanding and discriminating groups

Allen Sapp. Courtesy of Allen Sapp Gallery.

concerned with the arts in Canada, his own peers.'[12] Sapp received the Saskatchewan Order of Merit in 1985. Governor General Jeanne Sauvé appointed him an officer of the Order of Canada in 1987 for his outstanding achievements and his contributions to the citizens of Canada and to humanity at large.[13] He was given the Saskatchewan Arts Board's Lifetime Award for Excellence in Arts in 1996 and a National Aboriginal Achievement Award in 1999.[14] In November 2003 Allen Sapp received the governor general's Literary Award for his illustration of the book *The Song within My Heart*, co-authored with Dave Bouchard, which was based on his memories of his childhood.

Allen Sapp currently lives in North Battleford, Saskatchewan, where he continues to produce paintings depicting his Cree past and also dedicates his time to instructing young artists.

LAURA NIMILOWICH

Notes

1 Dean Bauche, 'Allen Sapp,' *Canadian Encyclopaedia 2000 World Edition* (Toronto: McClelland and Stewart 2000), 1.
2 www.allensapp.com/allen.htm.
3 Joan Black, 'Grandmother Believed in Boy's Artistic Talent,' *Windspeaker* 16, no.12: 2.
4 Bauche, 'Allen Sapp,' 1.
5 Black, 'Grandmother Believed in Boy's Artistic Talent,' 2.
6 Ibid.
7 www.allensapp.com/allen.htm.
8 Bauche, 'Allen Sapp,' 1.
9 Black, 'Grandmother Believed in Boy's Artistic Talent,' 3.
10 Ibid., 4.
11 Ibid., 2.
12 www.allensapp.com/allen.htm.
13 Ibid.
14 Ibid.

PART FOUR

LITERATURE

First Peoples Literature in Canada

KATERI AKIWENZIE-DAMM

How can we know if we're Canadian? I mean, how can we know what 'Canadian' is, unless all of us develop what we have.

(Campbell 1991, 58).

As Indigenous peoples, our connection to the land, our homeland, makes us who we are and connects us to each other and the web of life that surrounds and supports us. Land, community, culture, and spirituality are intricately woven together. This interconnectedness is expressed and reinforced through our language, arts, ceremonies, songs, prayers, dances, customs, values, and daily practices – all of which have been developed over generations, over thousands and thousands of years of living on the land. Who you are as an Indigenous person arises from your connection to the land and to all others who share it. Your community thus includes everything that is connected to the land: the human, the natural, and the supernatural. Your connection is complex because it is woven from strands of kinship.

Standing at the intersection, the centre of a web of ancestors and descendants, the intersections between past, present, and future, between the spiritual realm and the physical realm, we develop our sense of personal and social identity. We come to understand our relationship to all aspects of creation. This is how we come to know ourselves and our meaning and purpose as human beings. We are supported and sustained within a web of relationships. Our orature and literature reinforce, reflect, and are an integral manifestation of that web. It is part of a long tradition stretching backwards to our creation and forwards into forever.

In this way, Aboriginal literatures are unique.

Aboriginal literatures arise from a tradition unlike that of other literatures in Canada. They arise out of the culture, beliefs, values, aesthetics, humour, spirituality and experiences of the various Indigenous peoples of this land. Their traditions go back to the songs, stories, story cycles, prayers, invocations, speeches, anecdotes, and other orature of the people who have always lived on this land. Although contemporary Aboriginal literatures incorporate forms that may be recognizable from other traditions, such as the 'novel,' 'autobiography,' 'short fiction,' 'creative non-fiction,' 'poetry' and so on, many of these forms, as used by First Peoples writers, are influenced as much by our own traditional forms as by these more recent ones. Others may have named these forms, but many have been a part of our cultural expression since long before the newcomers arrived on this continent. Before it was named 'poetry,' our ancestors composed poetry in the form of songs and prayers. Before it was called 'creative non-fiction,' our ancestors told tales of personal and historical events in a style that was poetic and complex in its beauty. Our literatures come from our own sources both in style and content; although, of course, because we exist and operate in the world, we are influenced by other art forms from other cultures and traditions. Our literatures are part of a cultural continuum that continues to grow and develop.

While it is true that the act of writing down our stories and songs was not part of our ways of life before contact with Europeans (although many First Nations did use mnemonic devices as symbolic aids for remembering certain stories, information, or events), the simple act of writing words on paper is not literature. Literature is a creative art. The creativity that infuses literature has always been a part of our cultures, and we have always expressed it in various ways. Whether we sing it, speak it, or write it, that creative voice is ever present and unique.

Although our literatures are part of a continuum within our cultures, the development of our creative and artistic work was disrupted by the imposition of a colonizing culture. The resulting 'silence' that surrounded our peoples as a result of colonization and its impact has been misinterpreted by many who have failed to recognize a basic fact: we were 'silent' not because we had not yet learned how to write 'literature' or to use foreign art forms, but because our own artistic traditions had been banned, denigrated, and even outlawed. They were not accepted outside our communities. We were prevented from and discouraged from maintaining our own artistic traditions and telling our own stories. As curator Lee-Ann Martin says, 'the legacy of colonialism contributed to the collision between the worldviews of Aboriginal and Euro-Canadian communities. Eventually, many Aboriginal stories became silenced and the images invisible' (Martin 1999, 36).

This is a history that is part of our artistic tradition. It is one that is not shared by others in Canada, although it is true that other individuals and communities have had their artistic work banned at various times. Perhaps it is because of this, in part, that our relationship to language, to silence, and to the wider Canadian society and arts community is politicized. Not only do we come from cultures that have different views of the relationship between the speaker, the words/language, and the audience, but also our experience with the colonizing society is one that has repeatedly told us that our stories are deemed by that society to be unacceptable or inferior; that there is no audience (or a very small one) for our literatures; that we can be silenced by force if necessary; that others with greater 'power' in society will try to set the parameters for our literatures by containing, defining, and ignoring them; and that we have to assert our place within our homeland, not only politically and geographically, but artistically as well.

For many of us, creative language in written or spoken forms is used, not merely as a form of individual self-expression, but as a form of cultural expression that raises the communal consciousness of the people. We believe in the power of words. Not in the power of legal documents and signatures, but in the power of words. This is not something we learned through the process of treaty making or, in the case of the signatory governments, treaty breaking. We had in our traditions a respect for the power of words that, in a holistic world-view, is not separate from prayer or other aspects of physical and spiritual life.

Perhaps because of this, we recognize that writing, literature, and orature are important, not exclusively for our own peoples or even for other Indigenous peoples, but for all of us. For many Indigenous peoples, they are forms of activism, they are creative, and, therefore, they are positive and giving ways to maintain who we are, to connect us to each other, and to protest against colonization, hatred, and oppression in all its guises and forms. They are essential to our survival. Jeannette Armstrong has said, 'In Native philosophy, creative activity is a deep spiritual responsibility requiring as full an awareness as possible of its sacred nature and the necessity for pure love to be at its centre' (Armstrong and Cardinal 1991, 106).

Writing and other acts of creativity are a way to share, to reaffirm kinship, to connect with the sacredness of creation. Writing and orature are a part of this. Because WORDS ARE SACRED. As Metis architect Douglas Cardinal says: 'There is power in every individual because there is power in the words. Humans are very powerful in this way. To turn the realm of thought, which is abstract potential, into a thing in the physical world, through word, is powerful creativity as a natural act ... The word in that way is powerful. When we speak a word we declare something. We create it and then it can be. It can become action. So it is a sacred act (Armstrong and Cardinal 1991, 89).

Words are sacred. They can transform. Words can change peoples' attitudes, their thinking, their construction of reality, their actions. Words can change the world. As can silence.

I suspect that part of the essential uniqueness that makes the literatures of Aboriginal peoples in Canada so wonderfully different from other literatures in Canada has something to do with the creative process. I believe that, because of the different tradition from which it arises, and the different beliefs, values, and aesthetics upon which it is based, the context in which the writer creates, that is, the creative act itself, is different for Aboriginal writers. Therefore, the literature and orature are necessarily and fundamentally different. There is a different heart and spirit that goes into the creative act itself and the reader/audience's connection to that, through listening or reading, is necessarily different.

For me, creative writing is ceremony. There is a spiritual dimension to it that, although sometimes more strong and direct and other times less so, is never completely absent. I believe that the *autissokanuk*, the ancestors, the spirits, and the life force of all of creation, are around us as we work. This is true whether we are aware of it or not. It is true not only of writers and writing, of course, but also of all work that we undertake in a way that seeks connection (and really, what work does not?). The nature of creative work requires artists to open themselves, to, in a sense, call upon other realms, to transcend time and space, to reach deep within themselves and far out into creation, in order to find a truth and spirit upon which to form their work and speak. This is not intrinsically exclusive to those in the 'creative arts;' perhaps it is simply that, for such people, the connection with creation is more direct or, at least, more easily understood or accepted.

Despite the many ways in which Aboriginal literatures are vibrant, beautiful, and quietly but undoubtedly influential on the dominant literature in Canada, they are, for the most part, largely unknown, misunderstood, misinterpreted, ignored, and unacknowledged even as they are appropriated by some. Although Aboriginal literatures, and the traditions upon which they continue to develop, are a key element of what makes Canadian literature unique in the world, this contribution remains almost completely unrecognized. A few writers, such as E. Pauline Johnson, Thomas King, Tomson Highway, and Eden Robinson, are recognizable names. However, for the most part, the beauty, diversity depth of our literatures are lost to most Canadian readers. It is an ongoing struggle for Aboriginal writers to access the Canadian reading public through the Canadian publishing industry as well as through most other means (such as writing festivals, university reading lists, and so on). For those who do gain hard-won access to these opportunities or who create their own, few actually are able to attain any real, sustained, meaningful recognition. Fewer still would be considered part of the 'canon' of Canadian literature.

In the past decade, Aboriginal literatures have slowly begun to gain some recognition within the rubric of 'Canadian' literature. One sign of this is that more and more universities are offering courses in Aboriginal literatures. As a result of this and other factors, a 'canon' of Aboriginal literatures is beginning to take form. An example of this process of 'canonization' is *An Anthology of Canadian Native Literature in English*, which was first published by Oxford University Press in 1992. (The second edition was published in 1998.) In the preface to the first edition, co-editor Daniel David Moses says, 'the decisions on what should go in something that you might call the canon can be easily disguised as aesthetic decisions, but if we are making a canon the decisions are definitely political' (Moses 1992).

Politics seems to be an unavoidable reality in all aspects of Aboriginal peoples' lives, including our arts and literatures. This, I would argue, is the inescapable outcome of an imbalance of power in which the more powerful side seeks to control, dominate, define, and diminish the power of others. Of course, the nature of the politics in this case depends on who is doing the 'canonizing' and what they include and exclude. A fellow Anishnaabe writer and scholar, Rolland Nadjiwon, recognizes the politics of this process and argues that, 'if our literature is to be canonized, and it is being so, I would think we need to be in control of that naming and that content' (Nadjiwon 1999). I suspect that, in a sense, there may be two canons: one much smaller, extremely limited canon that is being developed outside the Indigenous community (through the influence of editors, publishers, reviewers, university professors, literary-awards juries, and so on), and one more fully developed and inclusive canon that is being formed and recognized within the local and international Indigenous communities.

One way in which Aboriginal peoples are taking control of that sort of decision making is through publishing companies that are controlled by Aboriginal owners, managers, and editors. Theytus Books, based in Penticton, British Columbia, was established in 1980 and is the oldest Aboriginal-controlled trade book publisher in Canada. Theytus is responsible for helping many writers gain valuable publishing credits as they work to become established writers. It published the first novel by a Native woman in Canada (*Slash* by Jeannette Armstrong), and the first book by an Inuk writer (*Arctic Dreams and Nightmares* by Alootook Ipellie). Theytus also published the ground-breaking collection of stories by the celebrated Metis 'storyteller' Maria Campbell, *Stories of the Road Allowance People,* which strove 'to put the Mother back in the language' (Campbell 1991, 49).

This collection of stories is told in a 'storytelling' style and in the common language of Campbell's people – what she refers to as a 'village English' that has a different sound and syntax from standard Canadian English. *Stories of the Road Allowance People* has influenced the thinking and writing of many First Peoples writers and marked a new development in the evolution of our literatures. At the time it was released and in the years since, there has been a definite trend among Indigenous writers to reclaim their authentic voices and decolonize the ways in which they use English, a foreign language that was forced upon our communities by colonizers.

Since her first book, a best-selling, 'somewhat fictional autobiography,' (Acoose 2001, 140), *Halfbreed*, was published by McClelland and Stewart in 1973, Campbell has influenced generations of First Peoples writers. In an interview with German scholar Hartmut Lutz, Anishnaabe writer Lenore Keeshig-Tobias says that her friend, fellow poet Daniel David Moses, calls Campbell '"The Mother of Us All" ... That's the way we all feel about her.' (Keeshig-Tobias 1991, 83). *Halfbreed* is a seminal text in Canadian literature and is widely considered a classic of Native Canadian literature and of Indigenous literature internationally. It was written, Maria says, to tell people 'what it is like to be a Halfbreed woman in our country' (Campbell 1973, 8). In doing so, Maria told a story that was essentially and intrinsically 'Canadian' but that other Canadians otherwise would not have known. Without knowing the stories of the people of this land, Canadians cannot know themselves.

Unfortunately, although *Halfbreed* was an early bestseller, it did not seem to have convinced the Canadian publishing industry that there could be a market for First Peoples writing in Canada. One might even argue that, although the marginalization of First Peoples literature is often dismissed as 'market driven,' this too involves decisions about where investments are made or not made. These decisions are, in large part, political rather than purely economic.

Kegedonce Press, established in 1993, and based at Neyaashiinigmiing, on Cape Croker Reserve in Ontario, is the only other national Aboriginal publisher in Canada. Kegedonce Press is committed to developing, promoting, and publishing Indigenous writers nationally and internationally. Among other accomplishments, Kegedonce, with Aboriginal Australian publisher Jukurrpa Books, published *Skins: Contemporary Indigenous Writing*, the first international co-publishing project between Indigenous publishers. This award-winning anthology features the writing of Inuit, Maori, Metis, Aboriginal Australian, First Nations, and Native American writers.

Pemmican Books in Manitoba and the Gabriel Dumont Institute in Saskatchewan are currently the only other established Aboriginal-controlled (in both cases, Metis) trade-book publishers in Canada. Both of them focus on publishing Metis writing. Pemmican is perhaps best known as the publisher of Beatrice (Mosioner) Culleton's novel *In Search of April Raintree*, one of the key pieces of Aboriginal writing in Canada and widely acknowledged and celebrated as an inspiration to generations of Aboriginal writers. Both Pemmican and Gabriel Dumont continue to provide publishing opportunities for Metis writers and to promote their work.

Through Aboriginal-controlled publishing programs in which books to be published are selected by Aboriginal peoples themselves, and through the support and promotion of Aboriginal literatures and writers, these four publishers are influencing the ways in which Aboriginal literatures are developing and being maintained. They are providing publishing opportunities to voices that otherwise would go unheard and are contributing to the diversity and definition of what Canadian literature is, or could be. They provide Canadian readers with access to Aboriginal writing that they might have little or no access to otherwise. Because extremely few Aboriginal writers, especially emerging writers, have been or are being published by other Canadian publishers, the important role of these publishers to Canadian culture seems obvious. However, all four continue to struggle to survive as they work to develop writers, to create and develop markets, and, against all odds and obstacles, to build an Aboriginal publishing industry. All four operate on the brink of imminent closure, yet they persist in the knowledge that the books they produce are beautiful and necessary. Without them, the voices of whole communities, whole generations of Aboriginal writers, could be shut out of the Canadian literary milieu.

Despite these many challenges, Aboriginal orature, literatures, and publishing continue. And as they do, they continue to challenge, influence, broaden, redefine, and contribute to Canadian literature, to Canadian arts and culture, and to this whole wider notion of what Canada is and what it means to be Canadian.

Although Aboriginal literatures in Canada have been kept on the edges of Canadian literature as a so-called 'marginalized' form, Aboriginal literatures are the grounding of Canadian literature. In truth, they are not at the margins, but at the centre. Aboriginal literatures and oratory are of the land and from the land. They are the land from which all other literatures in this place now known as Canada spring forth. Without this land, there is no Canada, and without the literatures of the people of this land, there is no true Canadian literature.

Bibliography

Acoose, Janice. 2001. 'Woman Standing above Ground.' In Armand G. Ruffo.,
(Ad)dressing Our Words: Aboriginal Perspectives on Aboriginal Literature(s). Penticton, BC.: Theytus Books, 140.

Armstrong, Jeanette, and Douglas Cardinal. 1991. *The Native Creative Process*. Penticton, BC.: Theytus Books.

Campbell, Maria. 1973. *Halfbreed*. Toronto: McClelland and Stewart.

– 1991. Interview by Hartmut Lutz. *Contemporary Challenges: Conversations with Canadian Native Authors*. Saskatoon: Fifth House Publishers.

Keeshig-Tobias, Lenore. 1991. Interview by Hartmut Lutz. *Contemporary Challenges: Conversations with Canadian Native Authors*. Saskatoon: Fifth House Publishers.

Martin, Lee-Ann. 1999. 'Reclaiming Desire.' *Exposed: Aesthetics of Aboriginal Erotic Art*. Regina: Mackenzie Art Gallery.

Moses, Daniel David. 1992. *An Anthology of Canadian Native Literature in English*. Toronto: Oxford University Press.

Nadjiwan, Rolland. 1999. Correspondence with author, 1 March.

Profile of Jeannette C. Armstrong (1948–)

Okanagan, Novelist, Teacher, and Activist

Jeannette Armstrong is an accomplished writer and an impassioned Indigenous rights activist who is concerned with land rights and democratic rights and improving the Aboriginal education system. Armstrong was deeply influenced by the powerful women within her family. She is the grandniece of Hum-Ishu-Ma (Mourning Dove, 1888–1936), who is believed to be the first Native American woman novelist.[1]

Armstrong was born in 1948 on the Okanagan Indian Reserve near Penticton, British Columbia.[2] She was first published at the age of fifteen when one of her poems was printed in the local paper.[3] She earned a Fine Arts diploma from Okanagan College and later a Bachelor of Fine Arts from the University of Victoria in 1978.[4]

As a writer and activist, her goal is to educate and empower Aboriginal people using history and culture. In 1978 Armstrong began work at the En'owkin Centre, a cultural and educational centre for the Okanagan people.[5] It is the first accredited creative writing program operated by Aboriginal people for Aboriginal people.[6] The En'owkin Centre also houses the first Aboriginal-owned and operated publishing house, Theytus Books.[7] Armstrong began working with the Okanagan Indian Curriculum Project in 1982, which stimulated her writing career.[8]

Among her many literary works, perhaps the best known is *Slash*, published in 1985. A tale about a young Okanagan man involved in the 1960s Aboriginal rights movement, *Slash* is widely used as course material in schools, universities, and colleges. Armstrong's most recent novel, *Whispering in Shadows* (published in 2000), chronicles the experiences of a young woman living on a reserve. An environmental theme runs throughout the book. Armstrong has published three children's books: *Enwisteetkwa* (1982), *Neekna and Chemai* (1984), and *Neekna and Chemai* (1991).[9]

Armstrong's publications include a collection of poetry entitled *Breath Tracks* (1991), as well as numerous poems in various anthologies. In 1991

Jeannette C. Armstrong. Courtesy of August Armstrong.

she also co-authored, with Douglas Cardinal, a non-fiction book entitled *A Collaborative Discourse between Douglas Cardinal and Jeannette Armstrong: The Native Creative Process.*

Armstrong's many essays include: 'Writing from a Native Woman's Perspective' (1985); 'Discipline and Sharing: Education in the Indian Way' (1985); 'Traditional Indigenous Education: A Natural Process' (1988); 'Voices of Native Women in Literature' (1988); 'Bridging Cultures, Cultural Robbery: Imperialism – Voices of Native Women' (1989); 'Real Power: Aboriginal Women – Past, Present and Future' (1990); 'The Disempowerment of First North American Native Peoples' (1990); 'Empowerment through Their Writing' (1990); 'Words, Racism: Racial Exclusivity and Cultural Supremacy' (1992); 'C is for Culture' (1993); 'Sharing one Skin' (1996); 'Speaking for the Generations, Native Writers on Writing' (1998); and, most recently, 'The Importance of Community: Development and Sustainment in an Age of Globalization' (2000).[10]

Her videos and sound recordings include songs such as 'Snpinktn' and the spoken poem 'Wind Woman' (Moving Images Productions 2001). She is co-director of 'In Our Territory,' a documentary about the Treaty 8 territory (1999); 'Turning Earth,' a video of music, song, dance, and words (1995); and 'Grandmothers,' a Much Music video special (1995). She also wrote the words for 'Till the Bars Break,' a collaboration produced on cassette and compact disk that was nominated for a 1991 Juno Music Award.

Armstrong has won two awards recognizing excellence in art: the Mungo Martin Award in 1974, and the Helen Pitt Memorial Award in 1978. She received an honorary doctorate from St Thomas University, Fredericton, in 2000.[11]

She lives in the Okanagan region of British Columbia.

ANGELA SHEPARD

Notes

1 Karin Beeler, www.quarles.unbc.edu/kbeeler_html/research/arm4.html

2 Hartmut Lutz, 'Jeannette Armstrong.' In Gretchen M. Bataille and Laurie Lisa, ed., *Native American Women: A Biographical Dictionary* (New York: Garland Press 1993), 13–14.

3 Jolene Johnson Dupont, *Voices from the Gap*, 2002. www.voices.cla.umn.edu/authors/Jeanette Armstrong.html.

4 Ibid.

5 Connie Fife, *The Colour of Resistance: A Contemporary Collection of Writing by Aboriginal Women* (Toronto: Sisterhood Vision Press 1993), 274.

6 Johnson Dupont, *Voices from the Gap*.

7 Lutz, 'Jeannette Armstrong,' 13.

8 Janice Williamson, *Sounding Differences: Conversations with Seventeen Canadian Women Writers* (Toronto: University of Toronto Press 1993), 16.

9 Beeler, 1.

10 Ibid.

11 http://www.ipr.org/cgi/ref/nature/browse.pl/A9.

Aboriginal Literatures:
A Distinctive Genre within Canadian Literature

JEANNETTE C. ARMSTRONG

Central to the question whether Aboriginal literatures are a distinctive genre within Canadian literature is the basic issue of Aboriginal oral traditions' relevance and potency. Those Aboriginal literatures, in their contemporary written form, must first be positioned as an evolution of oral traditions. Constituting far more than just daily spoken conversation, oral traditions encompass ancient artistic disciplines of the primary cultures within which they occur.

Contrary to the predominant view, Aboriginal literatures are not 'emergent' Canadian literary voices arising as a result of Aboriginal peoples' literacy in an official language and their introduction to Canadian literature. Aboriginal literatures, in written form, must first be read as an authentic older, complex, Aboriginal spoken art form. As with other Aboriginal art disciplines, their distinctive features are rooted deep in a past practice of culture, and shaped by past conventions and precepts. It is these features of oral artistic tradition that are carried forward into the present by intergenerational transmission in Aboriginal community populations, and that continue regardless of the mother tongue the people speak or their literacy level.

An overarching question then arises about whether words must be written to be defined as 'literature.' Although 'literature' is customarily viewed as a written artistic tradition, perhaps defining it as such diminishes and subverts a wider definition of artistry in words. Features of oral fiction, oral non-fiction, oral poetry, oral sacred text, public oratory, theatrical rhetoric, and children's narrative occur in all cultures worldwide – because of communication, not because of a system of symbols for sounds and words. 'Literature' does not occur solely as the result of a writing system. Writing can be thought of simply as one 'medium' of 'word' artistic tradition. Writing does not somehow magically elevate word meaning into artistry. Nor is it the writing system that generates 'creative genius,' on the grounds that it is transmissible, independent of the word crafter's presence. To agree with this would be to agree that oral storytellers of all cultures and all ages could not have achieved 'creative genius.' Perhaps it is best to allow that 'literature,' in its fundamental reference, in fact includes all artistry in words, and proceed with the view that 'literature' occurs with or without a writing system.

The term 'literatures' then, as I use it, can be broadened to include artistic discipline contained in words – through perspective, subject, and contextual experience – encompassing all forms of Aboriginal oral tradition as a distinctive genre within Canadian literature. A wider definition of 'literatures' is being revealed, contextualized and exacted as authentic features of an 'oral literary tradition' in contemporary Aboriginal writing, which is making tremendous contributions as a distinctive genre within Canadian literature.

The contributions that Aboriginal literatures make as a distinctive genre can be positioned first in the context of their role in their original first-language communities. Without an existing, extensive body of research from an Aboriginal perspective on the oral literatures of antiquity, I draw on my own experience in order to comment on the role of such literatures in Aboriginal communities. I am a fluent mother-tongue speaker of N'silxcen (Okanagan), and I have the good fortune of being a descendant of a family with a strong storytelling tradition. My great-aunt is a well-known Okanagan storyteller, Christine Quintasket, known as Mourning Dove. She published a collection of Okanagan legends translated into English, and other works, including a novel, in the early part of the last century. The storytelling tradition was maintained in my family and continues to inform my own writing and oral tradition.

The primary role of Aboriginal literatures within community is one of the most important of contributions. It is my view that oral literatures of community play a different role than contemporary written literatures in the world of market-driven parameters that shape what becomes mass product and define what survives. Oral literatures require a teller and an audience fluent in the cultural idiom of the telling, free of the 'widest marketability' considerations permeating much of written literatures. Oral literatures seek and require community and context. By their essence, they seek to draw community together around the familiar, the known, and the trusted. Oral literatures are performed by tellers – real people who have a place in community – rather than reflecting the distance of words on paper. Story 'telling,' in that sense, draws community together, generation to generation, in the knowledge of each other and of the land and the principles that they share. Persons who carry story magic bring the valued knowledge of antiquity, which has informed and sustained generations, forward into new generations, within a community contextualization. It is in the transmission of that knowledge that the greatest contributions are made. Written Aboriginal narrative, grounded in the oral tradition, carries with it the foundational integrity of story 'telling,' speaking from within collective principles, compelling audiences towards the common ideals of sustaining the community and land.

Humans construct the world through language. Language is a window through which we see and understand the world. Culturally, society is constructed by what the 'window' of language reveals, and this 'window' deeply influences all human action and interaction. The transmission of historical oral 'literatures,' in either the original language or official languages, contributes new dimensions to language patterns and cultural meaning, as a natural occurrence. Within each separate Aboriginal language and cultural group are cultural differences which are refined into contemporary literary manifestations. There are many distinctive language families in Canada. The profound influences of original language patterns and precepts upon communities are carried from generation to generation through ongoing community interaction. They remain as social construct and practice, regardless of language loss and generational transition to a foreign language, and they contribute to the vast pool of literary creation and language use. The richness and complex variety of Aboriginal literatures, from the perspective of their contemporary manifestations, are yet to be fully appreciated and explored as a facet of post-colonial literatures in Canada.

Reading and literacy serve to standardize the use of language across boundaries. One of the effects of high illiteracy in Aboriginal communities is that spoken foreign-language use overrides written foreign-language use. Contemporary Aboriginal spoken-language use, arising out of orally learned foreign language, evolved through a slow, generation-to-generation transition from Aboriginal-language use. The outcome is a hybridity of spoken use combining grammatical structural components of both Aboriginal-language use and the foreign language. The American literary term 'Rez-English' has been used to describe the wonderful dialectal hybridity which occurs throughout Aboriginal country. A veritable bounty of Aboriginal literatures exists written in 'Rez-English.' However, deviations from an 'accepted' Euro-format of content and language usage are critically conventionalized within the standard of Canadian literature, as substandard, 'emergent,' or 'naive.' Aboriginal literatures are wrongfully disregarded and – worse – discarded as 'literature.' Critical literary pedagogy is just beginning to explore the immense contributions to Canadian literature of this hybridization of language use in Aboriginal literatures.

The reason Aboriginal literary expression is not being read as a distinctive genre may lie in the fact that the only Aboriginal literatures accessible to Canadian culture are forced into one of the two official languages. As such, they are continuously 'culturally constructed' within Eurocentric aesthetic literary expectations. Attempts are being made to define Aboriginal literatures solely within the parameters of the 'accepted' Eurocentric literary conventions as a biased and restrictive practice lacking a coherent critical literary framework. In such a practice, Aboriginal literary format, subject, and genre are easily and erroneously categorized to Euro-literary genres, and deemed as such to be lacking sophistication. However, great strides are being made as vital Aboriginal literary criticism is published to assist in providing an Aboriginal critical view. These writings serve to elevate Aboriginal works to their rightful place as important literary contributions. They are valuable because they deconstruct the old definitions of what has 'literary' merit.

A common misconception about Aboriginal literature holds that it is a mono-voice of literary expression. Aboriginal literatures do not form a mono-voice within the canon of Canadian literature; however, Aboriginal literatures *can* be described as a distinctive genre within Canadian literature. Aboriginal cultures in their various contemporary forms – whether the experience is urban-modern, pan-Indian, or a clearly tribal, traditional past; whether it is Eastern Woodland, Subarctic, Plains, or West Coast – each have unique cultural sensibilities which shape the voices coming forward out of them. Therefore, Aboriginal literary voices, as one facet of cultural practice, have symbolic significance and relevance that are integral to the deconstruction of colonialism. Aboriginal literary voices also support the reconstruction of a new order of internal culture and a relationship that transcends colonial thought and practice.

It is common knowledge that Aboriginal peoples in North America were rendered powerless and subjugated through cultural aggression. The disintegration of family and community and nation was an inevitable outcome originating with the individual's internalized pain. Profound consequences of cultural aggression are evidenced in death statistics from suicide, violence, and alcohol and drug abuse, with Aboriginal peoples living in the poorest of conditions and suffering from the lowest life expectancies. Such systemic violence of cultural aggression is made possible through political will, reinforced and maintained through prevailing literary images. Literary images carried in education and the media are generated through a silencing and a cultural blindness; through a silencing and a demeaning of the story of ourselves and our worth. Through the politics of representation, cultural intolerance insinuates and manifests itself as a psychologically destructive force that only the culturally oppressed can articulate.

An effect of the continuous colonization of the Aboriginal voice is that Aboriginal peoples see the world through two separate realities. Writing becomes mediated and restricted by a 'standard' of literary practice defined and accepted principally by a dominant model of voice in the arts. This dominant model is represented daily in the array of literatures, magazine articles, creative journalism, news, advertising, television fiction, big screen fiction, political rhetoric, and everyday language.

Influences on Aboriginal literatures are not confined to the 'classic' written literatures alone. There are also influences from 'Canadian' culture in general. Aboriginal cultures, only recently removed from operating solely in the oral traditions, incorporate the contemporary manifestations of all word and language uses available. Aboriginal literatures are not constrained by a standard of classic literary convention principally defined and accepted by a 'literate' upper class. The vast array of influence moves their works through oratorical literary forms encompassing creative non-fiction, expressive journalism, poetic narrative and lyrical prose, and the oratorical prowess born of poetically melding public oratory speech and rhetoric. Hence, First Nations written literature is taking exciting, unique shapes through these influences not only because it is open to them without literary prejudice but also because it is in a position to influence the shape of a Canadian literature ghettoized by old world and colonial literary standards.

Another significant influence on Aboriginal literatures is the fact that these literatures lack access to their own primary community as a reading audience. One reason for this is the high rate of illiteracy, compounded by a deep generational influence of orality; while orality strengthens people-to-people communication, one effect of illiteracy, in most Aboriginal communities, is that not many people read books. Books written from a perspective intended for the smaller Aboriginal community do not survive economically, and consequently Aboriginal writers must write for a wider audience in order to be published. The primary cultural audience's lack of access to written Aboriginal literatures remains a serious obstacle and thus affects what is written and for whom. There are few examples of Aboriginal peoples' literatures written from the perspective of their own audience; however, those that do exist have created excitement and generated audiences for such works. Most commonly categorized and described as postmodern and post-colonial, these works contribute greatly to Canadian literature as a distinctive genre.

Another factor constricting written Aboriginal literatures is that they are read continuously from within a context of mainstream Canadian cultures, rather than within a context of cultural voice internal to each Aboriginal group. Aboriginal literatures thus become easily categorized, lumped as 'Native literature,' without reference to each unique internal potency of ancestral Aboriginal culture. One effect of this is to restrict the opportunity, within a process of cultural fragmentation, for the decolonization of the internal voice in the formation of identity. I suggest that such literatures not be defined by Canadian cultural experience and read as 'Native Litera- ture.' Instead, Aboriginal literatures should be appreciated as unique forms of Aboriginal literary expression emanating from within the cultural language family where it originates. In this way, the literary contributions of Canada's various Aboriginal language families as distinct cultural groups can be truly appreciated.

So much of the Aboriginal writing voice is concerned with, and thereby constrained within, a larger context of resistance to mainstream politics, while simultaneously having to comply with assimilation measures. Con- temporary Aboriginal writing moves continually into an externally reac- tionist framework of format, concern, and content. Resistance is the wellspring of literary inspiration, though much of this literature is read without reference to the unique potency of ancestral voice it contains.

Contemporary themes that predominate as a result of the common con- ditions of hegemony and marginalization are: political struggle; colonial oppression; social fragmentation; cultural renewal; and identity and crisis. Contemporary Aboriginal literatures thematically create intersections between literature and political struggles. Many Aboriginal works of fic- tion, non-fiction, and poetry thematically explore the story of political struggle as subject; however, works that embody a convergence between literature and political struggle are distinctly different. Such works present a positioning of 'artistic' intent in an emerging particularized body of Aboriginal literary works, whose central artistic aim is political struggle. Framed within the communities' demands for recognition of the narrative integrity defining their oral literatures, these Aboriginal literatures form an important body of work bridging gaps between different communities.

It is proposed that these 'bridging-between-cultures' voices, grounded in orality, reservation language use, regional symbolisms, and cultural metaphor, offer an exciting pathway to the exploration of a true multicul- tural communicative art form. Their importance as a contribution to Cana- dian literature is paramount in the restructuring towards a new order of human thought, beyond racial, ethnic, and cultural attempts to dominate and assimilate. Hence, these literatures may be the kind of story magic which draws us together across vast chasms of intolerance and ignorance.

In the literary arts, there is an opportunity to free us all from old world notions of power and its systemic mechanisms. Freedom of voice may be a possibility here in Canada when constraints on cultural practice are no longer dictated by a shrinking segment of the population intrinsically Eurocentric in its interpretations of Canadian culture. Aboriginal literatures are not only taking exciting unique shapes, but are also in a position to have a qualitative influence on the Canadian literary arts. It is highly likely that this contribution will be transformative for both Aboriginal cultures and Canadian cultures.

Although damage has been wrought, healing can take place through cultural affirmation. I have found immense strength and beauty in Aboriginal writers, in their dispelling of lies and their telling of what really happened. They choose to preserve images that protect and treasure the splendour of difference. The purpose is to tell a better story than the one being told about us. To speak about the old knowledge of community and this land. To give that to the people and to the next generations. The voices of the grandmothers and grandfathers compel the writers to speak of the worth of our peoples and to resist those who profane them, to cherish beauty and all life, and to ease the pain. Aboriginal writers carry the languages of the voice of the land and of the people. Theirs is a contribution that will not be silenced by the language of oppression.

At a time when there is a growing apprehension about the impact on 'Canadian culture' of 'global monoculturing,' we can see a multiplicity of healthy cultures in Canada as an essential component in a post-colonial society. The perception of a majority Canadian culture and literature is a construct which does not truthfully reflect the wonderfully pluralistic nature of the peoples who co-exist on a daily basis, and who find wonderful ways to communicate that to each other through their literatures despite great barriers. Implicit in that is the reality that culture is a process of defining and discovery, not a static state of being. This suggests, therefore, a unique vision in a literary gathering of voices focused on tomorrow's cultural possibility of peaceful co-existence and intent on celebrating the many literatures that are reflective of that experience. An immense knowledge of the past, and a vision of the present rooted in Aboriginal literatures, are transforming both Aboriginal cultures and Canadian cultures, and are the best of reasons to support Aboriginal writing in all its forms.

Profile of Tomson Highway (1951–)

Cree, Playwright, and Artistic Director

As Canada's pre-eminent Native playwright, Tomson Highway has fought to give voice to Aboriginal peoples' plight through provocative and insightful plays while at the same time trying to 'make the rez cool and celebrate what funky folk Canada's Indian people really are.'[1]

Tomson Highway was born on 6 December 1951, on the Brocket Reserve in northern Manitoba. He was the eleventh of twelve children born to Joe and Pelagie Philomene Highway.[2] His father, a fisherman, struggled with the daunting task of providing for a family of fourteen, a difficult chore by any standard.

Although members of his family excelled at dogsled racing, Highway found his calling in the arts.[3] At six years of age, he was sent to the Guy Hill Indian Residential School in The Pas, Manitoba.[4]

Highway remained in residential school until age fifteen and during this time made only sporadic visits to his parent's home. He was then sent to Winnipeg to attend high school and was there placed under the care and supervision of several white foster families.[5] After graduation in 1970, he studied piano at the University of Manitoba's Faculty of Music. He later attended the University of Western Ontario, where he graduated with a Bachelor of Music honours degree and a Bachelor of Arts in English in the mid-1970s.[6]

His restlessness prompted extensive overseas travel.[7] Upon returning to Canada, he met the playwright James Reaney, who encouraged him to pursue his writing talent under his tutelage.[8] Over the next few years, Highway reconnected with fellow Native brothers and sisters in Native Friendship Centres and correctional facilities. These interactions served as the basis for his plays.[9] A biographical note written about him recalls this experience: 'He loved and was deeply moved by the hundreds of Native Americans he met during his travels.'[10] He found himself 'falling in love all over again with Native people on reserves, on the streets and in the bars.'[11]

Tomson Highway. Photographer: V. Tony Hauser. Courtesy of the National Archives of Canada, PA207837.

His plays are widely recognized and include *New Song – New Dance* (1988), *Dry Lips Oughta Move to Kapuskasing* (1989), *Annie and the Old One* (1989), *The Sage* (1989), and *The Dancer and The Fool* (1989).[12] He won acclaim with *The Rez Sisters* (1986),[13] a production that centred around the high jinks, hopes, and dreams of seven Aboriginal women hoping to win the $1,000,000 jackpot at THE BIGGEST BINGO IN THE WORLD. It played to sold-out audiences. *The Rez Sisters* won the prestigious Dora Mavor Moore Award for best new play in Toronto's 1986–7 theatre season.[14] Not only was it a 1988 finalist for the Governor General's Literary Award,[15] it was also one of two productions that played on the mainstage to sold-out audiences at the Edinburgh International Festival.[16] Highway is also the author of *Kiss of the Fur Queen*, a novel about growing up aboriginal in norhern Manitoba.

Highway's work confronts the social problems prevalent in contemporary Native communities and gives an insider's glimpse into the sometimes tragic world of reserve life.[17] His characters are seldom heroes but a rather desperate lot forced to address the futility of their existence, their elusive dreams, and the demons of their colonized past. He succeeds in combining the mythical and spiritual elements of the Native world alongside present social ills, mixing equal parts of comedy and pathos to create a touching yet grim portrait of Native life.

Tomson Highway currently divides his time between Canada and France.

NANCY LUU

Notes

1 Tomson Highway, 'Prefatory Pages,' *The Rez Sisters* (Calgary: Fifth House Publishers 1988), ix.
2 'Tomson Highway.' In Elizabeth Lumley, ed., *Who's Who in Canada*, 35 (Toronto: University of Toronto Press 2000), 357.
3 Highway, 'Prefatory Pages,' ix.
4 'Tomson Highway,' *Biographical Dictionary of Indians of the Americas* (Newport Beach, Calif.: American Indian Publishers 1991), 278.
5 'Tomson Highway,' 278.
6 Ibid.
7 Lumley, ed., *Who's Who in Canada*, 357.
8 Colin Boyd, 'Highway, Tomson,' *The Canadian Encyclopaedia 2000 World Edition* (Toronto: McClelland and Stewart 2000), 1.
9 'Tomson Highway,' 278.
10 Ibid.

11 Highway, 'Prefatory Pages,' viii.
12 Boyd, 'Highway, Tomson,' 1.
13 Lumley, ed., *Who's Who in Canada*, 357.
14 Boyd, 'Highway, Tomson,' 1.
15 'Tomson Highway,' 278.
16 Ibid.
17 Highway, 'Prefatory Pages,' ix.

Aboriginal Voices:
Canada's Aboriginal Peoples in Their Own Words

CHERYL ISAACS

For almost six years from 1993 to 1999, it occupied magazine racks across this country. At first glance, it was virtually indistinguishable from its bright, shiny neighbours that touted fashion models and the latest gadgets. *Aboriginal Voices* magazine was different, though. By virtue of its content and the fact that it was the only one of its kind, it remains a milestone in Canadian culture.

The brainchild of actor Gary Farmer, *Aboriginal Voices* succeeded in giving Native people a voice, and a mass audience. It also gave that uninitiated mainstream audience a source of new information. By bringing the speakers and the listeners together, *Aboriginal Voices* accomplished what no other Canadian publication has before or since. It gave both Native and non-Native people a message essential to our shared Canadian culture and identity: 'As Native people, we are different, but we are not less.'

Aboriginal Voices was a magazine published by Native people, but not exclusively for them. For the Native community, the magazine was meant to be both entertainment and resource. In its pages, readers could find out what their favourite Native singer/actor/writer was up to, or check out the pow wow circuits, or the latest news items. There were also numerous advertisements scattered throughout the issues – on academic programs, grants and business opportunities – all geared to Native people. *Aboriginal Voices* was like a glossy message board for the nation's Native community.

At the same time, *Aboriginal Voices* was aimed at a different market. The magazine was a wonderful opportunity to educate non-Native readers. No doubt many mainstream readers were surprised to discover, for instance, the scope of the Native music or film industries. *Aboriginal Voices's* glossy, colourful pages reached out to readers eager to share what is – for many in this country – an unexplored world. Able to entertain and educate, *Aboriginal Voices* was one of the most important magazines on the rack. As Gary Farmer put it:

Our people have come into their own – there's no doubt about it – but now we have to build an audience. We have to do what we can to ensure that the beautiful power of our voices is heard. Aboriginal artists are some of the best in the world, yet so many of us remain unknown outside of our own communities. As many of us are only too aware, the mainstream media is full of the words and images of others who attempt to portray us. Yet, the only ones who can really know Aboriginal reality are Aboriginal people who live and breathe it every day. Our stories are full of both sorrow and joy and it is important that we share them (Farmer 1999).

This is where it started: the misrepresentation of Native people and their stories is what initially drove actor Gary Farmer to create *Aboriginal Voices* in 1993. It was, he says, 'an effort to take back our creative ways and make them our own' (Farmer 2001). As a remedy, he set out to found a magazine devoted to Native arts and culture that was produced by Native people – an authentic representation of Native arts.

Looking back, Farmer sees *Aboriginal Voices* as 'a tool of empowerment to take us into the communications age. It brought a circle of our artists together. It gave us a vision and a start. It had a dramatic impact, not only on our Native society, but on our society at llarge' (Farmer 2001). Farmer believes that *Aboriginal Voices* took Canada in the right direction – searching for new and better ways to resolve issues: 'There are creative ways to handle all of our problems, from diabetes to land claims' (Farmer 2001). Creativity and evolution are key ideas for Farmer. For the magazine to work, he knew that it would have to change with the times, to become what the community needed.

At its inception in 1993, *Aboriginal Voices* focused solely on the arts. However, given requests for more news and coverage of current events, Farmer realized that 'we could be *Entertainment Weekly* in the back, and *Time* up front' (Farmer 2001). As a result, the magazine's format was redesigned. News, sports, books, music, film, theatre, art, classifieds, and feature articles all appeared as regular items. In this way, *Aboriginal Voices* satisfied its Native readers and continued its quest for accessibility. For mainstream readers, even if the content was not familiar, the format was.

With the magazine's two audiences in mind, issues of *Aboriginal Voices* always carefully balanced the familiar with the unknown. Feature articles with celebrities such as Tina Keeper (*North of 60*), Tamara Podemski (*The Rez, Rent*), Irene Bedard (*Pocahontas*), and Elaine Miles (*Northern Exposure*) served as a common denominator. Anyone who watched television, Native or not, was familiar with these faces and names. Literary legends Vine Deloria, Jr and Tomson Highway, celebrated artists Daphne Odjig and

Gary Farmer, *Aboriginal Voices* vol. 4 no. 3 (July / August 1997), 4. Courtesy of
Aboriginal Voices.

Maxine Noel, and noted musicians Buffy Sainte-Marie and Robbie Robertson were also among the high-profile names that *Aboriginal Voices* featured.

Alongside the big names, the magazine focused on lesser-known faces, individuals who might not be known to those new to Native arts and culture. Among these were Ulali and Indigenous, musical groups who are wildly popular in Native circles but virtually unknown outside. And how many mainstream readers knew about Dinawo, the Aboriginal version of Roots?

Themed issues were another aspect of the magazine's evolution, with several issues devoted to sports, music, and film. For example, the new territory of Nunavut was the focus of a special themed issue. This gave readers the chance to learn about Arctic life: Inuit food, sports, art, culture, and the basic facts about Nunavut. Most readers would know that 'Eskimo' is a derogatory term, but how about the fact that 'Inuit' is the plural form of 'Inuk'? Themed issues such as these allowed readers interested in one particular area to get a huge dose of information – a crash course in their chosen topic. There was something for everyone.

It was through this union of disparate tastes and interests that *Aboriginal Voices* enjoyed its greatest successes. Unlike most other publications, it did not look to profit or notoriety as its principal goals. The magazine will instead be remembered for the effects it had on Canadian society.

One of those effects was that *Aboriginal Voices* helped strengthen the Canadian Native community. Individuals and small organizations gained nationwide exposure. The magazine provided a comfortable forum where new connections were made, experiences and ideas shared, and business conducted. Courses on film and writing, small business grants, academic bursaries, and employment programs – the magazine brought all these to the attention of the people they were meant for.

The impact that *Aboriginal Voices* had on the Native community's view of itself should not be underestimated. For the first time, young Native people were able to go to a bookstore and pick up a magazine just as glossy and colourful as any other on the rack, and read about people who shared their heritage. *Aboriginal Voices* proved to young musicians that there is a thriving Native music scene; young actors saw that Native actors can and do get great parts in great films. The magazine portrayed Native people as the writers, artists, journalists, athletes, and scholars that they are. It not only provided options; it proved that they were achievable.

The magazine also proved to the nation that we can do it ourselves. The team that produced *Aboriginal Voices* varied over the years but was always composed of Native people. Countless writers, photographers, graphic designers, and editors were given the opportunity to hone their skills with

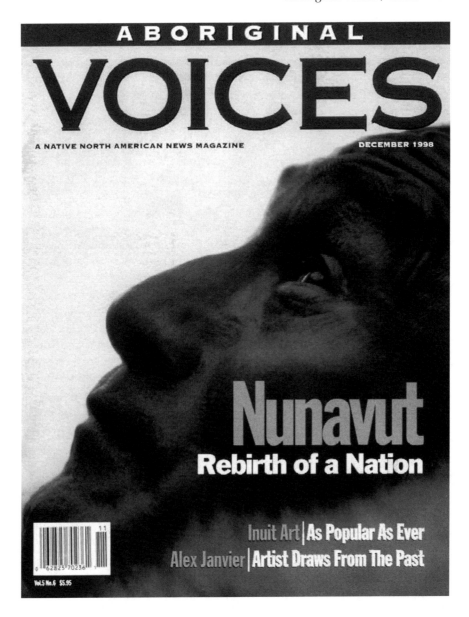

Aboriginal Voices cover, vol. 5 no. 6 (December 1998). Courtesy of *Aboriginal Voices*.

the magazine. As founder Farmer says, *Aboriginal Voices* 'was creative employment. It wasn't standing in a smoky room serving drinks or dealing cards' (Farmer 2001). Native staff was crucial. Native people producing a Native-focused magazine sent a message to the country. With *Aboriginal Voices*, we proved that Native people do not need to be spoken for or written about – we can do both quite well for ourselves.

The events and ideas the magazine explored also played a big part in *Aboriginal Voices'* impact on the Native community. As a publication that devoted itself to Native culture, *Aboriginal Voices's* did not shy away from issues such as suicide, cultural appropriation, treaties and land claims, and the adoption of Native children by non-Natives. Sadly, these things have become part of our culture and need to be addressed. By laying out the facts and discussing their ramifications, the magazine tried to do its part to help. Through educating readers and facilitating a dialogue, *Aboriginal Voices* aimed to stimulate some serious thought about some serious issues, before readers flipped to the music section.

Aboriginal Voices's most significant effect on Canadian culture and identity relates to this country's ethnic diversity. Diversity has long been a source of pride for Canadians, who delight in the many colours and faces of this country's citizens. Yet this makes it all the more surprising for so long, only one voice spoke for all of us. The countless minorities who make this nation what it is have generally not been given the opportunity to speak for themselves. For Native Canadians, it has been no different.

For many years, Canadian children have been taught about this country's First Peoples with books written by non-Native people, which often contain puzzling information. Certainly, the Iroquois, for example, once commonly lived in longhouses. But, while true enough, that fact has limited relevance to the Iroquois of today, about whom little is taught. History is important, but the Iroquois are not extinct – we have made history since the longhouses, and continue to make it today. Early prairie settlers once lived in sod houses, but no one would suggest that this is an essential fact about today's prairie dwellers.

In most cases, the school system taught limited facts and information of questionable relevance, because that was all there was. It is hard to describe someone if you don't know him or her. This is why *Aboriginal Voices* was so important. It was a real opportunity for Native people to speak for themselves, to tell the country who they are today. If every minority in Canada were able to produce its own version of *Aboriginal Voices*, if we all had the opportunity to understand more about each other – from the intricacies of Islam to the merits of Bollywood – would we not be stronger as a nation?

Aboriginal Voices cover, vol. 3, no. 3 (July/August/September 1996). Courtesy of *Aboriginal Voices*.

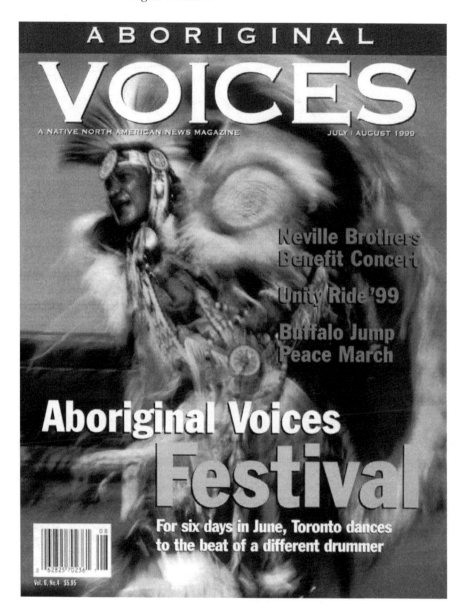

Aboriginal Voices cover, vol. 6, no. 4 (July/August 1999). Courtesy of *Aboriginal Voices*.

Mainstream Canada cannot ever hope to understand the Native perspective unless we ourselves have the opportunity to explain it. Only those who have climbed a mountain can truly understand and appreciate the experience. The rest of us can imagine, but perhaps our imaginings are misguided or unrealistic. We can never really *know.* The best we can do is listen to a mountain climber describe for us what it is like. It isn't the same as experiencing it ourselves, but it's the closest that most of us will ever get. And we're hearing from someone who knows. This seems absurdly obvious. Why, then, have we for so long listened to scuba divers tell us what it's like to climb a mountain? *Aboriginal Voices* was the first time Canada heard the mountain climbers speak.

Although no other publication has emerged to pick up where *Aboriginal Voices* left off, there is a feeling that it is only a matter of time. The arrival of Aboriginal Voices Radio Network and the Aboriginal Peoples Television Network point to a growing understanding in this country of the need, not only to speak to one another, but to listen. *Aboriginal Voices* contributed much to Canadian culture and identity. It began as an opportunity for Native people to speak for themselves. It evolved into a forum for sharing and learning about each other. In a nation of such vastness and such diversity, we must not underestimate the value of anything that enables us to learn about our fellow Canadians as individuals. It is the only way we will learn who we are as a whole.

Profile of Basil H. Johnston (1929–)

Anishinabe (Ojibwa), Author, and Storyteller

Basil H. Johnston is a man of many stories. He has addressed audiences for more than three decades using either written or spoken narratives and is among the few individuals who can both write and speak the Ojibwa language. These abilities, along with his commitment to preserve Ojibwa culture, have placed him in the unique position of recording Anishinabe stories. Johnston came by his information the traditional way – by listening to his grandmother, Rosa McLeod, and other Anishinabe storytellers including John Angus, Sam Ozawamik, Frank Shawbadees, Alex McKay, Tom Medicine, Ron Wakegijig, William Meawassige, Joe Migwanabe, Jane Rivers, Maria Seymour, Flora Tabobandung, Pauline Pelly, and many others.[1]

He was born to Rufus and Mary Toby Johnston on the Parry Island Indian Reserve in 1929.[2] While living on the Cape Croker Indian Reserve, Ontario, his parents separated. Basil and his younger sister, Marilyn, were sent to the St Peter Claver Indian Residential School in Spanish, Ontario, some two hundred miles away, where they remained under the care of nuns and priests for five years.[3]

When he was thirteen, he returned to the Cape Croker Reserve where he lived with his grandmother Rosa and his Uncle Dave.[4] Johnston's happy family life was short-lived, for his beloved grandmother passed away in 1946. At age seventeen, seeking a more rewarding life than cutting trees and gutting fish, Johnston returned to school and graduated valedictorian from Garnier Residential School for Indian Boys in Spanish, Ontario, in 1950.[5] He earned a Bachelor of Arts degree from Loyola College in Montreal, Quebec, in 1954.[6] He was one of only two Indian students enrolled there. Later, he obtained a teaching certificate and taught school for nineteen years.

While teaching secondary school, Johnston was invited to view an exhibit mounted by Churchill Avenue Public School Grade 5 students who

Basil H. Johnston. Courtesy of Canadian Press/*Toronto Star*.

had just completed a five-week study of Indians. One student, who had aspired to be an Indian, was disappointed. He asked, 'Is that all there is to Indians, sir?' It was then that Johnston decided to write about his people's beliefs, perceptions, institutions, and understandings to dispel the opinion that there was little to Indian life.

In 1970 he was seconded to the Royal Ontario Museum in Toronto to initiate a Native program for the museum's ethnology department.[7] It was there that Johnston had the opportunity to show that there was more to Native life than social organization, hunting and fishing, food preparation, dwellings, clothing, and transportation.

There was much to tell about the rich Anishinabe legacy. His first book, *Ojibway Heritage* (1976), includes stories such as 'The Vision of Kitche Manitou and Man's World.' He also wrote *Moose Meat and Wild Rice* (1978), *Tales the Elders Told: Ojibway Legends* (1981), *Ojibway Ceremonies* (1987), *Indian School Days* (1988), *Tales of the Anishinaubaek* (1993), *The Bear-walker and Other Stories* (1995), *The Manitous* (1995), and *Crazy Dave* (1999).[8] As well, he has written children's books: *How the Birds Got Their Colours* (1978), *Tales the Elders Told* (1981), and *Starman and Other Tales* (1997).[9]

Basil H. Johnston has been honoured as a distinguished author and for his contributions to society. He received the Centennial Medal in 1967 for his efforts on behalf of the Aboriginal community.[10] He was awarded the Order of Ontario in 1989 and honorary doctorates from the University of Toronto in 1994 and Laurentian University in 1998.[11]

Johnston lives at the Cape Croker Reserve where he continues to write because, as he says, 'I know no other life or occupation.'[12]

KIMBERLY BRUCE

Notes

1 Basil H. Johnston, telephone interview with Cora Voyageur (Calgary: 10 Oct. 2002).
2 Lisa A. Wroble, 'Basil H. Johnston.' In Sharon Malinowski, ed., *Notable Native Americans*, (New York: Gale Research 1995), 212–13.
3 Ibid., 212.
4 Ibid.
5 Johnston, telephone interview.
6 'Basil H. Johnston,' *Internet Public Library: Native American Authors Project (2002).* www.ipl.org/cgi/ref/native/browse.pl/A4.
7 Jon C. Stott, 'Basil H. Johnston,' *The Canadian Encyclopaedia 2000 World Edition* (Toronto: McClelland and Stewart Inc., 2000), 1.
8 *The Internet Public Library: Native American Authors Project.*
9 Ibid.
10 Wroble, 'Basil H. Johnston,' 212.
11 Ibid.
12 Johnston, telephone interview.

Laughing Till Your Face Is Red

DREW HAYDEN TAYLOR

The one universal thing about Native Americans, from tribe to tribe, is the survived humour.

– Louise Erdrich

A smile is Sacred

– Hopi Elder

It seems that some people have no sense of humour. I am tempted to say some 'white people' but that would be racist – though I'm told that it is politically impossible for a member of an oppressed minority to be racist against a dominant culture because of some socio-political reason ... but I digress.

A year or two ago, a play of mine titled *alterNATIVES* was produced in Vancouver. It was about cultural conflicts between Native people and non-Native people and the stereotypes each group held of the other, presented in a somewhat comedic manner. Or so I thought. A few days into its run, one reviewer referred to it as 'witless white bashing' (though other critics responded embarrassingly well both to this performance of the play and to its previous production), and practically accused me of having it in for white people (I am still trying to understand that logic, since I am half white). On the same day the review came out, the theatre actually received a bomb threat, accusing the company of producing a play that was racist against white people. Some days, it just doesn't pay to get out of bed and write a play.

I don't know why I was so surprised. Non-Native reaction to Native humour, specifically that presented in theatre, has always involved something of a perception problem. With the ongoing debate over the suitability of political correctness, the dominant culture's willingness to enjoy, appreciate, and accept the unique Native sense of humour can quickly become a political minefield. Add to that the volatile atmosphere in British Columbia

at the time owing to the fallout over the Nisga'a Treaty and the turmoil surrounding the Musqueam landowners, and it's no wonder that a few people
in Vancouver were less than enthused by a Native comedy/drama.

But if we look at the larger picture, this particular reaction to Native
humour goes beyond Vancouver and the tensions of that time, at least in
my experience. Several years ago, in 1993, I was fortunate enough to have
an early play of mine produced at the Lighthouse Theatre in Port Dover,
Ontario. A small, innocuous comedy called *The Bootlegger Blues*, it detailed
the adventures of a fifty-eight-year-old, good, Christian Ojibwa woman
named Martha, who, through a series of circumstances, finds herself boot-
legging 143 cases of beer to raise money to buy an organ for the church. Not
exactly Sam Sheppard, but it was based on an actual incident that happened on a reserve, which for legal reasons I won't get into, or my mother
will kill me.

In this play, there were no searing insights into Aboriginal existence, or
tragic portrayals of a culture 'done wrong by' that we have come to expect
on the stage. In fact, it was the opposite of that. My mentor, Larry Lewis, the
director/dramaturge with whom I developed the project, came to me one
day after having just directed a remount of a little play you may have heard
of, *Drylips Oughta Move to Kapuskasing*. He was somewhat burnt out by the
process, and said to me, 'Drew, I want you to write something for me that
has people leaving the theatre holding their sore stomachs from laughing so
much, not drying their eyes from crying or scratching their heads from
thinking too much.' Thus was born *The Bootlegger Blues*.

This play, I was proud to say, had no socially redeeming qualities what-
soever. It was simply a celebration of the Native sense of humour. Not my
best work, in retrospect, but it was funny enough to beat the theatre's audience projections and subtly (don't tell anybody) raise some awareness.

But the thing I especially remember about that particular production
was that it introduced me to the racially divisive line that sometimes
appears when a non-Native audience is presented with Native humour on
stage. Basically, pigment-challenged audiences didn't quite know how to
react to a Native comedy. And since Native theatre was still quite young,
many of us Aboriginal theatre practitioners weren't too experienced in that
field either. Prior to this production, *The Bootlegger Blues* had been produced on Manitoulin Island by a Native theatre company, so the audience
were either primarily Native or sympathetic/interested people of pallor.
After a two-week run, it then went on tour for a month.

In fact, it was on that tour that I received what I consider to be the best
review of my life. Somewhere in Ottawa, an old man, an elder I believe,
shuffled out after seeing the play, walked up to me, shook my hand, and

told me that my play had made him homesick. It was then it occurred to me that maybe this play was more than just a frothy comedy.

But in Port Dover, a small town located on the shores of Lake Erie, most of the pallid theatre patrons sported white or blue-rinsed hair and were expecting the kind of normal summer theatre epitomized by frothy British comedies or mindless musicals. While my humble offering was a comedy (though I hesitate to say mindless), it wasn't what they were expecting. I still remember the discussions with the artistic director, who was concerned about some of the 'strong' language in the show. Now those who know my work can attest that I am not one of the more profane playwrights. Hell no!

The strong language consisted, I think, of one 'shit' and one 'F.O.A.D.' (fuck off and die) in the two-hour play. But that was enough to scandalize the audience. A wall of beer, two Indians climbing into the same bed, and a veritable plethora of jokes about alcohol and drinking from a race of people most of the audience more than likely associated with drunkenness didn't make the play any more accessible. And it was also a touch uncomfortable.

But what I remember most was the white audience's puzzled reaction to the show. The play had a talented cast and a fabulous director. Overall, it was a very good production. You would never know it from the audience response. Their reaction to the first ten or fifteen minutes of the play was silence. All you could hear was the cast trying vainly to engage the audience, and the audience's breathing. For all the cast's enthusiasm, this could have been a murder mystery.

For some time, I puzzled over this unexpected lack of audience involvement in the play; opening minutes. I knew that it couldn't be the actors or the production. Heaven forbid, was it my writing? But the show had done well on Manitoulin Island. Then, after one afternoon matinée, it occurred to me. It wasn't me. It was them, the audience. Proving my point, I overheard one pigment-challenged lady coming downstairs from the balcony, talking to her friend, saying, 'I guess its funny, but I can't help thinking that if a white man had written that, he'd be in deep trouble.'

That was it. Political correctness had invaded my career. Most of the audience was afraid to laugh, or was uncomfortable with the prospect of laughing at Native people, regardless of the context. After so many years of being told about the miseries and tribulations we have gone through, the concept of funny or entertaining Aboriginal people (outside the pow wow circuit) was problematic. Other plays that had been produced, like Tomson Highway's, had some humour, but they were darker, or more critical. It seems that that was what the audience was expecting, and I was failing to provide it.

Perhaps in some way, they wanted to feel guilty about what they saw, to be kicked in the ribs by social tragedy that their ancestors had caused, rather than give in to the healing powers of humour. They did not expect Native people to be funny, let alone laugh at themselves. The audience had landed on Mars.

In that post-Oka era, people were still coming to grips with the concept that Native people were no longer victimized; they could be dangerous and volatile. These are definitely non-humorous notions. Maybe the wounds of Oka were still healing.

As an afterthought, I considered maybe doing a quick rewrite and throwing in a rape or murder somewhere in the text to shake the patrons up. Maybe blockading the bar or bathroom, giving the overwhelmed audience a familiar reference point. In fact, even though the play was about an aging female bootlegger, nowhere in the play does she, or anybody, actually drink beer on stage. I didn't even give the audience that.

The other interesting aspect of this production was that, as I've said, it exceeded the projected audience attendance by several important per cents. So obviously people must have liked it. I started to watch the audiences more closely in an attempt to answer this conundrum, and that's where I made my second observation. After about twenty minutes into the play, people began to laugh. Finally, the politically correct non-Natives were laughing at the Native actors doing the Native comedy. Laughing a lot, I might add. Above all else, true humour must be universal.

What the audience was waiting for – seeking in fact – was permission. They were looking for permission to laugh at this strange story about oppressed people who, political correctness told them, should not tickle their funny bone. As the Fates would have it, practically every audience included several Native people enjoying the show. Luckily, Port Dover is half an hour from Six Nations, one of the largest Native communities in Canada, if not the largest. And with two members of the cast from that community, there were, needless to say, always a few people from Six Nations trickling in to see their friends/relatives appear on stage. And they needed no permission to laugh. In fact, try and stop them.

In this audience of usually over two hundred (on a good night), it was always the Indians who would start the chuckling and giggling. It was the laughter of recognition, because seldom had this world been seen outside their own kitchens. Other than the rare movie like *Pow Wow Highway*, the humorous Indian was a rarely seen though thoroughly enjoyed creature. Mainstream audiences were used to seeing the tragic, downtrodden, and victimized Indian. According to the media, that was the only kind out there.

The laughter would at first be scattered, with people sometimes sounding embarrassed at being the only ones laughing. But eventually the rest of the audience got the hint that this was a comedy and that they were supposed to laugh. By the end of the performance, the whole audience was enjoying the play. A round of applause and an occasional standing ovation would follow.

I think that part of the catharsis was also due to the Caucasian patrons' sense of relief that everything they had seen in the media wasn't always true. The fact was that Native people weren't continually depressed, suppressed, and oppressed. Yes, they found out, Native people have a sense of humour and a joy for life. That production was a learning experience for both me, the cast, and, I hope, the audiences.

Several years later, I wrote a sequel to *The Bootlegger Blues*, called *The Baby Blues*, part of a four-part series I'm working on called *The Blues Quartet*. Its American premiere was at Pennsylvania Centre Stage at Penn State University, deep in the heart of Amish country. And everybody knows what theatre animals the Amish are. Not exactly optimum territory for Native theatre, but I was getting paid in American dollars.

Again, this play was a celebration of Native humour in a country that knows practically nothing of its Aboriginal inhabitants post-1880 (except for Wayne Newton). Again, I witnessed that awesome silence of an audience trying to connect, trying to find some neutral ground. It didn't help that there were numerous Canadianisms in the text – references to *The Beachcombers*, Canadian Tire Money, Graham Greene (for some reason, most American people thought that I was referring to the English novelist, not the Iroquois actor), to name a few. But, overall, I still felt that it should have been an accessible play. It worked in Toronto.

I even ended up quickly putting together a glossary of Canadian and Native words with explanations – sweetgrass, drumming, Oka, fancy dancing – to help the audience. But, still, a Native comedy was difficult for them to grasp. Oddly enough, my production was sandwiched between *Man of La Mancha* and *Forever Plaid*. Maybe if my characters were insane and wore tartans, it would have been a different story. Anyway, in this case, there were precious few American Indians around to act as guides for the confused theatre customers.

One theory I came up with, and then discarded, was that Native comedies, seen in a more metropolitan environment, might be a different story. Theatre patrons in urban climates tend to be more accepting and willing to embrace styles and forms of expression that are perhaps less well known, or familiar. I've seen plays with seventeenth-century people trapped in a plastic room, with no dialogue, just bouncing back and forth. A Native comedy, then, seems almost pedestrian. Yet witness the bomb threat in Vancouver – how does one explain that?

Unfortunately, there's a double-edged sword involved with performing comedies in the city. Though there are exceptions, urban companies prefer a more serious interpretation of life. As a result, most theatre companies tend not to feature comedies, since they are often seen as too lightweight and frothy. The complaint I have heard is, 'It's more summer theatre.' Thus I end up in Port Dover, trying to explain what an inter tribal dance is.

Native theatre as a whole has developed a fair amount of cachet in the last decade. With Ian Ross winning the Governor General's Award for his play *fareWel* (which admittedly had much humour), and the success of Tomson Highway and Daniel David Moses, to name just a few, most major theatre companies (and many of the smaller ones) try to program a certain amount of Aboriginal theatre in their line-up. But, again, their preferences lean more toward the angry, dark, and often disheartening view of Native life. Thus, I remember one Aboriginal woman telling me that she refused to see any more Native theatre because she found the plays 'too depressing.'

A few years ago, I wrote the play *alterNATIVES*. It was more than a simple comedy; it was what I called an intellectual satire, meaning that it dealt with serious and complex issues, but through humour. I've always thought that the best way to reach somebody wasn't through preaching or instructing, but through humour. It seems to make the message more palatable – spoonful of sugar and all that.

The play premiered in two different small towns via a co-production, with primarily non-Native audiences. This time, the result was markedly different. People – again mostly non-Native – laughed from the moment the lights came up. There was no waiting for permission or dealing with political guilt. In just six years, colour-denied people had learned that it's okay to laugh at Native comedies. God will not strike them down and send them to work at the Department of Indian Affairs if they laugh. It's amazing what can happen in a little over half a decade. The public looks at us now as being almost three-dimensional! It's astonishing what a good laugh will get you.

I think that part of the reason, if not the whole one, is the change in perceptions through the avenues of broadcasting. Witness the number of television and radio programs that have embraced the Native appetite for humour: *Dance Me Outside*, and *The Rez* – both of which were more or less successful – the delightful movie *Smoke Signals*, even the CBC Radio show *Dead Dog Cafe*, written and hosted by Mr Amusing, Tom King. This is substantially more programming than was seen in 1993.

Currently, I am in the early stages of developing a television series of my own, a sketch comedy show titled *Seeing Red*. I see it as a combination of *Air Farce* and America's *In Living Colour*, but with Native-oriented humour, where we make fun of the perceptions and stereotypes surrounding First Nations culture. It could be dangerous because the other two writers and I plan to pull the legs of white and Native peoples to the point of dislocation.

The CBC seems very interested, and we are proceeding down the long and winding path of development and – optimistically – production. I think that this shows the public's willingness now not only to embrace the Aboriginal sense of humour but also to appreciate and revel in it. So much so, in fact, that the powers that be at the CBC have specifically told me to avoid writing any sketches not dealing specifically with Native issues. Perhaps we've gone a little too far in the other direction.

Add to that the documentary I directed for the National Film Board of Canada on Native humour, called *Redskins, Tricksters and Puppy Stew*, and by golly, it's almost enough to make you think that Canadian society has developed somewhat in the last decade. What was once the exception has become a widely excepted rule. There is definite hope.

In my research, I have come across a term used by some Native academics to describe humour, specifically Native humour. They call it 'permitted disrespect.' You have the other people's permission to tease or joke about them without getting into a fight. Maybe that's what some audiences need to understand. We Native writers are part of a specific community and have to answer to that community. We are allowed a certain amount of 'permitted disrespect.'

But it was Tom King who also told me in a recent interview that most of the negative letters that *Dead Dog Cafe* receives come from the non-Native population. Most of them say something to the effect, 'If you guys (the producers/writers/ actors) are white, you're not funny.' Then Tom would tell them that, in fact, they are Native. These people would then respond grudgingly, 'Oh, that's okay then.'

If I understand the meaning of that sentence correctly, it's nice to know, finally, that you're funny only if you're Native. People are catching on. Except in Vancouver, I guess.

Profile of Emily Pauline Johnson (1861–1913)

Mohawk, Author, and Performer

Emily Pauline Johnson is considered the 'unofficial' *Poet Laureate* of Canada.[1] During the latter part of the nineteenth century, she captured readers' imaginations with writings of Indigenous themes and traditional cultures. Her poetry recitals captivated sold-out audiences in Canada, England, and the United States[2] and she was the first Aboriginal woman to write 'long works of prose.'[3] Her writing is sometimes called 'a printed museum' that wove Indian customs and traditional stories together into a linguistic art.[4]

This critically acclaimed poet was also known as Tekahionwake (Double Wampum). She was born on 10 March 1861 in Chiefswood, Ontario, to an English mother, Emily Howells, and a Mohawk chief, Henry Martin Johnson (Onwanonsyshen).[5] Her creative talents were shaped at home.[6] By the age of twelve, Johnson had read most of the classic works such as Shakespeare and Romantic writers who stressed nature, art, and imagination.[7] This influenced her Victorian writing style. Another influence for Johnson was her grandfather, John 'Smoke' Johnson. His traditional stories and his words appeared in her written stories, legends, and poems.[8] In her mid-teens, Johnson honed her writing skills at Brantford College, while drama classes helped set her charismatic delivery style.[9]

In the mid-1870s, Johnson sent a poem to a newspaper publisher who appraised her talent and encouraged her to set her dreams higher.[10] Shortly thereafter, her poems were featured in *Athenaeum and Harper's Weekly.*[11] This led to poetry recitals and an invitation to read at a Canadian literature forum in Toronto (1892). Johnson, wearing traditional buckskin clothing, recited her poem *A Cry from an Indian Wife*. She was a hit. *The Song My Paddle Makes*, her most popular poem, brought some audience members to tears. Over the next seventeen years, Johnson gave hundreds of poetry recitals and became one of the best-known performers of the time.[12] In addition to her poetry recitals, Johnson published many books, including *Songs of the Great Dominion* (1889), *White Wampum* (1895), *Canadian Born* (1903), *Legends of Vancouver*

Emily Pauline Johnson. Courtesy of the National Archives of Canada. Image no.
PA127297.

(1911), *Flint and Feather* (1912), *Moccasin Maker* (1913), and *The Shagganappi* (1913).[13]

Johnson died of breast cancer on March 1913, at the age of fifty-two. in Vancouver, British Columbia.[14] All flags across Vancouver flew at half-mast on the day she was buried.[15] In 1961 the Canadian government honoured the centenary of her birth by issuing a commemorative five-cent stamp.[16] That was the first time an author or Native Canadian had been honoured in this way.[17] Johnson is remembered for her contributions to and support of Native literature, and for giving Indians a thundering voice through her captivating and charismatic spirit.

CASH ROWE

Notes

1   Cynthia Kas, 'Emily Pauline Johnsen.' In Sharon Malinowski, ed., *Notable Native Americans.* (New York: Gale Research 1995), 210.

2   Ibid., 211.

3   Bruce E. Johansen and Donald A. Grinde, Jr, 'Emily Pauline Johnson,' *Encyclopedia of Native American Biography: 600 Life Stories of Important People, from Powhatan to Wilma Mankiller* (New York: Henry Holt 1997), 203.

4   Ibid., 205.

5   Ibid., 203.

6   Ibid., 203.

7   'Emily Pauline Johnson,' *Biographical Dictionary of Indians of the Americas* (Newport Beach, Calif.: American Indian Publishers 1991), 318.

8   'E. Pauline Johnson's Life,' *The Pauline Johnson Archive* (Hamilton, Ont.: McMaster University 2002). www.humanities.mcmaster.ca/~pjohnson/life.htm.

9   Kas, 'Emily Pauline Johnson,' 211.

10   Ibid., 211.

11   Johansen and Grindle, *Encyclopedia of Native American Biography*, 203–204.

12   'E. Pauline Johnson's Life.'

13   Kas, 'Emily Pauline Johnson,' 211.

14   'Emily Pauline Johnson,' 319.

15   Ibid.

16   Ibid.

17   Kas, 'Emily Pauline Johnson,' 210.

PART FIVE

JUSTICE

Profile of Anna Mae Pictou Aquash (1945–76)

Mi'kmaq, Aboriginal Rights Activist

In the early 1970s, during the heyday of 'political activism and militancy,'[1] an advocate for Aboriginal rights emerged – Anna Mae Pictou Aquash – who was to continue to fight for the rights of her people until her death. As an Aboriginal rights activist, she struggled against the bitter injustices of racism and in so doing inspired Aboriginal people across Canada and the United States. To some, she became a 'symbol of the movement for Indian rights.'[2]

Anna Mae Pictou was born on 27 March 1945 to Mary Ellen Pictou and Francis Thomas Levi on a Mi'kmaq reserve near Shubenacadie, Nova Scotia.[3] Her stepfather, Noel Sapier, a Mi'kmaq traditionalist, was influential in conveying the importance of the Mi'kmaq culture and beliefs to his stepdaughter.[4] Like many others, she suffered many indignities at the hands of racist fellow students when she attended an off-reserve school as a child.[5]

Having been abandoned by her mother, she quit school and began working as a farm hand – a common practice for Mi'kmaq. During this period, she met and married Jake Maloney. The coupled moved to Boston and had two children,[6] but in 1969 they divorced.[7] Overwhelmed by poverty faced by Aboriginals, Anna became 'increasingly intent on doing something for her people.'[8] In 1969 she became proactive by becoming an early organizer of the Boston Indian Council and also served as a volunteer community worker.[9] Anna participated in numerous protests including the 1972 Trail of Broken Treaties and the 1973 American Indian Movement (AIM) demonstration that resulted in a violent confrontation with police, destruction of property, and increased Federal Bureau of Investigation (FBI) efforts to 'disrupt AIM, discredit its leaders and strike fear' into its supporters.[10]

In 1975 violence erupted on the Pine Ridge Reservation in South Dakota, resulting in the killing of two FBI agents. Leonard Peltier was later arrested and convicted of the murders but, shortly after, rumors arose that an FBI informant was behind the conviction. 'Rumors of informers and suspected

Anna Mae Pictou Aquash. Courtesy of the Anna Mae Justice Fund.

informers were widespread'[11] within the AIM camp and heightened by animosities and jealousies. Many began to incriminate Anna as the possible the FBI informant.[12]

On 24 February 24 1976 a body was found on the Pine Ridge Reservation in South Dakota.[13] It was taken to the Pine Ridge Health Service, where an autopsy determined exposure as the cause of death.[14] The body was not identified and was buried as 'Jane Doe.'[15] Before burial, a hand was severed and taken to FBI headquarters for identification.[16] A week later, the body was identified as Anna Mae Aquash. Pressure from her family and from AIM caused the body to be exhumed for a second autopsy. The cause of death was reclassified as homicide when a .32 caliber bullet hole was located at the base of her skull.[17]

Years later, Anna Mae Aquash's murder still is under investigation; however, there have been new developments. In February 2003 Arlo Looking Cloud was arrested in Denver, Colorado, on a charge of first-degree murder.[18] Looking Cloud's case was heard in federal court in Rapid City, South Dakota, in February 2004;[19] he was found guilty and sentenced to life imprisonment. On 2 December 2003 a lengthy international manhunt ended with the arrest of John Graham, an Aboriginal Canadian also wanted on first-degree murder charges for the murder of Anna Mae Aquash.[20] He is currently fighting extradition to the United States.

Anna Mae Aquash's life has been inspirational to a number of Aboriginal peoples and her work continues to be remembered almost three decades, after her death.

NATASHA JOACHIM

Notes

1 Cynthia R. Kas, 'Anna Mae Pictou Aquash,' In Sharon Malinowski, ed., *Notable Native American*, (New York: Gale Research 1995), 16.
2 Jordan Dill, 'A Warrior Is Born,' www.dickshovel.com/bio.
3 Kas,'Anna Mae Pictou Aquash,' 16.
4 Ibid, 17.
5 Johanna Brand, *The Life and Death of Anna Mae Aquash* (Toronto: James Lorimer and Company 1978), 54.
6 Ibid.
7 Ibid, 57–8.
8 Ibid, 59.
9 Kas, 'Anna Mae Pictou Aquash,' 17.
10 Gretchen Bataille, 'Anna Mae Aquash' *Native American Women: A Biographical Dictionary* (New York: Garland Publishing 1993) 12.
11 Katz, Anna Mae Pictou Aquash,' 18.
12 Brand, *Life and Death*, 122.
13 Battille, 'Anna Mae Aquash,' 12.
14 Ibid, 15.
15 Ibid, 12.
16 Ibid, 15.
17 Kas, 'Ann Mae Pictou Aquash,' 18.
18 *Ottawa Citizen*, 3 April 2003.
19 Ibid.
20 Ibid., 3 Dec. 2003.

Getting Tough on Crime the Aboriginal Way: Alternative Justice Initiatives in Canada

KATHERINE BEATY CHISTE

Few areas of Canadian government activity attract as much attention as the multiple institutions that administer the justice system, particularly those with criminal justice responsibility. Scarcely a day goes by without a sensational case – domestic abuse, workplace violence, youth crime – prompting calls for politicians to 'get tougher on crime.' The truth that many such crimes are isolated incidents, and do not represent a larger social trend, seems lost in the fray. The public outcry for more punitive, 'tougher' criminal measures continues unabated, based in a bedrock faith in the effectiveness of deterrence as a principle of criminal sentencing. This faith in turn rests on the belief that both potential and experienced criminals will be deterred from committing criminal acts because they fear the denunciation of their fellow citizens, incarceration, or indeed execution. The call for toughness is also plainly a cry for vengeance, what David Paciocco describes as 'the deep, unflattering human thirst to punish' (Paciocco 1999, 36).

But as well as the 'get tougher' proponents, there is another voice in the justice debate – one whose agenda can broadly be characterized as 'alternative' to the mainstream system. The alternative voice also calls for us to get tougher on crime, but in a different way: not by isolating offenders from their crime and its consequences, but by *connecting* them to the victims and community their criminal act has disturbed. There are various kinds of 'alternativeness' on offer. Alternative participants may be involved. They may have alternative goals for their participation. And they may use alternative processes in their decision making. We commonly understand 'alternative' to mean a justice outcome alternative to imprisonment (see, for example, David Cayley's recent book, *The Expanding Prison: The Crisis in Crime and Punishment and the Search for Alternatives*).[1] 'Alternative' suggests a choice between two or more possibilities, sometimes defined as mutually exclusive; here, I am using the word in the sense of 'doing something different' in response to a justice problem. In the new millenium, Canadian

Aboriginal communities, more consistently than any other segment of Canadian society, are trying to do something different on their own justice homefronts.

The first alternative justice experiments, in the late twentieth century, focused on the relationship between Aboriginal peoples and the justice system. There were attempts to increase Aboriginal participation in administration of that system and to decrease the number of Aboriginal offenders mired within it. More recently, we have seen an exploration of ways in which Aboriginal peoples might develop and control their own institutions of justice. Evidence on these experiments, although scattered and largely anecdotal at present, suggests that Canadian jurisdictions are going in different directions at different speeds, and that where 'good personal chemistry' exists between potential participants, it is a catalyst. Initiatives may be led by police, by lawyers, by judges, by court workers, and by community leaders. Their efforts are focused at the community level. They are not part of a national constitutional debate – their concerns are local and immediate – and I believe that, collectively, these locally led (and in many cases Aboriginally led) initiatives are making a significant contribution to the practice of justice in Canada. This chapter will review five such 'on the ground' justice alternatives, keeping in mind a basic question: What exactly is it that makes them 'alternative?'

Aboriginal Justices of the Peace

One of the first experiments was the use of Aboriginal justices of the peace (JPs) and an expansion of the historical role of the English JP. The federal Indian Act provides for appointment of JPs for by-law and minor Criminal Code infractions, although the federal government no longer makes such appointments. Some provinces appoint Aboriginal and other JPs in the same manner; others have special programs that recruit and train Aboriginal justices of the peace. Cost has been a motivator here, especially in northern and remote communities. The 'flying circus' of mainstream circuit court is a highly expensive proposition. Moreover, there may be little agreement between the professional justice participants and community members about what has happened, who is involved, and what should be done about it.

In English history, the justice of the peace was the leading citizen in a particular geographical jurisdiction, the lord of the manor who represented king and church in the lives of the local peasantry. *Black's Law Dictionary* describes the JP's role as follows: 'Judges of record appointed by the crown to be justices within a certain district (e.g. a county or a borough) for the conservation of the peace, and for the execution of divers things' (Black 1951, 1003). The 'divers things' that occupied the JP included both civil and criminal matters. The assignment of his local landholding as a judicial district meant that the original JP was a person *known to* those who came before him, and, if he were a conscientious landowner, this meant that he *knew them* in turn.

Here lies another motivator – beyond cost or convenience – for developing Aboriginal JP programs. The aim is to have offenders dealt with by people who know their life's circumstances and how the various responses to an offence can affect a community's well-being. This is a true alternative perspective: rather than be blind, justice should view a case with the insight born of a personal and cultural perspective. Supporters of these programs argue that an Aboriginal JP from an Aboriginal community is more likely to understand the reasons for a wrongdoing and to identify a response that might be helpful to all those involved.

But finding community members who are prepared to act in the JP's role is difficult. In my home province of Alberta, a 1991 task force report on Aboriginal peoples and the criminal justice system reported that only four of Alberta's 398 justices of the peace were Aboriginal. The two jurisdictions where Aboriginal JP programs have prospered are the province of Ontario and the Northwest Territories. Ontario's Native Justices of the Peace Program dates to 1984, when specially recruited and trained Aboriginal JPs began to be appointed based on the Aboriginal percentage of a district's population. The Northwest Territories' one hundred or so JPs, a majority of whom are Aboriginal, are part of an overall 'community-based justice' approach; they have assumed unprecedented responsibilities in areas such as child welfare and young offender matters – with the option of sitting on JP panels where a solo JP feels uncomfortable.

To some extent, the purpose of these programs is to change the 'face' of the Canadian justice system, a result that does not seem to present an alternative per se (and that was criticized before the Royal Commission on Aboriginal Peoples on precisely the grounds that 'nothing has changed' [Royal Commission on Aboriginal Peoples 1996, 95]). But as well as the changing face of the courts ('Indigenization' is one term), I believe that what *has* changed in a community – Aboriginal or otherwise – with a homegrown JP is that he or she knows the community and its members. Moreover, these JPs have a mandate to use that personal knowledge purposefully, rather than setting it aside in the service of neutrality and legal abstraction. The extensive testimony before the royal commission, and other Aboriginally focused justice inquiries, suggests that this alternative stance is one of the main contributions Aboriginal peoples are making to the contemporary justice debate in Canada. There is also evidence that offenders find it tougher to be held accountable to knowledgeable community members than to outside justice professionals.[2]

Tribal Courts

A second kind of alternative justice initiative, well developed in the United States but a newcomer to modern Canada, is also Aboriginally centred: the tribal court. Most of the two hundred or so American Indian reservations have active tribal courts, which come in three variants. First are the so-called 'traditional courts,' established by and administering customary tribal law. These courts are characterized by mediation as an alternative to litigation or other adversarial procedures. The best-known of the traditional courts is the Navajo Peacemaking Court. There is also a small number of Courts of Indian Offenses still in existence, an anachronistic artifact established by the U.S. federal government because its officials lacked jurisdiction over 'Indian versus Indian ' disputes located on Indian reservations; Indian agents acted as judges in these courts. Finally, there are modern-day tribal courts established by individual tribal constitutions under the Indian Reorganization Act of 1934; this is the most common kind of tribal court. They have potentially broad contemporary jurisdiction, both civil and criminal, and have the option of implementing 'traditional' dispute resolution as well.

The territorial jurisdiction of tribal courts is usually limited to matters that arise within the boundaries of the reservations, with some exceptions such as child welfare and hunting and fishing. Personal jurisdiction is usually limited to tribal members, although if a case meets the 'tribal interest test' the courts may deal with 'non-Indians' as well. In criminal matters, the courts have no jurisdiction over non-members or over cases arising under the U.S. Major Crimes Act. Still, there are jurisdictional voids in criminal matters, and in theory the courts have full civil jurisdiction. The courts operate in various ways. Some are entirely staffed by lay people and use mediation as their process of preference. Some are staffed with lawyers acting as judges, prosecutors, and defence counsel, and produce jurisprudence hardly distinguishable from that of the state courts. Some have their own bar associations whose members must pass exams on tribal law. The courts have varying degrees of connection with the tribal councils that govern the reservations, and the extent of their independence from tribal politics is hotly debated.

But do these courts present an 'alternative'? Some of them deliberately staff themselves with participants who are not mainstream legal professionals (more specifically, with personnel who do *not* have legal training). Some operate with processes alternative to litigation. Some, such as the Peacemaking Court, pursue the goal of 'sacred justice and harmonious relations,' which strikes me not as alternative to, but somewhat advanced over, 'peace, order, and good government.'

In Canada, tribal governments operate under a different statutory and constitutional regime than do their American counterparts, and attempts to develop a 'tribal court' are rare. One of the few in existence is located on the Tsuu T'ina Reserve outside Calgary, where in November 1999 a provincial court opened with two local 'peacekeepers' and an Ojibwa provincial judge originally from Ontario. The partnership between the Alberta Department of Justice and the reserve seeks to incorporate Aboriginal traditions into the court system, in particular the involvement of the community and elders in dispute resolution and sentencing. The court, however, is still part of the mainstream Alberta system and Alberta decisions will take precedence over Aboriginal traditions in the event of any conflict (Melting Tallow 1999).

Community Justice Committees

A third alternative to mainstream processes has been springing up here and there across Canada: a community-based justice organization appearing variously as the community justice committee, the youth justice committee, and the elders' advisory panel.[3] These committees or panels are basically ongoing structures which call on senior and respected volunteers in a community; they can be distinguished from 'sentencing circles' or 'Family Group Conferences' (FGC) – both discussed below – which are a one-time response to a particular event. The committee structure first began appearing in the north, where remoteness from the apparatus of mainstream justice meant that months could go by before outstanding offences and disputes were dealt with formally; meanwhile, the communities themselves had to come to some internal accommodation with what had happened. The initiative for their development – or, in the case of Aboriginal communities, their redevelopment – came from a variety of change agents: judges who were tired of ineffectually sentencing the same old people for the same old things; community members who saw their young people drifting and lost, and wanted to get involved purposefully and personally; police who were frustrated and disconnected with the people they served. Many northern communities see the justice committees as a return to traditional ways, when an entire community and its respected leaders were collectively responsible for restoring harmony after a harm had been committed. As T'suu T'ina leaders describe their new court, this is precisely what that particular tribal court is aiming for.

The justice committee approach has also spread to southern and urban jurisdictions, where, predictably, closer contact with the legal profession throws up roadblocks to the process. As an example, my hometown Community Justice Committee was barely a year old when it was discovered the committee volunteers had no liability insurance, should one of their 'clients' misbehave; the committee's work was then shut down until the province arranged for insurance coverage.[4] In another southern jurisdiction, a small town had successfully incorporated domestic violence cases into this innovative structure when the provincial attorney general found out and told the town to stop the practice; reporting of domestic violence in the community immediately declined.[5]

The justice committee structure has been used primarily to deal with young offenders, youths aged twelve to seventeen. The Young Offenders Act 1984 provided that 'alternative measures,' rather than court proceedings, can be used to deal with a young offender: that is, through establishment of a Youth Justice Committee composed of citizens to assist without remuneration in administration of the act. Certain Canadian jurisdictions have embraced the Youth Justice Committee more enthusiastically than others. Manitoba and northern Alberta have been in the forefront, while Quebec also takes a distinctive preventive and rehabilitative approach to youth crime. Some youth committees are Aboriginal in composition and clientele; others are culturally diverse. The focus of these initiatives is to get input into the sentencing process from those who know and understand the young person, and from those who are affected by his or her conduct.

Canadian development of youth committees was influenced by the New Zealand experience with the Family Group Conference referred to above. In 1989 that country passed the Children, Young Persons and Their Families Act, which initiated the process known as the FGC. This process was rooted in the traditional Maori philosophy of restorative justice and applied to all offenders in the fourteen- to sixteen-year age group, regardless of cultural origin.[6] The FGC brings together a young offender, the victim, their families, and their 'supporters.' It then designs a disposition for an offence which improves the chances that the offender will stay out of trouble in the future, and that the victim of a crime will find some kind of resolution as well: a healing approach rather than a punitive one. The FGC, which has the strong support of the New Zealand police, has shown remarkable effectiveness.

Bringing a committee into the justice process changes the physical and psychological configuration of the court. Consider a typical courtroom layout: judge elevated on the bench, lawyers facing him, duelling parties with their backs to families and friends, the latter relegated to the role of spectators. Committees, on the other hand, sit around a table so that their members can talk face to face, and the community need no longer be a spectator. The dynamics of the justice committee engage offenders in a discussion, and they face not impersonal outsiders but people they know are respected in their community, as well as those their offence has hurt. The committee calls in family members – parents who were unaware of their teenager's escapades, for example. Rupert Ross describes crime as having a whirlpool effect, pulling many people into 'a common vortex of injury, anger and fear.'[7] Seeing an offender not as an isolated 'case' but as part of a network – even a dysfunctional one – is an alternative vision with which the committee tries to deal. This is a defining contribution of the Aboriginal perspective to justice alternatives in contemporary Canada.

Selection of committee members is an issue. Inappropriate persons might volunteer or be chosen, for example, those with unresolved personal problems of their own. In addition, there is the potential for abuse of power by community members from dominant families. One of the most commonly expressed fears about alternative justice practices in the Aboriginal context is precisely that they will allow community 'bigwigs' to pervert the process into a vehicle for preventing corrupt friends and relatives from being called to account for their behaviour. Aboriginal women's groups were particularly vocal on this point during testimony before the royal commission.

I see the community justice committee as a more inclusive way of achieving the *alternative* aspect of the Aboriginal JP programs, displacing judicial neutrality in favour of a personally knowledgeable perspective and a personal stake in the outcome of a case. Elders' panels and community committees have a real stake in what happens to the people who come before them; professional justice practitioners have only a distant one. One First Nation that developed its own Community Justice Panel – the Waswanipi Cree of Quebec – reasoned this way, according to its deputy chief: 'People felt it was time to put in place an institution that would deal with our problems locally. After all, they are our problems' (Saganash 1998).

Sentencing Circles

Sentencing circles convene on a case-by-case basis, rather than serving as an ongoing community structure, although they may meet more than once. The circles allow offenders, victims, family, community members, and justice professionals to meet face to face to talk about what has happened during (and before) a crime and establish a plan for dealing with its aftermath. Offenders and victims participate voluntarily, and offenders must admit their responsibility for an act before they are 'diverted' into the process; circles are not considered appropriate where there is doubt about guilt or innocence, or if the victim is unwilling to participate. The use of sentencing circles after an accused has disputed guilt, but was convicted in the end, is also viewed unfavourably by the courts. Critics see a call for circle sentencing as an attempt to get a more lenient sentence, and in a couple of cases this has been the obvious intent.

The first formal sentencing circle was introduced to Canadian courts in 1992, in *R. v. Moses*. (*R. v. Moses* 1992). This case, in the Yukon Territorial Court, involved a N-cho Ny-A'K-Dun First Nation member charged with theft and carrying a weapon for the purpose of assaulting a police officer. The circle suspended his sentence and put him under a two-year probation order requiring: first, time spent with his family on their trapline ninety-six kilometres outside town; second, participation in a two-month residential program for alcoholics; and third, a return to his family and First Nation, who would provide an alcohol-free home and further substance-abuse counselling.

As it did in the *Moses* case, a circle consists of several interested parties, besides the legal professionals. Sometimes one large circle will be assembled; sometimes there is an inner circle of those directly affected and an outer circle of community members. Either the judge or a community moderator kicks off the proceedings; the circle may also start with a prayer. People speak in turn around the circle, not interrupting each other. There may be four different rounds of talk: one in which participants introduce themselves and their reasons for being present; a second in which they speak directly to the offender; a third in which they speak to the victim; and a fourth in which they offer suggestions for an appropriate resolution. An effort is made to reach a consensus, but, at the end of the day, it is up to the presiding judge whether he or she will accept the sentence of the circle.

The purpose of holding a sentencing circle is not just to obtain community input in fashioning an appropriate sentence, nor simply to allow Aboriginal culture and tradition to be brought to bear for an Aboriginal offender. The organizational dynamics of the circle bring an offender face to face with the consequences of his or her act. This is an aspect that can be almost entirely avoided in mainstream justice processes – and the circles appear to have a chance at actually changing people's behaviour. Moreover, the circle offers an community a opportunity to recover from the aftermath of a criminal act. The reason for including so many participants is that many people may be affected by a crime; a judicial response that touches only the offender may leave serious problems unresolved. As Rupert Ross argues persuasively, most people live within networks of relationships; where those relationships have been damaged by a criminal act, the individual perpetrator cannot heal all by himself or herself (where healing is indeed possible), nor does a justice protocol that ignores the victim resolve very much.

The process of circle sentencing can be a great deal harder on offenders than a normal criminal sentencing. The structure of the process means that an offender hears first-person remarks – addressed to himself or herself – directly from the people who have been injured. This is a different experience from a victim's testimony in court or the reading of a victim-impact statement.[8] The circle process seeks that the offender accept emotional responsibility; it is not intended as an easy way out. In contrast, the mainstream system allows offenders to shut down emotionally behind a façade of cooperation.

In Canada, two jurisdictions have pioneered the use of sentencing circles – the Yukon Territory and the province of Saskatchewan – and some British Columbia and Quebec courts have also become active in this area. Sentencing-circle judgments are coming out of regions characterized by small communities with significant Aboriginal populations, and some courts have begun to identify the circumstances in such communities under which holding a circle is appropriate and endorsable. Judge Cunliffe Barnett (of British Columbia) has identified three requirements (Barnett 1995, 1). First, the judge involved in a circle sentencing cannot abandon basic principles, such as holding an open court and recording what is said. Second, the circle should be community-driven, rather than the initiative of a well-meaning judge. Third, the judge must *know* the community, so that she or he is not subject to manipulation by community factions seeking leniency for one of their own. Judge Jean-L. Dutil of Quebec has identified two other requirements: first that the offender must have a clear intent to rehabilitate himself or herself, and second, that his or her community clearly wants to become involved in the process (*R. v. Alaku* 1994).

In both cases, the judges take as a starting point the fact of a community actively taking responsibility for its membership. I think that sentencing circles present a clear alternative: it is either the local community, or the Canadian state, as the lead player in a justice situation. And, certainly, there are legitimate criticisms of the prospect of locally controlled justice.[9] The question can also be raised whether 'community justice' is achievable only for a geographically isolated, culturally homogeneous group of people. One of the features of the New Zealand FGC was precisely that the process was applied to everybody in the target age group – rural or urban,

Maori or something else – by recreating in the conferences the 'personal communities' of victims and offenders. And, as Judge Barry Stuart argues, 'those who believe the Circle process can only be successful in small, isolated communities, fail to appreciate either the flexibility of the Circle process or the dynamics of small isolated communities' (Stuart 1997, ix).

Alternative Sentences

A fifth alternative to be examined is not the process of disposing of a case but the disposition itself, involving something other than an incarceration or a fine.[10] Alternative sentences can be classified into five different categories: restitution, community service, loss of privileges, treatment, and banishment. In fact, the first four of these fit within existing legal frameworks. Restitution and community service blur into each other, particularly when the community in which an offence occurs is itself deemed to be one of the victims of a crime; the restitution offered a victim may come in the form of community service rather than financial compensation. A creative example in British Columbia involved a case where angry First Nations members assaulted their leadership at the band office (Barnett 1995, 6). They were sentenced for assault and offered the option of 200 hours of community work or hosting a traditional 'shame feast' to compensate their victims for the injury. They chose the feast, and a report later praised the effect that the traditional justice mechanism had on the community. Community service, offered without expectation of pay, can mean working for schools, women's centres, or recreational facilities; it can also mean a more face-to-face kind of service, such as shovelling snow or cutting wood for elderly community members. In other cases, offenders have been asked to provide traditional foods for those they have injured, bagging a moose for the justice committee, for instance.

The general category of loss of privileges offers many opportunities for creative sentencing, although enforcement is a problem outside a community-controlled setting. Assignment of curfew is standard. But, on occasion, communities have crafted novel and effective responses along this line. In *Doing Things the Right Way*, Joan Ryan describes a couple of alternative sentences in the community of Lac La Martre, a small fly-in community northwest of Yellowknife. In a case of theft by the local postmistress, the elders imposed a prohibition on gambling, drinking, and playing bingo; in northern communities where there are few modern recreational opportunities, a prohibition from gaming is a serious punishment. Ryan reported one youth as saying, 'I'd rather go to jail than not be allowed to play bingo or cards' (Ryan 1995, 74). A second case involved a boy who stole some marten pelts from the community gym. The Community Education Committee responded by closing the building to all users. After a couple of weeks, the young men of Lac La Martre, annoyed because they couldn't play basketball, confronted the offender. They decided to collect enough money among themselves to replace the pelts, and banned him from community activities until he repaid them.

Alternative sentences may include orders for an offender to participate in treatment; this is nothing foreign to mainstream justice, which often orders abstention from alcohol and drug use or participation in a treatment program. But there are other possibilities. Under the broad rubric of a probation order, an offender may be sentenced to participate in traditional Aboriginal activities – shipped off to a trapline, sent salmon fishing or moose hunting with an elder, or confined to a bush camp. A Yukon court, for example, held a sentencing circle in a domestic violence case involving alcohol abuse. As a part of the sentence, the man (the accused) and woman involved were to be sent to a wilderness camp together to try to work out their relationship problems under the supervision and protection of community elders (Northern Native Broadcasting Yukon 1993).

Banishment from the community was a traditional Aboriginal last-resort response to anti-social and dangerous behaviour, effectively a death sentence. Modern interpretations of banishment run immediately into logistical problems, as well as the resentment of neighbouring communities if a violent offender is merely thrust out of one community and into the next. Attempts at rehabilitative banishment are one thing; straightforward attempts to rid a community of a dangerous member are another. (The current police practice of informing the public of the location of 'dangerous offenders,' upon their release from prison, may result in 'serial banishment' as the offender is driven out of one location and into another.)

In both Canada and the United States, there have been a couple of cases of Aboriginal offenders being banished to remote islands. This was intended not as a death sentence but as a way of forcing them to come to terms with their destructive behaviour in a setting free from the distractions of modern life. One early example took place in British Columbia in 1978, when a fourteen-year-old Heiltsuk appeared in provincial court on an armed robbery charge. The presiding judge sentenced him to an eight-month term on an uninhabited island under the supervision of an uncle, and the video later produced by Frank Brown speaks well to the possibilities of such a sentence (NFB 1993). However, as Canada's Aboriginal population becomes increasingly urbanized, the limits of this approach are apparent.

A notorious case in Saskatchewan made its way through the court system in the mid-1990s; on that occasion, it was reported that this was only the second time a Canadian court had accepted a sentence of banishment. In *R. v. Taylor*, a Cree community member convicted of sexual assault and death threats was sentenced by a sentencing circle to a year in the remote bush and three years' probation, a disposition that was twice appealed by the crown (*R. v. Taylor* 1996). American experiments with banishment have also been rare. Around the time of Taylor, a case from the state of Washington drew attention when a Superior Court judge publicly expressed second thoughts about having banished a pair of young robbers to remote Alaskan islands; apparently, the two had been spotted off the islands in nearby communities ('Banishment May Not Be Working' 1995).

The very notion of 'alternative sentencing' implies that an 'alternative' is on offer, and it appears that the recipients of alternative sentences may regard them as tougher than jail sentences. Indeed, they may see an 'upside' to incarceration as one way to get out of a small, remote town (Nolen 2000). Either you go to jail, or you do something else to atone for a crime – in the short term, these can be mutually exclusive possibilities for the offender. But I think it is also 'alternative' that it is a community, not the provincial or national justice professionals, which meaningfully supervises and enforces an alternative sentence. David Cayley has observed that, where justice professionals take over a community's responsibility for internal-dispute resolution, that community is weakened: 'The criminal justice system, by appropriating conflict, steals the very means by which community is created' (Cayley 1998, 348). The disciplines of alternative sentences, and the demands they place on community members and resources, offer a path for strength and growth of Aboriginal and many other communities.

Tougher Alternatives

Aboriginal communities are not the only ones – geographically or culturally – who are actively involved in alternative justice processes. Religious groups such as the Salvation Army, the Mennonite Central Committee, and the Society of Friends (Quakers) are also active in justice issues with a special emphasis on mediation and restorative justice. Secular organizations such as the John Howard and the Elizabeth Fry societies also play a role. Nor do Aboriginal communities and individuals uniformly endorse alternative processes and sentences over mainstream sanctions.[11]

But, viewed as a rough collective, Aboriginal justice initiatives in Canada do offer an alternative approach: knowledgeable stakeholders, not neutral professionals; mediation and consensus, not adversarial processes; local community, not remote bureaucracy; and, ultimately, healing and harmony, not coercion and revenge. I see all four of the 'Aboriginal' elements of this alternative approach as being much more demanding, much more challenging, much 'tougher' on participants than anything the mainstream justice system has on offer. I also see the tougher Aboriginal perspective as having particular potential for effectiveness in youth justice matters, a perennial topic for public debate and one that the new Youth Criminal Justice Act (2003) will no doubt keep at the forefront. The main thrust of the act is a move away from the toughness of punishment and incarceration and towards the toughness provided by genuine rehabilitation and community involvement; fortunately, it is not only Aboriginal youth but all Canadian youth who may benefit from this change.

Notes

1 David Cayley, *The Expanding Prison: The Crisis in Crime and Punishment and the Search for Alternatives.* (Toronto: House of Anansi Press 1998).
2 Illustrated, for example, in the video series *Youth Justice Committees* (Native Counselling Services of Alberta 1993).
3 These organizations can play both advisory and decision-making roles. For a much more detailed analysis, see Ross Gordon Green, *Justice in Aboriginal Communities: Sentencing Alternatives* (Saskatoon: Purich Publishing 1998).
4 Personal communication with direct participants.
5 Ibid.
6 For one description of the Family Group Conference, see Rupert Ross, *Returning to the Teachings: Exploring Aboriginal Justice* (Toronto: Penguin Books, 1996), 19–24.
7 Ibid., 173.
8 The video, *Circle Sentencing: A Yukon Justice Experiment* (Kelowna, B.C.: Filmwest Associates 1993), illustrates the painful dynamics involved in a circle sentencing.
9 David Paciocco, *Getting Away with Murder*, makes this argument strongly.
10 I am not, in this chapter, attempting to enter the discussion over the Supreme Court's *R. v. Gladue* decision urging judges to consider the 'circumstances' of Aboriginal offenders in their sentencing decisions.
11 See, for example, Robert Matas, 'Native Man Should Go to Jail, Chief Says,' *Globe and Mail*, 17 March 2001.

Bibliography

Aboriginal Justice Learning Network (AJLN), Department of Justice, Canada. C. 1998. *The Donald Marshall Youth Camp*. Ottawa: AJLN. Videocassette.
– *LINK* (newsletter). 1999. January and following.
Alberta. 1991. *Justice on Trial: Report of the Task Force on the Criminal Justice System and Its Impact on the Indian and Metis People of Alberta*. Vol. 1, Main Report. March.

'Banishment May Not Be Working.' 1995. Lethbridge Herald, 4 August. Barnett, Cunliffe. [1995]. 'Circle Sentencing/Alternative Sentencing.' 3 C.N.L.R.

Black, Henry Campbell. 1951. *Black's Law Dictionary*, 4th ed. St Paul, Minn.: West Publishing.

Brodeur, Jean-Paul, Carol La Prairie, and Roger McDonnell. 1991. *Justice for the Cree: Final Report*. Ottawa: Grand Council of the Crees (Quebec). August.

Canada, Solicitor General. 1997. *Building Bridges: Off-Reserve Policing*. Ottawa: Aboriginal Policing Directorate.

Cayley, David. 1998. *The Expanding Prison: The Crisis in Crime and Punishment and the Search for Alternatives*. Toronto: House of Anansi Press.

Goff, Colin. 2001. *Criminal Justice in Canada*, 2nd ed. Scarborough, Ont.: Nelson Thomson Learning.

Green, Ross Gordon. 1998. *Justice in Aboriginal Communities: Sentencing Alternatives*. Saskatoon: Purich Publishing.

Manitoba. 1991. *Public Inquiry into the Administration of Justice and Aboriginal People: Report of the Aboriginal Justice Inquiry of Manitoba. vol. 1, The Justice System and Aboriginal People*. Winnipeg: Province of Manitoba.

Melting Tallow, Paul. 1999. 'New Court Employs Aboriginal Traditions.' *Alberta Sweetgrass*, 14 November.

Native Counseling Services of Alberta. 1993. *Youth Justice Committees*. Edmonton: Alberta Law Foundation. Videocassette.

National Film Board of Canada (NFB). 1997. *Circles*. Montreal: NFB. Videocassette.
– 1996. *First Nation Blue*. Montreal: NFB. Videocassette.
– 1993. *First Nations: The Circle Unbroken*. video 2, 'Voyage of Rediscovery.' Montreal: NFB. Videocassette.
– 1997. *Glimmer of Hope*. Montreal: NFB. Videocassette.
– 2000. *Hollow Water*. Montreal: NFB. Videocassette.
– 1990. *The Spirit within*. Montreal: NFB. Videocassette.

Nolen, Stephanie. 'Where Jail Is Sometimes the Only Way out of Town.' *Globe and Mail*, 21 March 2000.

Northern Native Broadcasting Yukon. 1993. *Circle Sentencing: A Yukon Justice Experiment*. Kelowna, B.C.: Filmwest Associates. Videocassette.

Paciocco, David. 1999. *Getting Away with Murder: The Canadian Criminal Justice System*. Toronto: Irwin Law.

R. v. Alaku [1994] 112 D.L.R. (4th) 732.

R. v. Moses [1992] 3 C.N.L.R. 116, 71 C.C.C. (3rd) 347, 11 C.R. (4th) 357.

R. v. Taylor [1996] 2 C.N.L.R. 208.

Ross, Rupert. 1992. *Dancing with a Ghost: Exploring Indian Reality*. Markham, Ont.: Reed Books.
– 1996. *Returning to the Teachings: Exploring Aboriginal Justice*. Toronto: Penguin Books.

Royal Commission on Aboriginal Peoples. 1996. *Bridging the Cultural Divide: A*

Report on Aboriginal People and Criminal Justice in Canada. Ottawa: Ministry of Supply and Services.

Ryan, Joan. 1995. *Doing Things the Right Way: Dene Traditional Justice in Lac La Martre, N.W.T.* Calgary: University of Calgary Press and Arctic Institute of North America.

Saganash, Romeo. 1998. Quoted in John Gray, 'They're a Law unto Themselves.' *Globe and Mail*, 16 November.

Saskatchewan. 1992. *Report of the Saskatchewan Indian Justice Review Committee*. January.

Stuart, Barry. 1997. *Building Community Justice Partnerships: Community Peacemaking Circles*. Ottawa: Department of Justice and the Aboriginal Justice Directorate.

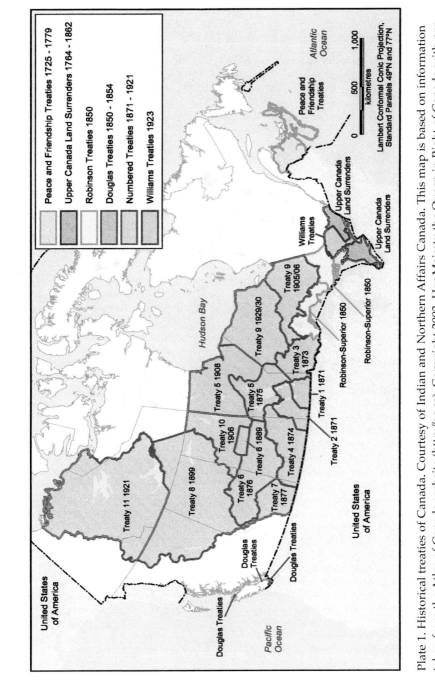

Plate 1. Historical treaties of Canada. Courtesy of Indian and Northern Affairs Canada. This map is based on information taken from the Atlas of Canada website (http://gc.ca). Copyright 2003. Her Majesty the Queen in Right of Canada with permission of Natural Resources Canada.

Plate 2. *Coyote*, 1995, by Edward Poitras. Courtesy of the artist.

Plate 3. Alwyn Morris receiving his Olympic gold medal in 1984. Courtesy of the Canadian Olympic Committee, Alwyn Morris, and the Canadian Canoe Association.

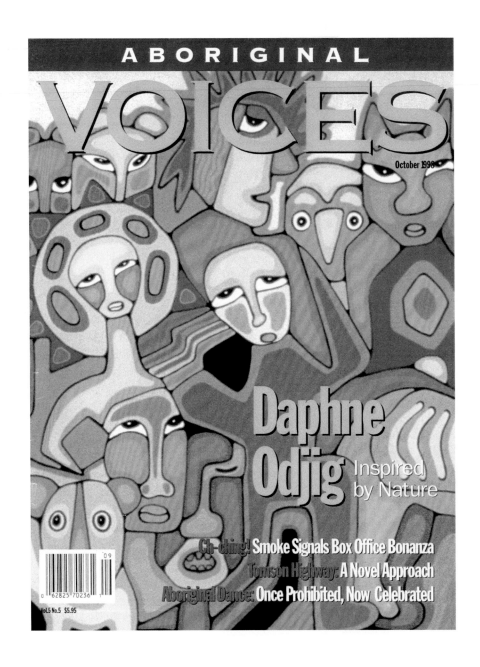

ABORIGINAL

VOICES

October 1998

Daphne
Odjig Inspired
by Nature

Ch-ching! Smoke Signals Box Office Bonanza
Tomson Highway: A Novel Approach
Aboriginal Dance: Once Prohibited, Now Celebrated

Vol.5 No.5 $5.95

Plate 4. *Aboriginal Voices* cover, vol. 5, no. 5 (October 1998). Courtesy of *Aboriginal Voices*.

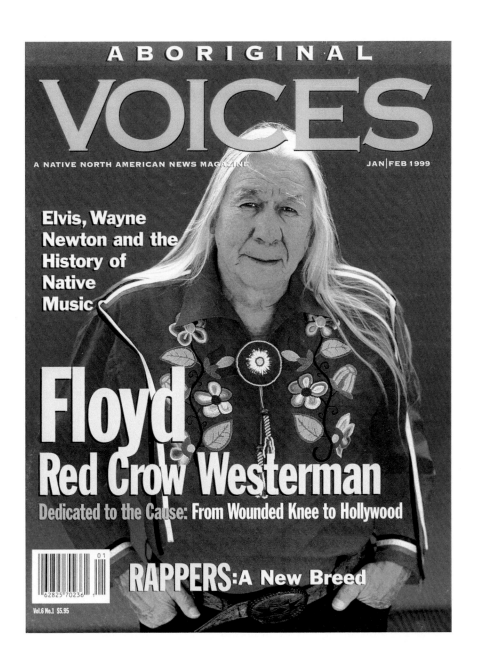

ABORIGINAL

VOICES

A NATIVE NORTH AMERICAN NEWS MAGAZINE   JAN|FEB 1999

Elvis, Wayne
Newton and the
History of
Native
Music

Floyd
Red Crow Westerman
Dedicated to the Cause: From Wounded Knee to Hollywood

RAPPERS:A New Breed

Vol.6 No.1 $5.95

Plate 5. *Aboriginal Voices* cover, vol. 6, no. 1 (January/February 1999). Courtesy of *Aboriginal Voices*.

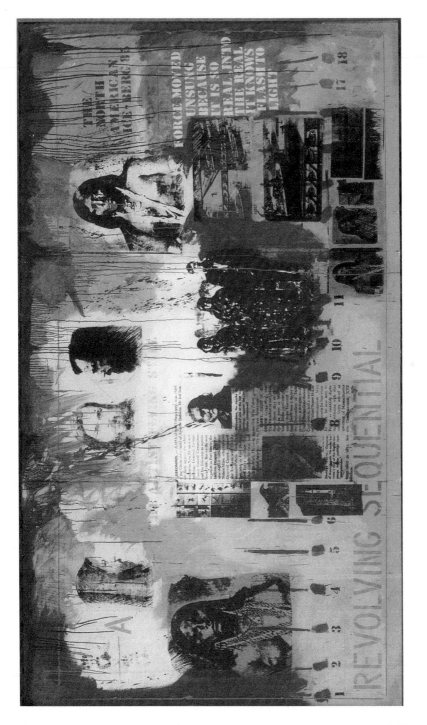

Plate 6. *The North American Iceberg*, by Carl Beam. Courtesy of the artist and the National Gallery of Canada.

Plate 7. *Sundance*, 1987, by Allen Sapp. Courtesy of Indian and Northern Affairs Canada.

Plate 8. *The Storyteller – The Artist and His Grandfather*, 1978, by Norval Morrisseau. Courtesy of Indian and Northern Affairs Canada.

Profile of John Joseph ('J.J.') Harper (1952–88)

Ojibwa-Cree, Chief, and Executive Director

John Joseph (J.J.) Harper was born into a large family with fifteen brothers and sisters. His early years were spent with his family fishing, hunting, and trapping at Wasagamack, one of four reserves with a combined population of about 5,000, known collectively as Island Lake, located four hundred kilometres northeast of Winnipeg.[1] This isolated community is accessible only by air for most of the year; however, land access is available in winter by an ice road.

When Harper was four years old, an airplane arrived in the community to take local children to the Jack River Residential School at Norway House, about one hundred and seventy kilometres away. Later, he began high school at Winnipeg's Assiniboine Residential School but transferred to Vincent Massey Collegiate. As fate would have it, fellow student Robert Cross, the person who would later shoot and kill J.J. Harper, attended this same school.[2]

Harper served as Wasagamack chief from 1982 to 1984. After resigning in 1984, he and his wife Lois moved to Winnipeg. There, he worked as executive director of the Island Lake Tribal Council and co-manager of Nor-win Construction, the band-owned company responsible for building and maintaining the winter road into the reserve.[3]

On 9 March 1988 J.J. Harper died from a gunshot fired from a policeman's gun.[4] It seems that the police were pursuing two males seen running from a stolen car. Both suspects, Allan and Melvin Pruden, were apprehended within minutes of fleeing the vehicle.[5] Seemingly unaware of the police pursuit, Harper was walking on a nearby street when a policeman approached him. Within minutes, he was shot in what was later described as a struggle over the policeman's gun.[6] The following day, the Winnipeg Police Department's Firearms Board of Inquiry reviewed the circumstances surrounding the shooting and cleared the policeman involved, Constable Robert Andrew Cross, of any wrongdoing.[7] The Aboriginal community

John Joseph (J.J.) Harper. Courtesy of Canadian Press/*Winnipeg Free Press*.

was outraged and felt that there were many unanswered questions during the police's internal investigation into the shooting.[8] Among those questioning the police's decision was a close friend (but no relation), Manitoba MLA Elijah Harper. After hearing of the shooting, Elijah Harper pressured Manitoba's attorney general, Vic Schroeder, to launch an inquiry into the treatment of Natives in the Manitoba justice system. The resulting Manitoba Aboriginal Justice Inquiry was launched in April 1988. Costing almost $3 million, it became 'the most far-reaching inquiry into the treatment of Natives in Canada's justice system.'[9]

The Manitoba Aboriginal Justice Inquiry, headed by justices Al Hamilton and Murray Sinclair, investigated racism within the Canadian criminal justice system. Its report, released on 29 August 1991, found racism to be a central cause for the overrepresentation of Native people in Canadian jails.[10] Hamilton and Sinclair concluded that the actions by Robert Cross that led to Harper's death were racially motivated and that there was subsequent collusion of some police officers in their handling of the investigation. The inquiry proposed thirty-six recommendations to the police force.

The tragic death of J.J. Harper caused Manitoba to examine its treatment of Native peoples. Phil Fontaine, former grand chief of the Manitoba Assembly of Chiefs, stated that it marked a turning point for Aboriginal peoples.[11] The story of Harper's death reached an international audience when a report by Amnesty International regarding human-rights violations made specific mention of his shooting.[12]

JANET TRACE

Notes

1 'The Death of John Joseph Harper: The Aboriginal Justice Implementation Commission,' *Report of the Aboriginal Justice Inquiry of Manitoba* (1991), 1. www.ajic.mb.ca/volumeIII/chapter1.html.
2 Gordon Sinclair, Jr, *Cowboys and Indians: The Shooting of J.J. Harper* (Toronto: McClelland and Stewart 1999), 12–17.
3 Ibid., 42.
4 Ibid.
5 Ibid., 12–17.
6 'Death of John Joseph Harper,' 1.
7 'The Justice System and Aboriginal People,' 2. http://ajic.mb.ca/volumeI/chapter1.html.
8 Ibid.
9 Sinclair, *Cowboys and Indians*, 41–4.
10 Patricia A. Monture-Angus, 'Lessons in Decolonization: Aboriginal Overrepresentation in Canadian Criminal Justice.' In Olive Patricia Dickason and David Allan Long, ed., *Visions of the Heart: Canadian Aboriginal Issue* (Toronto: Harcourt 2000), 379.
11 Sinclair, *Cowboys and Indians*, 385.
12 Ibid., 364.

Aboriginal Peoples and the Canadian Criminal Justice System

CAROL LAPRAIRIE

From Aboriginal politicians and judges to victims and offenders, the voices of Aboriginal peoples have profoundly reshaped the criminal justice landscape in Canada. This has happened largely because of concerns about the overrepresentation of Aboriginal people as offenders in the Canadian criminal justice and correctional systems, a reality first identified by the Hawthorne Commission of 1969. Since then, the overrepresentation issue has been the subject of many conferences, commissions, and inquiries. It has also been the starting point for most of the mainstream reforms in the criminal justice system as well as for Aboriginal community initiatives and self-government discussions about Aboriginal-controlled systems of justice. The efforts of Aboriginal peoples have been at the heart of all these initiatives and activities.

. The past three decades have witnessed important Aboriginal criminal justice reforms. Some of these have been stimulated by, and in turn have stimulated, more broad-based reform of the criminal justice system. Although the results are still relatively unknown – in terms of decreasing Aboriginal representation in the criminal justice system, reducing reoffending and the use of incarceration, and, more generally, making the system more humane and people safer – criminal justice in Canada is clearly on the road to change.

While other countries with large Indigenous populations, such as Australia and New Zealand, have undertaken many similar reforms, perhaps what makes Canada distinctive is the activism of the Aboriginal political organizations, service agencies, and communities that are driving this kind of change. The reforms can be seen most clearly outside the institutions of criminal justice; however, their effects inside the system have also been profound. The most notable changes have been in policing and corrections, but prosecutions and courts have felt the impact, too, both in practice and in judicial decision making.

There are two thrusts to the contribution that Aboriginal peoples have made in shaping criminal justice and promoting criminal justice reforms. The first involves the institutions of criminal justice, such as policing, court processing (including prosecution and sentencing), and corrections. The second is the emergence of alternative approaches (restorative justice) and processes (healing and sentencing circles).

The Institutions of Criminal Justice

Some of the first Aboriginal justice initiatives emerged in the early 1970s, 1980s, and early 1990s, primarily in response to what was increasingly described as the 'overrepresentation problem.' Aboriginal organizations, such as the Native Counselling Services of Alberta, promoted these initiatives – which at that time were more focused on law than on restorative justice. The best-known is the nationally implemented Native Courtworkers Program, established in the mid-1970s to assist Aboriginal accused. This program was rooted in the belief that culture, language, and other factors specific to Aboriginal peoples put Aboriginal individuals at a disadvantage when they became involved with the criminal justice system. The focus of the program was to counteract that disadvantage.

Other programs that provided legal services to Aboriginal peoples and communities followed creation of the Native Courtworkers Program, and these often served specific geographic areas. Once again, it was the activism of Aboriginal peoples and organizations that brought the initiatives about. One example is the Nishnawbe-Aski Legal Services Corporation, which provides legal services to a large number of tribally affiliated communities in the Treaty 5 and 9 areas in northern Ontario. Many of these are isolated or fly-in communities, and all are small and rural.

The Nishnawbe-Aski Legal Services Corporation was established after years of negotiation between the Nishnawbe-Aski Nation and the governments of Canada and Ontario. It was formally incorporated in 1990 to deliver a wide range of services – legal, paralegal, and others – to the Nishnawbe-Aski Nation. Legal and paralegal services encompassed criminal, family, administrative and civil legal aid, interpreter services, referrals, and information about rights under the law and public legal education. The corporation also had a research arm, which examined Aboriginal systems of justice based on custom (Campbell Research Associates 1994). Another region-wide initiative was the Dakota-Ojibway Probation Service, implemented in 1985. It differed from the Nishnawbe-Aski Legal Services Corporation approach in that, like many initiatives in policing, it was 'Indigenized.' In this case, 'Indigenization' involved attaching an Aboriginal probation service to the existing service, rather than creating a stand-alone unit.

The mid-1980s brought constitutional discussions on Aboriginal rights and a developing interest around the world in customary law, led most often by legal anthropologists and Aboriginal activists. Every newly funded Aboriginal justice project implemented thereafter paid particular attention to these issues. Even the law-focused programs usually had strong social-justice and public-education components. These programs were consistent both with the emerging Aboriginal self-government agenda and the attention given to customary law. A related emerging interest was popular justice, which in the 1980s and early 1990s often took the form and title of alternate dispute resolution (ADR). Popular justice increasingly gave way in title – if not form – to restorative justice. The 'new' justice, as these alternatives to mainstream criminal justice commonly called, encompasses principles of victim and community involvement, with a focus on repairing harm rather than punishing offenders. Counselling and attendant activities of the 'new' justice have led to what are now usually described as 'healing,' 'reintegration,' and 'reconciliation' – terms commonly used to explain the objectives of Aboriginal justice projects.

As noted above, the first attempts to incorporate an Aboriginal 'perspective' in the criminal justice system were mostly within 'Indigenized' structures, where an Aboriginal component was attached to an existing organization, such as the Royal Canadian Mounted Police. More recent reform, however, has increasingly promoted an autonomous approach. Today, we see Aboriginal police forces and the emergence of community courts, such as the one recently in Alberta. This more autonomous approach better reflects the political movement to Aboriginal self-government than does the Indigenized approach. The driving force behind it has largely been the recommendations of various reports on Aboriginal people relationship with the criminal justice system.

The idea of culture underlies most Aboriginal criminal justice reform, and there are two primary justifications for this. The first relates to one of the possible explanations for overrepresentation, about which we hear quite often – that discrimination in the criminal justice system is a result of culture conflict. Although the causes of overrepresentation are varied and complex, Aboriginal peoples have, for the most part, promoted this emphasis on culture, together with their concerns about culture conflict. Their demands have led to the implementation of culturally related reforms, such as cultural-sensitivity training for criminal justice personnel like police, judges, prosecutors, and probation officers. The aim of these measures is to help criminal justice personnel better understand Aboriginal culture, thus reducing the potential for culture conflict and discrimination.

The second justification for emphasizing culture is the widely held conviction that Aboriginal offenders will respond better when the system or the programs they are offered have a distinct cultural content. Indeed, the history of Aboriginal programming in federal institutions in Canada can best be described as having a cultural/spiritual focus. Aboriginal culture has influenced the principles of effective correctional programming, mainly in relation to learning and 'responsivity.' These principles ensure that offender's learning styles are matched with programs that target their needs. Aboriginal programming also endeavours to facilitate the release of Aboriginal offenders and to help connect and reintegrate them into their communities. This approach is based on the belief that unique solutions are needed to reflect the unique backgrounds of Aboriginal inmates, and that loss and lack of cultural roots and identity are the primary causes for their involvement in the criminal justice system. Most provincial and territorial institutions have followed the same path in developing and implementing programs for Aboriginal inmates, and their cultural and spiritual programs are usually focused on groups rather than on individuals.

To date, there have been no evaluations either of sensitivity training, to assess whether education translates into behavioural change, or of cultural programming, to determine whether Aboriginal content is the critical factor in bringing about changed behaviour. The impact of these kinds of cultural initiatives is thus still relatively unknown. However, this in no way detracts from the vital role Aboriginal peoples have played in promoting culture in the training of criminal justice personnel or in creating programs and services for Aboriginal offenders and Aboriginal victims.

Perhaps the most valuable contribution that Aboriginal peoples have made over the past three decades – and one that has emerged out of the overrepresentation debate – is in increasing the public's awareness of the extent to which the Canadian criminal justice system uses imprisonment. While the length of the average sentence is short, Canada nevertheless stands out for its high dependence on prison-based sentences. It is difficult to make a direct causal connection between Aboriginal concerns and broader pressures for change in this area. Nevertheless, it is clear that the raising of attention to Aboriginal justice issues influenced the implementation of the Sentencing Reform acts of 1996 and 2003. This legislation provided, for the first time, a direct alternative to imprisonment in the form of conditional-sentence orders.

Aboriginal pressures for change have also influenced the implementation of restorative-justice practices and stimulated a wider search for alternatives to formal criminal justice processing and imprisonment. Some specific examples of alternatives to mainstream processing for Aboriginal offenders are justices of the peace courts and sentencing panels. Other alternatives, such as diversion, sentencing circles, healing circles, Family Group Conferences (FGCs), and various other restorative-justice initiatives, have attracted widespread interest and been applied over the past two decades. Some of these options, and Aboriginal peoples' role in influencing them, are discussed in more detail below.

Alternative Approaches

Aboriginal groups, both nationally and internationally, have been forceful vocal advocates for finding alternative ways of dealing with the justice problems facing their communities, notably youth crime, sexual abuse, and family violence. For example, the Family Group Decision-Making Project in Newfoundland and Labrador was based in part on traditional practices of the Maori in New Zealand. It is widely believed that the Maori people successfully lobbied the government to modify legislation so that Maori families, extended families, and tribes could be involved in decisions taken about Maori children (Pennell and Burford 1994). These restorative-justice and community-based initiatives represent the 'new wave' in justice. Their ideas are exemplified in the Labrador and Newfoundland projects, which adopted a form of FGCs to deal with cases of family violence.

Restorative Justice

Restorative justice has been identified as a new 'paradigm' in justice in Canada. It has become integrated with, and is in many respects indistinguishable from, other current justice initiatives, such as safe communities, crime prevention, Aboriginal justice, and other locally/community-oriented justice initiatives. Restorative justice is the accepted new approach in several provinces, including Saskatchewan, British Columbia, Alberta, Nova Scotia, and New Brunswick. As noted above, restorative justice has become an important component of the Canadian criminal justice landscape, in part because of the efforts of Aboriginal groups. It is now an accepted and welcome response to community, political, and government pressures for 'solutions' to the ever-increasing number of Aboriginal people imprisoned by, and involved in, the criminal justice system.

In Canada, the move to adopt or identify with restorative justice is closely aligned with Aboriginal self-government. It reflects the wish of Aboriginal peoples and Aboriginal politicians, in particular, to build self-governing institutions around something that stands in stark contrast to the system adopted by mainstream society. The move to Aboriginal self-government has put culture and community at the forefront of justice as the legitimate means (and incorporating the appropriate tools) for assuming greater control over justice matters. Aboriginal, and many non-Aboriginal, commentators on justice issues feel that the state lacks the capacity to deliver justice to Aboriginal peoples and communities in a satisfactory and appropriate manner. Indeed, the common perception is that the state has 'forced Aboriginal dependence on dominant, adversarial and coercive, non-Aboriginal justice authorities, institutions and processes' (Depew 1994). These commentators see restorative justice as incorporating the most appropriate practices, and local institutions as the most appropriate vehicles for its delivery.

Among the most widely used forms of restorative justice are Family Group Conferences. As noted earlier, this initiative has its roots in New Zealand and apparently derives directly from a concern that the criminal justice system was not culturally sensitive to the needs and circumstances of Maori communities and youth. By contrast, FGCs were seen to mesh with traditional Maori culture and to give communities the opportunity to provide support and guidance to youth (Alder and Wundersitz 1994).

Unlike New Zealand, Aboriginal community-justice initiatives in Canada have been less fixed on adoption of a single model, such as FGCs. Descriptions of Aboriginal community-justice projects reveal a wide range of activities, although many incorporate the same principles as those found in the New Zealand model. The projects that have been implemented across the country over the past fifteen years are variously described as diversion, alternative measures, healing circles, FGCs, mediation, and dispute resolution. Most existing projects are pre-adjudication and may come into effect before or after an individual is charged; however, programs that take effect prior to the charge are clearly preferable. Most projects target both adults and youth. Some, however – mainly those described as alternative measures or diversion – are designed specifically for one or the other. Their descriptions and stated objectives do not differ greatly from those of alternative measures, FGCs, healing circles, and various types of dispute resolution.

As noted, the justice projects implemented in Canadian Aboriginal communities reflect the quest for self-government and the accompanying desire to exercise control over justice matters. This control may involve collaboration with the mainstream system (sentencing panels, sentencing circles, advisory panels, supervision of probationers and parolees). It may also involve a community taking direct responsibility, at least in the first instance, for particular activities such as community courts or for focusing on particular groups. Culture is a critical component of most of these initiatives, which, according to their project descriptions, incorporate 'traditional' responses, 'culturally relevant' interventions, and activities that reflect and support cultural traditions. Aboriginal languages may be used in meetings and other justice forums. Some justice activities open with prayers and the use of sweet grass. Traditional teachings may also be used to encourage offenders to change their behaviour, and elders often advise on the cultural components of projects.

Community-Based Initiatives

Community control is seen as key to Aboriginal people exercising greater control over justice and, ultimately, to reducing the Aboriginal prison populations. It is not surprising, therefore, that the most significant change over the past two decades has taken the form of emerging community-based justice initiatives. While many of the local projects are funded by large government initiatives, such as the Department of Justice's Aboriginal Justice and National Crime Prevention Strategies, the important point is that they are community-focused and require community members' involvement and commitment. The majority of these local projects are on reserves, but there are others that address the criminal justice problems and needs of Aboriginal peoples in urban centres.

Arguably, the best-known of the urban 'community' projects is the Toronto Aboriginal Legal Services Community Council program. This is a diversion program where the offender who admits the offences receives a 'community' disposition such as counselling treatment and/or restitution. Its approach is a model of criminal justice reform that is gaining wide acceptance. The stated objectives of the program are to return criminal justice responsibility to the Aboriginal community, to reduce recidivism, and to make offenders more accountable – three objectives common to most Aboriginal criminal justice reforms. The program's mandate is to accept Aboriginal adults who have been charged with an offence under the Criminal Code of Canada, and to arrange a hearing with Community Council members who will determine the conditions the offender must fulfil. Breach of these conditions may return the case to the mainstream system. Similar programs have been implemented in Vancouver and Winnipeg. Vancouver's Aboriginal Transformative Justice Services offers an alternative to the formal court process for Aboriginal accused and also involves the use of a community council that is responsible in part for developing a healing plan. Other models of justice for Aboriginal people living in urban areas include the Regina Alternatives Measures Program, which is Aboriginal-administered and staffed and diverts adults and youth to Family Group Conferences and mediation.

Perhaps the most famous and frequently cited community-justice project is the Hollow Water Community Holistic Circle Healing Program. The Hollow Water First Nation in Manitoba started it in 1986, as a response to problems of sexual abuse and family violence. The program has thirteen steps, from disclosure through various activities for victims, offenders, and the community, concluding with a healing contract and a cleansing ceremony (Griffiths 1996, 202). The Hollow Water project has been the subject of many restorative-justice discussions involving Aboriginal peoples and communities, and it is regarded by government and other agencies and commentators (Ross 1994) as the epitome of a successful restorative-justice program operating in an Aboriginal community. The Canim Lake Violence Program in British Columbia is also considered a successful community-based justice project. It is designed for the management and treatment of adult and youth sex offenders and for the victims of sexual abuse. The treatment interventions blend modern clinical techniques with traditional Aboriginal healing practices. The offender must sign a contract agreeing to complete the treatment program and if this is breached, formal prosecution follows (Griffiths 1996, 202–3).

Many community-justice projects in Canada, and in other countries with Indigenous populations such as Australia and New Zealand, involve community members in various positions of responsibility. Some positions are adjudicatory and make decisions about offenders; others, such as sentencing panels, are advisory and provide judges with advice and input. Still others use clan members in a variety of justice roles, while some involve council formats or councils where decisions are made about community-justice approaches, particularly crime-prevention strategies. Because problems are closely interrelated with needs in Aboriginal communities and populations, the justice strategies are often part of a broader strategy focusing on health, employment, alcohol abuse, and suicide. Given self-government interests, the goal of many of these local justice strategies is to lead to greater community empowerment and institutional control. The community groups concerned also have responsibility for ensuring that justice strategies and approaches are culturally relevant, and elders usually have some role in the delivery of justice.

The crucial benefit of community-based justice projects is that local Aboriginal peoples become involved in identifying the crime-and-order problems in their own communities. Government and non-government initiatives and funds are used to try to address these problems so as to decrease their members' involvement with the mainstream criminal justice system and to increase community control over justice matters.

It is now well known that justice programs are more effective where there is a homogenous community with a sense of social responsibility and some common, identifiable community goals. Even where community members hold diverse views and opinions (as is the case in virtually all communities except in the most closed ones), the ability to accommodate this diversity reveals the community's internal strength and cohesiveness. Linden (n.d.) and others emphasize the need for local communities to be involved in defining problems, determining strategies, and implementing programs. They suggest that the most effective community programs are those that are decentralized, involve the participation of local people, and link their clients to other community institutions.

Soon as many local projects are still in their infancy, however, there is still little hard evidence about their effectiveness in dealing with offenders and victims and, their capacity to promote institution building in communities. The next few years of their development are therefore critical. The ultimate question will be whether reform in the shape of restorative justice needs to be substantially different in the Aboriginal community context, and if so, what it would look like. One important aspect of that question is whether local justice can support the development of democratic institutions and an active citizenry, and not become a meaningless symbol of local control or, worse still, a coercive tool of repression for the powerful. Aboriginal peoples themselves will have to decide on the direction it takes.

Bibliography

Alder, Christine, and Joy Wundersitz, ed. 1994. *Family Conferencing and Juvenile Justice: The Way Forward or Misplaced Optimism?* Canberra: Australian Studies in Law, Crime and Justice. Australian Institute of Criminology.

Campbell and Associates. 1994. *Evaluation of the Nishnawbe-Aski Legal Services Corporation.* Toronto and Ottawa: Ministry of the Attorney General of Ontario and the Department of Justice, Canada.

Depew, R.C. 1994. *Popular Justice and Aboriginal Communities: Some Preliminary Considerations.* Ottawa: Department of Justice: Aboriginal Justice Directorate.

Griffiths, C.T. 1996. 'Sanctioning and Healing: Restorative Justice in Canadian Aboriginal Communities.' *International Journal of Comparative and Applied Criminal Justice,* 20, no.2:195–208.

Hawthorn, H. 1967. *A Survey of Contemporary Indians of Canada,* volume 2. Ottawa: Queen's Printer.

Linden, R. N.d. *The Role of Strategic Planning, Policy Implementation and Evaluation in Crime Prevention.* Winnipeg: University of Manitoba, Criminology Research Centre, unpublished.

Pennell, J., and G. Burford. 1994. 'Widening the Circle: The Family Group Decision-making Project.' *Journal of Child and Youth Care*, 9, no.1:1–12.

Ross, R. 1994. 'Duelling Paradigms? Western Criminal Justice versus Aboriginal Community Healing.' In R. Gosse, J. Henderson, and R. Carter, ed., *Continuing Poundmaker and Riel's Quest*. Saskatoon: Purich.

Profile of Helen Betty Osborne (1952–71)

Cree, Student

The Irish philosopher Edmund Burke once said, 'The only thing necessary for the triumph of evil is for good men to do nothing.'[1] The circumstances surrounding the tragic death of Helen Betty Osborne bring the struggles between Aboriginal peoples and the Canadian judicial system to the forefront. This event, along with the death of J.J. Harper, served as a catalyst for Manitoba's judicial system to examine its attitudes and practices towards Aboriginal peoples.

The eldest of twelve children, Helen Betty Osborne was born to Justine and Joe Osborne on 16 July 1952, on the Norway House Indian Reserve in Manitoba.[2] After completing as much school as possible on the reserve,[3] Osborne wanted to become a teacher so she left to continue her education.[4] In 1969, at the age of seventeen, she moved to the Guy Hill Residential School, located twenty-nine kilometres from The Pas, Manitoba.[5] After two years at residential school, she moved into The Pas where she attended Margaret Barbour Collegiate.[6] The Pas was a town fraught with racism between whites and Indians.[7]

Helen Betty Osborne was last seen walking towards home on 13 November 1971. Her badly beaten body was found the next morning with multiple stab wounds.

Although an investigation was started at that time, all the people questioned in the Osborne murder were Aboriginal.[8] No whites were questioned.

Police received an anonymous letter six months after the murder that named three teenagers, Lee Colgan, Frank Houghton, and Norman Manger as being responsible. A fourth teen, Dwayne Archie Johnston, was later implicated. Although the killers' identities were widely known throughout the town, and questions about them abounded, charges would not be laid for another sixteen years.[9] Further, only one of four involved in the killing was ever found guilty and sentenced.[10] Some say that it is because the victim was an Indian woman and therefore expendable.[11]

Helen Betty Osborne. Courtesy of Canadian Press/*Winnipeg Free Press*.

For many, the Osborne case is symbolic 'of the ugliness of the north, the lack of social fabric of a group of people that has been reduced in the eyes of Whites as unemployed, unintelligent, and therefore people who are not worthy to care about. They are only to be dealt with.'[12] The Manitoba Aboriginal Justice Inquiry was created to examine the circumstances surrounding the investigation of Osborne's death.[13] The commissioners concluded that the non-Aboriginal community of The Pas 'must learn to respect Aboriginal people and their culture.'[14] They further concluded that Helen Betty Osborne would not have been killed if she had not been Aboriginal.[15]

STEPHANIE PYNE

Notes

1 Edmond Burke, *The Columbia Book of Quotations* (New York: Columbia University Press 1996), 181.
2 'The Death of Helen Betty Osborne: The Aboriginal Justice Implementation Commission,' *Report of the Aboriginal Justice Inquiry of Manitoba* (1991), 1. www.//ajic.mb.ca/volumeII/chapter2.html.
3 Ibid. The reserve school went to Grade 8.
4 L. Priest, *Conspiracy of Silence* (Toronto: McClelland and Stewart 1989), 22–6.
5 Death of Helen Betty Osborne,' 1.
6 Ibid.
7 Priest, *Conspiracy of Silence*, 21.
8 'Death of Helen Betty Osborne,' 3.
9 Priest, *Conspiracy of Silence*, 188.
10 Ibid.
11 'Death of Helen Betty Osborne,' 2.
12 B. Bergman and D. McGillivray, 'A Scathing Indictment,' *Maclean's* 104, no. 36 (1991): 12.
13 'Death of Helen Betty Osborne,' chapter 1, 3.
14 Ibid., chapter 10, 1.
15 Ibid.

PART SIX

CULTURE AND IDENTITY

Inuit Names: The People Who Love You

VALERIE ALIA

... identity shows a lot in your Inuktitut name, because those are the names that are given to you when you're born by the people who love you.
                                              – Peesee Pitseolak (Pitseolak interview, 1994)

Names are the heart and soul of Inuit culture, and the richness of the Inuit naming system, which developed over hundreds of years and is one of the most intricate naming systems in the world, provides non-Inuit Canadians with a unique opportunity to better understand their own personal and cultural identities. Visitors to the north have long studied and observed, praised and criticized, confused and distorted, regulated and registered, revised and amended Inuit names. In the 1920s, missionaries introduced Christian names, which were added to people's existing Inuktitut names. In the 1940s, the government brought in 'disc numbers.' Each Inuk was given an identity tag with a number prefixed by 'E' (for Eastern) or 'W' (for Western) on the front and 'Eskimo Identification Canada' on the back. In the 1960s, 'Project Surname' was organized to make the Inuit like other Canadians, as a way of celebrating the 1970 centennial of the Northwest Territories.

Many people predicted that all this interference would mean the death of Inuit culture. They were mistaken. Throughout all of the changes, the Inuit kept their traditions alive. Today, they are naming babies in the old ways, reclaiming names that were lost or changed through Project Surname, and continuing naming practices which for a time became less public but were never lost.[1] In so doing, the Inuit have enhanced the richness of the Canadian cultural tapestry. Today, cultural revival – or recognition— is a dominant theme in Nunavut, which in 1999 became Canada's newest territory.

The intricate naming system is based on *sauniq* – a powerful form of namesake commemoration that has been described as a kind of reincarnation. Names are passed from one generation to the next, regardless of gender (except among the Polar Inuit, who developed separate names for men and women). The namesake, or *atiq*, can continue her or his life through many people. When a child is named, he or she becomes the *sauniq* or 'bone' of all those who have shared that name. Those with the same name-giver are *atia'uaaluq* or 'namesharers.' People linked by names help each other in time of need and are bound together in a complex and permanent set of relationships (Guemple 1965). 'No child is only a child. If I give my grandfather's *atiq* to my baby daughter, she *is* my grandfather. I will call her *ataatassiaq*, grandfather. She is entitled to call me grandson' (Brody 1987).

Naming Stories

Minnie Aodla Freeman was born in 1936 on Cape Hope Island in James Bay. In her 1978 book, *Life among the Qallunaat*, she recalled the naming traditions of her childhood: 'Our belief is that no one really dies until someone is named after the dead person. So, to leave the dead in peace and to prevent their spirits from being scattered all over the community, we give their names to the newborn. The minds of the people do not rest until the dead have been renamed' (Freeman 1978). Sometimes, the namesake is a living elder: 'Before I was born, my mother had to decide who would be involved at my birth ... The first person who has to be there is a mid-wife, man or woman. In my case it was my grandmother ... Also present at my birth was the person I was named after, my other grandmother. This automatically meant that I would never call her "grandmother" nor would she call me "grandchild." Instead, we called each other *sauniq*, *namesake*, *bone-to-bone* relation' (Freeman 1978).

Alexina Kublu's naming stories convey the complexity of the Inuit naming system and its link to a network of kinship reference that, to the outsider, is an incomprehensible tangle of interwoven identities. A linguist and educator, she comes from Igloolik. Her husband and teaching colleague, Mick Mallon, said, 'Kublu and I are fellow old men. I'm an old man because I've reached that stage all on my own. Kublu started life as an old man because she is her own great-grandfather' (Mallon interview, 1995). Kublu herself says:

I am my *paniq's atatukulu*. My *paniq's* my grandmother ... my grandmother is my *paniq*, which is daughter. I'm her *atatukulu* because I'm named after her stepfather. Her biological father was lost out at sea when she was a baby, so she never knew her father. The only father she knew was Kublu and so to her he was her father. My younger daughter calls me *inni* (son), and I in turn, call her *atatta* (father).

Some people call me Apuk and it's through Apuk that she's my *atata*. And through Apuk that I'm her *inni*. But first of all, I was always going to be Kublu because my *atiq* [namesake] died before I was born ... and so my family knew who I was going to be. I was born already about to be Kublu, so when I became born, so naturally I became Kublu ... My mother's midwife ... the first person who held me ... told my mother that she wanted her son to live with her ... my mother by name [told] my mother by birth that she wanted ... to have her son living with her. So that's how I became Kublu. (Kublu interview, 1995).

Martha Flaherty explains how the practice worked in her family: 'When my father died, there was a little boy born ... who was named after my father. So, everybody calls him my father: he is my father; my mother calls him husband. When he got his first seal, he gave a piece of that to my mother, gave the skin to my mother so my mother could make something for him. If he goes to the store, he'll buy sugar or tea for my mother. He calls all of us his children, according to how our father named us' (Flaherty interview, 1995).

The ties between an Inuk and his or her namesake are so strong that kinship terms, dress, and behaviour often follow the relationship rather than the person's biological sex. Jose Kusugak says that 'traditionally, because I was named after a woman, I would have gotten a mark on my right thumb, a tattoo. But I was one generation too late for that, so I never got a tattoo. It would be a nice thing, I think, to bring that back: having a tattoo on the thumb to signify that, if you're a man and you have a tattoo on your right thumb, then people would know that you are named after a woman' (Kusugak Alia interview, 1995). Napatchie Akeego MacRae describes how cross-gender naming worked in her family:

A lot of the names are about a hundred years old that I know of ... My father's sisters call me Akeego. When I was born, [a man] had just recently died ... called Napatchie ... Akeego was my dad's younger sister, and my middle name is named after her. I don't know how many names I've got so far. I know only about a few, but not all of them, but they are not used as often ... Napatchie was a man – the person I'm named after – his relatives call me his younger brother. One of the midwives that helped my mum was [his] mother ... my parents decided to name me after him. It's almost like reincarnation in the name's way. And that's how it works ... they feel like to respect the dead they let the name carry on for their family's sake.

Her identities are even more complicated because, in addition to being a 'younger brother,' she is also a 'younger sister.'

> My middle name is Akeewok ... after my dad's youngest sister. All of my dad's relatives treated me like I was their little princess because I was named after their younger sister. My grandfather showed his love towards me more than towards my other siblings because I was named after his youngest daughter ... And my dad ... me being his first daughter, treats me with better respect than his other kids. I don't call him 'Dad' in Inuktitut; I call him 'Brother' ... And ... I call them my aunts in English but in Inuktitut I call them older [or younger] sister.

Her biological family treats her as female, but the family whose brother is her namesake treats her as male.

> The older brother would ask me if I want to go hunting with him, or catch my first caribou or seal ... but the way I saw myself, I was more female, so I didn't want to do that. It's kind of hard to explain how it really works. There's some people I've noticed that had a daughter ... named after a boy ... they would make them grow up as if they were boys right from the birth ... A family ... adopted my youngest sister, and she was named after the brother of the adopted mother. They made her dress up like a boy ... gave her a haircut like a boy ... from the time she was old enough to get a haircut. It went on and on and on until she was old enough to decide which way she wants to dress up.
>   If a child was named after a female it would work the same way ... dress him up like a female ... let him grow his hair long ... That's how it works with some people, but other people ... with me it was different cause I had two names [one male, one female] ... it confused me for a while, but I got my mom to explain ... why this man was calling me his younger brother even though I'm a girl ...
>   The first pair of kamiks [sealskin boots] my little girl got from my mom were in a boy's kamiks style. There's two different ways of making kamiks, the female and the male styles. She was getting the male style ... because of her name. Once the person that is named after a person [of the] opposite sex, once they are beginning to feel that they are too old to be treated the way were treated when they were younger ... they would grow out of it. and they would let the parents know. But it's up to the child ... We would still have that name ... she'll know that ... For the child's emotional or mental stability, they have got to stop somewhere ... to make them understand how it really works so they won't be confused all their lives.

While continuing the Inuit naming traditions, she has adapted them to the cultural differences in her family and community.

> My oldest is 17. His first name is Patrick ... that's the name I picked 'cause he
> was born on St. Patrick's Day. But traditionally he's named after my dad's
> cousin, who died not too long before Patrick was born ... a lot of Inuit people
> say that if a baby has been born ... if he started crying...for no reason...we
> know that that person who passed away, even after the baby was born, prob-
> ably wants to be named through that baby. So a lot of babies are named after
> the person who has died, even after the baby was born. And they would stop
> crying and we would know that person wanted to be among the family ...
> named with that baby. My youngest daughter, we named her Kirsten, but she
> uses her middle name more often ... because that's the way she acts – she's
> got the personality of that person that we named her after ... Ninyurapiq, and
> she prefers Ninyurapiq to her English name ... (Akeego interview, 1995)

Project Surname and Its Aftermath[2]

Abraham (Abe) Okpik, the government's first Inuit Area Administrator at
Spence Bay, was a translator and interpreter for the Department of Indian
and Northern Affairs and a broadcaster. In 1965 he was appointed the first
Aboriginal member of the Territorial Council (Crowe 1991). In 1969 Northwest Territorial Commissioner Stuart Hodgson hired him to implement
Project Surname (some called it 'Operation Surname'). In thirteen months,
Okpik had travelled more than 70,000 kilometres and interviewed close to
17,000 people. Only the settlements of Whale Cove and Repulse Bay were
omitted because weather conditions prevented him from getting there.

In 1984 Pangnirtung Elder Etoangat Aksaiyuk[3] told me that despite
being given a surname,

> I've never been given a white man's name. Aksaiyuk was still not a white
> man's name. It's my name. It's nobody else's name. My wife had a powerful
> grandfather who was the boss. He did the naming. He was a real hunter, a
> real good hunter and that put him way up in society. I grew up with meat
> always there. I was never hungry. The way it used to be was most people
> were named after people who had passed away.
>
> A person that passed away, even though he wasn't a relative of yours, your
> child could take that person's name. And when the birth registration got
> started we kept going with the naming from deceased people but we would
> put a different name on the birth certificate (Alia 1994, 83–4).

Another Pangnirtung elder, Kudlu Pitseolak, recalled,

I was baptized by Reverend Peck as Malaya. But a person by the name of Kudlu who was my relative died before I was born, so I got Kudlu ... and kept Kudlu instead of Malaya ever since. [During Project Surname] my husband left town along with some of the other hunters with some of the art that they had made to sell. And when he came back he called, 'Hey, guess what? I just got a last name!' My husband told me that we would be having a second name of his father ... Pitseolak...We were amazed ... How could I be named another name while my husband was still alive? I didn't like this ...

The women weren't involved at all, only the men ... Because Abe Okpik was a man, he worked with the men. (Alia 1994, 85–6)

Kudlu was not the only person who was dissatisfied with the surname project. Elise Attagutaluk told me that she was stunned when, as a young adult, she received a birth certificate with her *husband's* surname on it. 'I sent it back and asked for correction and they just sent it back to me unchanged.' She said, 'When they did Project Surname, kids came back from school with new names. You go away and you come home, and suddenly, you're somebody else' (Alia 1994, 96). She was one of the first people to attempt to address the problems. In 1985 she presented a resolution to the annual general meeting of Pauktuutit (Inuit Women's Association):

RESOLUTION #85–15

Many Inuit in the Northwest Territories have been obliged under Project Surname to have erroneous last names. They now are forced to pay money to change their names as a result of government incompetence.

BE IT RESOLVED THAT: the federal and territorial governments set up a programme to support Inuit in the Northwest Territories to have their surnames changed back to the real names of their families.

AND THAT: the necessary costs in legally changing these surnames be fully assumed by the governments.

MOVED BY: Elise Attagutaluk

SECONDED BY: Leonie Qrunnut (Alia 1994, 91)

Continuing, Reclaiming, and Reasserting Cultural Traditions

The resolution passed. Its purpose was taken up by others, among them Peter Irniq, who changed his name legally from *Ernerk* to Irniq to reflect its proper pronunciation. A long-time advocate of cultural continuity and respect for naming traditions, he explains: 'Inuit had several names from, since time immemorial. When the missionaries came, they gave us Christian names. Peter ... was not the chosen name for me by my parents; it was a chosen name for me by a priest who baptized me in 1947.

George Quviq Qulaut is equally determined to help keep Inuit naming traditions, and the people who carry the names, alive. 'Two or three years after my father's death [Project Surname] came along and it was very hard for us ... It was very hard for me to say my father's name, it was so recent ago that he had passed away; it was very emotional ... not only for myself but for my mother and my sister.' His family agreed to take a surname, but avoided actually using the name for several years.

Peter Irniq also discussed this tension between the new surnames and traditional avoidance taboos: 'You are forced to say [the names] and it makes you feel very uncomfortable. Some people's names, you can never say them at all, even alone [because] if they could hear you through the spirits, they would be insulted if they knew that you had mentioned their name. We would never use those as surnames' (Qulaut interview, 1994).Traditional naming is strong in his family: 'My brother, who died about forty years ago, was named after my grandfather. When my parents adopted a child ... they named him again so ... he continues to have this new life each time. Same person, but living. He drowned in 1968. In 1969 they were given[4] a baby ... They named him my grandfather again ... I named my grandfather in our own family so that he's alive in our own family ...' His mother's name was given to his daughter, his father's name was given to his son, and so on. 'These are the names that I have carried because these are the people who were my leaders, my role models. They provided direction for me all my life, so they're in my family, all of them.'[5]

George Quviq Qulaut's oldest daughter carries the name of an elder who passed away a few months before she was born and was also named after George's father. Like many Inuit, she carries the names of female and male relatives because 'all Inuktitut names are unisex ... there is no woman's name or man's name. It works well.' His commitment to continuing the culture is strengthened by his knowledge that he himself almost lost it. 'At the age of ten, I couldn't speak my language ... Inuktitut ... my culture was completely gone. In order to be with my parents, I had to re-learn the whole thing ... I had no one to talk to. The only people that spoke Inuktitut were my parents and the only person who spoke English was my grandfather. I went back home and played with the children and relearned the pronunciation and the whole system' (Qulaut interview, 1994).

Deborah Evaluardjuk describes how namesakes can communicate directly to the family through dreams: 'My mother had a dream that my namesake came to lie down beside her and my father. He had this great big beard, one of the few Inuit who had a great big beard [his grandfather was a whaling captain from Scotland] ... One month later, when they adopted me, she knew what it meant ... that my namesake wanted to come back to them, because they were very, very close to him.' A month before her daughter was born, she had a dream: 'I saw my uncle, Calepee Apak, who had recently passed away with cancer, coming toward me. And he was healthy. All of a sudden I looked down in my dream and the baby came out. It was a girl, and I knew it ... I looked on the sand-type ground and I saw this tree twig; and right there it spelled A-P-A-K: Apak; and I knew right then and there that that's what the baby's name was supposed to be' (Evaluardjuk interview, 1995) Alexina Kublu's story also shows the strength of the connections between namesakes and recipients of the name. The namesake of one of her daughters had died in a plane crash.

> When my daughter was about eleven, we were flying down to Winnipeg from Rankin and it was pretty turbulent. They didn't know if we were going to land ... And ... [she] says, 'I was in a plane crash, wasn't I?' And I said, 'No, you weren't in a plane crash.' And she goes, 'I *know* I was in a plane crash ... I keep on dreaming about it.' I said, tell me about the dream. And she goes, 'I'm in the airplane, I'm looking out the window, I know we're going to crash, we crash, I get to the door and that's it.' She said she'd had the same dream over and over again. And I'm holding her and I said, 'Yes, you were in a plane crash, but not you as you. You as your *atiq*. You were in a plane crash.' He was found at the door of the airplane, and she said every time she got to the door, everything would go black and that was it. I held her and she started crying and she said, 'That's how I died, wasn't it?'

She explains why it is virtually impossible to describe Inuit relationships in terms Qallunaat – non-Inuit – can understand. In *Qallunaat* society, you are a person; a person who marries your uncle is also your aunt. But the system does not account for one of Kublu's relatives, who is

> my dad's uncle's wife, whom I called ... cousin, but she was my sister. She was my sister because she was the sister of the person I am named after. As a child, I considered the two people who were the name – who were the mother and father of my *atiq* – as my parents. I honestly thought that they were my parents, that I was their child and my biological parents were just looking after me for them. I felt ... at home with them. I was their child. They were my parents. Their children were my brothers and sisters. My brothers' and sisters' children were my nieces and nephews. I very much felt part of the family and I'd go in there and I knew I was home ... You know before the child is born who they are going to be. My [fifteen-year-old] daughter was in a bit of a dilemma a few years ago when a little girl who was named after my sister was killed ... [it] brought back ... the memory of my sister's death because she was named after her ... my daughter [asked], 'What am I going to

do ... when I have a baby? What names are my child going to have?' ... we don't have any other babies in the family, and so there's this backlog of names to be given, for us to keep, for us to have, because I have my uncle, I have my parents by name ... I do not have my mother, I do not have my sister and she's going, 'Well, I have two sisters, my mother and my aunt and then there's my aunt ... I want them all,' and she goes, 'Is my baby going to have all these names?' [I said], 'I don't know, I think so,' so we ... put that on the shelf to be thought about when the time comes ...

The way we name in Igoolik is still very strong ... it's part of the healing process, part of the grieving process. It gives me a lot of joy to have a little child come to me and I can put my arm around them and say ... this is my mother ... or the children that come up to me and say, 'Hi sis.' I don't know how to describe the feeling ... you know that this is not the sister that you had, but this is still your sister.[6]

And ... to have people refer to my own daughters through their name ... that bond ... there is no biological bond, yet they're not just my child ... I found very upsetting ... the use of our names as pieces of identity. Also ... it was extremely disrespectful to call a person older than you by name. You did not say those people's names. But when it becomes an identity marker, the respect ... just kind of disappeared.

My sister Elise was Kunatuloitok ... She didn't care how difficult it was to say. It was her name. And then she became Attagutaluk.[7] She was very upset ... she was told when you marry, you take your husband's name. Then, the following year, we had new recruits into the school, a new teaching couple, different last names. And so she goes up to them ... 'Aren't you married?' 'Yes, we are.' 'So how come you have different last names?' 'Because I chose to keep my last name.' 'You *chose* to keep your last names?' Oh, she was livid ... she became Attagutaluk because Project Surname was getting us Inuit like the rest of Canadians ... and then they turn around and say, 'Oh, I should decide to not change my name.'

In 1994 Martha Flaherty, then president of Pauktuutit, addressed the ninth annual Inuit Studies Conference, which was being held in Nunavut for the first time:

During a couple of annual meetings, we have discussed the topic of kinship in the North, of the Inuit people. I think this is only a tip of the problem in the North. I think it's very important that we deal with the whole situation ... not just ... surnaming of the Inuit people but also the kinship of the Inuit. And I think this should be dealt with by the real people of the communities.

[One of the objectives of the Nunavut Final Agreement is] 'To encourage self-reliance and cultural and social well-being of Inuit.' I think this ... is perhaps much more important than the land ownership rights and billion dollars Inuit receive as compensation. (Flaherty 1994)

Names and the Politics of Place

It is not just personal names that have deep meaning for Inuit. As George Kuvik Qulaut explains, 'Each one of our names means something, they all have meaning; geographical names are the same way.' Since 1972, Linna Weber and Ludger Müller-Wille have worked with Inuit elders and with the Avataq Cultural Institute in northern Quebec (now Nunavik) on mapping projects aimed at recording traditional place names.[8] Ludger's view is that 'place names are political symbols ... [they] are dynamic; they change ... depending on who is in a place or ... region to name ... spaces and places, so there are ... dimensions ... which we could call political identity (Müller-Wille interview, 1995). Inuit have put forward the claim that places that ... carry ... non-Inuit names should be changed back to the Inuit names that are being used by the local Inuit community ... I would say that place names are one element of personal identity.' The elders, most of whom were hunters, started from a place where they had camped and 'travelled' on the maps, following their travelling and hunting routes. They did not need maps to find these places. 'The maps were all in their heads. Through the oral tradition you have the names memorized ... and the sequence in which they appear ... and when you have this you can't possibly get lost' (Weber interview, 1995). There are traditional songs that record the places and their locations and special qualities. Some of the elders on the mapping project sang songs in which all of the place names of a given area were sung, in the sequence in which they were travelled. Place names contain important spiritual and environmental information. 'There are references to sacred sites ... [and] gravesites ... or references to spirits ...' (Müller-Wille interview, 1995).

> The names themselves contain warnings for hazards where there might be places on the lakes where there is always open water ... covered by snow ... They have warnings about bad water conditions, tidal conditions, wind conditions, information about places where you won't get good fish, [or] a lake that might yield fish [that] are always skinny and no good to eat, so you better avoid it if you have hungry. Then there is all the good information: good places to fish, good places to hunt, what kind of animals are in those places, what kind of hunting methods are the best to use in that place. [It's] all in the names. (Weber interview, 1995)

In traditional Inuit society, land and person are almost inseparable. The world is divided not between persons and places but between named and unnamed things. The particular band or dialect group is defined by a prefix followed by a common suffix, -*miut* ('the people of' or 'the inhabitants of'). As Thomas C. Correll explains, 'boundaries between the haunts of neighbouring groups are ... rather clearly formed – at least *in the minds* of the constituents – by the termination of place names relating to one group and the beginning of those of another' (Correll 1976).

Keith Basso calls names 'a mnemonic peg on which to hang a social history ...' (Basso 1996), a view extended by Mark Nuttall's observation that names show 'ownership by a person or group' but, more important, 'establish power and territorial claim ...' (Nuttall 1992). As Hugh Brody reminds us, 'a map is neither artifact nor romance. It is a political document, tied to past and present power relations, at the very centre of economic (land claims, etc.) and cultural progress' (Brody 1987).

In the Unalakleet community Correll visited, he was told that each person had a personal name with a place-name counterpart 'somewhere in the surrounding country.' Place names were spoken only in the dialect of the group that was identified with the area. Speakers of one dialect who were visiting the territory of another dialect group used the host group's pronunciation of place names. One group taught the place names to children by chanting the names of topographic features in sequence as they occurred in nature.

Place names express and identify the Canadian landscape. Northern place names reflect the activities and travels of residents and visitors. Over the centuries, visitors sometimes put their own names on places that the Inuit had known and named. Indigenous people have not always welcomed the renaming of their ancestral lands: 'Alexander Mackenzie came to our land. He described us in his Journal as a "meagre, ill-made people ..." My people probably wondered at this strange, pale man in his ridiculous clothes, asking about some great waters he was searching for. He recorded his views on the people, but we'll never know exactly how my people saw him. I know they'd never understand why their river is named after such an insignificant fellow' (Kakfwi in Dene Cultural Institute 1989, back cover).

In the western Arctic and subarctic region comprising today's Northwest Territories, Dene peoples had called the river Dehcho long before it became known to others as the Mackenzie. In the eastern Arctic, the sixteenth-century explorer Martin Frobisher left his name on a body of water and a community that would later become the capital of Nunavut. The Native Geographical Names Symposia, convened in Ottawa in 1985 and 1986 by Alan Rayburn, then executive secretary of the Canadian Permanent Committee on Geographical Names, had a permanent impact on Canada's maps. The remapping program accompanied nationwide efforts to clarify the enduring presence of Aboriginal peoples in what is now Canada. In the 1980s and 1990s, the Inuktitut names of most Inuit communities became official, and in 1987 Frobisher Bay was officially renamed Iqaluit. The change reasserted Inuit sovereignty and removed the name of a visitor from the map and the mental landscape. It heralded bigger change to come: creation of the Canadian territory named for the Inuit homeland, Nunavut ('our land').

Today, Nunavut's capital city of Iqaluit has turned its attention to the task of naming its streets. As the population and government infrastructure grow, the grid of streets expands and finding one's way becomes more difficult. In the spring of 2002, the Iqaluit city council asked residents to suggest possible street names. Not all of the residents are Inuit, and, although all names will appear in Inuktitut syllabics, some are likely to reflect the *Qallunaat* community as well. The syllabic spellings are checked with Nunavut Language Commissioner Eva Aariak; linguist and educator Mick Mallon has produced a cd for public distribution, to aid non-Inuktitut speakers in pronouncing the names.

Other Nunavut communities remain small enough not to require street names. At the time of this writing, Iqaluit's street names are still being discussed in public meetings, with extensive debate about appropriateness of various names. Some (such as those of *Qallunaat* explorers) remain controversial, and there are demands for better representation of women (Rideout 2002, 41). The introduction of Inuktitut place names redefines Nunavut's mental and physical landscape for residents, visitors, and those who visit only cartographically. The impression given by older maps, of a north more *visited* than *lived in*, has changed. Today's multilingual maps reveal the diversity of linguistic and cultural influences – and people. They present a more accurate picture, placing Inuktitut front and centre as befits a region whose population is 85 per cent Inuit.

Conclusion: It's All in the Names

Canada has long been portrayed – from inside and from without – as a quintessentially *northern* nation. Imbedded in what some have called the 'idea of North' is the *reality* of north. While the northern 'idea' is often focused on landscape, the northern reality is primarily concerned with *people* and their relationship to the life-giving and life-challenging land – less the 'scape' of visiting painters and poets than the named and located home of its indigenous inhabitants. The north that permeates Canadian literature, identity, and culture is a mix of 'idea' and lived experiences of northerners and visitors.

Visitors from Europe, southern Canada, and other parts of North America wrote about their northern experiences and carried photographs of Inuit with them when they returned home. Few of them named the people they had photographed – either because they were unable to gather, understand, or spell Inuktitut names or because they did not care enough to ask. (It is often said that the Inuit are the world's most photographed people.) As for the Inuit themselves, they all working to find and restore their original names. In 2000 Nunavut Tunngavik Inc. and the Department of Indian and Northern Affairs developed Nunavut Sivuniksavut, an educational program for young beneficiaries of the Nunavut Land Claim Agreement. Participants study Inuit history, the Nunavut agreements, and current issues and conduct research (Angus 2000). One project involves working with elders (and the help of the Internet) to find the names of Inuit whose faces populate hundreds of thousands of photographs taken in the early 1900s and stored for decades in the National Archives in Ottawa. Putting names on anonymous images is more than a research exercise – it is a way of reclaiming the images (and their link to families and communities) for Inuit while sharing them with Qallunaat and recording them for history.

The Archives project is one of many strategies the Inuit have developed to keep their names and ways of naming alive and teach them to each new generation. In the years since Project Surname, some people have kept their government-given names (often correcting the spelling). Others choose to adopt names of other cultures or combine them with Inuktitut names. Still others prefer to give and carry only Inuktitut names. Regardless of the particular choices of individuals and families, one thing is clear: in the Canadian north, Inuit names and naming traditions – and the people whose lives they perpetuate and honour – are alive and well and likely to remain strong for decades and generations to come. Canada's identity has always been founded on the diversity of its people, their shared Canadianness, and their cultural differences. The Inuit contribution to Canadian identity and culture is nowhere more evident than in the continuity of Inuit names and the strength of Inuit voices such as those recorded here.

> We started listening to our Elders ... they don't want us to lose our culture, language, and our identity ...
>
> – Deborah Evaluardjuk

> My identity is in that I am Peesee, named after my grandmother. I also have four other names that were given to me when I was born ... For a long time, I kept thinking, should I say Katherine is my name...even though it's not – because everybody else has a *Qallunaatitut* name. But no, it's part of my identity that I am Peesee.
>
> – Peesee Pitseolak

I think many people in Nunavut, especially the Inuit, are going to reclaim their traditions in order to be stronger in life. I want to ... make sure that our names, our community names, are properly spelled ... so that they mean something fifty years from now. My ancestors left this land for us and we are borrowing it from our children and grandchildren, so we must do it right. We must leave those proper names the way they are, for them to remember.

– Peter Irniq

... In the schools [children are registered] with their given names in Inuktitut ... I don't think it's a matter of bringing it back: I don't think there was ever a time that it got lost.

– Jose Kusugak

Inuit have experienced, over the years, a severe loss of pride and a crisis of identity ... We have a unique language, which is surviving incredible odds: wave upon wave of other languages have made it very difficult for our language to survive, because we're so small in numbers and others are so enormous ... people kept telling us, 'You're going to be extinct. You're going to die in fifty years' ... We decided to prove them wrong.

– John Amagoalik

Notes

1 In his monograph, *Eskimo Underground*, the anthropologist Robert Williamson used the term 'underground naming' to refer to the Inuit's maintenance of traditional names in private while they publicly complied with the dominant society's naming practices.

2 For a detailed discussion of various government identification programs, including Project Surname, see Valerie Alia, *Names, Numbers, and Northern Policy: Inuit Project Surname, and the Politics of Identity* (Halifax: Fernwood Books 1994).

3 This was the spelling he gave me. Over the years, his name has been spelled in a number of different ways in Roman orthography, which at best can only approximate Inuktitut pronounciation.

4 By traditional, or 'custom,' adoption.

5 At the time of the interview, Peter Imiq's name was spelled 'Emerk,' as it had been recorded during Project Surname. He has since corrected the spelling to have it more accurately reflect the correct pronounciation of his name.

6 The sister to whom Kublu is referring is Elise, whose resolution on Inuit names is mentioned earlier and whose life and work inspired and influenced many people, including this author.

7 Her husband's (post-Project Surname) surname.

8 In the mid-1980s, Ludger Müller-Wille and this author were members of a team of Aboriginal and non-Aboriginal people who worked with the Canadian Permanent Committee on Geographical Names, Surveys and Mapping Canada to correct, add, and restore Aboriginal place names on Canada's official maps.

Bibliography

Akeego, Napatchie. 1995. Interview by Kjersti Strømmen in Valerie Alia, *Nunavut: Where Names Never Die*, Alison Moss, prod. Toronto: CBC 'Ideas.'

Alia, Valerie. 1995. Interviews conducted during research for CBC radio documentary.

– 1984–96. Interviews conducted in Iqaluit, Pangnirtung, Igloolik and other locations in Nunavut, Greenland, and southern Canada.

– 1994. *Names, Numbers and Northern Policy: Inuit, Project Surname and the Politics of Identity.* Halifax: Fernwood Books.

– 1995. *Nunavut: Where Names Never Die*, Alison Moss, prod. Toronto: CBC 'Ideas.' Radio Documentary Transcript.

Angus, Murray. 2000. 'Inuit Students Naming the Past.' *Nunatsiaq News*, 14 Jan.

Basso, Keith H. 1996. *Wisdom Sits in Places.* Albuquerque: University of New Mexico Press.

Brody, Hugh. 1987. *Living Arctic: Hunters of the Canadian North.* Vancouver/Toronto: Douglas and McIntyre.

Correll, Thomas C. 1976. 'Language and Location in Traditional Inuit Societies.' In M.R. Freedman, ed., *Inuit Land Use and Occupancy Study.* Vol. 2. Ottawa: Department of Indian Affairs and Northern Development, 173–9.

Crowe, Keith. 1991. *A History of the Original Peoples of Northern Canada.* Rev. ed. Montreal and Kingston: McGill-Queen's University Press.

Dene Cultural Institute. 1989. *Dehcho: 'Mom, We've Been Discovered.'* Yellowknife, N.W.T.: Dene Cultural Centre.

Evaluardjuk, Deborah. 1995. Interview by Kjersti Strømmen in Valerie Alia, *Nunavut: Where Names Never Die*, Alison Moss, prod. Toronto: CBC 'Ideas.'

– 1994. Address to 9th Inuit Studies Conference, Iqaluit.

Flaherty, Martha. 1995. Interview by Kjersti Strømmen in Valerie Alia, *Nunavut: Where Names Never Die*, Alison Moss, prod. Toronto: CBC 'Ideas.'

Freeman, Minnie Aodla. 1978. *Life among the Qallunaat.* Edmonton: Hurtig.

Guemple, D.L. 1965. 'Saunik: Name Sharing as a Factor Governing Eskimo Kinship Terms.' *Ethnology* 4, no. 3: 323–35.

Irniq, Peter. 1994. Interview with author.

Isaacs, Harold. 1989. *Idols of the Tribe: Group Identity and Political Change.* Cambridge, Mass.: Harvard University Press.

Kublu, Alexina. 1995. Interview with author.

Kusugak, Jose. 1995. Interview with author.

Mallon, Mick. 1995. Interview with author.

Müller-Wille, Ludger. 1995. Interview with author.

Nuttall, Mark. 1992. *Arctic Homeland: Kinship, Community and Development in Northwest Greenland.* Toronto: University of Toronto Press.

Pitseolak, Peesee. 1995. Interview by Valerie Alia in *Nunavut: Where Names Never Die*, Alison Moss, prod. Toronto: CBC 'Ideas.' Comments to the session on Project Surname organized by Valerie Alia at the 9th Inuit Studies Conference in Iqaluit, 1994.

Pullen, Thomas C. 1987. Quoted in 'Editorial.' *Nunatsiaq News*, 26 Jan. Letter to the editor of the *Globe and Mail*.

Qulaut, George Quviq. 1994. Interview with author.

Rideout, Denise. 2002. 'Street-naming Project Hits Road Bumps.' *Nunatsiaq News*, 26 April, 41.

Strømmen, Kjersti. 1995. Interviews conducted during research for CBC radio documentary.

Weber, Linna. 1995. Interview with author.

Williamson, Robert. 1974. *Eskimo Underground: Socio-Cultural Change in the Canadian Central Arctic.* Uppsala, Sweden: Institutionen förallmen ochjamforand etnografi vid Uppsala Universitet.

Profile of John Kim Bell (1952–)

Mohawk, Conductor, Composer, and Foundation President

As the first Aboriginal symphony conductor, John Kim Bell is a trailblazer. He was born in the Mohawk community of Kahnawake, Quebec, on 8 October 1952 to Carl Donald and Beth Isabelle (Hamilton) Bell.[1] As a child, Bell studied keyboard, violin, and saxophone.[2] He earned a bachelor of music on scholarship from Ohio State University in 1975 and attended the Academy of Music in Siena, Italy, where he obtained a performance certificate in 1981.[3]

He began his career by conducting a New York City Broadway musical touring company in 1972, thus making him the youngest professional conductor in the United States.[4] That same year he was guest conductor for the National Ballet of Canada.[5] He worked as apprentice opera coach with the Chautauqua Opera Association in 1974.[6] At the age of twenty-eight, he was appointed apprentice conductor to the Toronto Symphony, making him the first Aboriginal person to conduct a symphony orchestra.[7]

A 1983 Canadian Broadcasting Corporation documentary featured Bell in his position as an Aboriginal symphony conductor. This program piqued the interest of many Aboriginal people wanting to know how they or their children could pursue training in the arts. Bell was flooded with inquiries.[8] In 1985 Bell endeavoured to provide access and financial support to Aboriginal Canadians seeking careers in the arts by establishing the Canadian Aboriginal Achievement Foundation (CNAF). The foundation began with a card table in his basement and $35,000 of his own money.[9] With the assistance of the foundation, many Aboriginal youth have been able to fulfil their own dreams by receiving education and training scholarships.[10]

The year 1988 was a busy one for Bell. During this period, he co-composed, directed, and conducted Canada's first Aboriginal ballet, 'In the Land of the Spirits.'[11] The contemporary ballet premiered at the National Arts Centre in Ottawa, Ontario, and was financed with $1 million raised by the CNAF.[12] Also in 1988, the National Aboriginal Achievement Foundation

John Kim Bell. Courtesy of the National Aboriginal Achievement Foundation.

(NAAF) was formed to 'fulfill the dreams of Aboriginal youth' by placing an emphasis on education. In 1994 the National Aboriginal Achievement Awards (NAAA) was televised, with Bell as the executive producer.[13] Annually, the NAAA recognizes the achievements of Aboriginal people in a variety of categories, including agriculture, arts and culture, business and commerce, community development, education, energy, environment, fisheries, forestry and natural resources, health services, heritage and spirituality, housing, law and justice, lifetime achievement, media and communications, medicine, public service, science and technology, social services, and sports.

John Kim Bell is widely recognized and has received many honours throughout his career: the William Oxley Thompson Alumni Award from Ohio State University (1987), Four Seasons Music Festival Award (1989), Award of Merit from the City of Toronto (1994), Member of the Order of Canada (1991), Officer of the Order of Canada (1997), and the Royal Bank Award for Canadian Achievement (1998). He received an honorary doctorate of music from Lakeland University (1990) and an honorary doctorate of laws and letters from Trent University (1992), Mount Allison University (1999), the University of Toronto (1999), and the University of Alberta (1999).[14]

John Kim Bell currently resides in Toronto, Ontario.

NASHILA DHARSHI

Notes

1 'John Kim Bell.' In Elizabeth Lumley., *Who's Who in Canada* (Toronto: University of Toronto Press 2000), 95.
2 Brett A. Lealand, 'John Kim Bell.' In Sharon Malinowski, ed., *Notable Native Americans* (New York: Gale Research 1995), 29–30.
3 Lumley, ed., *Who's Who in Canada*, 95.
4 Lealand, 'John Kim Bell,' 29.
5 Lumley, ed., *Who's Who in Canada*, 95.
6 Ibid.
7 Lealand, 'John Kim Bell,' 29.
8 Ibid.
9 Ibid.
10 National Aboriginal Achievement Foundation, 2002. www.naaf.ca/cnaf.html.
11 Lealand, 'John Kim Bell,' 30.
12 www.naaf.ca/cnaf.html.
13 Ibid.
14 Marie Burke, 'Bell Appointed to CBC Board,' *Windspeaker* 16 no. 7: 21.

Aboriginal Peoples and Canada's Conscience

RUSSEL LAWRENCE BARSH

When we say that Aboriginal peoples have contributed to Canadian society, we implicitly argue that there *is* a Canadian society to receive Aboriginal peoples' gifts. The statement necessarily implies an exchange between two separate and distinct worlds: that there was a Canada before Aboriginal peoples encountered it, and that there would be a reasonably recognizable Canada had Aboriginal peoples never existed. It implies that the main story of Canada took place somewhere else, neither on Aboriginal land nor in conflict or cooperation with Aboriginal nations – somewhere in Europe, perhaps. Yet it is difficult to imagine how Canada can be understood except as a direct product – from the beginning – of immigrants' encounters with Aboriginal peoples.

In this chapter, I suggest that the emerging national identity and shared discourse of Canadians, to the extent it exists today at all, does more than merely incorporate elements of Aboriginal philosophy or politely acknowledge the value of Aboriginal cultures. In this context, Canadians seem to me to have become peculiarly occupied with questions of justice – justice among themselves, and justice for peoples elsewhere in the world. This is not to say that Canada has fully achieved domestic justice, or that Canadians act altruistically in all situations abroad. What I am prepared to argue is that the shadow of Aboriginal rights looms over Canadian history and Canadian life in a way that results in ambivalence and a distinctively Canadian dialectic of justice and national legitimacy. Moreover, I believe that this argument over original national sin – the settlement of the land – has affected the way Canadians have approached all subsequent moral challenges, from Québécois nationalism and 'new immigrants' to Canada's global responsibilities.

Canadianité

'We *have* a meaning, however often we may forget it,' Vincent Massey (1948, 12–13) confidently maintained, for Canada 'may be a mosaic composed of different sizes and shapes and colours, and sometimes the cement between the bits has seemed to wear thin, but for all that the mosaic has a national pattern.' Since that time, Canadians have expressed confidence that they have a unifying national core culture, while failing to agree what it is. Although a majority of Canadians today approve of diversity and multiculturalism, 71 per cent feel strongly that immigrants must 'adopt Canadian values.' This figure is up from 61 per cent ten years earlier (Sheppard 2000; Bibby 1990, 52; Decima Research 1989).

It was only in the 1950s that most Canadians began to feel the need to adopt public symbols of independence, such as a distinctive national flag (Schwartz 1967, 250–1).[1] Canadians are neither an ancient nation that coalesced in ages past nor a self-invented revolutionary society like the United States. Americans declared their identity in 1776, and then opened their doors to immigration. Canada actively recruited immigrants for generations to fill its vast spaces but did not adopt a statement of fundamental principles until 1982, almost as an afterthought. Hence, 'the two main temporal rhetorics of nationhood are denied to us,' as Ian Angus (1997, 143) put it concisely, and 'we are left with, on the one side, a rhetoric of historical continuity imbedded in the British tradition that emphasizes rejection of the American Revolution and the conservative virtues of order, tradition, and parliamentary sovereignty and, on the other side, a rhetoric of the multiple origins of presently existing ethnocultures.'

Canadians clearly no longer conceive of themselves as Britons, and certainly not in Quebec. Defining Canada as a haphazard historical collection of ethnic particularities implies not only an absence of shared values, but the unlikelihood of agreeing to share any values (Keohane 1997, 162–3). Is Canada merely an anglophilic hotchpotch of ethnics? Or a state stripped of any pretence of nationhood, united by its administrative system and neutral procedural norms?

Whiteness

In a 1999 essay, Rhoda Howard-Hassman purports to identify the shared experiences and fundamental values that constitute a distinctive Canadian ethnic identity. Her list begins with predominantly European ancestry, Christian religion, English language, and the experience of living in the same northern geographical area: whiteness, nordicity, and anglophilia (compare Saul 1997, 69, 185–96). What Eva Mackey (1999, 30–1) has describes as 'icy white nationalism' excludes at least one-third of Canadian citizens from *canadianité*, however, and fails to distinguish Canadians adequately from Britons or (heaven forbid) Americans. Howard-Hassman suggests refining her definition by adding one ideological factor: 'To be

Canadian, increasingly, is in state ideology and public practice to be a multiculturalist: multiculturalism is a key Canadian value' (1999, 531). Canadianism is therefore a unique variety of *tolerant* whiteness: whiteness with a conscience.

A Canadian who teaches Canadian studies in the United States had this to say on the topic of whiteness: 'Left pretty much to its own devices, the white majority in Canada exudes a kind of ideal whiteness, ready for export. All my life, I've considered Canada to be a kind of discount warehouse where American networks and film companies go to purchase images of immaculate, politic whiteness ... Polite, pacific, respectable, Canadian whites are abundantly available for Americans who want to glorify whiteness without alienating African Americans' (Clarke 1998, 100).

In other words, Canada makes whiteness look good. To be sure, there are several other countries that might be said to give whiteness a good name in terms of pacifism, human rights, and generosity; the Nordic countries, certainly. Canada does not compare itself to Norway or Sweden, however, but to the United States, which everyone knows is violent, racist, imperialistic, and extraordinarily selfish for a country of such vast wealth. There is abundant corroboration of American faults in history and the mass media, but the real test is demonstrating that Canada abstained from the evils of slavery, imperialism, racism, or ethnic bigotry. Canadians 'are self-righteous in maintaining their innocence' (Clarke 1998, 103; also Mackey 1999, 162), and Aboriginal peoples are the acid test of Canadian integrity and self-respect.

When the British empire launched its bid for territory and power in the Americas three centuries ago, one of its tools was propaganda. British apologists unleashed stories of Spanish cruelty to Indigenous peoples: the Black Legend, which British and American authors have repeated and embellished uncritically to this day (Kagan 1996). Implicit in the Black Legend was a *white* legend of Anglo-Saxon beneficence and trustworthiness vis-à-vis the Indians. This legend was captured by Benjamin West in his frequently copied canvas of William Penn negotiating with the Lenape for lands to settle the Quakers in 1682 (Barsh 1994, 473), as well as in countless more recent images of the North-West Mounted Police (Francis 1992, 61–82; Mackey 1999, 34–5; Hill-Tout 1907, 25–7). The truth of the matter, as American legal scholar Cyrus Thomas (1899, 539) established long ago, was that all European empires made public declarations of their good intentions towards the Indians, and all European empires were comparably unwilling or unable to keep their word.

Canada has evolved its own version of the Black Legend and the white legend, in which the United States substitutes for Spain. Canada settled its territory peacefully, the new white legend contends, while the United States fought many bloody Indian wars for greed and gold. Canada has been 'gentle, tolerant, just and impartial' in its treatment of its First Nations (Mackey 1999, 39), a statement which implies that Americans have been cruel, biased, and selfish. Through this alchemy, Canada claims superior legitimacy as a country made, and still ruled by, its earliest waves of immigrants. 'More than anything else there was a sense of national self-congratulation,' Eva Mackey recalls of the Centennial celebrations of 1967; "we" Canadians had a kinder, better, more international, more inclusive nation than the United States' (ibid., 63).

Ambivalence

Canadians have somehow disengaged their sense of national self-respect from any contemporary awareness of Aboriginal peoples. Respondents to a recent Macleans/CBC annual poll ranked Aboriginal peoples twelfth in terms of 'what makes us Canadian,' lower than the maple leaf flag, health care, 'the traditional family,' the wintry climate, hockey, gun control, Canada's role in international affairs, bilingualism, and 'multiculturalism,' in that order – albeit somewhat *higher* than either Canada's 'Christian heritage' or the queen (Wallace 1999, 49).

Daniel Francis (1992, 223) finds 'an ambivalence at the heart of our understanding of what Canadian civilization is all about.' It is a conflict between our sense of European cultural and intellectual superiority and the depressing human toll of Aboriginal peoples' dispossession, which is still apparent on reserves and city streets. 'On the one hand, the national dream has always been about not being Indian,' Francis explains. Settlers strove to transform the continent into a facsimile of the material comforts that many of them had left behind, or been denied, in their home countries.

On the other hand, Euro-American civilization has always had second thoughts. We have always been uncomfortable with our treatment of the Native peoples. But more than that, we have suspected that we could never be at home in America, because we were not Indians.

Vincent Massey (1948, 31) once identified what he saw as twenty-nine distinctly Canadian symbols. Eight of them are Aboriginal handicrafts, such as birch-bark scrolls, canoes, totem poles, moccasins, and lacrosse; five are associated with the fur trade. Half of what Massey considered genuinely Canadian is therefore more correctly Aboriginal.[2] Images of Aboriginal peoples still dominate Canada's souvenir market; 'Native aesthetics serves as a resource pool for Canadian identity, a pool that Canadians can dip into when they wish to give something "very Canadian" to someone else' (Keohane 1997, 61). Indeed, Canada has used Indians to *attract* tourism, beginning with the omnipresent prairie Indian chiefs on promotional posters of the Canadian Pacific Railway (Mackey 1999, 36).

Ambivalence is also evident in Canadian literature and folklore, where Aboriginal peoples are alternately depicted as ruthless savages and as virtuously 'natural,' often by the same writers (Woodcock 1989, 138–67; compare Moyles and Owram 1988, 167–85 on British writers). Alan Smith (1994, 198–200) sees ambivalence towards Aboriginal peoples as a psychological game of Euro-Canadian self-congratulation. The depiction of Aboriginal peoples as barbaric justified their inevitable conquest and disappearance, while their depiction as noble, tragic figures assuaged any guilt that Euro-Canadians might feel: 'it allowed them to derive satisfaction from the fact that they were sympathizing with the displaced while at the same time enabling them to feel superior,' both to their forebears and to, their victims, by virtue of their 'their tolerance and understanding' (ibid., 198). Indeed, Smith observes, there has been a long-standing tendency to characterize Indians as partners in the defence of the empire – that is, against the United States. Albeit doomed, the savages did their part to protect their betters.

Indians themselves played little part in this psychosocial drama until a generation ago, when Aboriginal writers and artists began to receive national attention as a result of the new 'multicultural' self-consciousness of Canadian leaders and intellectuals. Indian and Inuit art occupy most of Canada's public spaces, but is this mere decoration or, what is worse, state-sponsored appropriation? Imperial cities since Ur and Babylon have filled their *agoras*, temples, and museums with art looted from conquered territories to advertise their triumphs. Vanquished nations' artisans and scholars were carried back in chains to create new works flattering their captors; an example is the Greeks who spent bitter centuries obliging the Romans. Patronizing Aboriginal art is a way of possessing Aboriginal culture and taking symbolic possession of Canada; it is a manifestation of Canadian ambivalence (Mackey 1999, 82–5).

Decency and Order

What kind of a society can continue to amass other peoples and cultures without being transformed or overthrown by them? The apparent historical stability of Canada, in spite of its growing, refractory diversity, suggests one of two plausible explanations. It is conceivable that Canadian institutions are so perfectly just, and the Canadian economy so rewarding, that dissatisfaction would be irrational. This is the explanation promoted by a majority of federalist leaders today. The alternative explanation is that Canadians simply eschew dissent and abhor confrontation; continuity is preferred to change. Diversity will be accommodated, provided that it keeps to itself.

The challenge of Canadian identity has roots in the American Revolution and the choice that Loyalists made to defend an old monarchy against an upstart republic. What did constitutional monarchy offer to settlers in a new world? Tradition, stability, and an established legal order: 'peace, order and good government,' the same terms proffered to Aboriginal nations by the Victorian treaty commissions. But Canada is not the United Kingdom; it grew on different soil from a somewhat different combination of peoples and cultures. Even if Canada had not developed in the shadow of the United States, it would undoubtedly have developed a sense of distance from its British roots, as Australia and New Zealand did.

As Canada gradually coalesced as a territory in the nineteenth century, British visitors were struck by the 'Americanization' of Canadians' everyday lives (Moyles and Owram 1988, 218–23). Although Canada retained the Westminster system of government and its devotion to the empire, there was a manifest, distressing lack of propriety in their social manners. Canadians seemed too democratic, too middle-class, and 'unashamedly materialistic.' In the presence of aristocrats, Canadians were said to be alarmingly familiar to the point of rudeness. Yet from a Canadian perspective, measured always in the U.S. mirror, the truth was precisely the reverse: Canadians maintained high standards of moral decency and circumspection. The Americans were rude and crude.

During the Second World War, Vincent Massey (1948, 3) maintained that Canadians were distinguishable from Americans by their 'self-control, an air of discipline and good manners.' This moderate and decent 'Canadian type' transcended Canadians' ethnic and linguistic diversity, Massey maintained, reflecting Canada's stronger, unbroken political relationship with the British Isles. Until Canada's social-welfare revolution in the 1950s, Canada remained 'a country ruled by tradition' and by traditional elites, Dominique Clift (1989, 189–90) has argued, and one in which the imperial pledge of peace, order, and good government trumped individual rights in public attitudes and official policies.

International survey data show that Canadians *are* unusually sensitive to political extremism (Nevitte 1996, 238). This may reflect a Canadian perception that the state is relatively fragile. More likely, as Clift (1989, 16–17) suggests, Canadians persist in a Millsian, monarchical view of the state as benevolent and protective – a firm but fair welfare state, which must place some restrictions on diversity and conflict for the general good. By contrast, Americans prefer greater freedom of action, and trust in the free play of competitive political and economic forces. Ironically, then, Americans may conceive of themselves as a melting pot, but American ideology is generally *more* compatible with cultural diversity than the Canadian endorsement of authority, tradition, moderation, and social security. To the extent that Canadians demand more state socio-economic support, they implicitly demand a more managed, homogeneous society as well.

Kieran Keohane (1997, 165) has used the clever metaphor of the 'restaurant at the end of the Trans-Canada Highway,' where the decor is discretely bland and the tables are spaced at a modest distance. The diners avoid eye contact and keep their voices lowered. Every cuisine is represented, and you can eat whatever you like in modest amounts and tranquil security. Is this the end of Canada?

Multilateralism

The pursuit of domestic tranquillity means that Canadians must go abroad to seek revolutionary challenges and test their ideals. As a career diplomat concluded, 'the face that Canada presents to the world is what enables Canadians of all cultures to recognize each other, particularly abroad, and to distinguish themselves from any other nationality' (Andrew 1993, 165). Lacking a revolutionary ideology or a unified cultural nationalism, Canada looks for its identity in others' eyes, and measures its value and legitimacy against its works overseas. Seeking respect is accordingly an implicit factor in Canadian foreign policy. Thus, Lyon and Ismael (1976, xlvi) can argue that 'a Canada that did more to close the gap between rich and poor countries, and to contain violence, would be *more secure in her identity* and more confident of an independent future' (emphasis added; see also Melakopides 1998, 192–3).

Americans also groom themselves in the mirror of international affairs, but they seek a different kind of respect: as a great military power and the 'defenders of the free world.' By the reverse logic that has become inescapable in U.S.-Canadian relationships, Canada plays Cinderella to the United States's evil stepsister. If Americans confidently aspire to monopoly leadership of the world, Canadians will promote multilateralism and co-operation. Gérard Bergeron (1979, 54) observes: 'Le nationalisme pan-canadien s'affirme de plus en plus sur le plan international [et] il tend même à prendre l'allure d'un anti-américanisme, non pas certes virulent mais systématique.'

Lester Pearson identified Canada's 'international personality and prestige' as the country's most important achievement since Confederation, rivalling its high standard of living and undiminished loyalty to the crown (Pearson 1964, 253–4). Pearson was very conscious of the growing role of 'middle powers' in the post-1945 world of superpowers and poor, newly emancipated former colonies (Pearson 1969, 75–7). Canada has clearly been a middle power, but as a matter of principle or necessity? Massey (1948, 86) argued that 'peace means more to us than to many countries' because of Canada's inability to defend itself, even from its large southern neighbour. Canadian scholars have questioned Canada's commitment and consistency in the fields of human rights, the eradication of poverty, and international security. Linda Freeman (1997) concludes that Canadian leaders were ambivalent about efforts to dismantle apartheid in South Africa and Southern Rhodesia, for example, while Robert Matthews and Cranford Pratt (1988, 293) conclude that 'on balance there appears to have been a persistent bias against attaching much importance to human rights.'

'Canadians must first make up their own minds about what kind of society they want and how they propose to get it; then only will they see clearly how to harmonize their external and domestic policies,' F.R. Scott (1938, 151) observed prophetically at the last pre-war British Commonwealth Relations Conference. 'Canada is searching for a new basis on which to re-establish her national unity,' he explained, 'and until she finds it she has no accepted internal criterion with which to measure her external obligations.' What happened since Scott's time, I suggest, is that Canadians *did* render their judgment on the question of 'a new basis [for] national unity,' and it was not about justice.

In fact, while human rights and multiculturalism were becoming central issues in domestic politics in the 1970s, the main focus of Canadian diplomacy shifted from peace and security to trade promotion, domestic growth, and co-existence with the United States (Thordarson 1972; Matthew and Pratt 1988). This was good electoral politics: Canadians were achieving a high level of consensus on the need to increase employment (Schwartz 1967, 99). 'Canadian policy, just as much as that of any other nation, is determined by its national self-interest,' a study by the Canadian Institute of International Affairs concluded, and 'by fortunate coincidence, this has generally managed to put Canada on the side of the angels' (Reford 1968, 238). Canada has pursued a program of 'enlightened self-interest' in which concern for the underprivileged has won Canada influence, access and resources denied to the superpowers (Melakopides 1998, 191–3). This was only possible in a Cold War world order in which leadership and expertise counted for more than sheer size and military strength (Cooper, Higgott, and Nossal 1993, 172–3). After the collapse of the Soviet Union and emergence of a U.S.-dominated world regime in the 1990s, Canada lost much of its distinctive advantage and much of its idealism. Enlightened self-interest yielded to 'Team Canada' and a trade-dominated agenda (Andrew 1993, 165).

Canada has nonetheless cultivated a national myth of global good citizenship since the Pearson years. 'Sometimes naïvely, but with unquestioned sincerity, Canadians on the whole retained their own vision of the world' after 1945, according to Ivan Head and Pierre Elliott Trudeau (1995, 6). 'It was a vision that featured decency, fair play, and a role for rational initiatives.' As I have shown elsewhere, however, Canadian initiatives at the United Nations increasingly encountered resistance created by the Aboriginal political movement at home (Barsh 1995). Canadian diplomats confronted a growing perception that Canada was (as an Indonesian colleague once told me), 'no better than the rest of us.'

Multiculturalism

John Murray Gibbon, who coined the term 'mosaic' as a description of Canadian society, argued that Canada had become a 'refuge' for victims of persecution in Europe. This shared experience, together with a public spirit of tolerance and a national system of public education, would be the 'cement' of national unity (Gibbon 1938, 414, 425). In this version of Canadian history, British traditions of civility and fair play attracted immigrants, implicitly building a more diverse and tolerant society than the United States (Mackey 1999, 34).

Vincent Massey (1948, 24) agreed. 'We have a tradition of tolerance in Canada,' he argued; indeed, 'to no other country in the world does tolerance mean more than to ours.' Although he conceded that 'tolerance alone will not solve our problems for us,' Massey was optimistic that 'it will enable us to approach them in the spirit that brings about solutions,' which is to say a spirit of compromise. 'Nothing is more characteristic of Canadians than the inclination to moderation,' he noted; 'we are not given to extremes in Canada' (ibid. 30). Massey's association of tolerance with moderation is significant in that it implicitly attributes Canada's stability to the passivity of its elites. Immigrants are not welcomed, but tolerated, by established Canadians; and once here, they are expected to become moderate themselves, rather than challenging the Canadian power structure.

Most Canadians today believe that tolerance is a good thing, and more Canadians believe in tolerance today than a generation ago (Nevitte 1996, 223–8). Canadians, however, actually fall in the mid-range of Western countries with respect to their self-reported belief in the importance of tolerance. 'By these measures, Canadians *are* relatively tolerant, but there is nothing to suggest that tolerance is a uniquely Canadian national trait' (ibid., 238). If Canada is better than other countries it must be due to a more active engagement with cultural diversity than mere tolerance.

'Multiculturalism' has become such a mainstay of Canadian policy discourse that it is easy to forget that it has only been with us since Pierre Elliott Trudeau responded to the report of the Royal Commission on Bilingualism and Multiculturalism (Day 2000, 188–9). Trudeau moved Canada from its bilingual 'duopoly' to a broader conception of cultural rights as an element of individual freedom: 'multiculturalism within a bilingual framework.' Multiculturalism may have weakened the inherently polarizing effect of the 'two founding nations' discourse, but it alienated other groups who were seeking specific recognition, such as First Nations (Mackey 1999, 63–4).

At one extreme, multiculturalism implies a community of communities, or what Gandhi once described as 'an oceanic circle of villages,' bound together by mutual self-interest in commerce and defence, sharing only an minimal core of civic values (Smith 1994, 209). Canadian philosophers Will Kimlycka (1995) and James Tully (1995) have defended the logic of a constitutional framework of geometric equality, arguing that it is not necessarily incompatible with liberal values such as individual freedom and mobility. Indeed, robust multiculturalism implies a dynamic democracy in which Canadian values must change as Canadian demography changes: a never-ending process of compromise and accommodation (Angus 1997, 167). Such a Canada would truly be the world's 'first postmodern state' (Gwyn 1995, 243).

Critics of multiculturalism neither defend intolerance nor dispute the contribution of diversity to Canadian life. Rather, some argue that emphasizing ethnic differences and historical injustices weakens Canadians' sense of shared interests, which are necessary for compromise and cooperation (Bibby 1990; Fairfield 2000, 111). Other critics focus on the growth of the state's role as a cultural entrepreneur, which they fear will suppress creativity and standardize cultures (Cannon 1995, 245; Mackey 1999, 62–5). In any case, political and business leaders continue to speak as if *real* Canadians are either French or English (Karim 1993). They may also mention Aboriginal peoples, who serve as the officially designated underprivileged class. At the bottom of the pyramid, there is a *residual* category of hyphenated multicultural Canadians – the same eastern European and non-white communities that have historically suffered exclusion (Bissoondath 1994; Mackey 1999, 150–1), reduced to mere folkloric elements.

Eva Mackey (1999, 150–1) contends that multiculturalism represents a strategic shift from 'the erasure of culture difference [to] the proper management of culture – a hierarchy of cultures – within a *unified project.*' Within this project, high-status cultures (English and French) provide a core of unifying national ideals, while low-status cultures (Aboriginal, eastern European, Asian, African) are reduced to mere folkloric and artistic elements.

Multiculturalism is decidedly *not* what Canada practised before 1945. In the nineteenth century, the Canada First Movement claimed to represent the new 'Britain of the North,' superior to the United States because it was whiter, more Anglo-Saxon, less contaminated by Asian and African blood, its people culled through hardship and climate by a kind of natural selection to become tougher, stronger, and smarter than the Yanks (Berger 1966; Mackey 1999, 40–1). Early twentieth-century nationalists secured quotas and aggressively pursued the Anglicization of non-English immigrants (Hall 1977; Palmer 1982; Ward 1990; Mackey 1999, 32–4; Day 2000, 115–45, 156–70), although a common 'racial alloy' seemed increasingly elusive (Scott 1938, 24). Much of this kind of thinking survived until the 1960s (Smith 1994, 209–10).

In fact, multicultural Canada is nearly indistinguishable from the U.S. melting pot, except 'in the realm of ritual and symbolism' (Smith 1994, 219–23). Aboriginal people may have gained the opportunity to speak for themselves, and be seen more in public in connection with national icons, but this is not the same as wielding any power over their destiny; nevertheless, the emergence of Aboriginal voices in the arts and politics allows Canadians to feel that they have achieved something (Mackey 1999, 87).

Human Rights

The real story is Canadians' need to be perceived, and to perceive themselves, as more tolerant than Americans, more tolerant than their forebears, and more tolerant than other nations and peoples generally. What motivates this quest for national beatitude? If Canadians feel the need for a national virtue, what is it about *goodness* (as opposed to wealth or beauty or a fine sense of humour) that remains so appealing? I suggest that it is Canadians' response to their memory of Aboriginal peoples, and to Aboriginal peoples' increasing numbers, visibility, and assertiveness.

A country with a clear conscience does not go out of its way to defend its honour. Nor does it engage in hyperbole to convince others that it is not only innocent but also utterly incapable of sinning. In the year that the United Nations adopted the Universal Declaration of Human Rights, Vincent Massey wrote:

There is a continuity of principle which runs straight from the beginning [of Canada] to the present. The best example of this is the individual contribution we have made to the cause of freedom. Our French-speaking fellow-countrymen won freedom for their faith and language in Canada. The United Empire Loyalists found freedom here to live as they pleased. Canada achieved freedom for herself and in finding it quite unconsciously played a vital part in the creation of what came to be known as the British Commonwealth. We often forget our relationship to that monumental conception which has given the world so great a pattern of political liberty. *Canada was the laboratory in which this discovery took place.* (emphasis added; Massey 1948, 13)

It may seem strange today to think of Canada as the fountain of world freedom through its role in decolonizing the British Empire. The idealization of Canada as a beacon of hope to the world has remained with us, however.

The new idealism envisions Canada as a place 'to communicate with the world rather than to conquer it' (Powe 1997, 105). 'If we begin to perceive our strengths in the history of communications, in debate and experimentation, in the resistance to violent resolutions and arbitrary systems, then we may say that Canada is light, unburdened by constitutional weight and records of viciousness' (ibid. 101). Stéphane Dion (1996, 102–3) has defended national unity in similar terms, explaining that 'the reason I consider myself so fortunate to be Canadian is not because of what is distinctive and particular to this country, but because of our achievement of universal human ideals. Canada is the greatest example of what the world must become in terms of tolerance, openness, and capacity for harmony between different communities ... Canada is considered the world over to be a model of generosity and openness. Let us live up to our reputation and send the rest of the world a positive signal of reconciliation.'

As Peyton Lyon and Brian Tomlin (1979, 77) have observed, 'Canadians like to be liked' more than do other people. Wittingly or unwittingly, Canada has deployed a self-image of wholesomeness abroad (Lyon and Tomlin 1979, 83). Canada's neighbours are not entirely convinced, however, nor are large numbers of Canadians.

Two-thirds of the respondents to an Angus Reid survey of 4,510 citizens in sixteen of the most industrialized countries in 1992 agreed that Canadians are tolerant of minorities; however, one-fifth *strongly* agreed that Canada mistreats its Aboriginal peoples (Reid 1992, 29–30). Only one-sixth of the respondents strongly agreed that Canada is a world leader in the protection of human rights (ibid., 43). A larger proportion of Canadian respondents were convinced that Canada is tolerant (82 per cent), but a larger proportion of Canadian respondents also *strongly* agreed that Canada mistreats Aboriginal peoples (28 per cent; ibid., 81–2).

Similarly, three-fourths of the 1,200 Canadians who responded to the 1999 *Maclean's*/CBC year-end poll identified the need to improve Aboriginal peoples' economic welfare (social services, employment, and taxes) as the most important problem facing Canada (Wallace 1999, 48), rather than justice or unity at home or peace abroad. A year later, a majority of respondents to the 2000 *Maclean's*/CBC year-end poll strongly supported the idea of spending tax dollars on subsidizing Canadian skilled jobs (58 per cent), as opposed to international peacekeeping (48 per cent), environmental protection (44 per cent), eliminating homelessness (42 per cent), or affirmative action in employment (24 per cent; Sheppard 2000, 54).[3] Canada has become a stereotypically middle-class country, preoccupied with individual material gain.

Canadians persist in the belief that they have achieved a high level of justice, and this belief enables them to pursue a more egocentric and materialistic agenda than before. Twenty years ago, 36 per cent of Canadians believed that discrimination had *never* been a problem in Canada and 9 per cent stated that it had been a problem only in the past (Bibby 1983). Public education may have eroded Canadians' belief in a just past, but this belief has been replaced by greater confidence in a just present. The latest *Maclean's*/CBC year-end poll found that 66 per cent of Canadians believe that there have been improvements in the treatment of 'visible minorities' since 1975 (Sheppard 2000, 54) – despite the fact that as many as one in four Canadians have experienced some form of discrimination (Bibby 1990).[4]

Contradictions

Since 1989, when a public inquiry attributed the wrongful conviction of Donald Marshall, Jr to racism, Canadians have been confronted by mounting evidence of past and continuing iniquities towards Aboriginal peoples. According to the Royal Commission on Aboriginal Peoples (1996, xxv), 'contemporary Canadians reject the paternalism of yesterday and recognize that Aboriginal people know best how to define and promote their own interests.' However, public support for redress remains relatively low. Self-congratulation is deployed as a defence against unpleasant facts.

Decima Research and the University of Calgary conducted in-home, face-to-face surveys of Canadians' attitudes towards Aboriginal peoples in 1976 and 1986 (Ponting 1988). In 1976, 72 per cent of the respondents agreed that 'Indians deserve to be a lot better off economically,' but this had fallen to 48 per cent by 1986. Support for Indian control of school programs fell from 35 to 22 per cent. There was also a decline in public support for 'special cultural protection' for Indians, and greater opposition to the settlement of land claims. One-third of the respondents to the 1986 poll were opposed to 'Native self-government.' Fewer than half of the respondents were in favour of giving more resources or rights for Aboriginal peoples. On most questions, moreover, few respondents had strong views; in other words, Canadians are largely *indifferent* to Aboriginal peoples.

Langford and Ponting (1992) re-analysed the 1986 Decima survey data and found that respondents' beliefs about national unity and multiculturalism were *not* good predictors of their attitudes towards Aboriginal peoples. Respondents who opposed more Aboriginal rights also tended to feel that Aboriginal people already enjoy a lot of political power; that ordinary Canadian working people deserve more government aid; and that Indians are 'a bunch of complainers.'[5] Many Canadians seem to feel that they are competing with Aboriginal peoples for a limited fund of state aid. This is consistent with polls that indicate Canadians put a priority on their own economic status and on strengthening the state's role to provide them with economic security.

Canadian ambivalence towards Aboriginal peoples is also evident in Angus Reid surveys of Canadian attitudes conducted in 1998 (Martin and Adams 2000). One-third of the respondents strongly agreed that Canada should give priority to achieving Aboriginal self-government. One-third also agreed that Aboriginal governments should have the same kinds of legislative powers as the federal government. Yet a majority (55 per cent) believed that Aboriginal peoples would be better off simply assimilating into mainstream Canadian society, and this view was strongest in Alberta (72 per cent), British Columbia (65 per cent), and Quebec (62 per cent). Support for Aboriginal autonomy was strongest among older and better-educated Canadians, who may feel they have greater personal socio-economic security.

Similarly, one-third of the respondents to a 1997 Thompson Lightstone national opinion poll 'strongly opposed' increased funding for First Nations self-government, and one-sixth 'strongly opposed' First Nations self-government altogether. Responses were particularly negative in Quebec, where Aboriginal peoples continue to be identified as an obstacle to the aspirations of Québécois (Salée 1995; Laczko 1997; Barsh 1997),[6] and in Saskatchewan, where Aboriginal peoples are highly visible in provincial politics.

Ambivalence divides Canadians psychologically, politically, and demographically. Individual Canadians hold inconsistent beliefs and attitudes about Aboriginal peoples, acknowledging the virtue of policy reform while opposing initiatives that might tax their own pocketbooks. Canadians are almost equally divided between supporters and opponents of greater

Aboriginal power, although opponents tend to be most numerous in Quebec and the west. It is easy to appreciate Ottawa's preference for a strategy of self-congratulation: acknowledging the primacy of justice but insisting that justice has already been done – and, for that matter, done better than anywhere else in the world.

Rites of Passage

Until the 1960s, most immigrants to Canada were Europeans. Trudeau introduced multiculturalism just as South and East Asian immigration surged (Nevitte 1996, 17) and Aboriginal peoples built a nation-wide coalition for land and treaty rights (Cardinal 1977). White Canadians were invited to stake their identity on tolerance at precisely the moment that Canadian demography and politics were 'browning.' It was an ambivalent historical moment, which produced ambivalent results: broad popular commitment to an ideal, with little change in actual social behaviour.

Since the 1970s, Aboriginal peoples have challenged Canadian justice, and thus Canadian identity, not only through domestic political action but also through campaigns on the international stage (Barsh 1995). Every post-war initiative to build a mooring for Canadian identity – multilateralism, multiculturalism, tolerance, and human rights – has foundered on the rocks of Aboriginal criticism. The presence of Aboriginal peoples has intensified, undermining Canadians' efforts to be perceived as good and reverberating with the increasing challenges of Canada's growing ethnic diversity. Aboriginal peoples neither assimilate nor succeed: they are forever a skeleton in the closet of Canadian ambitions.

The panels on the Dominion Memorial Sculpture in Parliament's Hall of Honour, designed in 1932, reflect a familiar historical perspective. The story begins with a child-like Indian living in a state of nature; subsequent panels depict (white) settlers mapping and transforming the landscape – converting nature into civilization. (Mackey 1999, 37–8). Indians shrink to the background as mere spectators, and then disappear completely. Canada owes its conscience to the fact that Aboriginal peoples have *not* disappeared, but remain as witnesses to the efforts of successive waves of immigrants to create a country –witnesses who have grown increasingly outspoken and critical. I imagine an additional panel for the Dominion Memorial Sculpture, an update for the early twentieth century, showing Elijah Harper holding his eagle feather as he cast the deciding vote in the Manitoba Assembly on the Meech Lake Accord. The message: *we are still with you, and you cannot have a country without us.*

James Tully (1995) has invoked Bill Reid's famous sculptural representation of the Haida canoe as a metaphor for a genuinely post-colonial Canada. In Reid's great black canoe, conveniently displayed at the Canadian Embassy in Washington, D.C., for Americans to ponder, a diverse crew of humans and animals hold the oars. The canoe has no commander; dialogue and compromise settle the course. Daniel Francis (1997, 128–51) suggests a darker interpretation of this sculpture. A canoe journey into the wilderness is a persistent trope in Canadian literature and folklore: 'the canoe carries us out of our European past deep into the wilderness where we are reborn as citizens of the New World' (ibid., 129). The canoe symbolizes a spiritual journey in search of national as well as personal identity, and a journey that is uniquely Canadian.

Like their immigrant forebears, Euro-Canadians are drawn to the wilderness – *the frontier* – because it lies beyond the borders of maps, outside the world of books, a place without labels, laws, or institutions; a place of unseen dangers, but also infinite possibilities. Europeans came to the wilderness with ambivalence in their hearts. They left Europe because they wanted something different, yet they reproduced the European landscape with all of its social conflicts wherever they went. The same ambivalence can be found in the writings of James Fenimore Cooper and his nineteenth-century contemporaries in the United States (Barsh 1996), but Americans got over it. They consumed the land and went on to achieve happiness as a dominant world power. Canadians continue to ask the land for a spiritual gift (Saul 1997, 185–96).

For Aboriginal peoples, there was no wilderness, nor was there any need for one. For them, the territory we now call Canada was a familiar, socially constructed landscape, densely embedded with stories and kinship (Barsh and Dormaar 2001). As long as Canadians see a wilderness extending beyond their cities and towns, they do not belong to the land and will continue to view Aboriginal peoples ambivalently, with envy and sometimes disgust. Before Canadians can feel comfortable with themselves and their territory, and cast away their obsessions with identity and goodness, Canada needs a rite of passage, a cathartic experience, through which non-Aboriginal Canadians earn Aboriginal peoples' respect.

I am not referring to 'truth and reconciliation,' at least in the way this concept has developed in South Africa. As the eminent Nigerian poet and playwright Wole Soyinka (1999) has explained, the South African process has sought truth but stopped far short of reconciliation. Reconciliation is more than a confession or apology, Soyinka contends; it must include some form of restitution. Beneficiaries of injustice must be willing to share their wealth and privileges with the victims; they must believe that by sharing, they, too, gain something: trust and a shared country.

Canada Unwrapped

In *Moses and Monotheism*, Sigmund Freud speculated that the Jews' experiences of oppression over the ages had made them keenly sensitive to the importance of justice – not only for themselves but also for others. If a tragic past can have this effect on the descendants of the victims, can it sometimes have the same effect on descendants of the oppressors? Young Germans suggest that this is the case. Deprived of a reputable national legacy, many have chosen to make a clear moral break with the past. They support the punishment of war criminals, finance the reconstruction of eastern Europe, and flock to various social movements. Others have chosen to deny or glorify their past, as skinheads and neo-Nazis; or to disguise their German nationality and pretend to be Aboriginal people as members of 'Indian clubs.' Justice is highly salient for these young Germans, but their historical conscience manifests itself in contradictory ways.

This, I believe, is also the case in Canada: our national conscience gives rise to both love and hate for Aboriginal peoples. It polarizes, and thereby seems to deprive, Canadians of any neat solution. Are Canadians condemned to what Richard Day (2000, 178) has aptly described as 'unhappy countriness'?

Canadian philosopher John Ralston Saul (1997, 81) refers to a 'triangular reality' in contemporary Canada: a shifting balance of power among anglophones, francophones and Aboriginal peoples. He argues that Canada's leaders must learn to abandon ethnonationalism; a 'colonial mind-set' that emphasizes bureaucratic economy, stability, certainty, and order; and the categorical thinking generally associated with Platonic intellectual traditions. Instead, he advocates a Socratic paradigm of persistent dialogue in which truth emerges dialectically from multiple perspectives (ibid., 443–53, 464).

I agree. Canada will never be able to say to the world, 'We fixed that and it is behind us – now we *are* truly the most tolerant and just nation on earth.' This is not a uniquely Canadian misfortune. No state has survived for long without internal adjustments or realignments; states survive by being flexible enough to change without resorting to extreme violence. When Canada is finally unwrapped, then, will it simply be like any other liberal-democratic society? Yes and no. A future Canada will necessarily be flexible and responsive like other societies, but it will (I suggest) always be unusually sensitive to issues of justice.

Canada continually tries to use Aboriginal peoples to assuage its conscience, and they continually disappoint Canadians by reasserting their claims with redoubled force. Aboriginal peoples have not given Canadians a *good* conscience as such; rather, they have created a dialectic about justice in Canadian society that refuses to go away and forces Canadians to continue to grapple in each generation with the problem of doing something to demonstrate, in some meaningful and lasting way, that Canada is Canada because Canadians firmly choose to be just. This may not make Canada unique among countries, but it will make Canada an important and influential country.

'Conscience is much more than a guide for human behaviour; at the conclusion of the twentieth century, it is the elevated – and only certain – path towards the survival of civilization' (Head and Trudeau 1995, 319).

Notes

1 Indeed, it was only in the early years of the twentieth century that leading British Columbians such as Emily Carr began to think of themselves as 'Canadian' at all (Magaret A. Ormsby, *British Columbia A History* [Vancouver: Macmillan 1958], 329, 402).

2 Only five of Massey's 'Canadian' symbols are distinctly Québécois. It may be argued that Metis are the most *genuine* Canadians, since they are a hybrid people of multiple European and Indigenous ancestries (Nicolas van Schendel, 'L'identité métisse ou l'histoire oubliée de la canadianité.' In Jocelyn Létourneau, ed., *La question identitaire au Canada francophone: récits, parcours, enjeux, lors-lieux* [Sainte-Foy, Que.: Presses de l'Université Laval 1994] 101–21). Yet they, too, have been banished to the margins of Canadian society.

3 A decade earlier, a majority (57 per cent) of Canadians identified (in descending order) pollution, unemployment, free trade, the national debt, and moral integrity as Canada's 'most important problems,' (Decima Research, 1989). References to immigration, multiculturalism, and Aboriginal peoples were negligible. But Canadians polled in 1985 were more concerned about freedom, than material comfort (Reginald W. Bibby, *Mosaic Madness: The Poverty and Potential of Life in Canada* [Toronto: Stoddart 1990], 158). Johnson (Richard Johnson, *Public Opinion and Public Policy in Canada: Questions of Confidence* [Toronto: University of Toronto Press 1986], 19) argues that, until the 1970s, Canadians viewed big government as a greater threat to their well-being than big business. Echoes of mistrust of government were detected in the Angus Reid poll: Canadians were no more confident in their freedom of speech or judicial system than Russians or Americans (Angus Reid, *Canada and the World: An International Perspective on Canada and Canadians* [Toronto: Canadian Institute of International Affairs 1992], 122–5).

4 A 1989 *Maclean's* poll reported only 11 per cent victimization (Decima Research, *Canadian-American Survey, 1989*), and other surveys have reported figures somewhere in-between. This presumably reflects the effects of survey methods (phone, mail, face-to-face) and the phrasing of questions.

5 Bibby's 1981 survey similarly found that nearly one-third of Canadians felt that Indians were lazy and undeserving of further rights or benefits (Bibby, *Mosaic Madness*).

6 Quebeckers were *more* supportive of Aboriginal peoples than were other Canadians in 1986 (J. Rick Ponting, 'Public Opinion on Aboriginal Peoples' Issues in Canada,' *Canadian Social Trends* [winter 1998]: 9–17 at 16), and more supportive of Aboriginal self-government in 1998 (David Martin and Chris Adams, 'Canadian Public Opinion Regarding Aboriginal Self-Government: Diverging Viewpoints as Found in National Survey Results,' *American Review of Canadian Studies* 30, no. 1 [2000]: 79–88 at 81), despite some public blame of Aboriginal people for the failure of the 1995 referendum on sovereignty (Russel L. Barsh, 'Aboriginal Peoples and Quebec: Competing for Legitimacy as Emerging Nations, *American Indian Culture and Research Journal*, 21, no. 1 [1997]: 1–29).

Bibliography

Andrew, Arthur. 1993. *The Rise and Fall of a Middle Power: Canadian Diplomacy from King to Mulroney.* Toronto: James Lorimer and Company.

Angus, Ian. 1997. *A Border Within: National Identity, Cultural Plurality, and Wilderness.* Montreal and Kingston: McGill-Queen's University Press.

Barsh, Russel L. 1997. 'Aboriginal Peoples and Quebec: Competing for Legitimacy as Emerging Nations.' *American Indian Culture & Research Journal*, 21, no.1: 1–29.

– 1996. 'James Fenimore Cooper in Canada.' *Literary Review of Canada* 5, no.1: 11–13.

– 1995. 'The Aboriginal Issue in Canadian Foreign Policy.' *International Journal of Canadian Studies* 12: 107–33.

– 1994. 'The Legal Significance of U.S. Indian Treaties.' In Duane Champagne ed., *The Native North American Almanac*. Detroit: Gale Research, 461–86.

Barsh, Russel L., and John F. Dormaar. 2001. *The Prairie Landscape: Perceptions of Reality.* Prairie Conservation Forum, Occasional Paper no.3. Edmonton.

Berger, Carl. 1996. 'The True North Strong and Free.' In Peter Russell, ed., *Nationalism in Canada*. Toronto: McGraw-Hill, 3–260

Bergeron, Gérard. 1974. *Incertitudes d'un certain pays: le Québec et le Canada dans le monde (1958–1978).* Quebec: Presses de l'Université Laval.

Bibby, Reginald W. 1990. *Mosaic Madness; The Poverty and Potential of Life in Canada.* Toronto: Stoddart.

– 1983. 'The Precarious Mosaic: Divergence and Convergence in the Canadian 80s.' *Social Indicators Research*, 12, no.2: 169–81.

Bissoondath, Neil. 1994. *Selling Illusions: The Cult of Multiculturalism in Canada.* Toronto: Penguin Books.

Cannon, Margaret. 1995. *The Invisible Empire: Racism in Canada.* Toronto: Random House.

Cardinal, Harold. 1977. *The Rebirth of Canada's Indians.* Edmonton: Hurtig.

Clarke, George Elliott. 1998. 'White Like Canada.' *Transition; An International Review* 73: 98–109.

Clift, Dominique. 1989. *The Secret Kingdom: Interpretations of the Canadian Character*. Toronto: McClelland and Stewart.

Cooper, Andrew F., Richard A. Higgott, and Kim R. Nossal. 1993. *Relocating Middle Powers: Australia and Canada in a Changing World Order*. Vancouver:University of British Columbia Press.

Day, Richard J.F. 2000. *Multiculturalism and the History of Canadian Diversity*. Toronto: University of Toronto Press.

Decima Research. 1989. *Canadian-American Survey, 1989*. Storrs, Conn.: Roper Center for Public Opinion Research.

Dion, Stéphane. 1999. *Straight Talk on Canadian Unity*. Montreal and Kingston: McGill-Queen's University Press.

Fairfield, Paul. 2000. 'Nationalism and the Politics of Identity.' In G.B. Madison, Paul Fairfield, and Ingrid Harris, ed., *Is There a Canadian Philosophy?* Ottawa: University of Ottawa Press, 89–116.

Francis, Daniel. 1992. *The Imaginary Indian; The Image of the Indian in Canadian Culture*. Vancouver: Arsenal Pulp Press.

– 1997. *National Dreams: Myth, Memory, and Canadian History*. Vancouver: Arsenal Pulp Press.

Freeman, Linda. 1997. *An Ambiguous Champion: Canada and South Africa in the Trudeau and Mulroney Years*. Toronto: University of Toronto Press.

Gibbon, John Murray. 1938. *Canadian Mosaic; The Making of a Northern Nation*. New York: Dodd, Mead.

Gwyn, Richard. 1995. *Nationalism without Walls: The Unbearable Lightness of Being Canadian*. Toronto: McClelland and Stewart.

Hall, D.J. 1997. 'Clifford Sifton: Immigration and Settlement Policy.' In Howard Palmer, ed., *The Settlement of the West*. Calgary: University of Calgary, 60–85.

Head, Ivan L., and Pierre Elliott Trudeau. 1995. *The Canadian Way; Shaping Canada's Foreign Policy, 1968–1984*. Toronto: McClelland and Stewart.

Hill-Tout, C. 1907. *Native Races of the British Empire: British North America 1, The Far West, Home of the Salish and Déné*. London: Archibald Constable.

Howard-Hassman, Rhoda E. 1999. '"Canadian" as an Ethnic Category: Implications for Multiculturalism and National Unity.' *Canadian Public Policy/Analyse de Politiques* 25, no.4: 523–37.

Johnston, Richard. 1986. *Public Opinion and Public Policy in Canada: Questions of Confidence*. Toronto: University of Toronto Press.

Kagan, Richard L. 1996. 'Prescott's Paradigm: American Historical Scholarship and the Decline of Spain.' *American Historical Review* 101, no.2: 423–446.

Karim, Karim H. 1993. 'Reconstructing the Multicultural Community in Canada: Discursive Strategies of Inclusion and Exclusion.' *International Journal of Politics, Culture and Society*, 7, no.2: 189–207.

Keating, Thomas F. 1993. *Canada and World Order: The Multilateralist Tradition in Canadian Foreign Policy*. Toronto: McClelland and Stewart.

Keohane, Kieran. 1997. *Symptoms of Canada: An Essay on the Canadian Identity*. Toronto: University of Toronto Press.

Kymlicka, Will. 1995. *Multicultural Citizenship*. Oxford, U.K.: Oxford University Press.

Laczko, Leslie S. 1999. 'Attitudes towards Aboriginal Issues in Canada: The Changing Role of the Language Cleavage.' *Québec Studies*, 23: 3–12.

Langford, Tom, and J. Rick Ponting. 1996. 'Canadians' Responses to Aboriginal Issues: The Roles of Prejudice, Perceived Group Conflict and Economic Conservatism.' *Canadian Review of Sociology and Anthropology/Revue canadiènne de sociologie et anthropologie*, 29, no.2: 140–66.

Lyon, Peyton V., and Brian W Tomlin. 1979. *Canada as an International Actor*. Toronto: Macmillan.

– and Tareq Y. Ismael, ed. 1976. *Canada and the Third World*. Toronto: Macmillan.

Mackey, Eva. 1999. *The House of Difference: Cultural Politics and National Identity in Canada*. London and New York: Routledge.

Martin, David, and Chris Adams. 2000. 'Canadian Public Opinion regarding Aboriginal Self-Government: Diverging Viewpoints as Found in National Survey Results.' *American Review of Canadian Studies*, 30, no.1: 79–88.

Massey, Vincent. 1948. *On Being Canadian*. Toronto and Vancouver: J.M. Dent and Sons.

Matthews, Robert O., and Cranford Pratt ed. 1988. *Human Rights in Canadian Foreign Policy*. Montreal and Kingston: McGill-Queen's University Press.

Melakopides, Costas. 1998. *Pragmatic Idealism: Canadian Foreign Policy, 1945–1995*. Montreal and Kingston: McGill-Queen's University Press.

Moyles, R.G., and Doug Owram. 1988. *Imperial Dreams and Colonial Realities: British Views of Canada, 1880–1914*. Toronto: University of Toronto Press.

Nevitte, Neil. 1996. *The Decline of Deference: Canadian Value Change in Cross-National Perspective*. Peterborough, Ont.: Broadview Press.

Ormsby, Margaret A. 1958. *British Columbia: A History*. Vancouver: Macmillan.

Palmer, Howard. 1982. *Patterns of Prejudice; A History of Nativism in Alberta*. Toronto: McClelland and Stewart.

Pearson, Lester B. 1964. *The Four Faces of Peace and the International Outlook*. New York: Dodd, Mead.

– 1969. *Peace in the Family of Man: The Reith Lectures 1968*. Toronto and New York: Oxford University Press.

Ponting, J. Rick. 1998. 'Public Opinion on Aboriginal Peoples' Issues in Canada.' *Canadian Social Trends* (winter): 9–17.

Powe, B[ruce] WA. 1997. *Canada of Light*. Toronto: Somerville House.

Reford, Robert W. 1968. *Canada and Three Crises*. Toronto: Canadian Institute of International Affairs.

Reid, Angus. 1997. *Canada and the World: An International Perspective on Canada and Canadians*. Winnipeg: Angus Reid Group.

Royal Commission on Aboriginal Peoples. 1996. *The Report of the Royal Commission on Aboriginal Peoples, Volume 1*. Ottawa: Queen's Printer.

Salée, Daniel. 1995. 'Identité québécoise, identité autochtone et territorialité: entre

les and frontières subjectives et objectives de l'espace québécois.' In Alain-G.
Gagnon and Alain Noël, ed., *L'espace québécois.* Montreal and Quebec: Editions
Québec/Amérique.

Saul, John Ralston. 1997. *Reflections of a Siamese Twin: Canada at the End of the Twentieth Century.* Toronto: Penguin Books Canada.

Schwartz, Mildred A. 1967. *Public Opinion and Canadian Identity.* Berkeley: University of California Press.

Scott, F.R. 1938. *Canada Today: A Study of Her National Interests and National Policy.*
Toronto: Oxford University Press.

Sheppard, Robert. 2000. 'We Are Canadian.' *Macleans Magazine,* 113, no.152 (25
Dec.): 26–32, 52–4.

Smith, Allan. 1994. *Canada – An American Nation? Essays on Continentalism, Identity,
and the Canadian Frame of Mind.* Montreal and Kingston: McGill-Queen's University Press.

Soyinka, Wole. 1999. *The Burden of Memory, the Muse of Forgiveness.* Oxford and New
York: Oxford University Press.

Thomas, Cyrus. 1899. 'Introduction' to Charles C. Royce's *Indian Land Cessions in the
United States; 18th Annual Report of the Bureau of American Ethnology, Part 2.* Washington: Government Printing Office, 527–644.

Thompson Lightstone Co. 1997. 'Canadians Support Royal Commission Proposals
to Recognize Native Rights.' Press release, Toronto. 14 Jan.

Thordarson, Bruce. 1972. *Trudeau and Foreign Policy: A Study in Decision-Making.* Toronto: Oxford University Press.

Tully, James. 1995. *Strange Multiplicity: Constitutionalism in an Age of Diversity.* Cambridge and New York: Cambridge University Press.

Van Schendel, Nicolas. 1994. 'L'identité métisse ou l'histoire oubliée de la canadianité.' In Jocelyn Létourneau, ed., *La question identitaire au Canada francophone: récits,
parcours, enjeux, hors-lieux.* Sainte-Foy, Quebec: Presses de l'Université Laval, 101–
21.

Wallace, Bruce. 1999. 'What Makes A Canadian?' *Maclean's,* 112, no.51 (20 Dec.):
32–6, 48–9.

Ward, Peter W. 1990. *White Canada Forever: Popular Attitudes and Public Policy
Towards Orientals in British Columbia.* 2nd ed. Montreal: McGill-Queen's University Press.

Woodcock, George. 1989. *The Century That Made Us: Canada 1814–1914.* Toronto:
Oxford University Press.

Profile of Freda Ahenakew (1932–)

Cree, Educator, Novelist, and Children's Author

Language is essential for cultural maintenance and preservation and as a vehicle for transmitting cultural values. Many of Canada's languages are threatened with extinction and concerted efforts must be made to conserve them. Fearing the disappearance of her culture, Freda Ahenakew has documented the Cree language and produced an indispensable collection of instructional and leisure books.

Freda Ahenakew was born in 1932 on the Atâhkakohp First Nation in central Saskatchewan.[1] Her passion for the Cree language began at a young age when her grandfather, Edward Ahenakew, began teaching her Cree.[2] Although she enjoyed going to school, she left Marcelin High School during her final year to marry. Many years later, Ahenakew decided to return to high school after some of her twelve children had dropped out.[3]

Inspired by her high school graduation, Ahenakew pursued an academic career at the University of Saskatchewan where she completed a bachelor of education degree in 1979.[4] Then, in 1984, Ahenakew graduated with a master of arts degree in Cree linguistics from the University of Manitoba. While working as the director for the Saskatchewan Indian Languages Institute, Ahenakew published an instructional guide for the Cree language entitled, *Cree Language Structures: A Cree Approach* (1987). The book was reprinted seventeen times.[5]

As associate professor of Native studies at the University of Manitoba, Ahenakew surprisingly found the time to publish a collection of literature on the Cree language.[6] Ahenakew's teaching materials include *Native Voices: A Teacher's Guide* (1993) and *The Student's Dictionary of Literary Plains Cree* (1998). To complement her teaching tools, Ahenakew created a valuable collection of children's books which includes *How the Birch Tree Got Its Stripes* (1988), *How the Mouse Got Brown Teeth* (1988), and *Wisahkecahk Flies to the Moon* (1999). In addition to her children's books, Ahenakew wrote books for an adult audience: *Our Grandmothers' Lives As Told in Their Own Words*

Freda Ahenakew. Courtesy of the National Aboriginal Achievement Foundation.

(1992), a collection of narratives detailing the daily lives of seven Native women; and *Voices of the First Nations* (1995), an anthology of stories, poems, articles, plays, and interviews. A valuable feature of Ahenakew's publications is the translated glossary found in the back of all her books.

Ahenakew's outstanding work has resulted in her receiving many awards such as the Federation of Saskatchewan Indian Nations Citizen of the Year Award, and an honorary doctorate of laws degree from the University of Saskatchewan in 1997.[7] In 1999 Ahenakew received the Order of Canada for her many contributions to Cree culture. Most recently, she was honoured by her own community when she received the National Aboriginal Achievement Award for education in 2001.[8] Currently, Ahenakew works for the Cree Retention Committee, a group designed to maintain the Cree language and culture by producing reading and writing materials. In addition, Ahenakew also hosts Cree immersion camps during the summer at Muskeg Lake to encourage youth to exercise their Native language.[9]

Freda Ahenakew is a remarkable woman who deserves much recognition for her efforts to protect and promote the Cree language. As a result of her hard work, the Cree language will live forever in print.

AMBER MCGINNIS

Notes

1 John D. Nichols, 'Freda Ahenakew.' In Gretchen Bataille, ed., *Native American Women: A Pictorial Biography* (New York: Garland Publishing 1993), 2.
2 'Freda Ahenakew,' *Internet Public Library.* www.ipl.org/cgi/ref/native/browse.pl/A507.
3 'Cree Language Retention Committee: Freda Aenakew' (Saskatoon: Saskatchewan Indian Cultural Centre 2002). www.sicc.sk.ca/crcom.htm.
4 Nichols, 'Freda Ahenakew,' 2.
5 'Our Elders: Freda Ahenakew' (Saskatoon: Saskatchewan Indian Cultural Centre 2002). www.sicc.sk.ca/cgi-bin/siccepage.pl?171.
6 'Aboriginal Faces of Saskatchewan: Freda Ahenakew' (Saskatoon: Saskatchewan Indian Cultural Centre 2002). www.sicc.sk.ca/faces/wahenfr.htm.
7 'Aboriginal Faces of Saskatchewan.'
8 Lorie Ann LaRocque, 'Citizen of the Year: An Inspriation to All,' *Saskatchewan Indian* 22, no.3: 1.
9 'Aboriginal Faces of Saskatchewan.'

Hiding in 'Plane' View: Aboriginal Identities and a Fur-Trade Company Family through Seven Generations

DAVID T. MCNAB

In his *The Empire of Nature* (1988), John M. MacKenzie remarked that a 'cultural characteristic may be rendered nebulous by its very ubiquity.' Such is the case with hunting, an activity that, as MacKenzie shows, contributed to the spread of European imperialism and colonialism in the nineteenth and twentieth centuries and the strict control of Indigenous peoples. The newcomers steadily restricted Indigenous peoples' use of animal resources as the nineteenth century progressed. Indigenous peoples were imprisoned for hunting for food, sometimes even when they had an Aboriginal or a treaty right. This is still the situation in Canada today. However, it was not just the animals and Indigenous peoples' activities that suffered. By putting Native peoples' hunting activities on a lower scale of value, newcomers could regard Aboriginal peoples themselves as wild animals. Aboriginal peoples became not only illegal hunters but also the hunted. The newcomers applied the same principle to Indigenous trading – an offshoot of trapping that was another form of hunting. And trapping animals was an essential part of the fur trade.

As MacKenzie has also observed, hunting became part and parcel of nineteenth-century European imperial culture: 'An imperial and largely masculine elite attempted to reserve for itself access to hunting, adopted and transformed the concept of the Hunt as a ritual of prestige and dominance, and set about the separation of the human and animal worlds to promote "preservation" (later "conservation") as a continuing justification of its monopoly. A worldwide legislative authority, backed by military and technical power, enabled Europeans to take elite policies in existence intermittently from ancient times and attempt their global application.'

Notwithstanding the vaunted principles of protection and trusteeship espoused by English imperialist commentators such as Herman Merivale (1806–74) in his work *Lectures on Colonization and Colonies* (1841) (Merivale 1967)[1], it was also clear that when it came down to a matter of everyday policy and practices, principles gave way to determination of issues based on an 'immediate exigency' (McNab 1983, 85–103). The same is true for the racist stereotypes of the 'Indians' (Krech 1999) as well as for their identities which had been and still are based upon representations of Aboriginal peoples as 'good' or 'bad' Indians. There are actually three categories here that are wholly fictitious but ubiquitous – 'Indians,' 'good' ones, and 'bad' ones. The truth is that Aboriginal peoples are human beings who exhibit just as much diversity and complexity as Europeans and cannot be reduced to mere categories of thought rooted in European knowledge-based systems.[2] The present chapter will address these issues of identities and traditions through the history of seven generations of a fur trade company family – the Kennedys (Fixico 1998, x).

My grandmother, Mabel Kennedy, always used to ask me when I came back from visiting people on the reserve: 'Well David, how are the Indians doing?' Then she would always say to me: 'You know we are the true Natives of this country,' and 'we are the true Canadians.' The elders say that some people are slower learners than others, and I am a very slow learner. I did not find out what she meant until many years had passed. Thirteen years ago, my grandmother passed away. In her obituary, I was struck by the statement that she was the 'last of the Kennedys.' Kennedys ... the last of the Kennedys – like the last of the Mohicans? If I was still alive, I was a Kennedy. So why would anyone put that in the obituary? I got no answer from my family; they were exceedingly tight-lipped. Then I began to do some checking on the Kennedys ... who were they? Where were they from? Where were they buried? Things are not always what they appear to be. Often, in order to survive, Aboriginal peoples have been/are hiding in 'plane' view, in a different dimension of spirit memory, and cannot be seen except from their angle of vision.[3]

Both sides of my family have rich heritages. On my father's side, it is fairly easy; the McNabs, people of Mac An Aba, are from the Highlands of Scotland, on the southeastern shores of Loch Tay. My family on my father's side[4] is called in the Scottish language, Gaelic, Mac An Aba, which in English means 'Son of the Abbot.' My ancestors are buried on islands in the north where the river flows from the Highlands southward. My father, John McNab, named like his father before him, was born in Kirkcaldy, Scotland, the birthplace of Adam Smith, who is known as the father of free trade.[5] It was with this knowledge that I was raised as a Scottish person born in Canada, whose grandparents lived in Montreal and who spoke Gaelic and told stories in their language (not mine, since I grew up in a different place – Kitchener-Waterloo, part of the Six Nations Territory – learning only English and some German). My mother was simply a Canadian of mixed ancestry, which was not seen to be important; certainly, the name Kennedy was rarely spoken about, much less understood for its significance. For more than forty years, in spite of being by profession a Canadian historian of Aboriginal peoples, I did not know the history of my family in Canada. I believed that I was a Scottish Canadian, who, by an accident of birth, failed to learn the language and culture of his Scottish ancestors because his grandparents lived in Montreal.

On my mother's side, the situation is much more complicated and complex and hidden. The Kennedys, Hudson's Bay Company (HBC) traders, were originally from Aberdeen, Scotland. But also part of the family mix were the Cree, Bear clan; Algonquin, Bird clan; and probably Onondaga, Pigeonhawk clan, as well. These names and Aboriginal places are inextricably connected through spirit journeys. I discovered my family history after my mother and grandmother passed away in 1996 and 1993 respectively.

Margaret Aggathas, or Mary Bear, was a daughter of Old Muk-kwah and a Cree woman from Cumberland House, an ancient Aboriginal community and a place of trade and trading (Cooper 1989, 3–26). I know nothing of her mother who was likely Cree as well. In 1774, Samuel Hearne established the HBC's first inland post at Cumberland House, which was located strategically on the northern canoe routes (McNab 2001, 237–92). In time-honoured Aboriginal trading tradition, Old Muk-kwah, the trader, gave one of his daughters to Alexander Kennedy, the powerful chief factor at that post, to cement the trading relationship with the HBC. Kennedy was originally from Aberdeen, Scotland, the home of many of the Scottish fur traders and a fairly prominent seaport in the eighteenth and nineteenth centuries, with connections north to the Orkney Islands and beyond – to the northern parts of North America.

Situated on Pine Tree Island, Cumberland House is located in present-day northeastern Saskatchewan and it is the only Treaty 5 community in that province. Cree and Metis communities are still there today, located at the confluence of the Saskatchewan, Sturgeon, and Grass rivers (Waldram 1988, 55–7). Margaret Aggathas married Alexander Kennedy *à la façon du pays* at Cumberland House. In all, they had nine children, John Frederick Kennedy, born in 1801, being the eldest. The fifth child, William, my great-great-great-grandfather, was born in 1814.

As an extremely prominent chief factor of the HBC, Alexander Kennedy made large sums of money in the fur trading business. A tough trader, he was well-liked by Sir George Simpson, the head of the company in the nineteenth century. Yet, by all accounts, he treated his Aboriginal family well and never abandoned them, as sometimes happened with other Native-white fur trade families. By the early 1830s, he had amassed a small fortune in the business and today would be the equivalent of a millionaire. However, like other Europeans in that trade, he frequently drank to excess (Rich 1967, 151).[6]

The Scottish clan motto of the Kennedys is 'Consider the End.' Alexander died from the effects of alcoholic poisoning on the streets of London, England, in July 1832 (Cooper 1989, 3–26), while he was away from his family on furlough from the company. He left his wife and nine children at Cumberland House; the children's names were John Frederick, Mary, Alexander, Elizabeth, William, George, Philip, Isabella, and Roderick. But he provided for his family in his will, leaving £5,680 to be divided among the nine children. As a result, John Frederick, his eldest son, was able to go to the University of Edinburgh to study medicine and become the first Aboriginal person to obtain a medical degree from a European university. He subsequently (in the 1830s) became a HBC surgeon in the Nass valley as well as a trader with the Nisga'a and the people of Haida Gwaii. He married a Haida woman who was a daughter of a Haida trading captain. After a successful career as a doctor and trader, John Frederick retired to Fort Victoria in the early 1850s with his wife. There, they bought land, and John Frederick was elected as one of the first members of the legislature for the colony of Vancouver Island in 1857–8. Although he passed away in 1859, John Frederick Kennedy is still known today in the history of British Columbia as one of that province's Fathers of Confederation (Van Kirk 1997/98, 149–79).

William Kennedy wanted to go to the University of Edinburgh like his elder brother. But he was not so fortunate since there was only enough money for one education; he had to sign on to follow in his father's footsteps as a HBC trader. He worked at Fort Coulonge (Fort William) on the Ottawa River adjacent to Allumette Island, in 1834. He is known in Canadian historiography as 'a very simple fellow' and also as the first 'white' person to make successful use of Indigenous knowledge on one of the first Arctic expeditions in search of Sir John Franklin in the early 1850s. How the written records do lie. Owing to his mother, he was a Cree, Bear Clan and he 'married' *à la façon du pays* Sarah Stevens, an Algonquin woman, Bird clan. William met her on his first posting for the HBC at Forts Coulonge/William in 1834.[7] Sarah, the daughter of an Algonquin trading captain from the Morrison/Allumette islands, was given to William to cement the Algonquins' relationship to the HBC when the fur trade was in serious decline in southern Canada. Sarah is rumoured to be buried at the north end of the Morrison/Allumette islands, now a cottage subdivision.

By this country marriage to Sarah, William Kennedy had two children. The eldest, born in 1835, was named, as was the practice, William, after his father. The youngest, Anthony, born in 1837, was likely named by Sarah. Sometime after the latter's birth, likely 1838, William took up a posting with the HBC at Fort Chimo in the Ungava peninsula in Labrador. He left Sarah behind with two small children on a small fifty-acre farm, which he bought for them on the banks of the Grand River near present-day Winterbourne, in Waterloo County, Ontario. The area is still today known as Kaufman Flats after the prominent German businessmen, Jacob and A.R. Kaufman of the Kaufman Rubber Company, founded in Berlin in 1907.[8] His son married a daughter of the Kaufman family. In German the word 'Kaufman' means trader. My maternal grandfather, Edward Huehn, worked as a foreman for the Kaufman Rubber Company in its Kitchener plant and likely got his position through his wife's (Mabel Kennedy) family connections to the Kaufmans. My grandfather used to take me through the plant to meet Mr Kaufman in the 1950s. Trading families marry into trading families. By 1861, the Kennedy family farm on the Grand River was reported to have one cow, two pigs, $18 invested in livestock, and an overall investment of $200. They were very poor. Although Sarah listed William in the 1851 census as 'deceased,' there is no written record of his death or his burial in any of the written records in Ontario or in any of the local cemeteries.

In 1840 Indians were banned from Waterloo Township (later County) by an Upper Canadian government order-in-council based in a racist and colonialist context (Good 1998, 145–80). Thereafter, William Kennedy's family, now residing in the Six Nations Territory, went into hiding to survive into the twenty-first century. They resided in Waterloo County among the German immigrants, and were able to hide by having their sons marry German women who were born in Germany.[9] They became Christians and spoke both German and English, learning the newcomers' ways.

William Kennedy, my great-great-great grandfather, probably returned frequently to the farm on the Grand River during the late 1840s and 1850s, when he resided again in Toronto and other places in Upper Canada such as Southampton, where he is known as one of the founding fathers (along with Captain John Spence, who was his business partner) of that town, located near the Saugeen Reserve. His friend and colleague with the HBC in Labrador, John McLean, lived in Elora, only a few miles away. One of McLean's daughters married the Reverend James Evans, who was a nineteenth-century missionary among the Anishinabe and the Cree and who has been cited as the inventor of the Cree orthography. Besides Cree, Evans learned the Anishinabe language from the Kennedy and McLean families who resided on the Grand River. So at least a few fur trade company families resided in the Six Nations Territory on the Grand River, where their descendants still are today, including me.

William Kennedy fought the HBC on the use of alcohol in the fur trade during his career as one of its traders from 1832 to 1846. He had seen its devastating effects, especially among the Inuit at Fort Chimo. When the company failed to change its practices in their area, William resigned in protest from the company's service in 1846. Thereafter, he and his nephew Alexander Kennedy Isbister challenged the company's monopoly and the validity of its 1670 charter on the basis of Aboriginal title and rights.

William's career as an Arctic explorer ended at Valparaiso on his second expedition in search of Sir John Franklin, when his crew mutinied in August 1853. The primary cause of complaint was the lack of alcohol on board ship; their captain had banned its use, as he had done on his first expedition in search of Sir John Franklin. William, left with the legacy of his father's death from alcoholic poisoning, had become a teetotaller. This tradition of temperance continued in the Kennedy family through the next three generations.

Perhaps even more so than his elder brother, Dr John Frederick Kennedy, William Kennedy deserves to be remembered as one of the Fathers of the Canadian Confederation. In the late 1850s, he knew and worked with George Brown and William McDougall on both trade and political matters. It was William who helped bring about the Great Coalition of 1862 and the Canadian Confederation of 1867. It was William's vision of Canada as an Aboriginal place, and of confederation as a form of a treaty, that came to dominate the construction of Canada in the mid-nineteenth century. This history is part of the Aboriginal and family oral traditions that are generally unknown, and have not been given written form in Canadian historiography.

William Kennedy is not buried with his sons and grandsons in cemeteries in Elmira and Kitchener. Rather, he was buried in St Andrew's cemetery (in present-day Winnipeg) in 1890. William Kennedy, Cree, Bear clan, Aboriginal person, HBC trader, critic of the company, Arctic explorer, traveller, Great Lakes captain and trader, erstwhile Father of Confederation, Manitoba magistrate, is the only Canadian to have his portrait displayed in the National Portrait Gallery in London, England. But this prominent Canadian is forgotten in his own country as an Aboriginal person. His family had to hide to survive federal Aboriginal policies of racism and colonialism and today none of his descendants has any status under the Constitution Act as 'Indians' or 'Métis.' The family has been forgotten, except for William Kennedy's stone house on the banks of the Red River, which as a National Historic Site, is now reduced to a tea house.

William Kennedy's eldest son, William, was both a trader and a farmer. His father's purchase of the fifty-acre farm on the banks of the Grand River in the late 1830s marked a shift and a diversification of the family's economic interests, because the fur trade was declining. Yet, at the same time, the interest in trade and trading remained and survived with the family over the generations. The family stayed on the land until 1912, when the farm was sold and William Kennedy retired to the market town of Elmira. Then the family became part of the urban Indian experience in Elmira and Kitchener-Waterloo and Toronto.[10] William owned a feed-mill business which, at his death in 1925, he left to his son, John Frederick, my great-grandfather. Its headquarters came to be at 284 Duke Street in Berlin, later Kitchener, Ontario. It was primarily through their marriages that the Kennedys hid and survived in plane view in the Six Nations Territory.

John Frederick Kennedy was named after his great-uncle of the same name. I never knew him; he died before I was born. Nor did anyone ever tell me anything about him. One of his daughters was Florence, my great-aunt, and the other was Mabel, my grandmother. It was during John Frederick Kennedy's time in the late nineteenth century that my family's Aboriginal languages and cultures were lost. Marriages to German women – German-speaking people then dominated Waterloo County – led to the children speaking German and English. Kennedy's feed-mill business supplied the outlying farming district for the local agricultural area. John Frederick Kennedy did not live on a farm but in a small town where he, like his ancestors, worked as a trader.

I was born in Kitchener on 28 October 1947. By the 1950s, John Frederick's house had been in herited by my great-aunt Florence, who lived in Toronto and seemed to be the most mysterious person in the family. My own family rented this house from Florence, and my brother and I played in a nineteenth-century-style horse-drawn wagon belonging to my great-grandfather that was housed in the barn. Boys being boys, my brothers and I did our utmost, when playing in the barn with that wagon (The name 'Kennedy Feed Mill' was emblazoned on it), to try to burn both of them down. We never succeeded. The barn still stands now, used as a multiple garage behind the house. But the wagon is now no more.

I have very fond memories of the house at 284 Duke Street. The winters were long and cold. The house was fuelled by a coal furnace which grumbled constantly against the Arctic blasts of the 1950s, but we were always warm. Waking up early in the mornings was natural for me. I heard the sound of horses' hoofs and their bells as the Silverwood Dairies man came down the street to deliver milk at 6:00 A.M. To this day, I always am awake at this time. I have many vivid memories, such as playing outside when Hurricane Hazel came through in 1954. Kitchener was a market town and still a trading place in the 1950s. Every Saturday morning, I walked with my grandparents to the Kitchener market to see the Mennonites with their buggies and horses and the many stands of meats and fruits and vegetables and flowers. Now all of this is gone. We live in a different world, with only the memories of what we have lost. It was for me a sad day when we bought our own house in 1958 and moved to the 'suburbs': no more milkman and his horse with singing bells on delivery.

I met Aunt Flo only once or twice at her place on King Street West in Toronto where her partner (I do not believe they were ever married), perhaps a Native American from New York State, operated a custom-shirt factory. I always had the impression that they had never married except *à la façon du pays*. She was small and extremely dark-looking. She was known as the family radical and an eccentric, always acting contrary to the rest of her relatives. She must have taken after Mary Bear in many ways. In retrospect, I believe that Aunt Flo exhibited many 'Indian' cultural characteristics and Aboriginal identities that still remained in the family. But, like her sister, she never spoke to me about the Kennedys. I liked her instantly and enjoyed my train trips to Toronto to see her. I was in awe of the large powerful steam engines which arrived at the Kitchener station to take us to Toronto. They hissed and snorted like dark monsters.

Perhaps out of fear of the big city, my family, with the exception of my grandmother, disliked going to Toronto. But for me, it was a grand adventure. One of the places I remember my grandmother taking me on one of our trips was to the old Toronto Zoo, which was located in Riverdale Park in the Don valley. I now work and live only a few blocks away from this Aboriginal place, an ancient Mississauga fishing spot which, under David Boyle, became one of the first archaeological sites in Canada. It was also the place where William Kennedy (1814–90) resided in the mid-nineteenth century. Aboriginal people always return to their places.

I was very close to my grandmother, Mabel. Whenever I have ever mentioned 'Indians' to my grandmother and mother – the Kennedys – there was always a strange look, something like fear, in their eyes. This is not surprising, since Sarah had been left alone with two small children by William in 1838. Born in 1898, Grandma Mabel must have learned from her grandfather, William, who lived until 1925, about the Kennedys and the family miscegenation with 'Indians.' But there has been a great deal of hiding of the family story, especially by the Kennedy women. The women, who were in fact the offspring of Cree and Algonquin, always kept the family secret. They never shared it with anyone else, even the males in the family. Publicly, they denied their identity. After all, 'what if Grandma was an Indian?' (Van Kirk 1985, 207–20). This denial created long-term psychological problems for the children within and across generations. Presumably, the family story was hidden because, since Canadian society was then predominantly white and racist, the children would be better off by being passed off as whites, rather than as 'Indians.' This may have been true. But it was a survival strategy that had great costs. In my own case, my mother appeared to become upset every time I talked about the 'Indians.' In retrospect, I suppose that her attitude reflected fear – fear of being discovered to be an 'Indian.' But it caused estrangement and deep wounds. This story is filled with both sadness and tragedy for those of the sixth and seventh generations, who did not know who they were, or where they were going, having lost their languages and cultures. It has also deeply affected my professional career as a historian.

My father, like his father before him, was a stonemason, working on various construction sites in Ontario as a construction foreman. His own father had reached only Grade 3 and could barely read or write. My father made it to Grade 8, and then the Second World War intervened. He went off to the North Atlantic as a nurse on the corvette, *H.M.C.S. Lindsay.* My first summer job was alongside my father, as a bricklayer's helper in 1963, and I needed to spend some time helping him read the architectural drawings. But he could always visualize his work very precisely, which is a skill that he must have learned from his father.

In the Cold War of the 1950s, many of the construction sites my father worked on were used for military training. They included Fenelon Falls and Balsam Lake near the Rama Reserve on Lake Simcoe, and Seaforth and Balm Beach on Georgian Bay near Christian Island Reserve. We spent the summers at these places because my father worked on the military establishment at Penetang and Petawawa; one year, we lived for a long summer at a place outside Pembroke opposite Morrison/Allumette islands on the banks of the Ottawa River. It was at this place that I remember being connected through spirit memory to the spirit and the birthplace of Sarah Stevens. I returned in October 1999, almost forty years later, and then again in the winter of 2003 when I was appointed, not without a great deal of irony, the first HBC visiting professor of Metis studies in the School of Canadian Studies at Carleton University.

In retrospect, my childhood was full of joyous moments. My father was often away for months on end working on construction. He made his own cedar-strip motor boat and our summers were spent on the waters, swimming and fishing. We always seemed to be near Aboriginal people and places. This was one of the times, of strong memories and powerful, enduring images.

In 1958–9, at Sunnyside Public School in Kitchener, I took my first course in Canadian history in Grade 5 from Jim Moses, a Mohawk from the Six Nations of the Grand River. Jim, then in his twenties, taught history and physical education – he scared the wits out of us because he was such an incredible athlete. He taught us the history of Canada from the perspective of the Six Nations, all the while placing the textbook by George Tait, *From Breastplate to Buckskin*, in bold relief by studiously avoiding its imperialist and racist contents. I was lucky to have this experience at a time when far too many Aboriginal children were then in residential schools surviving untold abuses at the hands of their teachers. As my school experience with Jim Moses illustrated, it could have been otherwise.

My father died at the age of forty-four, killed by a drunk driver in Kitchener in June 1967. He left five children and I was the eldest. My mother was left alone, much like Mary Bear and then Sarah had been, more than 135 years before.

The history of the fragmentation of the family has continued through the generations. Once you leave your place, things disintegrate as the names and the places become disconnected ... But no one ever told me the truth; not my grandmother before she died, and not my mother. Sometimes fear is stronger than truth. I had to piece it together as the spirits and the spirit memory came back to me after the passing of my grandmother and then my mother.

On the other hand, the spirit memory is there right from one's birth. I received a PhD in 1998 from the University of Lancaster, England, making me, perhaps, the first Aboriginal person to have graduated from a British university with a PhD in history (just as my great-great-great uncle, John Frederick, had been the first Aboriginal British trained doctor). My doctoral dissertation was entitled 'Herman Merivale and the British Empire, 1806–1874, with special reference to British North America, Southern Africa and India.' Much of it focused on William Kennedy and Alexander Kennedy Isbister, as well as on the 'Native question' in British North America. And I have published nine articles focusing on the Metis in Canadian history. My professional career since 1970 has been as a writer, teacher, and researcher on Aboriginal land and treaty-rights issues, following and maintaining the family and the clan traditions through seven generations. Most of my work, in retrospect, is about family history and autobiographical. And it is connected to and based on the history of the Kennedy family. I have long been intrigued, even obsessed, by the relationship between Aboriginal peoples in Canada and the Scots – a theme that is such a dominant feature of the history of Canada.[11]

And so the family history of the Kennedys continues to survive and retain its continuity in spite of the tremendous losses of languages and cultures from generations of hiding in 'plane view' as a result of racism and colonialism. In the last few years I have discovered that many Kennedy descendants married McNabs in the nineteenth century. So there are cross-family marriages, as well through the generations, as well as connections of place through spirit journeys. The names and the places are today being reconnected through the spirits and spirit memory.

Retrospect

By the twenty-first century, four of the six fundamental elements of the paradigm of my family's connection to Indian society – the family, the clans or societies, community, and nation – had disappeared. The two that remained intact were person and spirituality. And when the spirits returned to that one person, and were connected once again, the missing elements began to return as well. What binds all of these elements together is the interconnectedness in many distinct dimensions of all my relations. The Anishinabe/Metis/Cree writer Louise Erdrich opens her stories this way in her collection *The Last Report on the Miracles at Little No Horse* with the following statement by Nanabush about the framework of Creation: 'Nindinawemaganidok There are four layers above the earth and four layers below. Sometimes in our dreams and creations we pass through the layers, which are also space and time. In saying the word nindinawemaganidok, or my relatives, we speak of everything that has existed in time, the known and the unknown, the unseen, the obvious, all that lived before or is living now in the worlds above and below.'

So, as you can see, fur trade company families do not die. Their descendants are still here and very much alive today. Yet, at the same time, many fur trade company families still remain hiding in 'plane view' as a direct result of Canada's Aboriginal policies from the mid-nineteenth century, and they still live today in fear of racism and colonialism. At the same time, they have no recognized status as Aboriginal people, except generally and unofficially, but hitherto without effect, as Metis in the constitution (except in the Pauley case in 2003). And their lives are still ruled by the inherent nineteenth-century ideology of blood quantum and racism that remains firmly imbedded in the *Indian Act* and within Canadian society to this day. But we have survived and resisted and hidden through many generations.

One thing is certain. The common denominator of this fur trade company family is that it has always been involved in trading, whether it be furs or any other material goods or in knowledge. Trade and the art of trading are part and parcel of Aboriginal identities, connecting them to Indigenous knowledge and places, from where that knowledge comes. It is a powerful and a significant legacy bequeathed by Aboriginal peoples to all Canadians.

Notes

1 See also David T. McNab, 'Herman Merivale and the British Empire, 1806–1874, with Special Reference to British North America, Southern Africa and India,' PhD thesis, University of Lancaster 1978.

2 I have shown how this view plays out in a policy context in my currently unpublished 'Stories and Reflections of Bear Island.'

3 An earlier version of this chapter was published as 'The Spirit of the Canadas: The Kennedys, a Fur Trade Company Family through Seven Generations,' in Louise Johnston, ed. *Aboriginal People and The Fur Trade: Proceedings of the Eighth North American Fur Trade Conference* (Akwesasne 2001), 114–21. Please note that I deliberately use the word 'plane,' meaning an imaginary flat surface in space, since this highlights the ambiguity of my family history. What seemed to be a one-dimensional flat space was in fact a multidimensional space within circles of time.

4 This paper is based on a larger unpublished manuscript which I completed in 1998 and was entitled 'Dreaming and Drawing: Autobiographical Fragments of Air and Fire.' On the Clan Kennedy, see Charles MacLean, *The Clan Almanac*, (New York: Crescent Books 1990), 45. Kennedy is 'Ceannaideach' or 'Ceann Dubh,' which means either 'Ugly Head' or 'Black Headed,' respectively. The clan motto is 'Consider the End' and the clan badge is the Oak.

5 His father was also called John. They were stone masons by trade and came to Canada in 1929. The Clan 'Mac An Aba,' in Gaelic, means 'Son of the Abbot.' The clan motto is 'Let fear be far from all' and the clan badge is the pine tree. See Fitzroy MacLean, *Highlanders: A History of the Scottish Clans* (New York: Penguin Books 1995), 229, 236, 262; Charles MacLean, *The Clan Almanac* (New York: Crescent Books 1990), 85.

6 See also his three-volume *History of the Hudson's Bay Company.*

7 I can find no evidence that they were ever married. This is not too surprising since William's father and his brother's also had 'country marriages.'

8 Kenneth McLaughlin and John English, *History of Kitchener, Ontario* (Kitchener, Ont., Wilfrid Laurier University Press 1983).

9 I am married to a German who was born in Germany, and so is one of my brothers. My youngest brother is married to a descendant of the family of A.T. Galt, a businessman and a prominent Father of Confederation.

10 On the urban American Indian experience, see Donald L. Fixico, *The Urban Indian Experience in America* (Albuquerque: University of New Mexico Press 2000). There is no similar study for Canada, although the family patterns and experiences appear to be alike.

11 This history is, as yet, not well documented. One has to look at Aboriginal history in microcosm or at the biographies of Scots who have figured prominently in Canada's history such as the first prime minister, Sir John A. Macdonald or Sir Allan Napier MacNab. See the biographies of Donald Creighton Donald R.

Beer, *Sir Allan Napier MacNab* [Hamilton: Dictionary of Hamilton Biography
1984], and Donald L. Beer (*John A. Macdonald: The Young Politician* and *John A.
MacDonald: The Old Chieftain* [Toronto: Macmillan 1952, 1955]) respectively. For
other prominent Scots, who had a relationship(s) with First Nations, there are
no biographies available; these omissions include Alexander Morris, William
McDougall, and Duncan Campbell Scott. See also W. Stanford Reid, ed., *The
Scottish Tradition in Canada* (Toronto: McIlelland and Stewart 1976). In Reid's
work there is no reference to Aboriginal people. In 1971 I met with Reid at the
University of Guelph, having applied at that institution to do my PhD with him
in Scottish-Canadian history. I have always had an interest in the subject and
my first published article was on 'Peter McArthur and Canadian Nationalism,'
Ontario History, 64, no.1 (March 1972): 1–10.

Bibliography

Cooper, Barry. 1989. *Alexander Kennedy Isbister: A Respectable Critic of the Honourable
   Company*. Carleton Library Series. Ottawa: Carleton University Press.
Erdich, Louise. 2002. *The Last Report on the Miracles at Little No Horse*. Toronto:
   HarperCollins Canada.
Fixico, Donald L. 1998. *The Invasion of Indian Country in the Twentieth Century:
   American Capitalism and Tribal Natural Resources*. Niwot: University Press of
   Colorado.
Good, E. Reginald. 1998. 'Colonizing a People: Mennonite Settlement in Waterloo
   Township.' In David T. McNab (editor for Nin.Da.Waab.Jig.), *Earth, Water, Air and
   Fire, Studies in Canadian Ethnohistory* (Waterloo, Ont.: Wilfrid Laurier University
   Press.
Krech, Sheppard III. 1999. *The Ecological Indian: Myth and History*. New York: Norton.
MacKenzie, John M. 1988. *The Empire of Nature: Hunting, Conservation, and British
   Imperialism*. Manchester, U.K.: Manchester University Press.
McNab, David T. 1983. 'Herman Merivale and Colonial Office Indian Policy in the
   Mid-Nineteenth Century.' *Canadian Journal of Native Studies*, 1, no.2 (1981): 277–
   93. Reprinted in Ian A.L. Getty and Antoine S. Lussier, ed., *As Long as the Sun
   Shines and Water Flows: a Reader in Canadian Native Studies*. Vancouver: University
   of British Columbia Press.
– 2001. Bruce W. Hodgins, and S. Dale Standen, '"Black with Canoes": Aboriginal
   Resistance and the Canoe: Diplomacy, Trade and Warfare in the Meeting
   Grounds of Northeastern North America, 1600–1820.' In George Raudzens, ed.,
   *Technology, Disease and Colonial Conquests, Sixteenth to Eighteenth Centuries: Essays
   Reappraising the Guns and Germs Theories*. Amsterdam: Brill International.
Merivale, Herman. 1967. *Lectures on Colonization and Colonies*, (1st ed., 1841; 2nd ed.,
   1862). New York: Augustus M. Kelley.
Rich, E.E. 1967. *The Fur Trade and the Northwest to 1857*. Canadian Centenary Series.
   Toronto: McClelland and Stewart.

– 1997/8. 'Tracing the Fortunes of First Founding Families of Victoria, British Columbia.' *B.C. Studies*, 15 and 16 (autumn, winter).

Van Kirk, Sylvia. 1985. '"What if Mama is an Indian?": The Cultural Ambivalence of the Alexander Ross Family.' In Jacqueline Peterson and Jennifer S.H. Brown, ed., *The New Peoples Being and Becoming Metis in North America*. Winnipeg: University of Manitoba Press.

– 1980. *Women in the Fur Trade*. Winnipeg: Watson and Dwyer.

Waldram, James B. 1988. *As Long as the Rivers Run: Hydro-electric Development and Native Communities in Western Canada*. Winnipeg: University of Manitoba Press.

Profile of Douglas Joseph Henry Cardinal (1934–)

Metis, Architect, and Author

Against the horizon of the prairies, his buildings, with the circle as the basis of their design, fit naturally into the landscape with an innovative artistry. The man behind these unique creations is Douglas Cardinal, a Metis architect who is recognized in fields ranging from educational philosophy and town planning to his pioneering work in the CADD (Computer Aided Drafting and Design) system of architecture. His buildings can be found across Canada in such communities as Hay River, Northwest Territories; La Ronge, Saskatchewan; Fort McMurray, Alberta; Grande Prairie, Alberta (Phase I of the Grande Prairie Regional College); and Red Deer, Alberta (St Mary's Roman Catholic Church).[1] Perhaps his most noted commission was the Canadian Museum of Civilization located in Hull, Quebec – across the Ottawa River from the Canadian Parliament Buildings. Cardinal has also designed buildings in other countries around the world, including Australia, New Zealand, the United States, and Bolivia.[2]

Douglas Joseph Henry Cardinal was born in Calgary in 1934 to Joseph and Frances Cardinal.[3] Although his parents were of Aboriginal descent (his father was mixed European and Blackfoot ancestry, while his mother was Metis), they did not openly acknowledge this aspect of their heritage.[4] As a result, Cardinal grew up in a '"conspiracy of silence" regarding his Indian roots. Only the obvious native legacy of facial features belied his all-white upbringing.'[5] When his mother became too ill to care for her family, he and his two younger brothers were sent to live at St Joseph's, a Catholic residential school near Red Deer, Alberta. During his four years at residential school, he received fine arts training from the Grey Nuns. This training would figure significantly for him in later life.[6]

After completing high school in 1952, Cardinal was accepted into the University of British Columbia School of Architecture at the age of eighteen.[7] In his third year of study, he was dismissed from the UBC program after failing a studio-design class.[8] After a Mexican holiday, Cardinal landed

Douglas Joseph Henry Cardinal. Courtesy of the Canadian Press. Photographer: Terry McEvoy.

a job as a draftsman with a prestigious architectural firm, Jessen, Jessen, Milhouse, and Greeven, in Austin, Texas.[9] He continued his university studies and graduated with an honours degree in architecture from the University of Texas in 1963.[10]

Early in his professional career, Cardinal took an active interest in Native culture and religion. He started attending sweat-lodge ceremonies in Hobbema and studied under a local medicine man. This spiritual awakening influenced his writing. His publications include: *Of the Spirit: Writings by Douglas Cardinal* (1977) and *The Native Creative Process* (1991).

Douglas Cardinal's architectural accomplishments have been recognized both nationally and internationally. Throughout his career he has received several honorary doctorates from Canadian universities, including the University of Windsor (1992), the University of Lethbridge (1994), Carleton University (1994), Trent University (1994), Concordia University (1998), and the Emily Carr Institute of Art and Design (2000).[11] Cardinal has also received numerous architectural awards, most recently the Governor General's Award in Visual and Media Arts.[12] He was honoured with a National Aboriginal Achievement Award in 1995.[13]

Douglas Cardinal currently lives in Aylmer, Quebec, and runs an Ottawa architectural firm.[14]

MARY CUMMINGS

Notes

1 Paul Melting Tallow, 'Activist by Design: Douglas Cardinal,' *Aboriginal Times* (2001): 22.
2 www.djcarchitect.com.
3 Trevor Boddy, *The Architecture of Douglas Cardinal* (Edmonton: NeWest Press 1989), 11.
4 Melting Tallow, 'Activist by Design,' 24.
5 Boddy, *The Architecture of Douglas Cardinal*, 7.
6 Ibid., 11.
7 Ibid., 13.
8 Ruth Rosenburg, 'Douglas Cardinal.' In Sharon Malinowsk:, ed., *Notable Native Americans* (New York: Gale Research 1995), 69.
9 Ibid., 22.
10 www.djcarchitect.com.
11 Ibid.
12 Ibid.
13 Melting Tallow, 'Activist by Design.'
14 Rosenburg, 'Douglas Cardinal,' 69.

Aboriginal Peoples and the Canoe

BRUCE W. HODGINS AND BRYAN POIRIER

Aboriginal peoples, the canoe, and the kayak are inextricably linked to an understanding of Canadian identities and cultures. In fact, the canoe has become one of the great Canadian icons, sharing pride of place with perhaps only the beaver, the skate, and the hockey stick – all emblematic of the 'true North.' More than just symbolic, the canoe and the kayak have also played a vital part in defining and developing the country. Even if often 'hidden in plain sight,' Aboriginal peoples are important in the iconography of the canoe, and in canoe travel and traditional canoe building – all of which continue to be vital in Canadian cultures. For so many Canadians, the canoe and canoeing is or has been a major part of their lives, both practically and metaphorically.

Long before contact with the Europeans, in what later became known as Canada, the canoe was of great significance, whether the vessels were fine eastern barks, the classic central birch-barks, or the Pacific coast giant cedar dugouts. In the Arctic, the Inuit kayak was central to coastal Inuit life – for travel, for hunting (seals and whales), and for fishing.

As David McNab, Bruce W. Hodgins, and Dale S. Standen argue in 'Black with Canoes,'[1] the canoe, especially the birch-bark canoe (but also later the skin kayak) of the Aboriginal peoples, made the ascendancy of the European newcomers in North America much different from the European conquest of the rest of the Americas. Certainly that was the case inland and upriver to the west and northwest of Montreal, and inland south and west of James Bay and Hudson Bay. Beyond the French-Canadian settlements on the St Lawrence, Europeans as a minority entered 'Indian Country' in Aboriginal canoes, with the approval and often the paddling of Aboriginal peoples. Because of the canoe (and the beaver), Aboriginal peoples were useful to the Anglo-Celtic-French traders and officers, and the traders were useful to Aboriginal peoples.

After 1816, in southern Upper Canada and Nova Scotia, the story would be somewhat different. There would be increasing settlement, but the pattern would not be at all very violent. In the northwest, at least until 1870, and in the far north and Arctic long after that, the canoe and the trade would remain supreme (Jennings 2002).

On the west coast, the great voyages and battles of the Haida and other Pacific coast First Nations were undertaken in their huge dugouts[2] (Shadholt 1998). In the Gulf of St Lawrence, the Bay of Fundy, and the valleys of the Saint John and the Mirimachi rivers, the Mi'kmaq, Maliseet, and Pasamaquoddy used both smallish dugouts and birch-bark canoes. The Mi'kmaq in their small dugouts made the frequent, and phenomenal, crossings of the stormy Cabot Straits between Cape Breton and southwestern Newfoundland.[3]

The Canoe and the (Fur) Trade

Long after contact with Europeans, Aboriginal peoples continued to build the birch-bark canoes used by European traders and travellers. During the trade (commonly called the fur trade), the Aboriginal birch-bark canoe, of various sizes, was a central factor in travel and commerce – facilitating a 'partnership in fur.' For more than a century, from 1670 until about 1775, Hudson's Bay Company (HBC) traders generally stayed at their Bay posts, expecting Aboriginal traders (and trappers) to paddle downriver to these posts to sell their beaver and other furs in exchange for European iron goods (including pots, pans and guns), special clothing, and ornaments. The Aboriginal traders would then paddle back upstream, through distant watersheds and over remote divides (that is, heights of land) to their homelands.

In the early years of the fur trade, when European traders ventured out, First Nations peoples, especially the Cree, did most of the paddling. Still later as voyageurs, whether they were in the *canot du maitre* (the Montreal canoe, about eleven metres long) or the *canot du nord* (about eight metres long), Aboriginal peoples, especially the Metis, were often paddlers along with French Canadians. By this time, Aboriginal peoples figured prominently as canoe builders together with the French Canadian majority in the Montreal-Trois-Rivières, Sault Ste Marie, and Lakehead areas.

To the north, the trade link between First Nations and the HBC remained paramount until the late 1770s. In 1715, according to James Knight at York Factory, 172 Indian canoes arrived at the post to trade. Nearly all had come down the Hayes River. Most were paddled by Cree and Assiniboine. Many of the Cree came from the upper Churchill River valley, and even farther north from Reindeer Lake. Many also came from what is now southeastern Manitoba and areas between the Saskatchewan and Churchill rivers. Blood and Blackfoot, too, came from the west. Thirty of the 172 canoes were filled with 'Mountain Indians' – Hidatsa and probably Mandan from the Upper Missouri and as far west as the Rocky Mountains. There were even 'Sarsi' (Sarcee) who came from farther to the southwest. This pattern continued. In 1717 James Knight indicated that the crews of twenty-two canoes of 'Mountain Indians' at the post reported that most of their compatriots had starved on the return journey in 1716, because the trip was so long and no supplies had arrived by European ships for them: 'It grieves me to the very heart to think how a country is ruin'd by a senseless blockhead not having thought, care nor consideration.' In 1721 Henry Kelsey at York Factory reported large numbers of Indian canoes arriving, including, for the last time, those of the Mandan. Although a few Blackfoot continued to travel to York Factory, increasingly travel on the Hayes River was done by Cree and Assiniboine. Plains Indians preferred horse travel, so they traded their furs to the Cree for transport northeastward. Between 1730 and 1754, there was a modest decline in the numbers of southern Indians travelling down the Hayes River because of competition from the La Vérendrye family and other French traders in the eastern prairies.[4] Yet in 1742 Joseph La France, a *coureur de bois*, travelled from Cedar Lake (Le Pas) down the Nelson River to York Factory with a fleet of 100 canoes carrying 200 Swampy Cree (Gibbon 1951, 38). Between 1757 and 1771, the numbers of Cree canoes on the Hayes River carrying furs to trade increased steadily (Ray 1974, 60–71).

The period from 1784 to 1821 was the heroic era of the North-West Company (the HBC's rival trading company), characterized by voyageurs paddling the *canots de maitre* and the *canots du nord*. They built a 'fur empire' far greater than that of the HBC, stretching from Montreal to the northwest, over the Methye Portage (now in northern Saskatchewan) between the source waters of the Churchill River and the Arctic-flowing Clearwater River of the Athabaska country and beyond (up what became known as the Peace River and also down what came to be called the Mackenzie River). This fur empire was held together by the Aboriginal canoe and its paddlers and by Aboriginal male trappers and their daughters. It was long alleged that the voyageurs were adventurous sons of French-speaking habitants from the St Lawrence seigneuries. A majority undoubtedly were. A few were also poor Scottish immigrants. Many, however, were Metis of the new mixed-blood nation born around Grand Portage and Fort William and the junction of the Red and Assiniboine rivers. Today, we also know that many of the canoeists were Mohawk from Oka-Kanasatake and some were Anishnabe from the same community, from around Mattawa, and from around Sault Ste Marie and Michilimackinac.

After the HBC merger with the North-West Company in 1821, the Montreal canoe-based trade and the voyageur travels declined radically. They still survived in the *petit-nord*, that is, northeastern Ontario and central Quebec, and in the northwest, to Hudson Bay and James Bay, supported by heavy Aboriginal involvement. However, on Lake Winnipeg and the Nelson and Hayes rivers north to York Factory, and on Hudson Bay, Orkney-crewed York boats (which were rowed, sailed, and hauled), rather than canoes, soon predominated. Of course, many of the 'Orkneymen' were themselves Metis (Cree-Scot).[5]

The Canoe, Diplomacy, and Nation Building

In so many ways, the Aboriginal canoe was instrumental in defining most of the boundaries of Canada. As well, Aboriginal canoe culture in central North America (and hence French trade and diplomacy to 1760, then briefly the Scottish and English trade and diplomacy from 1763 until 1783) stretched southwest across the current 'medicine line' (that is, the U.S.-Canadian border). From there, the canoe culture spread down the Mississippi Valley to New Orleans and also into the pre-Cambrian Shield country of current-day Minnesota. To a lesser extent, it penetrated into the Mohawk valley and other parts of what is now upstate New York. Despite strong Aboriginal military resistance, these territories were later lost to Canada during warfare between Britain and the United States.

Before that, the huge, so-called French North American empire, based on the lower St Lawrence (the little 'Canada'), was really a loose diplomatic system of independent First Nations linked by trade and defence to the numerically weak French-Canadian towns of Montreal and Quebec and the seigneurial lands in-between. The aim of both groups was to keep the Anglo-Americans confined to the broad coastal Atlantic area, inland to the Appalachians. The French strategy was geopolitical and, secondarily, trade. The First Nations strategy was to preserve their homelands from the expansive American 'longknives' and to make gains through trade. The Aboriginal canoe made French strategy possible. By 1758, however, after a century of the canoe working this imperial French/Aboriginal system, even it was not enough against British and Iroquoian arms. The efforts of Pontiac and other First Nation leaders, and the war-weariness of the distant British ruling class, led to the Anglo-Celts in Montreal and Quebec replacing the French traders. The Royal Proclamation of 1763 and the Treaty of Niagara of 1764 restored, for a time, the old mid/western system, held together primarily by the canoe, for the purpose of trade, diplomacy, and mutual defence.

The American victory in their War of Independence, from 1775 to 1783, shattered the inland superiority of Montreal. The canoe, however, helped sustain a portion of the alliance system through trade. It even helped maintain, after 1783, many of the British inland posts, which were technically in U.S. territory, in what Americans called the 'old northwest.' There was some interruption in the occupation of the posts and the trade from the late 1790s until the outbreak of war again in 1812. The posts were finally abandoned in 1816 following the Treaty of Ghent.

Nevertheless, in the 1820s, Chief Peterwegeschick of Walpole Island (Bkejwanong First Nation) told the story about his father as a boy going over to Detroit to trade, when 'the St. Clair was often black with canoes in their journeying to the trading post at Detroit.'[6] By then, and indeed from 1783 onwards, the canoe-facilitated Montreal-based fur trade had shifted its focus to the near north and the northwest.

The Canoe and Exploration

Virtually all the trade-inspired explorers, such as (Sir) Alexander Mackenzie, travelled with Aboriginal guides and paddlers. The same goes for overland explorers such as John Franklin on his two inland voyages searching for the Northwest Passage and Dr John Rae and the rest who later searched inland for the missing, and actually dead, John Franklin after his third and final seafaring expedition. Many of these Aboriginal paddlers have certainly become 'hidden in plain sight.' They were, however, indispensable and often 'more than guides' for traders and early explorers. This was true, for example, of the Dene or Chipewyan woman Thanadelthur, the 'Ambassadress of Peace.' Between 1714 and 1716, she led William Stewart (for HBC Governor James Knight) west from York Factory to Great Slave Lake, trying to bypass the Cree and open direct contact and trade with the Dene.

Samuel Hearne of the HBC, in 1771–2, had the great Matonnabbee and his Chipewyan entourage on his long overland trip down the Coppermine River. On Alexander Mackenzie's trip down the Athabaska and Mackenzie rivers, he had five First Nation associates, the 'English Chief,' two wives, and two young males.[7] Akaitche accompanied John Franklin on his first overland trip. Dr John Rae, on his diverse, far northern overland trips, was accompanied by many others including the Inuk Albert One-Eye, the Inuk William Ouligbuck, Jr, and the Cree Thomas Mistegan. Of course, Rae usually travelled by canoe, kayak, dog shed, or toboggan in the Inuit or Cree manner.

From 1874 to about 1939, Aboriginal peoples were canoe-bound guides. Nearly all the great voyages of European and Euro-Canadian exploration, commerce, survey, and administration (the Geological Survey of Canada, the Royal Canadian Mounted Police, northern treaty parties) used Aboriginal canoe guides and paddlers. This pattern continued as recreational, long-distance canoe tripping expanded around and after 1900 (Hodgins and Hobbs 1985).

The first great recreational long-distance canoe tripper was David Hanbury, who in 1899–1900 travelled around the Thelon, Hanbury, Coppermine, and Lockhart watersheds in the far north, nearly always with First Nation companions or guides. He wrote about his voyages in a huge, fascinating, and popularizing book, *Sport and Travel in the Northland of Canada*, which is full of wonderful maps and great adventures usually involving Native peoples (Hanbury 1904).[8]

The Canoe, Youth Camps, and Pauline Johnson

First Nations peoples in the early twentieth century guided many of the great youth camp canoe trips, particularly those such as Keewayden (from 1903) and Wabun (from 1934). Based in Temagami, and often American-owned, these camps took many youth on voyages north after 1911 to far James Bay.[9] Aboriginal guiding of youth campers also permeated the early youth camping movement in another sense. Through the efforts of Ernest Thompson Seton, Taylor Statten, Mary S. Edgar (founder of Glen Bernard Camp for Girls in Sundridge, Ontario), and others, camp programming of woodcraft and character-building and environmental stewardship were often modelled on Native peoples' traditions and rituals. This was a practice that was withdrawn from most camp programs during the 1970s out of respect and concern for the possible misrepresentation and unintentional trivialization of Aboriginal peoples (Benidickson 1997, 129–34, 139–43, 157–71).[10]

Mary Edgar's regard for Native traditions might have stemmed from her childhood encounters with Mohawk paddler and poet Pauline Johnson. When speaking of a time from her youth when she had attended one of Johnson's poetry readings, she confessed, 'I was fascinated and wished I were related to her' (Benidickson 1997). Born on the Six Nations Reserve on the Grand River near Brantford, in March 1861, Pauline Johnson (or Tekahionwake, her Mohawk name, meaning 'double wampum') is regarded as Canada's premier female Aboriginal poet and as the 'the first Aboriginal woman to write about her heritage in ways that non-Aboriginal people could understand.' Probably her most famous poem, *The Song My Paddle Sings*, did much to foster an appreciation of the canoe beyond its traditional application in work and commerce:

> The river rolls in its rocky bed;
> My paddle is plying its way ahead;
> Dip, dip,

Where the hills uplift
On either side of the current swift.
And up on the hills against the sky,
A fir tree rocking its lullaby,
Swings, swings,
Its emerald wings,
Swelling the song that my paddle sings.[11]

Arguably, however, it was poems such as *The Portage*, with its message of feminine skill and ability, that established her as a noted poet in the hearts of many:

Now for a careful beach, atween the towering
Grey rocks a'yawn like tombs.
Aft lies the lake, blurred by our paddles scouring.
Forward the Portage looms,
Beyond its fastnesses, a river creeping,
Then rapids leaping.
Now for a bracing up of stalwart shoulders,
And now a load to lift,
An uphill tramp through tangled briars and boulders,
The irksome weight to shift,
And through it all, the far incessant calling
Of waters falling.
What of the heat? The toil? The sun's red glaring,
The blistered fingers, too?
What of the muscles, teased and strained, in bearing
The fearless, fleet canoe?
Brief is the labor, then the wild sweet laughter
Of rapids after.[12]

The Voyage of the *Odeyak*

One of the greatest recent canoe voyages by Aboriginal peoples, in this case Cree and Inuit from northern Quebec, involved the voyage of the *Odeyak*, built in Kuujuaraapik, James Bay, transported to Ottawa and paddled from there to the United Nations headquarters in New York City. The trip was undertaken to raise Canadian and American awareness of the Cree-Inuit opposition to Quebec's Great Whale Hydro Electric Project, James Bay II. The voyage and 'voices from the Odeyak' was led by Matthew Coon Come, then the grand chief of the Cree of Quebec. The voyage was initiated by the Inuit of Kuujjuaraapik and the Cree of Whapmagoostui – the villages on opposite sides of the endangered Great Whale River, by its mouth. The craft was basically a large six-metre, ten-person, wood-canvas canoe with an Inuit kayak-style enclosed stern (with a cockpit). It was built by a Kuujjua-raapik Inuk, Billy Weetaltuk, who had learned the trade from his father, who himself had experience with the canoe builders of Moose Factory. Weetaltuk received great help from his twenty-eight-year-old daughter, Caroline, his two sons, Morris and Redfern, and his Cree friend, Andrew Natashaquan. The canoe was hauled over the James Bay ice on a sleigh by an Inuit-style dog team to the Cree town of Chisasibi (up from the mouth of the La Grande River downstream from James Bay I). From there, it was transported by truck to Ottawa and launched from Victoria Island on 24 March 1990.

After ceremonies, speeches, and meetings on Parliament Hill, the canoe was paddled down the Ottawa to Montreal and the Mohawk Reserve of Kahnawake. From there it was escorted by Mohawk canoeists (including Mike Canoe and Kenneth Deer) from the Kahnawake Canoe Club, up the Richilieu River, and onto Lake Champlain to Burlington, Vermont, in the United States. Here a side trip by van carried the *Odeyak* to Middlebury, Vermont, for speeches by the Cree and talks with the governor of Vermont and other authorities. The canoeists also spent a weekend at the American Camp Keewaydin (which runs canoe trips in Quebec through Cree and Inuit territories).

Back on the water, the canoe crew, which included Cree students such as Stella Masty and Randy Pepabano, as well as Cree elders, the Algonquin Roland Chamberlain, young Inuit paddlers, such as Mary Milkeyook and Heather Tukatuk, and, for most of the way, Grand Chief Coon Come, himself a great canoeist, proceeded down the Hudson River. After major stops for speeches and discussions at Albany, the New York state capital, the boat was paddled into New York City, landing with great ceremony beside the United Nations Building. There followed more speeches and discussions led by the grand chief. All this and more is described in Michael Poslun's *Voices from the Odeyak* and in the feature-length documentary film, *Power from the North: Two Peoples, One River*.

New York State reversed and repudiated any purchase of hydro power from a future Great Whale Project. Vermont also cut back its proposed purchases. The new Parti Québécios government permanently shelved the Great Whale Project, while the *Odeyak* itself was presented on permanent loan to the Canadian Canoe Museum in Peterborough, Ontario.[13]

Evolution of the Canoe

Through much of the French period, most of the canoes used for trade and diplomacy were made by the Aboriginal peoples themselves. Later, some

French habitants, such as the Maitres, and others living around Trois-Rivières and the lower Saint-Maurice began building canoes, learning the skills from Aboriginal peoples. During the era of the North-West Company (1784–1821), French-speaking Canadians were probably making most, but not all, of the Montreal canoes – often with Aboriginal help. This intercultural canoe building and canoe culture is described brilliantly, in four volumes, by Timothy J. Kent, himself a Metis (living in the United States).[14]

As Aboriginal birch-bark vessels evolved into cedar-strip and canvas-covered canoes, Aboriginal peoples still participated in their manufacture and played important roles. Indeed, many Aboriginal people, such as William Commanda and César Newashish, were making quality birch-bark canoes late into the twentieth century. Some of their products are displayed in the Canadian Canoe Museum.[15] In the late nineteenth and through most of the twentieth century, many other Native people have helped with or built cedar-strip canoes in the greater Peterborough and Temagami areas and wood-canvas canoes in the Saint John valley, New Brunswick, and nearby across the border around Old Town, Maine.[16] For example, the Abenaki birch-bark canoe, displayed at the Canadian Canoe Museum, was entirely restored by Possamaquoddy builder Lewie P. Sock at the Old Town Canoe Company in Maine, a manufacturer primarily identified by its cedar-canvas canoe construction. Sock's name can still be found etched on the end thwart of the canoe.[17] In the mid-twentieth-century, outboard motor-driven Rupert House or Prevost freight canoes (or Prevos) became crucial to Cree life and travel on coastal James Bay and Hudson Bay and on the great rivers flowing into these bays and west over the Arctic divide into the homeland of the Dene peoples of the Mackenzie valley.

Significant Modern-Day Canoe Builders

Highlighting the canoe as the great Canadian cultural icon that it is, the Canadian Canoe Museum, in liaison with Native communities across Canada, is attempting to preserve traditional skills and the stories of the peoples behind the canoe. The museum currently devotes about 40 per cent of its display area to the canoe's diverse Aboriginal origins and continuing uses.[18]

For example, in recent decades there have been many significant Native people building traditional canoes in the old ways or by using modern tools and processes. Two of the most famous are William Commanda (Ojigkwanong) and his wife, Mary (now deceased). They lived at Garden River (Kitigan Ziki) by Maniwake, north of Gatineau, Quebec. Commanda has a very high reputation. He is the most senior elder of the Algonquin

Algonquin Canoe. Courtesy of the Canadian Canoe Museum, Peterborough, Ontario.

Nation and keeper of Algonquin wampum belts, an impressive alignment when considered in tandem with his skill as a canoe builder (Gidmark 1980).[19] He has built over one hundred birch-bark canoes in the western Algonquin style, with split-root decklashing and decorative figures along the side. The Canadian Canoe Museum, which has honoured and fêted the Commandas, has a 1980 model on special display.[20]

César Newashish of Manouane, Quebec, has a similar reputation. The museum has a large, circa 1972, birch-bark North canoe (8.17 metres) of his also on special display, loaded with fur and trail goods. In the late 1960s, the National Film Board of Canada produced a documentary film, in both black-and-white and coloured versions, showing César Newashish actually building a birch-bark canoe (*César's Bark Canoe* 1971).

Beginning in 1969, Kirk Wipper, founder of the museum's canoe collection, worked successfully with a Haida, Victor Adams of Masset, to revive the building of the great red cedar dugouts on Haida Gwaii (Queen Charlotte Islands). Adams's first product, the huge Eagle canoe, which took three years to build, is on display in the Canadian Canoe Museum. Back then, the construction details existed only in the memory of old elders. One of them, Adam Bell, who was a mentor to Victor Adams, recalled that no such work had been undertaken since 'many decades ago.' These canoes became the image for Haida sculptor Bill Reid's *Lootaas* or *Wave Eater*, completed in 1986. Since the completion of Adams's Eagle canoe, the Haida have continued to build and paddle many more such boats. Indeed, with the parallel creation of their traditional giant totems, the Haida have their own living museum at Skidegate, where traditional canoe and totem building still continues.[21]

Near the Mackenzie valley, in Edzo, Northwest Territories, the Dogrib canoe project is reviving the Dogrib Dene's unique bark creations. One of the project's first canoes, built by Chief Jimmy Bruneau, is in the Prince of Wales Northern Heritage Centre in Yellowknife. The project is carried on by Joe and Julie Mackenzie, Elizabeth Rabesca, and Nick and Aimée Black – all Dogrib people. A Dogrib canoe is also in the Canadian Canoe Museum.[22]

The Canoe in Art

Along with the frequent appearance of the kayak as a motif in Inuit soapstone sculptures and print making, there are other Aboriginal artists for whom the canoe is a major motif. Patrick Maranda of Lac Rapide, La Vérendrye Park, Quebec, depicts canoes in the late Algonquin style in his paintings. The works of Rick Beaver, the noted Mississauga artist living in Alderville, Ontario, are frequently canoe-inspired. He uses 'colour and flowing lines' in all of his paintings. Many of his works are on display at the Canadian Canoe Museum. Frank Polson, an Algonquin artist from Long Point First Nation, also frequently depicted canoes. His *Old Style* painting in the museum has a young man and two young women, depicted in rich reds and oranges, standing expectantly beside a canoe on shore. The museum has works featuring canoes by Susan A. Point, the Musqueum Coast Salish artist. Art Thomson, a Nuu-chah-nulth Coast Salish from Vancouver Island, emphasizes the shapes and colours of the canoe paddle in her paintings. The Mi'kmaq artist Alan Sylibey gives a modern sensibility to canoe and paddle art, often depicting children in a canoe. Her *Voyage into the Mystic*, on display at the museum, is an example.[23]

The late Bill Reid magnificently combined the Haida canoe with Haida art and the Haida world-view. Of particular note is his monumental canoe sculpture, *The Spirit of Haida Gwaii*, which stands in front of the Canadian Embassy in Washington, D.C. James Tully describes it: 'Cast in bronze, it recreates a group of thirteen human, animal and bird figures interacting with each other as they head into the unknown in a Haida canoe, under the guidance of Chief Kilstlaai, wrapped in the skin of the mythical sea wolf and holding a speaker's staff that tells the Haida story of creation' (Tully 1995, 17–34, 202–12). This sculpture, often called the *Black Canoe*, also symbolizes Canada's remarkable unity amid multiplicity and multiculturalism. A full-size jade replica stands in the Vancouver International Airport (Bringhurst and Steltzer 1991).

The Canoe and Film

Aboriginal people kayaking and canoeing have been depicted in film, at least since Inuit starred in the 1922 epic, *Nanook of the North*. Then, in 1929, the equally epic, feature-length *Silent Enemy: Hunger*, though American-produced, was set in Temagami in northern Ontario. It shows, especially in its first half-hour, many scenes of young people and children of the Teme-Augama Anishnabe, paddling and shooting rapids on the Matabitchewan River. A few of those young canoeists are still alive. A former Teme-Augama Anishnabe chief, Gary Potts, himself a great canoeist, has helped keep alive the traditions of canoeing (now in modern canoes) among the people of Bear Island. Back in 1913, many of George Speck's photographs of Temagami Native people depicted the rather special Bear Island birch-bark canoes, paddled by Anishnabai.[24]

A survey of Aboriginal canoeists in film would be incomplete without mentioning Holling Clancy Holling's intrepid little character Paddle-to-the-Sea, in the book of the same name, who hailed from the Nipigon region. He has paddled his birch-bark canoe into the literary imagination of children since 1941, and via the silver screen since 1966, when well-known Canadian canoeist and filmmaker Bill Mason brought him to life in a cleverly crafted National Film Board movie.

Canoe Racing

First Nations peoples became involved in canoe racing as the sport developed – although the numbers are not as high as one might expect. Perhaps sports racing is too 'gentleman-oriented.' Yet many Mi'kmaq from the Dartmouth-Bedford Basin area of Nova Scotia have distinguished themselves in this sport.

Then there are the canoe racers from 'remote' Cumberland House on the North Saskatchewan River, 'a thriving First Nations community and the home of some of Canada's best marathon canoe racers, including Erasmus Solomon, who for years was the partner of the invincible Serge Corbin. Together these two men won most of the major canoe races in North America' (Finkelstein 2002).

Recently, competing Native canoe racers such as Alwyn Morris have emerged (see a profile of Alwyn Morris elsewhere in this volume). At the 1984 Summer Olympic Games in Los Angeles, Morris, after winning an Olympic bronze medal in the 500 metre two-man kayak race, climbed the gold medal podium for the 1,000 metre two-man kayak. He held aloft an eagle feather to honour his grandfather's teachings and his Mohawk heritage. Morris, the renowned kayaker, has since been working to guide and inspire Aboriginal youth across the country (INAC 2002).

Conclusion

Arguably, Aboriginal peoples, and by extension the canoe and the kayak, played a prominent role in the exploration, development, and early defence of Canada, and in the creation and expansion of Canada's first great economic venture – the fur trade. Before Canada was founded, and for many years thereafter, canoes and kayaks were the only means of domestic travel over long distances. For much of the French period, most of the trade canoes and the diplomatic canoes were made by the Aboriginal peoples themselves. Later, as the French-speaking Canadians began constructing some of their own vessels, they were actively assisted by Native peoples. Aboriginal peoples, including the Metis, were guides and paddlers. This has continued into the twentieth century, especially on the great youth camp canoe trips.

Today, Aboriginal peoples are reasserting their inherent rights and privileges, recognized under past treaties, and becoming actively involved in managing their lands and resources. The canoe has been a part of most of these past practices and traditions. Now, with an evolving lifestyle, Native peoples are redeveloping an enviable position in the social, economic, and cultural life of Canada. In this position, the canoe continues to be important as a reminder of traditional knowledge and ways, a unifying symbol advocating a spirit of cooperation and a source of pride and encouragement for many Aboriginal youth.

Notes

1 In George Raudzens, ed., *Technology, Disease and Colonial Conquests, Sixteen to Eighteenth Centuries: Essays Reappraising the Guns and Germs Theories* (Leiden, Netherlands: Brill 2001), 237–92.
2 Eugene Arima, 'Barkless Barques,' and Kenneth Lister, 'Extremely Cranky Craft: The James W. Tyrell Kayak, Big Islands, Hudsons Strait,' both in John Jennings, Bruce W. Hodgins, and Doreen Small, ed., *The Canoe in Canadian Cultures*

(Toronto: Natural Heritage 1999), 43–61 and 28–42 respectively, and David Neel, *The Great Canoes: Reviving a Northwest Coast Tradition* (Vancouver: Douglas and McIntyre 1995).

3 David McNab, 'Fragments of Time: The Mi'kmaq Nation and Ktagamkuk, "The Place of Fog"' (Historical Report for the Federation of Newfoundland Indians, 16 April 1996); idem., 'Black with Canoes,' and 'Aboriginal Resistance and the Canoe: Diplomacy, Trade and Warfare in the Meeting Grounds of Northeastern North America, 1660–1821,' in Raudzens, ed., *Technology, Disease and Colonial Conquests*, 258.

4 The material is taken from: Bruce W. Hodgins and Gwyneth Hoyle, *Canoeing North into the Unknown: A Record of River Travel 1874–1974* (Toronto: Natural Heritage 1994), 83, 89; J.M. Gibbon, *Romance of the Canadian Canoe* (Toronto: Ryerson 1951), 38–40; and Daniel Francis and Toby Morantz, *Partners in Furs* (Montreal and Kingston: McGill-Queen's University Press 1983); and especially A.J. Ray, *Indians and the Fur Trade* (Toronto: University of Toronto Press 1974), 51–72.

5 On canoeing the Orkneys, see Ken McGoogan, *John Rae, Fatal Passage: The Untold Story of John Rae, the Arctic Adventurer* (Toronto: Harper 2001).

6 Quoted in McNab, Hodgins, and Standen, '"Black with Canoes,"' 237.

7 Germaine Warkentin, ed., *Canadian Exploration Literature* (Toronto: Oxford University Press 1993); James Houston, *Running West* (Toronto: McClelland and Stewart 1989), a fact-based novel about Thanadeltur; and McGoogan, *Fatal Passage*. Also, note Theodore Binnema et al., ed., *From Rupert's Land to Canada: Essays in Honour of John E. Foster* (Edmonton: University of Alberta Press 2001).

8 See also Shawn P. Hodgins, 'David Hanbury's Life and Northern Travels,' unpublished Trent University Canadian Studies paper, 1984.

9 See Brian Back, *The Keewaydin Way: The Story of the World's Oldest Canoe-Trip Camp* (Temagami, Ont.: Keewaydin, 2004); Bruce W. Hodgins and Seana Irvine, 'Temagami Youth Camping, 1903–1973,' in Bruce W. Hodgins and Bernadine Dodge, ed., *Using Wilderness: Essays on the Evolution of Youth Camping in Ontario* (Peterborough, Ont.: Trent Frost Centre 1992).

10 See also Heather Dunlop, 'The Role and Image of Aborigines in Selected Ontario Shield Camps,' MA thesis, Trent University, 1998.

11 Quoted from E. Pauline Johnson, *The White Wampum*, in Sheila M.F. Johnston, *Buckskin and Broadcloth: A Celebration of E. Pauline Johnson – Tekahionwake, 1861–1913* (Toronto: Natural Heritage 1997), 107.

12 Quoted from Marcus Van Steen, 'Pauline Johnson and Her Life and Work,' in Johnston, *Buckskin and Broadcloth*.

13 Canadian Canoe Museum, Peterborough, Ont., text panel, 'Matthew Coon Come' (Reflections Gallery). See also Michael Polsan's *Voices from the Odeyak* (Toronto: NC Press 1993). The *Odeyak* itself is in storage at the Canadian Canoe Museum.

14 Timothy J. Kent, *Birchbark Canoes of the Fur Trade*, vols. 1 and 2 (Ossineke, Mich.: Silver Fox Enterprises 1997); *Tahquamenon Tales: Experiences of an Early French Trader and his Native Family* (Ossineke, Mich.: Silver Fox Enterprises 1997, 1998); and *Ft. Ponchartrain at Detroit: A Guide to the Lakes Lives of Fur Trade and Military Personnel, Settlers and Missionaries at French Post* (Ossineke, Mich.: Silver Fox Enterprises 1997, 1999).

15 Canadian Canoe Museum, Peterborough, Ont., text panel, 'William and Mary Commanda'; National Film Board of Canada, *Césars Bark Canoe* [film] (Montreal: National Film Board of Canada 1971).

16 Canadian Canoe Museum, Peterborough, Ont., text panel, 'Peoples of the Rising Sun.'

17 Canadian Canoe Museum, Peterborough, Ont., file no.977.44.1, 'Possamoquoddy Birchbark Canoe.'

18 Canadian Canoe Museum, Peterborough, Ont., 'Legacy' and John Jennings, 'The Canadian Canoe Museum and Canada's National Symbol,' in Jennings, Hodgins and Small, ed., *The Canoe in Canadian Cultures.*

19 See also David Gidmark, *Birchbark Canoe: Living among the Algonquins* (Toronto: Firefly 1997).

20 Canadian Canoe Museum, Peterborough, Ont., text panel, 'William and Mary Commanda.'

21 Canadian Canoe Museum, Peterborough, Ont., file no.977.1.1, 'Haida Dugout Canoe: The Eagle,' and David Neel, *The Great Canoes: Reviving a Northwest Coast Tradition* (Vancouver: Douglas and McIntyre 1995).

22 Canadian Canoe Museum, Peterborough, Ont., text panel O/21, *The Dogrib Birchbark Canoe Project*. Also, note the video *Thicho Kielà: The Dogrib Birchbark Canoe* (Rae Edzo 1997). Furthermore, note the Shotah Dene video by Gabe Etchivelle, *The Last Mooseskin Boat* (Fort Norman, c. 1998).

23 Examples of art by Patrick Moranda, Rick Beaver, and Alan Sylibey are on display at the Canadian Canoe Museum, Peterborough, Ont., with accompanying interpretive information. Concerning the canoe in Aboriginal art, see Donald Burry, 'The Canoe in Canadian Art,' PhD thesis, University of Alberta, 1993; and Liz Wylie, *In the Wilds: Canoeing and Canadian Art* (Kleinburg, Ont.: McMichael Art Gallery 1998).

24 More than two hundred photographs were taken by Speck during his visit to Bear Island, now archived at the Geological Survey of Canada and the Smithsonian Institute, with copies in the possession of the Temagami First Nation. Also, note Bruce W. Hodgins and Jamie Benidickson, *The Temagami Experience* (Toronto: University of Toronto Press 1989).

Bibliography

Benidickson, Jamie. 1997. *Idleness, Water, and a Canoe: Reflections on Paddling for Pleasure*. Toronto: University of Toronto Press.

Bringhurst, Robert, and Ulli Steltzer. 1991. *The Black Canoe: Bill Reid and the Spirit of the Haida Gwaii*. Vancouver: Douglas and McIntyre.

Césars Bark Canoe. 1971. Montreal: National Film Board of Canada.

Finkelstein, Max. 2002. *Canoeing a Continent: In the Footsteps of Alexander Mackenzie*. Toronto: Natural Heritage.

Gibbon, J.M. 1951. *Romance of the Canadian Canoe*. Toronto: Ryerson.

Gidmark, David. 1980. *The Indian Crafts of William and Mary Commanda*. Toronto: McGraw-Hill Ryerson.

Hanbury, David. 1904. *Sport and Travel in the Northland of Canada*. London: Arnold.

Hodgins, Bruce W., and Margaret Hobbs. 1985. *Nawstagan: The Canadian North by Canoe and Snowshoe*. Toronto: Betelgeuse.

Indian and Northern Affairs Canada. 2002. 'Alwyn Morris.' Ottawa. Available from www.ainc-inac.gc.ca/ks/english/3052_e.html.

Jennings, John. 2002. *The North American Canoe: A Living Tradition*. Toronto: Firefly.

Ray, A.J. 1974. *Indians and the Fur Trade*. Toronto: University of Toronto Press.

Shadholt, Doris. 1998. *Bill Reid*. Vancouver: Douglas and McIntyre.

Tully, James. 1995. *Strange Multiplicity: Constitutionalism in an Age of Diversity*. Cambridge, U.K.: Cambridge University Press.

PART SEVEN

SPORTS

Profile of Sharon Anne and Shirley Anne Firth (1953–)

Loucheaux-Metis, Olympic Cross-Country Skiers

For more than two decades, twin sisters Sharon Anne and Shirley Anne Firth were among the top cross-country skiers in Canada. They represented their country in four consecutive Winter Olympics from 1972 to 1984 and their contributions to the sport are still felt today.

The Firth twins were born New Year's Eve, 1953, in Aklavik, Northwest Territories, to Fanny Rose and Stephen Firth.[1] They, along with their ten siblings, had a traditional upbringing and were taught to trap by their father and to track animals by their mother. Their childhood experiences prepared them for the hard work and dedication needed to succeed at elite-level sports.[2]

A Roman Catholic priest, Father Jean-Marie Mouchet, believing that the harsh life led by the area's trapping families could produce great skiers,[3] began the Territorial Experimental Ski Training (TEST) program in 1965. Getting the Firth sisters to try out for the ski team took some encouragement. Although they wanted to travel and saw the ski team as an opportunity, the Anglican sisters felt they had little chance of winning spots on the ski team since it was dominated by Catholics. Their mother eventually convinced them to try for the team by telling them that religion had little to do with athletic ability.[4] They began cross-country skiing in 1967. Father Mouchet also introduced them to Bjorger Petterson, the Norwegian coach of the Canadian Ski Federation. Petterson would coach them throughout their skiing careers.

Their first racing success came when Shirley, seen as an underdog, won a race in Anchorage, Alaska. This was only the beginning of the racing success the Firths would enjoy. By the end of their careers, they had captured forty-eight Canadian championships between them.[5] They participated in the Olympic Games from 1972 until 1984, making them the first Canadian women to participate in four straight Olympiads.[6] Although they failed to capture Olympic medals, they obtained the highest-ever ranking by Cana-

Sharon Anne and Shirley Anne Firth. Courtesy of Cross Country Canada; photographer: Jarl Omholt Hensen.

dian female skiers at that time. Sharon Firth's twenty-fourth-place finish in the five-kilometre event at the 1972 Games in Sapporo, Japan, stood as Canada's best showing until the record was broken in 2002.[7] In 1976 the Firths' efforts as members of Canada's 4x5 kilometre relay women's team brought our country's highest ski race ranking – seventh place – in Innsbruck, Austria.[8] They are also record holders for Canada's best Olympic finishes – Shirley in the ten kilometre and Sharon in the twenty kilometre – in race events that are no longer part of the Olympic program.[9] In their final Olympic appearance, at the 1984 games in Sarajevo, Yugoslavia, Sharon finished twenty-first in the twenty-kilometre race. Both retired from competitive skiing in the mid-1980s.

Success in Canadian and international athletics has garnered the Firth sisters many awards. They were inducted as members of the Canadian Skiing Hall of Fame in 1990[10] and appointed as members of the Order of Canada in 1988.[11] Their contributions to cross-country skiing have resulted in an award being named in their honour. The Firth Award is given annually to women who have made an outstanding contribution to Canadian cross-country skiing.[12]

ROLAND SIMON

Notes

1 Brenda Zeman, 'That Long Distance Feeling: Sharon and Shirley Firth.' In Zeman (with David Williams, ed.) *To Run with Longboat: Twelve Stories of Indian Athletes in Canada* (Edmonton: GMS2 Venture 1988), 99–120.
2 Ibid.
3 Ibid.
4 Ibid., 103.
5 www.canadagames.ca/enghome/thegames/Notable%20Alumni/firth.html.
6 Ibid.
7 Telephone conversation with former Team Canada women's cross-country ski coach Tom Holland. Canmore, Alta., Nordic Ski Centre, 25 Feb. 2003.
8 www.canoe.ca/2002GamesNordicCombined/dec14_cro-sun.html.
9 www.canada.x-c.com/nst/canadas.html.
10 www.nwt2000.com/skiyellowknife/westerns.html.
11 www.wysiwg://4/http://www.gg.ca.
12 www.canada.x-c.com/womens/volapp.htm.

The Qimmiq[1]

BRYAN CUMMINS

The Inuit of Arctic Canada called this dog 'Qimmiq.' The breed ... occupied the coastal and archipelago area of what is now Arctic Canada. – The Canadian Kennel Club Breed Standard for the Qimmiq – Canadian Eskimo Dog, cited in the Canadian Kennel Club's *Book of Dogs – Centennial Edition* (1988), 353.

The Canadian Kennel Club (CKC) recognizes over 160 breeds of dogs.[2] Of these, the breed names typically suggest the animal's country of origin and/or purpose. For example, we have the Australian Cattle Dog, the Irish Wolfhound, the German Shepherd, and the Old English Sheepdog. Of the scores of breeds recognized by the CKC, only one can claim to be truly indigenous to this country. Despite their names, the Labrador Retriever, the Newfoundland, and the Nova Scotia Duck Tolling Retriever are essentially breeds of European derivation that, at some stage of their development as purebreds, became associated with specific regions of this country. All have old world breeds somewhere in their ancestry. In contrast, the Qimmiq was developed in Canada's Arctic regions by the Inuit.

The Canadian Eskimo Dog bears this name courtesy of the Canadian Kennel Club. It is one of the oldest pure breeds. Recent evidence from the Arctic indicates that the dog has been resident there for at least 4,000 years (Carpenter 2000; Nunavut Legislative Assembly). The dog's real name then, that given him by Inuit, is *Qimmiq* (or Kimmiq). It is interesting that we long ago discarded the use of 'Eskimo' – a pejorative term – in favour of the proper 'Inuit' but still use the former in the breed name for their dog.

Identifying the Qimmiq

The two earliest discussions of the Qimmiq date from the early nineteenth century. The first is an article by J.G. Children in 1827; the second is John

Kimmiq, pencil sketch by Joanne Briggs, 2002.

Richardson's discussion of the breed in the important (and exceedingly rare) *Fauna Boreali Americana* (1829).

Children's brief article has been praised as the first scientific treatment of the Qimmiq. He notes that there had been a previous discussion of the breed in *L'Histoire Naturelle des Mammifières, Livraison XII* under the title 'Chien des Esquimaux de la Baie de Baffin.' However, closer examination revealed that the actual dog described was the product of a Qimmiq bitch and a Newfoundland dog, leaving the discussion somewhat null and void. Thus, Children's 'On the Esquimaux Dog' (1827) emerges as the first legitimate treatment of the breed.

Children's discussion is based on an 'unquestionably genuine male [Qimmiq], brought from the Polar sea' (Children 1827, 55). The dog's name was Akshelli, and, in the manner of the era, Children provides us with the requisite measurements of the animal: twenty-eight inches from the occiput to the root of the tail, eleven inches from the occiput to the extremity of the nose, four inches from the eyes to the point of the nose, four and a half inches between the ears, and twenty-four inches in height. The tail was approximately eighteen inches in length. Children goes on to describe the dog in considerable detail, noting the animal's erect and pointed ears, full curled tail, and 'very stout legs.' The coat was rather long, thick and soft, and 'somewhat woolly.' While Akshelli was black and white, Children noted that the breed was, of course, subject to variation in colour.

Particularly interesting are Children's observations of the dog's character and physical gifts. These are worth citing in full:

> Akshelli is good humoured, but rather impatient of restraint, and seems particularly to dislike being examined about the head, snapping at my hands somewhat angrily, on my applying the rule to measure its length. He seldom barks, but if displeased utters a low wolfish growl. He takes very little notice of strangers, and is of no use whatever as a guard. He feeds on carrion, and prefers raw fish to such as has been cooked. The strength of this dog is very great; when taken from his kennel, he appears extremely anxious to get at liberty, and when held back by his chain and collar, exerts himself with great power, increasing his efforts in proportion to the resistance that restrains him. A stout Boy [sic] of fourteen ... was unable, when the dog exerted his utmost strength, to hold him back; the animal dragged him forward several paces, in spite of all his efforts to prevent it. (Children 1827)

In his work, Richardson (1829) discusses three indigenous breeds, including the 'Esquimaux Dog' or *Canis familiaris americana borealis*. He noted, as did so many of his contemporaries, the similarity between Aboriginal breeds of dogs and wolves. Nowhere was this more apparent than at 'the *very northern extremity of the Continent*, the Esquimaux dogs being not only extremely like the gray wolves of the Arctic Circle, in form and colour, but nearly equaling them in size' (author's emphasis).

Richardson devotes much of his discussion of the breed to observations provided by Captain Lyon, who 'had so many opportunities of studying the habits of the Esquimaux dog.' We are particularly indebted to Lyon for his observations on the training of sled dogs. Incredibly, as soon as puppies could walk, they were harnessed and thus learned to pull, in their quest for freedom and in order to follow their dams. At the age of two months – an age, incidentally, when most Westerners bring their puppies home for the first time – the Qimmiq was harnessed to the sled with adult dogs. Sometimes, he noted, 'eight or ten little ones are under the charge of some steady old animal, where ... they soon receive a competent education.'

Lyon suggests the value of the Qimmiq in traditional Inuit society. Three or four dogs could haul a walrus, and he once witnessed a single dog carrying 'the greater part' of a seal in panniers on his back. Backpacking was the traditional task of the dogs in summer. However, it was in winter, when sledges could be equipped with runners that were shod or iced, that the dogs demonstrated their real worth. To illustrate, Lyon states that three of his dogs carried him, on a 100-pound sled, one mile in six minutes, while his lead dog hauled 196 pounds one mile in eight minutes. In another instance, seven dogs ran one mile in four minutes while hauling 'a heavy sledge full of men.' To give an idea of strength in numbers, nine of his dogs hauled 1,611 pounds one mile in nine minutes. What was remarkable in this case is that the runners on the sledge had been neither shod nor iced. Had they been, Lyon claims, 40 pounds per dog could have been added to the sledge for a total weight of nearly 2,000 pounds.

Tanner (personal communication, 2001) relates a true story that reflects the resourcefulness and hardiness of Inuit and their dogs. One November day in the late 1950s, some Inuit men were hunting seals at the floe edge near Inukjuak. They had with them a dog sled and team, as well as a kayak that was used in harpooning and retrieving seals. The ice on which they were standing began to break and drift into Hudson Bay. They started ferrying people back from the drifting ice to the larger ice attached to the mainland. However, given that they had only a kayak, which cannot carry that much, and that they were fighting a wind, progress was slow. In the end, all the hunters except one, and the dog team, reached the mainland. But there was nothing the survivors could do as the stranded hunter and the dogs started drifting away.

The men returned to Inukjuak and notified the Royal Canadian Mounted Police (RCMP). Because it was early in the year, they could not land a fixed wing plane on the ice. They sent for a helicopter from the south, but it was necessary to bring fuel for the aircraft, which necessitated caching fuel every seventy-five kilometres or so. As well, it could fly only during daylight hours. It took over a week for the helicopter to arrive and to pick up the police officer for a search.

The Inuk was located quite soon after the search began. His ice floe had run aground on a sand bar, where he had built an igloo and killed one of the dogs for food. All things considered, he had done well. The helicopter picked him up, but the pilot would not transport the dogs since he was afraid that they might become unruly during the flight and thereby jeopardize everyone's survival. The dogs were thus left behind.

When the RCMP officer reported the events to his superiors, he was given a stern reprimand for having left the dogs behind. He was informed that he should have asked the man to kill his dogs, and, if he had refused, the officer should have shot them for him. The reason for this harsh measure was that, if the media had received the full account of what had transpired, the RCMP would have come under fire from humane societies for having left the dogs to starve.

In the end, the officer was vindicated. By mid-January, two months later, the ice had formed all the way to the sand bar where the dogs had been left. They came trotting back into the settlement, none the worse for their ordeal. This dramatic account speaks volumes about the hardiness and resourcefulness of the breed.

The Qimmiq and Other Northern Sled Dogs

Glover M. Allen, in the important *Dogs of the American Aborigines* (1920), suggests that the 'Eskimo Dog' was originally found in Arctic America, co-extensively with the Inuit nations from the barrens of Alaska to Labrador, chiefly along the coast. In the east, Allen then states, the breed probably reached its southern limit on the east coast of Newfoundland, and then ranged northward, accompanying the Inuit, to Smith Sound in Greenland. In that region, the breed was found along the west coast southward, but by 1875 the draught dogs of the Danish settlements had been largely mongrelized through interbreeding with European breeds. This had happened as well in Alaska and southern Labrador (Allen 1920, 442).

We are faced with a problem, however, regarding Allen's assessment of the breed's distribution. The Federation Cynologique Internationale (FCI), essentially a United Nations of national kennel clubs, recognizes the Greenland Dog and the Canadian Eskimo Dog, suggesting a breed distinction between the two. Allen's description of the range of the 'Eskimo Dog' suggests – possibly – that the two are one and the same. The breeds are unavoidably similar, in that both are Arctic draught dogs. However, there are differences, notably in size and general configuration ('conformation,' in dog fancier terminology). Going a step further, some cynologists, Hubbard (1947) in particular, make the distinction between West Greenland Dogs (also called West Greenland Husky and Vestgronlands Hund) and East Greenland Dogs (or Husky), also called Angmagssalik Husky or Ostgronlands Husky. Hubbard states that both of these breeds bear greater similarity to the related breeds of Asia than to North American breeds, although the West Greenland shows some similarity to what Hubbard calls the Baffinland Husky, undoubtedly the Qimmiq. Incidentally, Hubbard claims that the East Greenland Dog is, in his view, the purest of the northern breeds of the Western Hemisphere.

All of this, of course, asks us to distinguish between 'breed' and 'type,' making us either a 'lumper' or 'splitter.' For many people there is the 'Husky' or 'Eskimo' dog, essentially a type of generic draught animal indigenous to a similarly generic 'north.' These are the lumpers. Splitters note the fine distinctions that exist among physical and cultural environments, as well as the dogs found in each one. For them, the Qimmiq is the draught dog of the Inuit of Canada, hence, the breed indigenous to the tundra, especially the coastal regions and the adjoining archipelagoes. The breed is thus distinct from the Alaskan dogs, such as the Malamute, and the Greenland Dog. It is, as the English name suggests, the *Canadian* Inuit Dog.

Allen makes another point clear. The Qimmiq, despite its appearance, is not a wolf. He notes that, in the wild, wolves are aggressive towards dogs and will kill them if they can. Samuel Hearne (1958) stated that they were 'great enemies to the Indian dogs, and frequently kill and eat them.' Allen adds that there is no evidence that wolf pups were habitually reared by either 'Indian' or 'Eskimo' (Allen 1920, 446, 447). Decades later, Ian Mac-Rury (1991) would reach the same conclusion while conducting research for a master's thesis on the Qimmiq at Darwin College, Cambridge University.

The Inuit and Their Dogs

Dogs were not evenly distributed throughout the Canadian Arctic before (or even after) Europeans arrived on this continent. Contrary to popular belief, the Inuit had relatively few dogs, although their importance cannot be overstated. The number of dogs that each nation had was largely a function of the resources available to support them.

The Mackenzie Delta Inuit had a moderate number of dogs in their teams, generally about five or six animals. This compares favourably with the one or two dogs of some other Inuit nations. They hauled sleds with iced bone or antler runners. The Mackenzie Delta Inuit used dogs, and dog-sledding technology, especially during the sealing season and for land-mammal hunting (Smith 1984, 349).

The situation was different among the Copper Inuit, who live on the islands and along the coast of the central Arctic. In traditional times, a hunter would have only one to three dogs, while, in the more recent past, this number doubled or tripled (Damas 1984). Richard G. Condon provides a most dramatic example of a hunter and a single dog (1996, 112, 113). This hunter, Povotag, a Copper Inuk, never grew to more than thirty-six inches and fifty-nine pounds, allegedly because of a curse placed on him. In the mid-1930s he had a very small sled and a single dog named Kavrak. With these, and a .22 calibre rifle, he maintained a small trap line.

The main reason for the relative paucity of dogs among the Copper was the environment, which is harsh even by Arctic standards. Condon (1996) suggests that, because the Copper did not hunt larger marine mammals such as walrus and whales, they were unable to feed large numbers of dogs (unlike, for example, the Iglulik or Baffinland Inuit, who live on Baffin Island, in the Melville peninsula, and along the northwest coast of Hudson Bay). Thus, mid-winter travel meant that men, women, and older children, assisted by only a couple of dogs, pulled the sleds. This also meant that trading expeditions, which were conducted with other Copper groups, as well as with other nations, might take months or even years. These trips occurred in stages, perhaps initially with sleds and then backpacking as the snow disappeared. Sleds would be cached near the coast and the gear backpacked. In the latter stage, dogs as well carried backpacks, typically including tents (Condon 1996, 74, 80, 90).

During the 1920s, the Netsilik, like many other Inuit nations, had relatively few dogs. The need to find food for the animals meant that most families had only a single animal, and some perhaps two to four. Only the most successful of hunters had as many as seven or eight (Rasmussen 1931, 148). It was the absence of large sea mammals, such as walrus, that kept the number of dogs to a minimum. As a result, their value lay in their worth not as draught animals but as hunters. Indeed, assisted by a dog or two, people typically pulled sleds. If a longer trip were undertaken, a team would be assembled by borrowing dogs from other people. Knud Rasmussen suggests that, even during the 1920s, the Netsilik did not practise any real sledge driving, for the dogs rarely would pull without a person leading the way (1931, 148). According to Asen Balikci (1970, 56) this would be a woman, typically walking five to ten yards ahead of her husband and dogs.

Regarding the Qimmiq's usefulness to the Netsilik in terms of hunting, Rasmussen notes: 'As a draught animal it might well be dispensed with. But a breathing-hole hunter without a dog might just as well stay at home and suck his thumb. If he has a dog, a hungry one for preference, it will lead him over the ice with distended nostrils in order to get the scent of something eatable, and it is from wonderfully long distances that it will suddenly prick its ears, lift its tail and rush away, not stopping until with unfailing certainty and without wavering a moment it has taken its master to a breathing hole' (1931: 148).

Breathing-hole seal hunting was a group effort. Men set out with dogs on leads towards a selected site, usually within walking distance of the camp. Once there, the group split up, each man going in a different direction with his dog or dogs, which were of 'crucial importance' in the hunt. Once a dog had located a hole, it either stopped and circled the hole or lay down beside it. Then, the hunter alerted his comrades to his discovery and they began probing the snow to locate the breathing hole. The dog was then removed

and tied to a block of snow or ice until the seal came up for air and was har-
pooned. Following the successful hunt, the hunters held a small feast on the
ice. They then strapped the seal to the dogs and brought it home. It is important to note that not all dogs were expert at locating breathing holes and a
particularly good dog was highly valued (Balikci 1970, 72–8).

Dogs also played an 'indispensable part' in the hunting of musk-oxen.
These animals naturally form a defensive circle when pursued or threatened. Cows and calves occupy the middle of the circle, with the bulls on
the outside, facing the threat. The animals rarely charge, so when the dogs
had brought the musk-oxen to bay, the Netsilik could target a particular
animal and shoot arrows at it. If it did eventually break rank and charge, it
could be killed with a spear. The same strategy worked with a single animal. If a solitary musk-ox were found near a cliff or steep hill, the hunter
and his dogs would drive it over the precipice (Balikci 1970, 51, 52).

Therkel Mathiassen (1928) states that, as a rule, the Iglulik did not have
many dogs. Only a few had teams of ten or more dogs, the norm being four
to six per family. While this number may seem low to Mathiassen, it is certainly more than other groups, such as the Netsilik, the Copper, and the
Caribou, had. In brief, it is likely that only the Labrador Inuit had more
dogs. The allegedly small number of animals among the Iglulik was again
attributed to the difficulties of procuring food, particularly during the caribou hunting season. It was among the Iglulingmuit that one found the big-
gest and best dog teams, because these people most often had large stores
of walrus meat. Nevertheless, on long journeys it was common for two
Iglulingmuit families to share a sled.

The Caribou kept only a few dogs and, at the time of the Fifth Thule
Expedition (1921–4), they were all the indigenous, or Qimmiq, breed. Even
if other larger and more amenable breeds were available, the coat and paws
alone made the traditional Inuit dog far better adapted to the Arctic environment (Birket-Smith 1929, 170). The small number of Qimmiq kept by the
Caribou was due to the fact that the dogs had to be fed caribou meat, which
is not nearly as nutritious as seal or walrus, and even less so in winter when
it was fed to them frozen. Without firearms to assist in the procurement of
game, the Caribou typically never had more than three dogs per family.
Later, even when the Caribou had rifles, the number of dogs per family was
no greater. As a result, when a long journey was undertaken, it was common for several families to combine their teams. Another reason for the relatively small number of dogs was the prevalence of distemper. In the early
1920s, distemper had wrought havoc among the dog teams of the Caribou.
Birket-Smith reported seeing one dog hauling two sleds with, of course,
some help from the people (1929, 170).

The Labrador Inuit differed in one major way from many other Inuit peoples, namely, in the number of dogs they owned. The size of the average team in Labrador, in the late eighteenth century, was more than fifteen dogs. J. Garth Taylor (1974, 37, 38) provides data on sixteen teams in the early contact period. These ranged in size from two dogs, owned by a couple and their child, who are described as 'very poor people,' to a pair of teams with twenty-eight dogs. The size of these teams contrasts dramatically with most parts of the Arctic, where the norm was well under half a dozen. Consistent with these large teams were large sleds and heavy loads. Again, Taylor refers to sleds measuring sixteen feet in length and thirty inches wide, and one was twenty-one feet long with crossbars eighteen inches wide. References to one sled returning from a hunting trip with a cargo of twelve seals, suggests a minimum weight of 1,800 pounds being hauled by the dogs. Unfortunately, in this case, the number of dogs is not given. But the facts suggest a sizeable team.

Given the lengthy period of contact between the Labrador Inuit and Europeans, it is safe to assume that it was not long before the traditional Inuit dog, the Qimmiq, was forever altered through cross-breeding with foreign breeds. Thus, virtually any reference made to dogs in the historical record indicates a mongrelized animal. Evidence for this contention is found in the polar literature in which writers refer to 'Labrador Huskies,' often implying a much shaggier animal than the Qimmiq. Photos of these dogs suggest a Qimmiq that mated with an Old English Sheepdog. But, in reality, they are probably the result of Qimmiq/Newfoundland or Qimmiq/St Bernard crosses, or simply the end result of centuries of contact. Regardless, they were not pure Qimmiq.

The Qimmiq in Religious Belief

The Qimmiq played a role in Netsilik religious beliefs. Nuliajuk, Narssuk, and Tatqeq are the three major deities in Netsilik religion. Nuliajuk is considered the mother of all animals and the mistress of both land and sea; Narssuk is the weather god; and Tatqeq is the moon spirit. There are two stories that account for the origin of Nuliajuk, both of which include a dog. They were both related to Rasmussen. In the more common version, people long ago left the settlement at Qingmertoq in Sherman Inlet. They were going to cross the water, so they made a large raft of several kayaks that were tied together. The people were in a hurry since they were anxious to reach new hunting grounds. As the crowded rafts were pulling away, a little girl named Nuliajuk jumped on a raft carrying the other children. But she had no family, so nobody cared about her. The children threw her off the raft and, as she tried to climb back on, chopped her fingers off. As she sank to the bottom of the sea, the stumps of her fingers became alive as they bobbed about in the water like seals. In this way, seals came into existence. Nuliajuk herself sank to the bottom of the sea where she became the sea spirit and the mother of all sea beasts. She also became mistress of everything else that lives, including land beasts, which people need to hunt. Because of the way she was treated, she has no affection for people. Given that she is the most powerful spirit, she exerts considerable control over the destinies of people and is thus the most feared of all spirits. She lives in a house on the bed of the sea. Along the passageway of the house, there is a big black dog that keeps watch. No one but the greatest of shamans, of whom the dog is afraid, can enter the house.

The Dog-Husband story is common throughout the Subarctic and Arctic and is found to a lesser degree on the Plains, along the Northwest Coast, and on the Canadian plateau. A man named Nakasuk related the Netsilik version of the myth to Rasmussen (1931, 227, 228), who viewed Nakasuk as a highly credible informant. In many ways, it is an interesting and intriguing story insofar as it explains not only the origin of Nuliajuk but also the origins of First Nations and Europeans and, intriguingly perhaps, Netsilik perceptions of them. Of course, the inclusion of references to whites indicates that this is a post-contact story, suggesting the dynamism of Netsilik culture.

An angry father once yelled at his daughter that he wanted a dog, not a husband, for her. That night, after everybody had gone to bed, the man's dog came in, but in human form, and wearing a dog's tooth on his breast as an amulet. He laid down beside the girl, embracing her and 'hung fast' to her, dragging the girl into the passageway. 'In that way they became man and wife.' The Dog-Husband continued to come to her every night. Soon, the girl became pregnant and when she was about to give birth, her father rowed her to an island, because he did not want to take care of her children. On the island, the girl gave birth to a litter of young who would eventually become White men and 'Indians.' The father (from what follows, it is assumed that the girl's father is meant, not the children's father) used to go to the island in his kayak and bring meat to them.

The girl, though, resented the way that she had been treated and when her children had grown up, she told them what had transpired. She then ordered her offspring to attack her father when he next arrived. When he pulled his kayak up on shore, they licked the boat and then threw themselves upon him and tore him to shreds. After this, she sent her children out into the world. To those who would become 'Indians,' she gave her inner kamiks for boats and let them leave, telling them that they should be hostile to all men. To those who would become white men, she gave her outer kamiks, which would become their ships. She exhorted them to be friendly. However, when she tried to board one of her children's boats, they threw her into the water. When she tried to save herself by holding onto the edge of the boat, they chopped off the first joint of her fingers. These later surfaced as seals. Again, the mother tried to board the boat but her children chopped off the next finger joint. It took a while, but these surfaced as bearded seals. A third time it happened, and the dismembered joint appeared, after a long time, as walruses. Finally, the woman sank to the bottom of the sea where she became Nuliajuk, the mother of the beasts.

Rasmussen adds that, in this version, the woman built a house in a bubble at the bottom of the sea. It is her husband, the dog, who guards the entrance to the house so that she may not be disturbed when she is angry (1931, 227).

The Qimmiq's Contribution to Polar Exploration

Given the Qimmiq's unparalleled qualities as a draught animal, it is not surprising that it became the favoured breed for Arctic and Antarctic exploration. It served in a number of polar excursions, not only in the Canadian Arctic, but elsewhere. The British used the breed in their Falkland Islands Dependency Survey, while American and New Zealand exploration teams used the Qimmiq in Antarctica and found them superior to all other breeds. This is consistent with what many people have observed about the breed: while not as speedy as the Siberian Husky (or Chukchi), nor as powerful as the Alaskan Malamute, the Qimmiq is probably the most durable breed in the world.[3]

One need only consider the ill-fated Scott expedition to Antarctica in 1912 to appreciate the Qimmiq. It is generally recognized that Roald Amundsen was successful in reaching the South Pole because of his reliance upon sled dogs, while Scott preferred to use ponies for the heavy draught work. Scott had dogs on his expedition, but he fully believed that the tough, durable Siberian-bred ponies were suitable for Antarctica. More than one observer has noted that Scott had a relatively low opinion of dogs, although he acknowledged that the ones he had seen at work impressed him. His expedition employed them for setting up food caches that were to be used on the assault on the South Pole. In the end, the ponies proved completely unsuitable, many dying in blizzards, while the Qimmiq simply curled up in the snow, oblivious of the weather. When some of them did die, for whatever reason, they were fed to their team-mates.

Between 1957 and 1959, the Canadian Defence Research Board used the Qimmiq in northern Ellesmere Island (about as far north as one can get in this country) while conducting scientific studies. During this time, they were used for both draught and backpacking work. Few breeds, if any, have proven so useful to humankind under the harshest of conditions. Furthermore, it is quite simply the case that polar exploration could not have occurred without the aid of the northern sled dogs. And of these, the Qimmiq is the undisputed king. The breed's contributions not only to Canadian culture, but to the world, are beyond dispute.

More recently, the Qimmiq has been called back into harness for polar journeys, albeit for other reasons. Some were as ill-conceived as Scott's expedition. Lonnie Dupre (2000) attempted a journey along the Arctic Coast, beginning in Point Barrow, Alaska, in 1992. In part, it was to recreate (although eastwards) Rasmussen's Fifth Thule Expedition and to document changes in Inuit life since that time, but also to assess environmental damage by collecting and analysing plant samples.

The expedition had thirty-four dogs, some Alaskan Huskies, the rest Qimmiq. Beset with difficulties, nineteen dogs died of hypothermia and starvation. Those that survived and made it as far as Churchill, Manitoba, were all Qimmiq. As Peary (1910) had observed decades earlier after witnessing his own Qimmiq in harness, 'there is no dog that can work so long in the lowest temperatures on practically nothing to eat.'

Other, better-conceived ventures, have succeeded. One four-person team, accompanied by three Qimmiq, traversed the Penny Ice Cap off Baffin Island in 1992. The Qimmiq hauled small sleds loaded with supplies. When travelling over ice and snow, the dogs backpacked the supplies. The expedition was well planned and successful, with the Qimmiq and people finishing in fine shape. Elsewhere, Qimmiq are used today in a number of eco-travel and sporting ventures. Dog-sledding excursions are increasingly popular in the Arctic, and the Qimmiq is a natural for this task. As well, a limited amount of polar bear hunting is allowed for people from outside the Territories. The law stipulates, however, that the animals cannot be pursued from motorized vehicles. Thus, sports hunting has opened the door to income opportunities for Inuit, while also producing a revival in traditional means of transportation and increased demand for the working Qimmiq.

Saving the Qimmiq from Extinction

In 1935 S. Hadwen wrote a two-part article about the Qimmiq for *The Beaver*, the Hudson's Bay Company magazine. He observed how, following a study, it was decided that the Siberian Husky (Chukchi) had been deemed a better breed for work in the Canadian Arctic, because of its greater speed. This, he alleges, was a grave mistake, and, as a consequence, the Qimmiq was suffering. The solution, he proposed, was a total embargo on foreign dogs in the Arctic. He had no idea how prescient his observations were to be.

By 1970, the Qimmiq was in real danger of going the way of so many other indigenous breeds of dog. The estimate is that the population had dropped from an estimated 20,000 dogs in 1920 to fewer than 200. The American Kennel Club had dropped the 'Eskimo Dog' from the list of registered breeds in 1950, because of a lack of registrations. Its existence today is attributable to one man, a biologist and Springer Spaniel fancier by the name of William (Bill) J. Carpenter. Carpenter related his story in the February 1976 issue of *North/Nord*.

Carpenter embarked on a one-person crusade to save the breed, eventually working with a number of individuals and organizations, including John McGrath, Ken MacRury, the Canadian Kennel Club, and the city of Yellowknife. Through sheer diligence and hard work, he brought the breed back from the brink of extinction, although it is still threatened. Today, there are approximately five hundred purebred Qimmiq in existence.

The Qimmiq's Contribution to Canadian Identity and Culture

In the early 1950s, Yukon Territory's coat of arms was commissioned by the federal Department of Indian Affairs and Northern Development. It was granted approval by Queen Elizabeth in February 1956. The Qimmiq – or a related breed – is part of the coat of arms of the territory. Standing on a snow bank at the top of the coat of arms is a dog that has been variously described as a 'sled dog,' a 'Husky,' or a 'Malamute.' This dog is said to be representative of the 'traditional means of transportation' in the territory. The terms used for the emblematic dog are all problematic, of course, for a number of reasons. A sled dog theoretically may be any breed capable of doing the work. The term 'Husky' is more properly applied to the Alaskan Husky (in reality, a type rather than a breed) or the Siberian Husky. The Malamute is more properly known as the Alaskan Malamute. Finally, only a fraction of the Qimmiq's original homeland was found in Yukon. Nearly the whole of its homeland territory is in present-day Nunavut.

If confusion reigns over the animal on Yukon's coat of arms, there was no such doubt at the end of the twentieth century when Canada's newest territory was formed. The Qimmiq became the official animal of Nunavut at the time of the territory's creation on 1 April 1999. As noted in the Legislative Assembly's literature, the 'dog has been essential to the survival of the Inuit for generations, being the only draft animal for long-range travel and a willing and capable hunting companion.' It was a fitting recognition for the Qimmiq. Not only was the dog essential for Inuit survival, but the territory also includes 99 per cent of the breed's original homeland.

In addition to official recognition by various governments, the Qimmiq has found its place in popular culture as well. The Qimmiq has featured prominently in the literature and folklore of the north, from the novels by Jack London to the legend of Sergeant Preston of the Yukon. While the media have misrepresented the dogs at times (Sergeant Preston's Yukon King, for example, was played by a Malamute and Constable Benton Fraser's Diefenbaker, in the television program 'Due South' [1994–8], was a Siberian Husky playing a 'wolf'), there is clearly an assumption that the 'Husky' is meant to represent all that is Canadian and northern. If Canada is the 'true North,' then there is no fitter icon than the Qimmiq, indigenous to the Arctic and recognized the world over as truly 'Canadian.'

Perhaps the last words should go to John McGrath, Bill Carpenter's partner in saving the Qimmiq. He has written: 'The future of the [Qimmiq] is not in the dog show world with dogs on a leash instead of a sealskin or webbing harness – although this display may help in the needed dissemination of information about this noble breed – but in the north. We cannot separate the dogs, the place and the people.'

Notes

1 The illustration of the Qimmiq dog was provided by Joanne Briggs, a multi-media artist born and educated in Canada. Briggs's work has been displayed at galleries and exhibits in Ontario and may be found in private collections throughout Canada, Great Britain, and the United States. She is currently majoring in anthropology at Trent University and her illustrations have been published in Bryan D. Cummins's *First Nations, First Dogs* (Calgary: Detselig Enterprises 2002).
2 The Federation Cynologique Internationale, a global organization, recognizes over four hundred breeds of dogs.
3 The Siberian Husky is a smaller, lighter dog than the Qimmiq, standing approximately fifty-one to sixty centimetres and weighing fifteen to twenty-seven kilograms. It is well adapted to sled-dog racing. The Alaskan Malamute generally stands between fifty-eight and sixty-three centimetres and weighs in the neighbourhood of thirty-four to thirty-nine kilograms. It excels at heavy draught work. The Qimmiq is generally between these two in height and weight although, being a natural breed, there is considerable range in size.

Bibliography

Allen, Glover M. 1920. 'Dogs of the American Aborigines.' *Bulletin of the Museum of Comparative Zoology* 63.
Balikci, Asen. 1970. *The Netsilik Eskimo*. Garden City, N.Y.: The Natural History Press.

Birket-Smith, K. 1929. *The Caribou Eskimo: Material and Social Life and Their Cultural Position*. Copenhagen: Gyldenalske Boghandel, Nordisk Forlag (Report of the Fifth Thule Expedition, 1921–4, vol. 5).

Canadian Kennel Club. 1988. *Book of Dogs – Centennial Edition*. Toronto: Stoddart.

Carpenter, William J. 1976. 'Canada's Own Eskimo Dog ... On The Brink of Extinction.' *North/Nord* (February).

– 2000. Personal communication.

Children, J.G. 1827. 'On the Esquimaux Dog.' *Zoological Journal* 3.

Condon, Richard G. 1996. *The Northern Copper Inuit*. Norman: University of Oklahoma Press.

Damas, David. 1984. 'Copper Eskimo.' In *Smithsonian Handbook of North American Indians*, vol. 5 (Arctic), ed. David Damas. Washington, D.C.: Smithsonian Institution.

Dupre, Lonnie. 2000. *Greenland Expedition: Where Ice Is Born*. Chanhassen, Minn.: NorthWorld Books.

Hadwen, S. 1935. 'The Eskimo Dogs of the Eastern Arctic – Part I.' *The Beaver* (June).

Hearne, Samuel. 1958. *A Journey from Prince of Wales Fort in Hudson's Bay to the Northern Ocean in the Years 1769, 1770, 1771, and 1772*, ed. R. Glover. Toronto: Macmillan.

Hubbard, C.L.B. 1947. *Working Dogs of the World*. London: Sidgwick and Jackson.

MacRury, Ian Kenneth. 1991. 'The Inuit Dog: Its Provenance, Environment and History.' Master of Philosophy thesis in Polar studies, Cambridge University.

Mathiassen, Therkel. 1928. *Material Culture of the Iglulik Eskimos*. Copenhagen: Gyldendalske Boghandel, Nordisk Forlag (Report of the Fifth Thule Expedition, 1921–4, vol. 6, no.1).

McGrath, John. 1998. *Notes for a Talk at a Meeting of Dog Enthusiasts in Connecticut* (3 Jan.). Courtesy of William Carpenter.

Peary, Robert E. 1910. *The North Pole*. New York: Fredrick and Stokes.

Rasmussen, Knud. 1931. *The Netsilik Eskimos – Social Life and Spiritual Culture*. Copenhagen: Gyldendalske Boghandel Nordisk Forlag (Report of the Fifth Thule Expedition, 1921–4, vol. 8, nos.1–2).

Nunavut Legislative Assembly. n.d. 'Symbols of Nunavut.'

Richardson, John. 1829. *Fauna Boreali-Americana or the Zoology of the Northern Parts of British North America*. London: John Murray.

Smith, Derek G. 1984. 'Mackenzie Delta Eskimo.' *Smithsonian Handbook of North American Indians*, vol. 5 (Arctic), ed. David Damas. Washington, D.C.: Smithsonian Institution.

Tanner, Adrian. 2001. Personal communication.

Taylor, J. Garth. 1974. *Labrador Eskimo Settlements of the Early Contact Period*. Ottawa: National Museums of Canada Publications in Ethnology, no.9.

Profile of Alwyn Morris (1957–)

Mohawk, Olympic Rower

World-class paddler Alwyn Morris put in a stellar performance at the 1984 Olympics in Los Angeles, California, where he became the third North American Indian after Jim Thorpe and Billy Mills to win a gold medal.[1] The gold medal was a reward for the many years of training, determination, and perseverance that helped him keep a promise he made to his grandfather when he was eleven years old.

Alwyn Morris, a Mohawk, was born in 1957 on the Kahnawake First Nations Reserve in Quebec.[2] At fourteen, he became interested in the Onake Paddling Club that operated on the Mohawk territory of Kahnawake. His grandfather asked him, 'Why not hockey, why not lacrosse?' Morris replied, 'Because I love to paddle.'[3] In 1968, while watching the Mexico City Olympics on television with his grandfather, he made a vow. He promised his grandfather that one day he would become an Olympian.[4]

Despite discouraging comments from coaches about his physical stature, Morris showed determination during the endless hours of training. At eighteen, Morris moved to Vancouver to train with Hugh Fisher, his future rowing partner.[5] Morris began winning competitions. In 1977 he won the K-1 1,000-metre and the K-1 500-metre junior national championships.[6] That same year he was named the 1977 recipient of the Tom Longboat Award as the top North American Indian athlete.[7]

In 1980 Alwyn Morris won a spot on the Canadian Olympic team but did not compete because the Canadian government joined a United States-led boycott that protested Russia's invasion of Afghanistan. The Canadian government's political stance had moved his goal of Olympic competition another four years down the road. This meant that Morris needed even more commitment to pursue his Olympic dream.

Morris, and his partner, Hugh Fisher, trained in Burnaby, British Columbia. They raced in the 1984 Summer Olympic paddling competition in the K-2 event (kayak pairs).[8] They were gold-medal favourites. They came in

Alwyn Morris. Courtesy of Windspeaker, Canada's National Aboriginal News Source.

third and won a bronze medal in the 500-metre race, but they went on to win the gold medal in the 1,000 metre competition. Morris proudly raised an eagle feather on the Olympic podium. He sent sports commentators scurrying to figure out what he was doing with 'the feather.' They asked, 'Is it some sort of "Red Power" gesture?'[9] Morris replied that it stood for the lessons he had learned from his grandfather – perseverance and dedication. His grandfather had passed away in 1980 and so would not see his grandson compete and win Olympic medals.

Today, Alwyn Morris lives on the Kahnawake Reserve and works with the Mohawk Council of the Kahnawake. He is chairman of the Aboriginal Sports Circle, a national organization that promotes athletics among Aboriginal youth. He continues to spread his message: 'There is opportunity. There are lots of hurdles. You can never quit on something you believe strongly in.'[10]

LEONA FURGASON

Notes

1   Brenda Zeman, 'Alwyn Morris: An Olympic Image.' In Brenda Zeman (with David Williams, ed.), *To Run with Longboat: Twelve Stories of Indian Athletes in Canada* (Edmonton: GMS2 Ventures 1998), 203.
2   'Alwyn Morris' (2002). www.cbc.sports/olympians/morris/shtml.
3   Zeman, 'Alwyn Morris,' 202.
4   'Alwyn Morris' (2002). www.olympic.org/uk/athletes.
5   Zeman, 'Alwyn Morris,' 207.
6   James Marsh, 'Morris, Alwyn,' *Canadian Encyclopaedia: 2000 World Edition* (Toronto: McClelland and Stewart 2000).
7   Ibid.
8   Zeman, 'Alwyn Morris,' 196.
9   Ibid.
10   www.cbc.sports/olympians/morris/shtml.

'Eminently Canadian': Indigenous Sports and Canadian Identity in Victorian Montreal

GILLIAN POULTER

From the ball play of the Indian have we inherited our national game, and from the snowshoe and the toboggan, their means of locomotion over the snows of winter, the white man has developed two glorious winter sports.
— William H. Whyte, *The MAAA* (Montreal: [Becket Bros?] 1905)[1]

In his account of the early history of the Montreal Amateur Athletics Association (MAAA), William Whyte clearly understood the contribution of Indigenous cultural activities such as lacrosse, snowshoeing, and tobogganing to the culture of the new Dominion of Canada. The enthusiasm with which immigrants from the British Isles adopted these activities and transformed them into organized sports might seem somewhat surprising in light of the cult-like appeal that cricket held for the British well into the twentieth century. Indeed, some historians argue that British sports were an important influence in the development of sport culture in Canada.[2] Nevertheless, the records of the MAAA and newspaper reports of sports activities in the second half of the nineteenth century show that British settlers in Canada did not just transplant their own sports onto North American soil; instead, they appropriated activities that were rooted in Canada and in so doing forged for themselves a new identity as Canadians.[3]

British colonists in nineteenth century Montreal were faced with a problem. They needed to develop an identity that would distinguish them from the British and the Americans, while still retaining commercial connections and family ties with the old country. Most did not wish to repudiate their connections with the British empire entirely, although the annexation crisis of 1849 indicates that amalgamating with the Americans in a continental union was a distinct alternative. Still, there was a strong desire to 'make Canadians' and to claim the 'new nationality' called for by nationalists such as D'Arcy McGee and Canada First.

How was this to be done? Although the characteristics of national identity might be posited on an ideological or intellectual level, national identity does not take form until it is made real through cultural practices. Thus, the process of forming Canadian national identity required that certain characteristics become identified as distinctively Canadian through being repeatedly enacted by individuals whose performance was recognized as 'Canadian' by spectators.[4] Aboriginal cultural activities such as hunting, snowshoeing, and lacrosse proved to be ideal for this purpose in three ways. First, they were visually distinctive activities; they were clearly not British and not American. Second, the performance of the activities was in itself an Indigenizing experience which legitimized colonists' claim to be 'native-Canadian.'[5] Third, they were activities that could be 'tamed' and made 'civilized' through the imposition of British values and ideology. Hence, on the one hand, Canadians emulated British values and the ideology of order, discipline, and fair play since these were considered the hallmarks of a civilized nation and counteracted the 'primitive' connotations associated with Native peoples; on the other hand, what was distinctively Canadian about Canadians was actually Native.

By examining what Indigenous cultural activities such as hunting, snowshoeing, and lacrosse meant to the white colonists who participated in them, we can discover the indispensable contribution that First Nations peoples made to Canadian identity.[6] In order to feel 'at home' in their new land, British colonists needed to learn how to navigate and survive in their new landscape. Early colonists learned these skills through the trials and travails of clearing the land for agriculture, but the urban middle classes in Victorian Montreal had not experienced this themselves. They relied instead on tales about the olden days of the fur trade, the heroic efforts of the Loyalists, the quaint and romantic past of 'Old Quebec,' and reports of contemporary scientific expeditions. Taking part in hunting parties and snowshoe tramps provided an opportunity for these city-dwellers to be Indigenized – through personal experience in the Canadian wilderness landscape and northern climate, they could learn Native skills and literally put themselves in the place of Native peoples as a new type of native Canadian. Playing lacrosse was another way to step into Native shoes and was a distinctive visual spectacle through which to display Canadian identity abroad. However, this was an identity restricted to affluent Montreal middle-class professionals, businessmen, managers and merchants who could afford the time and expense of club membership. Women, the working-class and French Canadians were largely excluded.

Caribou and Moose Hunting

At mid-century, Canada was popularly viewed as a northern land of cold and snow – a stereotype that Canadian entrepreneurs and politicians tried hard to dispel. Indeed, historian Carl Berger has shown that Canada's northern location became a positive attribute and veritable national characteristic in the vocabulary of advocates of imperialism and Canadian nationalism towards the end of the century (Berger 1970, 129). Robert Grant Haliburton, for instance, argued in an 1869 address entitled 'The Men of the North and Their Place in History' that Canadians were tough, strong, and hardy and destined to play a dominant role in the new world because they were all 'descendants of Northern races.' As Berger contends: 'Few of Haliburton's young friends could resist seizing upon his assurances that "we are the Northmen of the New World,"' and hunting in the northern bush was an enactment of this identity (53).

Hunting was, of course, a well-established sporting activity in Britain, and imperial 'big game hunting' was a familiar colonial pursuit.[7] But it took on new meaning and form in the Canadian context where the exotic animals were moose and caribou and the 'Great White Hunter' had his equivalent in the 'Great Northern Hunter' of the winter wilderness. Bagging Canadian game required special hunting techniques, for which British colonists needed the assistance of Native guides. A series of portraits created in 1866 in the Montreal photographic studio of William Notman visualized Colonel William Rhodes as the ideal model of the Great Northern Hunter, venturing out into the Laurentian wilderness in search of caribou, the Canadian game most in keeping with the gentlemanly tradition. Rhodes was the perfect choice of portrait subject. A former member of the British military, he had settled in Canada to become a prominent Quebec landowner and politician, and was already known as 'the Great Northern Hunter.'[8] Not surprisingly, given the history of discrimination and oppression suffered by First Nations in North America, several of the Notman photographs represent the Native guides as subordinate and subservient to their colonial employers (Figure 1).[9] However, the photographs also reveal the ways in which white hunters were indebted to the teachings of their Aboriginal guides.

The *Cariboo Hunting* series of nine photographs depicts a hunting party setting out into the bush on snowshoes, carrying supplies on toboggans. The two white hunters are accompanied by three Huron guides – three generations of the Gros-Louis family from Lorette, all named François. In some photographs, one of Notman's employees, Octave Dandurand, plays the part of a young Native guide.[10] On this staged hunting trip in Notman's studio, they set up a tent and the Gros-Louis men are seen in various scenarios: cooking, mending equipment, assisting in the hunt, and carrying home the bagged caribou. In the *Moose Hunting* series, which was taken in the same studio a few months later, the Native guides feature more prominently as

Figure 1. William Notman, *Colonel Rhodes and Octave the Guide*, Montreal, Quebec, 1866. Courtesy of the Notman Photographic Archives, McCord Museum of Canadian History, Montreal. Image no. I-19310.

Figure 2. William Notman, *The Chance Shot, Colonel Rhodes and Octave the Guide*, Caribou Hunting Series. Montreal, 1866. Courtesy of the Notman Photographic Archives, McCord Museum of Canadian History, Montreal. Image no. I-19323.

the sole subject of two of the seven images. Again they are shown in subservient roles: hunting, cooking, and preparing equipment; and this time they have built a lean-to shelter from pine boughs. And, once more, the portraits reveal that white hunters initially relied on Native people to teach them the hunting and camping skills required in the Canadian environment.[11]

The Chance Shot is an allegory of how Aboriginal knowledge was passed on to the new 'native Canadian' (Figure 2). Colonel Rhodes is shown crouching in the snow with his young Native guide. They are both staring ahead, presumably at caribou, judging by the trophy at their feet. Octave is leaning close to Rhodes, peering over his right shoulder. The iconographic allusion here is of the Native guide as classical Muse, literally inspiring or breathing into Rhodes Indigenous knowledge and wisdom.[12] The knowledge being transferred is the technique of still-hunting, the most common method used for hunting moose and caribou but one of the most difficult for non-Native hunters to learn. Grey Owl (the well-known British immigrant who took on the persona of a Canadian Native) claimed that 'still-hunting is an art learned from the Indian, an accomplishment in which few white men excel.'[13] The key to still-hunting is patience. Once the Native guides had found prey, the hunters would approach quietly, crouching or crawling on their stomachs, and wait for the chance to get off a perfect shot. This was obviously more difficult than running down caribou or moose in deep snow, which was considered unsporting because the animals were at such a disadvantage. The Quebec *Mercury* quoted Rhodes in an article describing one of his hunting trips: 'In some instances the caribou have to be approached by crawling on the ground. "On one occasion of this kind," says our friend, "previous to the final stalk, it being very cold weather, I had one of my men badly frost-bitten, as he dare not move for some time for fear of alarming the deer, so we had to retire, warm ourselves by running about and eating, and then recommence the attack"' (Quebec *Mercury*, 10 January 1866, 6–7). In this passage, Rhodes shows he has absorbed his training. In fact, he is better than 'his' men, because it is they who get frostbitten, not him. He is the Great Northern Hunter, the privileged possessor of knowledge which makes him a native Canadian; he has been Indigenized through learning Aboriginal skills.

In tracking animals in the bush, hunters like Rhodes became familiar with the land and gained mastery over the skills required to navigate it. The Notman hunting photographs show white colonists comfortable in the Canadian wilderness environment. *Around the Camp Fire* (Figure 3), for example, depicts the hunting party: 'After an exciting day, our heroes have seated themselves upon the ground to tell the adventures of the day's chase. The pipe is in nearly every mouth, and a happy, contented-looking group they are' (*Philadelphia Photographer* 3, 29 (May 1866), 130.[14] Whereas the wilderness had always been a source of danger and anxiety for early European visitors, these men are relaxed in their environment. They know how to be warm and sheltered in the forest because, thanks to their Native guides, they have learned the skills necessary to survive in the bush. From the time of first contact, white colonists were heavily dependent on Native peoples for their physical survival in the New World. These photographs show another, albeit less crucial, type of dependence among urban colonists of the mid-nineteenth century.

The photographs reached a wide audience because Notman submitted them to numerous international exhibitions and fairs, at which they invariably won prizes (Triggs 1992, 57). They were awarded medals at the Paris Universal Exposition of 1867, even though they were not advantageously displayed.[15] In addition, Notman sold the photographs in a variety of sizes

Figure 3. William Notman, *Around the Camp Fire*, Caribou Hunting Series, Montreal, Quebec, 1866. Courtesy of the Notman Photographic Archives, McCord Museum of Canadian History, Montreal. Image no.VIEW-596.A.

and formats to suit every pocketbook, and some were reproduced in large quantities to be sold as souvenir 'Views' in stationery and book stores, hotels, and train stations. His artistic ability and business acumen therefore ensured that these images of Canada and Canadians were circulated widely at home and abroad, establishing for their audiences the link between Canada and its distinctive wildlife, and reinforcing already established stereotypes about Canada as a snowy, northern land – but this time with a positive 'spin.'

Snowshoeing

The contribution of Native culture to Canadian identity is also obvious when we look at the way in which middle-class Montreal males adopted snowshoeing as a leisure pursuit. Snowshoes were a distinctive attribute of

Canada. They were on display at the Great Exhibition in the Crystal Palace in London in 1851; they were prominently featured in the Notman hunting photographs; and, along with an outdoor setting, they were enough to identify the scene as 'Canadian' in the hundreds of souvenir portraits taken by the Notman Studios and other photographers of the time.[16] The outdoor winter setting was chosen, for instance, by General Wyndham and family for a souvenir portrait taken in 1867 (Figure 4). Mrs Wyndham and her daughter hold snowshoes and the youngest child sits on a sleigh wearing a miniature snowshoe costume – a blanket coat with coloured epaulets and sash.

Apart from the snowshoes themselves, the uniform worn by the numerous snowshoe clubs formed in Montreal and other provincial centres in the second half of the nineteenth century also became a visual signifier of Canada. Every club adopted a similar outfit consisting of a coat cut from the blanket cloth originally produced for the fur trade, a wool tuque, leggings, moccasins, and sash. In donning this uniform, the snowshoe-club members were dressing up as composite natives: the moccasins and leggings were Aboriginal, the sash was the French-Canadian *ceinture flechée*, the tuque was a French liberty cap, and the coat resembled the French *capote* but was made from the striped blankets commonly associated with Native peoples.[17] To be sure, extensive transcultural borrowing had occurred between voyageurs, *coureurs de bois*, habitants, and First Nations peoples since the sixteenth century. Both habitants and voyageurs had adopted elements of Aboriginal clothing, particularly in foot and leg wear; both used pipes and beaded tobacco pouches; and, of course, both had adopted Aboriginal means of transport – birch-bark canoes, snowshoes, and toboggans. The uniform chosen by the snowshoe clubs was therefore remarkably similar to the winter clothing of these 'Canadians of old,' thus linking British colonists to the Aboriginal and French-Canadian past of the continent and to the Nor'Westers of the fur trade.

Like hunting, the weekly snowshoe tramps were a way that urbanites could become familiar with the rural landscape and learn the skills required to navigate it in winter. As they set off from their club headquarters on their Wednesday evening tramps over Mount Royal, the members of the Montreal Snow Shoe Club (MSSC) presented an 'eminently Canadian scene' as they fell into 'Indian-file' behind their leader.[18] Certainly it made sense to tramp in single file because it made travelling easier and was safer when the party was large or the weather or the going was bad. More significantly, tramping in 'Indian-file' was also part of the performance of snowshoeing. Club members could carry out an activity thought to be characteristic of Canadian Natives and at the same time demonstrate

Figure 4. William Notman, *General Wyndham and Family*, Montreal, Quebec, 1868. Courtesy of the Notman Photographic Archives, McCord Museum of Canadian History, Montreal. Image no. I-30495.

the discipline and hierarchy that were valued as part of what sport historian Don Morrow calls the 'snowshoe ethos'.[19] Stamina and pluck were part of this ethos and were also qualities associated with the North-West Company voyageurs. Snowshoe-club songs and reminiscences celebrated these qualities and valued tales of treks in the 'olden days,' when members had steadfastly faced and overcome obstacles of terrain and weather. One such favourite tale was the famous tramp to Saint Vincent de Paul in the early days of the MSSC, when the participants 'went fifteen miles astray' because they were caught in a blizzard: 'Such hair-breadth escapes and wonderful adventures as belong to it were surely never matched by any other excursion' (MAAA, MSSC Minutes 1868, 93).

The snowshoers' performance of Canadian identity was often enacted for the domestic audience. Every evening and weekend, clubs would muster on the city streets for their tramps, making the snowshoe outfit a familiar sight. Enthusiasm for the sport grew over time and dozens of clubs were formed, many of which commemorated their activities in composite club portraits (Figure 5). City newspapers regularly reported the clubs' exploits, and in the 1870s some of the clubs organized popular concerts at which they sang their club songs and presented re-enactments of their tramps and activities. A decade later, the snowshoe clubs participated in the Montreal Winter Carnival, which brought their activities and values to the attention of thousands of visitors from home and abroad and gave them a prominent stage on which to display Canadian identity.[20]

Through visual images and text, American and British readers also became familiar with the image of Canadians as a hardy, northern race devoted to outdoor winter sports. From the 1860s onward, articles about Canadian winter sports appeared in popular newspapers and magazines and evidenced a striking repetition of themes.[21] They are all basically variations on ideas first articulated by W. George Beers, a Montreal dentist and sports enthusiast. In an 1863 article entitled 'Canada in Winter,' published in the *British American Magazine*, Beers distinguished between imported winter sports like skating and curling and local sports like snowshoeing, tobogganing, ice-boating, and moose and bear hunting (Beers 1863, 68). The distinction between imported (British) and local (Canadian) sports was reiterated by subsequent newspaper and magazine articles for Canadian, British, and American audiences.[22] The consistent linking of climate, geography, and local sports with national identity reveals that these had become the distinguishing characteristics of 'Canadianness.' By 1886, American readers had evidently accepted this formula. Under the heading 'Our Winter Sports. How They Are Becoming Popular in Uncle Sam's Domains ... An American Picture of Our Leading Pastimes ...,' an article

Figure 5. Notman & Sandman, *Montreal Snow Shoe Club*, Mount Royal, Montreal, Quebec, composite, 1877. Courtesy of the Notman Photographic Archives, McCord Museum of Canadian History, Montreal. Image no. II-44798.

published by Newell B. Woodworth of the Saratoga Toboggan Club explained that 'the hardships and physical exercise of early Canadian life gave little time or inclination to the people to use the snowshoe and toboggan for pleasure. It was not until some forty years ago that a leisure class having developed, the Anglo-Saxon element, with their Norseman blood and natural love of out of doors sports, seized upon the Indian snowshoe and toboggan wherewith to utilize for sport the deep snows of the long Canadian winter ...' (MAAA Scrapbook 3, 1886, 16). Woodward clearly acknowledged the Indigenous origins and distinctive character of Canadian sports. Thus, through several means, snowshoeing became a signifier of Canada and Canadianness and its performance a 'meaningful dramatization' of Canadian identity (Gruneau 1980).[23]

Lacrosse

Pre-eminent among the cultural activities that white colonists appropriated from Native peoples, and then identified as characteristically Canadian, was *baggataway*. Native peoples throughout the North American continent played numerous variations of the game of *baggataway* or *tewaarathon*. The game played on the Native reserves at Caughnawaga and Saint-Regis (present-day Kahnawake and Akwesasne) became the model for the Western game called lacrosse when a group of Montrealers adopted the game and transformed it into the sport we know today.

Baggataway had important religious and ritual functions in Native society. The games were traditionally proceded by special training and rituals, for they were religious ceremonies initiated and directed by spiritual leaders for a variety of purposes (Vennum 1994, 28). For instance, one of the earliest nineteenth-century lacrosse games to be reported in the colonial press was played in 1833 by teams from Caughnawaga and Saint-Regis as part of a ceremony to initiate five new chiefs (Lindsay 1969, 115). Eastern Woodlands peoples used lacrosse as a means of influencing the weather (Salter 1983), and in other cases lacrosse was played to bestow name and rank or to honour the dead (Salter 1971). However, the spiritual significance of lacrosse was not recognized by white colonists, who sought to 'tame' the game for their own purposes.

Lacrosse was a 'primitive' game that could be 'tamed' and transformed into a 'modern' sport by imposing rules and regulations and 'scientific' training and play. By delineating temporal and spatial boundaries, by establishing rules that stipulated what constituted legal and illegal plays and the amount of physical force allowed, and by analysing positional play and strategy, the white players 'tamed' the primitive game and made it respectable while retaining its distinctive 'Native' qualities. Beers, the person who beyond all others was responsible for the modern form of lacrosse, understood the result of this: 'The Indians' old fierce *baggataway* has shared the fate of the Indian himself in having become civilized almost out of recognition into a more humane sport. It has lost its wild and wanton delirium, and though restless under regulations, has become tamed into the most exciting and varied of all modern field sports' (1877, 125).

Shortly after the Montreal Snow Shoe Club was organized formally, some of its members played a lacrosse game against a Native team in August 1844. Not surprisingly, the Native team won handily, even though they fielded five players to the Montrealers' seven. Over the next decade, Montrealers played the occasional match, but they did not take up the game seriously until the Montreal Lacrosse Club (MLC) was formed in 1856. A decade later, the formulation of the National Lacrosse Association in 1867 produced an explosion of interest in the game. In the spring of that year, there were ten clubs, and by November eighty clubs had been formed with over 2,000 members (Lindsay 1969, 123–4).[24] These clubs were founded in Quebec, Toronto, Hamilton, Paris, Brantford, Halifax, and other towns throughout central and eastern Canada. Lacrosse's wide appeal in central Canada led to clubs starting in Manitoba in 1871, in Alberta in 1883, and in British Columbia in 1886. With an estimated 20,000 players registered in 1884 (Vellathottam and Jones 1974, 40), lacrosse was vastly more popular than cricket or athletics as a spectator sport and regularly attracted huge crowds. A game played on 1 July 1867 in Montreal between the MLC and the Caughnawaga team attracted 5,000 spectators, while cricket matches attracted barely 100 (Lindsay 1969, 126). An audience of 5,500 watched a game between the Montreal Shamrocks and the Toronto Lacrosse Club in 1873 (MAAA Scrapbook 1, 41), and crowds of 8,000 to 9,000 were common for championship games in later years (Kidd 1996, 31). According to a Montreal *Gazette* article, lacrosse was also a popular recreation: 'Every Saturday afternoon particularly, the Parks and Commons are crowded with Lacrosse players, from the Professor who doffs the Gown for the occasion, to the little urchin who can barely scrape together 50 cents to purchase a crosse' (23 October 1867, quoted by Lindsay 1969, 126).

The connection between lacrosse and Canadian identity was made explicit by the publicizing efforts of the indefatigable George Beers, whose book entitled *Lacrosse: The National Game of Canada*, published in 1869, set out the rules and regulations that were adopted as the basis of the game. Lacrosse was even popularly (but incorrectly) believed to have been formally instituted as Canada's national game at Confederation.[25] The appeal of lacrosse was that it was distinctively Canadian, quite different from British cricket or American baseball. As Beers (1869, 59) opined: 'It may seem frivolous, at first consideration, to associate this feeling of nationality with a field game, but history proves it to be a strong and important influence ... If the Republic of Greece was indebted to the Olympian Games; if England has cause to bless the name of cricket, so may Canada be proud of lacrosse.'

Whereas hunting and snowshoeing had to be done *in situ*, the advantage of lacrosse was that it could be showed off abroad. Canadian lacrosse teams made several foreign tours and have been called 'the most widely travelled Canadian sporting teams' of their time (Cox 1969, 155).[26] Through these tours, lacrosse became known as the Canadian national game. Little is known about the first tour in 1867, organized by Captain W.B. Johnston and considered a financial failure by contemporaries.[27] However, the Kahnawake community remembers that Big John Rice led two teams from Kahnawake and Akwesasne on this tour, and that they played for Queen Victoria at the Crystal Palace and at the Paris World's Fair of 1937 (Beauvais 1985, 57, 44). As a result, three lacrosse clubs were started in England, and the English Lacrosse Association was formed the following year. Two further tours in 1876 and 1883 were organized and led by Beers, who saw them as a means to promote Canadian immigration. The Canadian government was a partner in the 1883 tour; it paid for public speakers to accompany the teams to give speeches and distribute brochures encouraging emigration to Canada.[28]

Both of Beers's tours were well received in Britain, and a number of new clubs were formed there. The British press portrayed the game as easy to follow, quickly understood, and fast moving (Morrow 1982, 15), and the fact that Queen Victoria and members of the royal family watched a game at Windsor Castle legitimized it further.[29] Beers was piqued on the first tour when the teams were received in Belfast by a crowd waving the American Stars and Stripes, and he made sure the team raised a Dominion flag at all future games 'to show a distinction between Americans and Canadians' (MAAC MLC Annual Report 1877, 17). With subsequent team visits to Australia and New Zealand, lacrosse became Canada's imperial sport – recognized as Canadian throughout the British empire (Brown 1987, 60).

Lacrosse teams also frequently visited American cities and in the process further spread the idea of lacrosse as a Canadian game. Native teams played an exhibition match in front of 10,000 spectators in 1867 in Troy, New York. As a result, the Mohawk Lacrosse Club of Troy was formed, and it visited Montreal in July of the following year (Cox 1969, 156). The Dominion Club of Montreal was invited to visit Brooklyn, and there were several tours of U.S. cities in 1869. In 1870 the New York Knickerbocker Lacrosse Club travelled north to play Canadian teams (Cox 1969, 157), and throughout the next two decades Canadian teams visited northern U.S. cities such as Boston, Portland, Baltimore, New York, Chicago, and Washington, as well as travelling westward to Winnipeg and St Paul, Minnesota. The formation of lacrosse teams in the United States was facilitated by the Montreal clubs, which sent them equipment and copies of Beers's rule book.[30] To achieve his ambition to make lacrosse Canada's national game, Beers had been wise to take teams abroad, because it was only through playing teams of an 'other' nationality that the game could be truly perceived as 'native Canadian.'[31] A 10 December 1878 article in the *Boston Post* noted that for 'years this exciting sport has been identified with Canadian life,' and a report in the *Acadian Recorder* of 18 July 1874, under the heading 'Canadian Nerve and Muscle,' stated: 'It is no new thing – the men of these Provinces taking vigorously to athletic exercises and sports. Unlike the people Southward of them, it has always seemed to come natural to them' (MAAA Scrapbook 1, 116). The writer stated what had become 'natural' and 'obvious' – Canadians have *always* been a *northern* people, *innately* predisposed to excel at sports, *unlike* their American neighbours.[32]

In the early years of club lacrosse, Native teams were indispensable: they provided the only challenging competition and were the source of all white knowledge about the game. As soon as enough white teams had been formed, Native peoples' importance as players waned.[33] However, they have never been totally dispensable as signifiers of Canadian identity. In the nineteenth century, important exhibition matches, major holiday games, and civic and state occasions where a lacrosse match was played inevitably included an appearance by a Native team.[34] If they did not actually play, Natives performed war dances, gave concerts, or competed in specially devised 'races.' They were paraded at home and abroad in 'full regalia' as an amusing entertainment for the crowd. On the tours abroad, Beers required members of the Native team to wear elaborately beaded feather headdresses and sashes in keeping with popular stereotypes of Native peoples (Figure 6). For, apart from providing challenging competition, Native lacrosse teams were also useful as exotic spectacle: they signified the national identity of the occasion and attracted a big crowd. Playing the Western game of lacrosse, often at major civic celebrations such as the visits of the Prince of Wales in 1860 and of Prince Arthur in 1869, Native peoples were distinctive signifiers of Canada. Because the white Canadian lacrosse teams played against Native players, they became elements in a series of equivalents whereby lacrosse itself came to signify 'Canada.'[35] When Native teams were invited to exhibitions, to the Montreal winter carnivals in the 1880s, or to other public events, it was the spectacular Native ceremonial dress that was important. The Native teams were present as

Figure 6. William Notman, *Caughnawaga Lacrosse Team*, Montreal, Quebec, 1876. The captain wears the beaded headdress and sash. Courtesy of the Notman Photographic Archives, McCord Museum of Canadian History, Montreal. Image no. II-41679.

colourful, nostalgic reminders of the pre-history of Indigenous peoples in Canada, the remnant of what was believed to be a dying race. By playing and watching lacrosse, white colonists could put themselves in the place of the 'real' Native people; by performing Indigenous activities, they could legitimize their own claim to be a new type of native Canadian.

Conclusion

In Victorian Canada, Indigenous sports were an important vehicle for constructing the 'new nationality' called for by Canadian nationalists. Owing to the example, instruction, and tools of Native peoples, and with their active cooperation, middle-class Victorian men appropriated and transformed hunting, snowshoeing, and lacrosse into organized sports which became recognized at home and abroad as distinctively Canadian. Although they were only 'playing Indian' when they tramped into the bush on showshoe expeditions or hunting trips, British colonists engaged in these Indigenous activities to enjoy an authentic experience in the wilderness.[36] Snowshoeing and hunting were Indigenizing experiences which brought them into contact with the landscape and climate, thus legitimizing their claim to be 'North Men of the New World.' Furthermore, because lacrosse and snowshoeing were Indigenous sports, they were sufficiently different from sports played in America or Britain to distinguish the players as Canadian. The 'primitive' associations of the games could be countered by imposing scientific rules and regulations which demonstrated the progressive and 'civilized' nature of Canadian society. Through these sports, British colonists made themselves native Canadians.

The Native contribution to Canadian national identity has largely gone unrecognized, because what was appropriated from Native culture was also transformed by its incorporation within a modern, Western ethos. Once it was part of 'us,' the 'other' lost its own identity. At times, Native peoples were able to profit from cooperating with the colonists: by hiring themselves out as hunting guides, by competing for prizes in snowshoe races, or by making snowshoe and lacrosse equipment for sale. But, once colonists had learned how to navigate and subsist in the new landscape and no longer needed Native peoples as their allies, Native peoples were expendable; by changing the rules in order to monopolize the field, colonists justified their exclusion.[37] Under the guise of conservation, hunting laws were imposed to make hunting a sport restricted to the relatively wealthy, thus excluding subsistence hunters. Similarly, in the early years of club snowshoeing, the annual races were open to First Nations competitors and the Indian Races were the most popular events, but, over time, the clubs made rules that banned Native participants from club competition. Native peoples were also said to be unable to play the modern, scientific game of lacrosse, and the amateur code adopted by the lacrosse clubs justified their exclusion from the playing field. The progressive exclusion of Native peoples from these sports paralleled their treatment in the political and economic life of the nation. Cultural practices can therefore be understood as part of the discourse that naturalized the subordination and exclusion of Native peoples, thus institutionalizing and justifying their treatment in the social and political realm.

In trying to characterize their national identity, Canadians today face similar problems to those of nineteenth-century British colonists. What

Canadian identity is, and should be, is enigmatic in the face of assertions of Quebec's sovereignty, Americanization, and globalization. Perhaps for want of something better, Canadians continue to use the very solutions devised by Victorians. Souvenir stores combine snowshoes, moccasins, 'Indian' dolls, and Inuit carvings with modern clothing emblazoned with Mounties, moose heads, and the Canadian flag.[38] First Nations peoples continue to play a role today as signifiers of Canada; along with RCMP in dress uniform, they are invited to most important ceremonies staged by the federal government. In the twentieth century, lacrosse was superseded by hockey as Canada's national sport. But recent European and American successes in world hockey competition have caused much angst because of the threat to Canadian dominance in ice hockey, and hence the game's effectiveness as a national signifier. Thus, it may not be coincidental that lacrosse is making a comeback as a professional Canadian sport and that snowshoeing is enjoying new popularity.[39] It was through participation in Indigenous activities such as these that British colonists in Victorian Canada first came to regard themselves as native in a foreign land.

Notes

1 The author gratefully acknowledges the financial support of the Social Sciences and Humanities Research Council of Canada, and research funds from York University, Toronto.

2 This is an argument made by Morris Mott, 'The British Protestant Pioneers and the Establishment of Manly Sports in Manitoba, 1870–1886,' *Journal of Sport History* 7, no.3 (1980): 25–36. Historians of nineteenth-century Canadian sport generally claim that the presence of British military garrisons encouraged the development of local sports. See, for example, Peter Lindsay, 'A History of Sport in Canada, 1807–1867,' PhD thesis, University of Alberta, 1969, and his 'The Impact of the Military Garrisons on the Development of Sport in British North America,' *Canadian Journal of History of Sport and Physical Education* 1, no.1 (May 1970): 33–44.

3 The records of the MAAA and its member clubs are held at the Library and Archives Canada under MG 28 I351. I use the term 'British' to denote English-speaking immigrants from all parts of the British Isles. The middle-class ranks of the Montreal population included a high proportion of Scots.

4 The importance and agency of performance are pointed out by Judith Butler, 'Performative Acts and Gender Constitution: An Essay in Phenomenology and Feminist Theory,' in Sue Ellen Case, ed., *Performing Feminisms: Feminist Critical Theory and Theatre* (Baltimore: Johns Hopkins University Press 1990), 270–82. See also John J. MacAloon, ed., *Rite, Drama, Festival, Spectacle, Rehearsals: Toward*

a Theory of Cultural Performance (Philadelphia: ISHI 1984); and Tom F. Driver, *The Magic of Ritual: Our Need for Liberating Rites That Transform Our Lives and Our Communities* (San Francisco: Harper 1991).

5 I use the term 'native Canadians' to denote those immigrants who sought to make themselves over as a new type of Canadian native. I employ the designation 'Native' as a synonym for First Nations peoples, and 'native' as a synonym for indigenous or autochthon (of the land).

6 Space precludes a discussion of tobogganing or canoeing in the list of Indigenous activities appropriated as 'Canadian.' I have also only alluded in passing to the contribution of French-Canadian culture to Canadian national identity and the way in which Native and French-Canadian identities were elided by British colonists. For these arguments, see Gillian Poulter, 'Becoming Native in a Foreign Land: Visual Culture, Sport and Spectacle in the Construction of National Identity in Montreal, 1840–1885,' PhD thesis. York University, 2000.

7 The general pattern after colonization in India, Africa, and elsewhere was the replacement of indigenous hunting techniques by European methods, along with a change in the relationship between peoples and animals. Hunting shifted from being a useful survival skill to a regulated, recreational activity accessible only to the mostly European elite. When game quickly began to disappear, colonial pressure groups were formed to 'protect' animal stocks through legislation, thereby denying Aboriginals access to hunting grounds. M. MacKenzie, *The Empire of Nature: Hunting, Conservation and British Imperialism* (Manchester, U.K.: Manchester University Press 1988), 298.

8 Rhodes was called the 'Great Northern Hunter' and 'Nimrod of the North' by J.M. LeMoine in *Maple Leaves: Canadian History and Quebec Scenery*, 3rd series (Quebec: Hunter, Rose 1865), 85.

9 A detailed analysis of the images can be found in Poulter, 'Becoming Native,' chapter 2.

10 Dandurand was a young man whom Notman regularly employed in the winter months, probably to cut wood and keep the fires going. Whether he was Native or French Canadian in real life is unclear from the historical record, but Notman did not find it necessary to make a *representational* distinction between the two because their identities served the same purpose. They were both historical identities, both natives in the eyes of British colonists.

11 The real hunting trips took place on Native hunting grounds; in fact, the land between Lac Saint-Jean and the St Lawrence that the photographs purported to represent was the hunting ground of the Huron, and the hunting rights to the territory between the Rivière Blanche, Saint-Anne, and Jacques Cartier rivers as far as the head of the Batiscan belonged to the Gros-Louis family: Frank G. Speck, 'Indian Notes – Huron Hunting Territories in Quebec,' typewritten manuscript, dated 1920 and 1923 (Notman Photographic Archives: Triggs files). Far from being subordinates, in European terms the Native guides owned the land on which the hunt occurred. Hence, images like these were part of the discourse that

naturalized and at the same time produced racist assumptions about the racial and cultural inferiority of Native peoples, as well colonial claims to the land.

12 This pose is repeated again in 'Early Morn – the Surprise,' 'Trapping the Carcajou,' and 'Trapping the Beaver.' A similar representational strategy was used by Benjamin West for his portrait of superintendent of Indian affairs Colonel Guy Johnson (c. 1767–76), in which a Native person in ceremonial dress stands as a shadowy figure behind Johnson's shoulder. J.C.H. King suggests that West intended the Native figure to represent 'civilization's antecedent.' J.C.H. King, 'Woodland Artifacts from the Studio of Benjamin West, 1738–1820,' *American Indian Art Magazine* 17, no.1 (winter 1991): 35–47.

13 Grey Owl, *Men of the Last Frontier* [1931] (Toronto: Macmillan 1976), 87. Grey Owl was the Native name taken by Archibald Belaney, an Englishman who falsely claimed to be the son of a Scot and an Apache. Belaney lived for many years in northern Ontario and, at the urging of Anahareo, his Iroquois wife, took up the cause of conservation and became a popular writer and public speaker. His assumed identity was not discovered until after his death.

14 Edmund Wilson, the editor of the *Philadelphia Photographer*, published a review of each of Notman's hunting series, providing a narrative for each of the images. His text is an indicator of how the contemporary audience would have understood and responded to the photographs.

15 G. Wharton Simpson reported that 'Mr. Notman sends a fine display of his cabinet pictures and fine hunting scenes but they are hung so high that they cannot receive any justice from inspection in the Exhibition.' 'Photography at the International Exhibition at Paris,' *Philadelphia Photographer*, 4 (1867): 207.

16 Over 450 photographs of sitters wearing blanket coats were taken by the Notman Studio between 1860 and 1900: Eileen Stack, 'The Significance of the Blanket Coat to Anglo-Canadian Identity,' paper presented at the 25th Annual Symposium, Costume Society of America, Sante Fe, New Mexico, 22–25 May 1999, 5. Many of these portraits were taken during the summer months, indicating that setting, clothing, and props were specifically chosen to create a recognizably Canadian image.

17 See, for instance, the representation of Native clothing in the paintings of Cornelius Krieghoff.

18 This remark was made in reference to a special torchlight tramp in honour of Lord and Lady Dufferin (MAAA Scrapbook 1, 4, *Boston Journal*, 20 Jan. 1873).

19 This is the term coined by the sport historian Don Morrow to describe the values of the snowshoe clubs. He claims that, in 1860, the ethos included manliness, skill, vigour, and a pronounced devotion to the activity. In accordance with the notion of 'muscular' Christianity, 'snowshoeing became an ethic, symbolic of right values, moral purity and all that was right and good for society' during the 1870s. Don Morrow, 'The Knights of the Snowshoe: A Study of the Evolution of Sport in Nineteenth-century Montreal,' *Journal of Sport History*, 15, no.1 (spring 1988): 5–40 at 16, 29.

20 Five separate week-long winter carnivals were held in Montreal during the 1880s. The snowshoe clubs were particularly instrumental in organizing and carrying out these events. See Poulter, 'Becoming Native,' chapter 4.

21 These include W.G. Beers's 'Canadian Sports,' *Century Magazine*, 14 (May–October 1877): 506–27, and 'Canada as a Winter Resort,' *Century Illustrated Monthly Magazine*, 29, no.50 (February 1885): 514–29. There is also an article by John C. Martin on the snowshoeing experience in Canada in *Outing*, February 1885, and about winter sports in George A. Buffum, 'Ralph's Winter Carnival,' *St. Nicholas*, February 1885, both cited in *The Week*, 29 Jan. 1885, 146.

22 For example: Frederick G. Mather, 'Winter Sports in Canada,' in *Harper's New Monthly Magazine* (February 1879): 391–400, notes the 'peculiarly Canadian' pastimes of tobogganing, sleighing, and snowshoeing. A similar comment is made in the *Illustrated London News* (11 Sept. 1886): 289–90. Charles Dudley Warner recognized 'a Canadian type which is neither English nor America' in 'Comments on Canada,' *Harper's New Monthly Magazine*, 78 (March 1889): 520–48. All are quoted in D. Brown, 'The Northern Character: Theme and Sport in nineteenth-century Canada,' *Canadian Journal of the History of Sport* 10, no.1 (1989): 49–51.

23 I have focused on national identity, but class, race, and gender identities were also imbricated in the performance.

24 Lindsay claims that Beers's publicity campaign and the founding of the National Lacrosse Association were the catalysts for this explosion of interest ('A History of Sport in Canada,' 123–4). Many of the Montreal clubs subsequently formed snowshoe clubs for the winter, seeing the two sports as complementary (*Montreal Gazette*, 6 Dec. 1867).

25 Contemporary scholars have failed to find any evidence that it was discussed in Parliament. See Kevin G. Jones and T. George Vellathottam, 'The Myth of Canada's National Sport,' *CAHPER Journal* (Sept.-Oct. 1974): 33–6.

26 David Brown claims that lacrosse tours to Britain were made in 1867, 1876, 1880, and 1883: 'Canadian Imperialism and Sporting Exchanges: The Nineteenth-Century Cultural Experience of Cricket and Lacrosse,' *Canadian Journal of History of Sport* 18, no.1 (1987): 61. The hectic schedule of the 1883 tour – sixty-two matches in forty-one different cities in a two-month period – is described by Don Morrow, 'The Canadian Image Abroad: The Great Lacrosse Tours of 1876 and 1883," *Proceedings of the Fifth Canadian Symposium on the History of Sport and Physical Education* (Toronto: University of Toronto, Aug. 1982), 17.

27 According to a letter written to a Montreal newspaper by Captain Johnston's son in 1876, this tour had proved financially disastrous: MAAA Scrapbook 1, 123, 340.

28 The lacrosse immigration scheme was 'a unique form of distribution and advertising in fierce competition with other immigration methods used by the United States, Australia and South Africa.' However, there is no direct evidence of federal financing of the tour (Morrow, 'The Canadian Image Abroad,' 15).

29 The symbolic importance of the royal gaze can be judged by the fact that afterwards the original MLC team annually commemorated its visit to Windsor Castle and the game they played for Queen Victoria (MAAA Scrapbook 2, 549). Johnny Beauvais's memoir of Big John Canadian (Sawatis) recounts how Native team members were introduced to Queen Victoria the night before the game. Despite the instructions he had received about formal behaviour, 'with a smile on his face, Sawatis walked with that smooth gait usually found in fine athletes, took the Queen's extended hand, and planted as gentle a kiss as he could on her unsuspecting cheek.' The queen 'was tickled by this display of fine warmth and "primitive" gallantry, despite the complete lack of protocol.' Johnny Beauvais, *Kahnawake: A Mohawk Look at Canada and Adventures of Big John Canadian, 1840–1919* ([Montreal?] 1985).

30 A copy of Beers's book was 'going the rounds among members' of a new team founded in Corinne, Utah (MAAA Scrapbook 1, 14 May 1873, 41). It was also issued in Britain and reprinted in Montreal in 1879.

31 Elias and Dunning argue that playing and watching sport constitutes a medium of collective identification in which 'a group's sense of "we-ness" or unity is strengthened by the presence of a group who are perceived as "them."' Norbert Elias and Eric Dunning, *Quest for Excitement: Sport and Leisure in the Civilizing Process* (Oxford, U.K.: Basil Blackwell 1986), 222–3.

32 Certain practices, attitudes, values, and beliefs become naturalized through the workings of ideology. Similarly, Bourdieu's notion of 'habitus' explains how 'a given culture produces and sustains belief in its own "obviousness"' through 'embodied rituals of everydayness.' Judith Butler, *Excitable Speech: A Politics of the Performative* (New York: Routledge 1997), 152.

33 The frequency of games between the Montreal Lacrosse Club teams and Native teams, noted in the minute books of the club, diminished over time. A graphic example of the waning importance of Native teams is recorded in May of 1887, when the Caughnawaga team was asked to play an MLC team at the Dominion Day celebrations for a fee of $50. The Native team asked for $60 instead, apparently to cover increased train fares. The MLC refused to pay more, and called the game off. The Caughnawaga team capitulated, but the MLC arranged 'a friendly match' with a white, working-class team instead. By 1887, the pleasurable excitement of the game and a class, rather than racial, confrontation would apparently draw in the crowds (MAAA, MLC Minute Book, 1887, 53–60).

34 For example, the Prescott Dominion Day celebrations for 1875 included a lacrosse match between the Prescott Club and a team from St Regis, played for a prize of $100 (MAAA Scrapbook 1, 340).

35 Indian = Lacrosse = Canada. 'Indians' signified Canada initially, but lacrosse was promoted so successfully as an 'Indian' sport that the game itself became a signifier of Canada. In combination with the concepts already discussed (northern character, vigorous, outdoor winter sports, and so on), a distinctive Canadian identity was produced.

36 Americans also employed the 'imaginary Indian' in constructing national identity, but they dressed up as Indians to act out political and economic discontent,
rather than appropriating Native activities as a way to become indigenized:
Philip J. Deloria, *Playing Indian* (New Haven, Lonn.: Yale University Press 1998).

37 The adverse effects of the appropriation of lacrosse are examined by Michael
Salter, 'The Effect of Acculturation on the Game of Lacrosse and on Its Role as
an Agent of Indian Survival,' *Canadian Journal of the History of Sport* 3, no.1 (May
1972): 28–43.

38 Images of Native peoples and culture employed to signify national (in this case,
Québécois) identity are illustrated in Bernard Arcand, Marc Laberge, and Sylvie
Vincent, 'L'Imagerie des Amérindiens: Un tour organisé,' *Recherches amérindi-
ennes au Québec* 10, no.2 (1980): 132–5; 10, no.3 (1980): 205–7; and 10, no.4 (1981):
278–85.

39 Lacrosse lost its popularity after the First World War, but it never died out completely and continues to be a popular game in small-town Ontario and in British
Columbia. However, by 1999, it had not been a significant game nationally for
many decades. Yet, in the team's first year in the National Lacrosse League, the
Toronto Rock beat an American team to win the title in front of a standing-room
only crowd at Maple Leaf Gardens. This was particularly significant since this
arena, considered by many to be an historic city landmark, had recently been
vacated by the Toronto professional ice hockey team. Newspaper reporting was
effusively nationalistic: 'What is truly wonderful about the Rock's success is
that it strums a chord in most of us that is uniquely, boldly and unapologetically
Canadian.' Mary Ormsby, 'Lacrosse Team Keeps the Gardens Rocking,' *Toronto
Star*, 3 April 1999, and, 'Rock Caps Triumphant, Raucous First Season,' ibid.,
24 April 1999. The popularity of lacrosse continues to grow in Toronto, so, at a
time when ice hockey has become an international rather than an exclusively
Canadian game, lacrosse has made a comeback in the popular imagination in a
key Canadian city.

Bibliography

Beauvais, Johnny. 1985. *Kahnawake. A Mohawk Look at Canada and Adventures of Big
John Canadian, 1840–1919*. Kahnawake, Que.: Khanata Industries.

Beers, W. George. 1863. 'Canada in Winter.' *British American Magazine* 2 (December):
166–71.

– 1877. 'Canadian Sports.' *Century Magazine* (May-October).

– 1869. *Lacrosse. The National Game of Canada*. Montreal: Dawson Bros.

Berger, Carl. 1970. *The Sense of Power: Studies in the Ideas of Canadian Imperialism
1867–1914*. Toronto: University of Toronto Press.

Brown, David. 1987. 'Canadian Imperialism and Sporting Exchanges : The Nineteenth-Century Cultural Experience of Cricket and Lacrosse.' *Canadian Journal of
History of Sport* 18, no.1 (1987): 55–66.

Cox, Allen E. 1969. 'A History of Sports in Canada, 1868–1900.' PhD thesis, University of Alberta.

Gruneau, Richard S. 1980. 'Power and Play in Canadian Society.' In Richard J. Ossenberg, ed., *Power and Change in Canada*. Toronto: University of Toronto Press, 146–94.

Kidd, Bruce. 1996. *The Struggle for Canadian Sport.* Toronto: University of Toronto Press.

Lindsay, Peter. 1969. 'A History of Sport in Canada, 1807–1867.' PhD thesis, University of Alberta.

Morrow, Don. 1982. 'The Canadian Image Abroad: The Great Lacrosse Tours of 1876 and 1883' *Proceedings of the Fifth Canadian Symposium on the History of Sport and Physical Education*. Toronto: University of Toronto, August, 11–23.

– 1988. 'The Knights of the Snowshoe: A Study of the Evolution of Sport in Nineteenth-century Montreal.' *Journal of Sport History* 15, no.1 (spring): 5–40.

North American Indian Travelling College. 1978. *Tewaarathon (Lacrosse).* Akwesasne: North American Indian Travelling College.

Salter, Michael A. 1983. 'Meteorological Play-Forms of the Eastern Woodlands.' In J.C. Harris and R.J. Park, ed., *Play, Games and Sports in Cultural Contexts*. Champaign, Ill.: Human Kinetics Publishers, 211–21.

– 1971. 'Mortuary Games of the Eastern Culture Area.' *Canadian Journal of the History of Sport* 2: 160–97.

Triggs, Stanley G. 1992. *William Notman's Studio: The Canadian Picture.* Montreal: McCord Museum.

Vellathottam, George T., and Kevin G. Jones. 1974. 'Highlights in the Development of Canadian Lacrosse to 1931.' *Canadian Journal of Sport and Physical Education* 5, no.2 (December): 31–47.

Vennum, Thomas Jr. 1994. *American Indian Lacrosse: Little Brother of War.* Washington: Smithsonian Institute Press.

Whyte, William H. 1905. *The MAAA.* Montreal: [Becket Bros.?].

Profile of Wayne ('Gino') Odjick (1970–)

Algonquin, National Hockey League Player

A sports figure accredited with changing the face of hard-hitting hockey, Gino Odjick established himself as one of the liveliest and arresting big-leaguers when he began playing for the Vancouver Canucks in the National Hockey League (NHL) in 1990.[1] He proved that you can accomplish anything if you put your mind to it and follow your dreams.

Wayne 'Gino' Odjick was born on 7 September 1970 in Maniwaki, Quebec. He is the middle child, and the only boy, born into a large family of five sisters and thirty-eight foster children.[2] He played hockey at an early age on his reserve and was coached by his father.[3]

After playing for the Laval Titans of the Quebec Major Junior Hockey League and the International Hockey League, he began his professional career in 1990 when he was named the fifth-round draft pick for the Vancouver Canucks and was chosen eighty-sixth overall in the NHL entry draft.[4] He played twelve seasons in the NHL with the Vancouver Canucks, New York Islanders, Philadelphia Flyers, and the Montreal Canadiens.[5]

Odjick is not only a professional hockey player and a role model for Aboriginal children throughout Canada, he also makes many contributions to his community. He runs the Aboriginal Role Model Hockey School for Aboriginal minor hockey players during the off-season.[6] Through this school, he demonstrates to young Aboriginals the importance of teamwork, involvement in sports, physical fitness, having fun, and believing in themselves. He instils confidence in young Aboriginal athletes.

Odjick also lectures Aboriginal children on the dangers of alcohol abuse. He has received much praise for his anti-drug and alcohol campaign. The chief of Little Shuswap, Felix Arnouse, says that Odjick's message got the attention of youth and that many Natives stopped drinking because of his dedication and hard work.[7]

Odjick has worked hard to prove that many Native stereotypes are untrue. For example, there is still a widely held belief that Indians' place is

Wayne 'Gino' Odjick. Courtesy of Canadian Press; photographer: Ryan Remiorz.

on the reserve and that they cannot fit into mainstream society. But Odjick knows that, if he had not left the reserve to play hockey, he may not have realized his role as a teacher and role model. Although his main NHL role was as an 'enforcer,' he has displayed that he is much more. He gives Aboriginal youth hope that they, too, can realize their dreams.

Odjick retired from the NHL in September 2003. He is currently running the Musqueam Golf and Learning Academy and lives just outside Vancouver.

AMY DELLER

Notes

1 Dan Diamond et al., 'Gino Odjick,' *Total Hockey: The Official Encyclopaedia of the National Hockey League* (Scarborough, Ont.: Total Sports Publishing 1998), 1358.
2 Ibid.
3 Stan Fischler, *Bad Boys 2: More Legends of Hockey's Toughest, Meanest, Most Feared Players!* (Toronto: McGraw-Hill Ryerson 1993), 26–33.
4 Ibid. 28.
5 Diamond, 'Gino Odjick,' 1358.
6 Sam Laskaris, 'Canucks Send Odjick East,' *Windspeaker* 15 no.12: 24.
7 Rick Hiebert, '"Angels Rescue the Enforcer" – Crusade Against Drinking,' *BC Report* 6, no.15: 42.

Aboriginal Rodeo Cowboys: The Good Times and the Bad[1]

MORGAN BAILLARGEON

The cowboy is a mythic figure, conjuring up romantic pastoral images of men riding their horses over dusty ranges, keeping watch over cattle quietly grazing on tall prairie grasses. Many wrongly believe that the original cowboys were exclusively of European descent. Although there were many cowboys of European descent, they were certainly not the first cattlemen, nor were they the only cowboys on the North American Plains during the famous cattle drives that followed the American Civil War.

During the 1860s, the North American cowboy was African-American, mixed African-American-Native American, Native American or First Nation, Metis, Spanish/Mexican, Mexican-Native American, Irish, Scot, English, Dutch, French, and a host of other nationalities. A few writers, such as Richard Slatta, Peter Iverson, Morgan Baillargeon, and Leslie Tepper, have made concerted efforts to move beyond the pale (no pun intended) and acknowledge the involvement of the 'other cowboy,' the Aboriginal cowboy.

It is odd that so many 'Western' historians and researchers, whose work focuses on the 'cowboy,' rarely consider the story of the 'first herdsmen' on the American continent. Of course, it would be foolish to argue that buffalo are the same as cattle. They certainly are not; North American Aboriginal people did not tend buffalo in the same manner as they would later come to tend cattle. However, the similarities buffalo and cattle shared in their inherent worth to Plains Aboriginal peoples is worth investigating because the ultimate product obtained from both species was the same – buffalo and cattle provided Aboriginal peoples with needed hide for leather and meat and tallow for consumption and trade.

Buffalo and cattle share other traits: buffalo were sometimes rounded up and directed into buffalo-pounds to be slaughtered, while cattle were rounded into corrals to be shipped to eastern markets to be slaughtered and consumed. Buffalo were and still are wild, despite the modern interest in buffalo ranching. Left to fend for themselves, cattle will also run wild, which they once did in great numbers. Those that escaped the large Spanish ranches in Mexico and California in the seventeenth and eighteenth centuries, and those from the American southwest that had been left unattended during the American Civil War, roamed freely across the southwestern Plains. Following the American Civil War, the need for men to help round up and drive the large herds of wild and domesticated cattle to shipping ports, where they could later be sent to market, was the event that led to the creation of the 'American cowboy.' Later, showmen and businessmen, such as Buffalo Bill Cody and Pawnee Bill to name but two, turned the once despised cowhand into a North American cultural hero by showcasing him in their famous Wild West performances.

In reality, 'cowboying' was a profession that was not exclusive to any one culture, contrary to what the motion picture industry would have us believe. Among those involved in this profession were a significantly large number of Aboriginal people, who were exceptional cowhands. After all, by the time the American cowboy appeared on the scene in the 1800s, Aboriginal peoples already had over 140 years of riding experience, not to mention expertise at hunting buffalo on horseback and raiding camps of neighbouring tribes and Spanish ranches for horses and cattle. Unfortunately, the habit of exclusion in myth-making is part of the mythology of the Caucasian 'blue-eyed' American cowboy.

For over 200,000 years (Foster et al. 1992, 4), enormous herds of bison or buffalo roamed the American continent, from Mexico to northern Alberta, Saskatchewan, and Manitoba, from the Rocky Mountains to New York State. North America's Aboriginal peoples hunted the bison on foot for over 12,000 years until the horse was reintroduced[2] to the continent. The horse, after first being brought to America in 1493 (Tyler 1976, 29), made its way onto the southern Plains in the early 1600s. In the early 1700s, they were found on the northern Plains, at which time Aboriginal peoples used them to hunt buffalo and to engage in warfare with enemies who were generally too far away to reach by foot. Some First Nations peoples used the horse to round up the bison into pens, or them over cliffs, or push them into deep snow where they could more easily be killed. Aboriginal peoples knew their horses and the buffalo they hunted, intimately. Given these facts, it is clear that North America's first herdsmen were its First Nations peoples.

When the Hudson Bay Company (HBC) established itself in the Red River district of what is now Manitoba, Wisconsin, Minnesota, and the Dakotas in the early 1800s, it introduced oxen to the area in order to pull the Red River carts along the north-south trail: 'As early as 1811 the Hudson Bay Company at Red River was raising cattle for milk for the use of the fort's personnel' (Baillargeon and Tepper 1998, 87). Within a short time, company employees as well as retired Metis company men, also known as 'halfbreeds,' began enterprises that included raising oxen for the HBC. 'In 1820 a Métis by the name of Alexis Bailly drove a herd of cattle north from Prairie du Chien (in what is now southeastern Wisconsin) and sold it profitably to the Selkirkers' (a community just south of Lake Winnipeg) (Howard 1994, 43). Owing to Bailly's entrepreneurial spirit, freighting by oxen was being carried out between the two settlements by 1823.

Between 1823 and the 1870s, Metis and retired HBC men and their families established cattle and oxen ranches along the Red River trail, on both sides of the border, in order to meet the demand for milk and oxen for HBC employees as well as the needs of the Red River cart freighting industry. The demand for oxen also carried over into the Plains 'Reservation Period,' which started in the 1860s in the United States and the mid-1870s in western Canada. With a government policy on both sides of the border that favoured farming, oxen were required to pull the plough.

When the buffalo herds all but disappeared on the northern Plains during the late 1870s and early 1880s, most northern Plains First Nations communities in both the United States and Canada had already acquiesced in their government's plan to convert then an agrarian lifestyle through relocation on reserves. Mandan communities such as the Nuptadi, Hidatsa, and Nuepta and the Sahnish or Arikara, which were long established as farmers before European settlement, adjusted well to this plan. However, those communities comprised of nomadic hunters struggled with the new demands placed upon them. Many people starved in the process.

While some communities adapted to a farming lifestyle, others prospered at raising cattle and horses. People who could not support themselves in their own communities found employment in other Aboriginal communities or through securing employment among non-Aboriginal ranchers. The same skills Aboriginal people used for herding and breaking wild horses and hunting buffalo or herding them into buffalo pounds were quickly transferred and used in the ranching industry. Aboriginal women were not excluded from working as ranch hands. They had always been competent at training their own horses. These skills proved to be valuable in the new circumstances facing Native people and many Aboriginal women came to be known as competent ranch hands and horse trainers.

First Nations and Metis peoples have been involved in competitive events for thousands of years. Quite often, some of these events took the form of running races that may have included distances of over 120 kilometres. When the horse appeared on the southern and northern Plains, these competitions naturally included the horse. Flat races over several kilometres were most common, but occasionally the distances were greater. Many of these racing competitions took place during special religious gatherings, such as the Sundance during the annual trade rendezvous. Following the 'Reservation Period' of the 1860–1870s, the skills of horsemanship continued to be important to Aboriginal peoples. Even today, in most Plains Aboriginal communities, the horse, cattle, and buffalo continue to be held in high regard. Social gatherings provide the opportunity to hold old-time horse races and rodeo events.

The History of Indian Rodeo in Canada

As in many sports, the skills developed for rodeo events emerged from a working environment. Aboriginal cowboys, like every other cowboy, had to work at developing riding skills, riding rough stock and breaking wild horses, roping horses and cattle, and cutting cattle from a herd. They also participated in roping and riding competitions held at the end of the day or at the end of the drive, on the ranch or on the range, or at holiday time. Many times, Aboriginal cowboys won those ranch competitions and remained undefeated. Unfortunately, their accomplishments were rarely acknowledged. Aboriginal women would compete against each other in flat races where they, too, proved themselves competent riders. Several women competed against the men in the bronco riding events and later in the steer-decorating and wrestling events.

It is not known with any certainly when or where the very first rodeo took place. We do know that William F. Cody, also known as Buffalo Bill Cody, began using the skill of the working cowboy in his 'Wild West' shows beginning in 1883. Although Buffalo Bill was not the first to bring the cowboy's skills into the public arena, he was certainly the man who popularized the 'working cowboy' and his skills. Buffalo Bill employed cowboys to demonstrate many things, including their riding and roping skills and their ability to break wild horses. And, from the beginning, he involved Aboriginal people in his shows as actors, riders, sharpshooters, and cowboys. What grew out of this was the sport known today as rodeo. Since the Wild West shows of the late nineteenth and early twentieth centuries, North America's Aboriginal peoples have been involved in various 'sports events' that were originally part of ranching life and, in some instances, of the buffalo-hunting era.

It has not been established when the first rodeo took place on an Indian reserve in Canada; however, there is a story of a rodeo taking place on the Blood Reserve in southern Alberta in 1896. The story was told in 1992 by Pete Standing Alone, now a seventy-four-year-old Blood cowboy, who heard it from his father. In an attempt to discourage people from attending the community's annual Sundance, the federal government organized a community rodeo. Families who attended the rodeo, and did not attend the Sundance, received fresh beef as food rations. The government-selected beef cattle was so skinny, however, that when it was boiled, little meat was left on the bone. A young boy was born shortly after the rodeo and, in memory of the 'lean meat' served by government officials, he was named 'Lean Boiled Meat' (English translation) (Standing Alone interview, 1992).

During the early days of the community rodeo, and long before organized rodeo, Aboriginal cowboys felt that they participated as the equals of non-Aboriginal cowboys. When the city of Calgary held its first stampede in 1912, Aboriginal people were there. Tom Three Persons, a Blood from Stand Off, Alberta, who was the only Canadian to place first in any of the events, won the Saddle Bronc competition. Not only was Three Persons the first Canadian to win an international title in rodeo, but he was also the first Aboriginal person in North American to win such a title. Four years later, in 1916, Jackson Sundown, a Nez Perce cowboy living on the Flathead Reservation, took the 'All-Around' title at the Pendleton Round-up in Oregon.

During the 1920s, 1930s, and 1940s, Aboriginal people participated in rodeos not only as contestants but also as stock contractors and promoters. When organized rodeo came into being in Calgary, Alberta, in 1944 with the Canadian Cowboys Insurance Association and the Cowboys' Protective Association, Aboriginal cowboys were there. However, during the 1950s, Aboriginal cowboys in both Canada and the United States had had enough of being discriminated against in the rodeo arena. In polite society, people excused the discrimination with words like, 'he wasn't a local boy' or 'he was from out of town.' But, in reality, Aboriginal cowboys faced outright discrimination. Often, Aboriginal cowboys would not be granted prize money, despite having won the event. Other times, they were not even acknowledged as having won the event or as having ridden an 'unrideable' horse. For example, Pete Bruised Head, a World Champion calf roper and bronco rider from the Blood Reserve in Stand Off, Alberta, had ridden the famous outlaw horse 'Midnight' at the Midnight Rodeo in Fort Macleod, Alberta, in front of a crowd of hundreds. However, Pete Knight, a World Champion non-Aboriginal bronco rider, was credited as being the first to ride the horse. In some cases, non-Aboriginal cowboys were allowed as many rides as required until they rode a horse (or bucking stock) successfully – not always the horse they drew that day. Aboriginal cowboys were not allowed this privilege.

In the mid-1950s a group of cowboys from the Blood Reserve, including Stephen Fox, Sr, Rufus Goodstriker, Ken Tailfeathers, Sr, Frank Many Fingers, and Fred Gladstone, who were committed to the sport of rodeo, wanted to pass their love for the sport to young Aboriginal people in the community. They formed the Lazy-B 70 Rodeo Club on the Blood Reserve for Blackfoot cowboys. With the goal of further fostering Aboriginal involvement in rodeo, the club expanded its membership to include Aboriginal peoples from other reserves. An executive was formed and members were chosen from different regions in the province of Alberta. Metis cowboys, American Indian cowboys, and Aboriginal cowboys from British Columbia who were not Treaty Indians[3] were also interested in joining this all-Indian organization (Goodstriker interview, 1993).

As dissatisfaction over unfair judges and timekeepers grew among the Aboriginal cowboys, Patty Rattlesnake, from the Ermineskin Reserve in Hobbema, Alberta, proposed to Rufus Goodstriker that an all-Indian rodeo association be formed. In 1962 the executive of the Lazy-B 70 Rodeo Club formed the All Indian Rodeo Cowboys Association (AIRCA), for Treaty Indians. In 1967 AIRCA changed its name to the Indian Rodeo Cowboys Association (IRCA). A new executive was formed with board members from different regions in the province. The Stoney, Cree, Metis, Tsuu T'ina, and Saulteaux were now allowed to join this organization, which until then had been a predominantly Blackfoot rodeo association. The association eventually expanded its membership to allow non-Treaty[4] Indians and Metis cowboys from other provinces and the United States to join. Some of the cowboys involved in the Indian Rodeo Cowboys Association were Gordon Crowchild, Cecil Currie, Alex and Helen Sherman, Bud Connelly, Him Gladstone, Fred Gladstone, Wilf MacDougall and Jim Twigg, to name but a few (Currie interview, 1995).

In 1969 the Indian Rodeo Cowboys' Association held its first International Rodeo Finals in Lethbridge, Alberta, and in the same year registered itself under the Societies Act of Alberta. In 1973 a second Indian rodeo association was formed – the Northern Indian Cowboys Association. In 1974 the Lazy B 70 Club amalgamated with the Indian Rodeo Cowboys Association under the Indian Rodeo Cowboys Association title (Bly interview, 1993). In 1982 the Western Indian Rodeo and Exhibition Association in British Columbia was incorporated and became the ninth Indian rodeo association to be represented at the Indian National Final Rodeo.

In 1974 several members of Indian rodeo associations in both Canada and the United States began negotiations to organize an international Indian rodeo finals in the fall of the year. A committee was established whose members included Pete and John Fredericks, Jay Harwood, Mel Samson, and Fred Gladstone. The next year, the first World Indian Rodeo Finals were held in Salt Lake City, Utah. The event came to be known as the Indian National Finals Rodeo (INFR) Commission. Today there are thirteen Indian rodeo associations in Canada and the United States that are recognized by the INFR Commission. The location of the Indian National Finals

Rodeo has moved around over the years. It has been held in Salt Lake City, Albuquerque, Rapid City, and Saskatoon.

Reflection on Rodeo Life

Becoming a first-class rodeo cowboy is a long and difficult process. Champions are not born overnight. Some say they are carved out of mud, blood, guts, and beer, although there have been many who have succeeded without the help of beer. Excelling in rodeo means dedicating oneself to the sport, just as any other world-class athlete would be expected to do. The hours spent driving, bussing, flying, or hiking is generally long and quite often lonely. The reality is that not everyone wins at a rodeo and, at the end of the day, few go home happy, with money in his or her pocket. Rodeo is also a dangerous sport and not everyone comes out alive. The late Charlie Roasting, a Cree rodeo promoter, horse racer, and rodeo announcer who lived in Hobbema, Alberta, offered this witty formulation when commentating on the sport of bull riding: 'Ladies and gentlemen, a person can get themselves *seriously* killed in this event!' Charlie's famous words may in fact apply to any of the rodeo events. Some people walk away from rodeo after a lengthy career with hardly a scratch. Others have broken almost every bone in their bodies. By the time some rodeo cowboys are thirty years old, they are total wrecks – physically, emotionally, spiritually, and mentally. Moreover, many cowboys and cowgirls have also lost their lives on the way to a rodeo event: when a person is entered in three or four rodeos in any given weekend, and the venues are several hundred miles apart, bad things can happen. However, despite the hardships, there are many joys. Above all, cowboys are unanimous in prizing the lifelong friendship they have made along the way.

The stories that follow are told by people who have travelled or are still travelling 'down the road' and have no regrets. They share their joys and sorrows, frustrations, and accomplishments.

Ann Lefthand (Nakoda, Eden Valley, Alberta)

This interview was conducted at the Calgary Stampede in 1993. Ann was with her father, John, who was wearing a new medal given to him for services to his people by the Canadian government at a dinner given in his honour.

My first rodeo experience was when I was seven years old. I wanted to ride so bad I asked my Dad and he wouldn't let me because I was too small. He said, 'No you are too small.' I said, 'No I want to go in there.' So I went and

Constable Tyrone Potts. Courtesy of the Canadian Museum of Civilization, CMC94-298. Photographer: Morgan Baillargeon.

Coy Fisher. Canadian Museum of Civilization, CMC93-1043. Photographer: Morgan Baillargeon.

signed myself up in the Ladies Barrel Racing and got on my old Queen and went up there and I did make a run, but I guess it was pretty embarrassing. But it felt good to me because I was only seven years old!

That was the start of my rodeo career and from then on I got myself a good horse and I travelled to all the local villages. Sometimes my dad would just throw me in the truck and we would leave early in the morning and I'd wake up at some rodeo grounds. Usually I was there with my Dad. I didn't have my Mom around because she came in a different car later or she just stayed home. I had to tough it out and get my own horse and really look after her. I placed in a few rodeos in the junior event and I did make it to the Finals a few times.

When I moved into the senior event I quit for about five years; I stayed away and had kids. Then I came back after a few years and began training horses myself. I did pretty good on the horses I trained the first year. The second year I went and bought a new one which took me to all the big rodeos around here and in the IRC [Indian Rodeo Cowboys] circuit. That horse took me to Albuquerque, New Mexico, to compete in the [Indian] National Finals. The first night I screwed it all up. I went and hit the barrel. The horse stumbled and I hit the barrel and left it. So I lost five seconds bounding through there. And it cost me! If I hadn't hit it I would have made good time. But after I knocked it over, I finished the race and said to myself, 'Well, I won't get the title, but I still tried.' And I won the championship in the end!

Barrel racing wasn't the only event I took part in. I used to rope at home when there was a branding, but I wasn't active in rodeo. When I used to take part in the Little Britches Rodeos, I would team rope. I also rode steers when I was fourteen and fifteen years old. That was something else! The men actually liked to see us do that sort of thing. They wanted to see us get dumped and stuff, so there was a whole bunch of guys standing around helping me get on and showing me how to ride. From my reserve, there were about three or four women who used to ride steers, but not in the rodeo show, just on the ranch or at home.

I loved the rodeo! That's where I grew up and I wouldn't know what I'd have done without it! Like right now I'm just wishing I could go out there and do it again. I had an accident in 1987 on my horse and I tore all my ligaments right across my knee and broke some bones. So I had to go through surgery, I was on crutches for six months and then I had to take physical therapy for six months. It took me the whole year to recover and the following year I was pregnant with my baby. Ever since I haven't been able to get back into it. Right now I'm at a point where I would like to get back into it. I'm hoping.

As a child, my parents and I also took part in the Banff Indian Days. That's where my Dad did all the work. He ran the rodeo and the Indian Days. They used to have horse races too and I took part in the Ladies' Relay-race. We'd race around the track, jump off and somebody else would jump on and race around the track again. Another race they had was the Rawhide Race. They'd drag a rawhide from the back of a horse with a person sitting on it, and race around the track. Yes, that's how they raced. Both men and women entered this race.

I also danced in the pow wows at Banff Indian Days and at Calgary Stampede. I took first place here in Calgary in 1985 in the Ladies Traditional Dance. I don't have much time for that anymore. I have four kids, three boys and one girl and today they dance here at the Calgary Stampede. One of the boys is starting to rodeo, he travels, so I hope he'll carry on the tradition. My father ran the Banff Indian Days and Rodeo for thirty years. I've also promoted [organized] rodeos. I ran the Morley rodeo and I used to run professional rodeos in the area.

Last month the federal government of Canada just awarded my dad, John Left Hand, with this medal for all the work he did for the band in the last thirty years. They told him he served his people well and did a good job. They invited him to a dinner in High River. In 1932 Dad accompanied Doug Kootenay from the Stoneys, Jim Starlight, and Ed One Spot from Tsuu T'ina Reserve, John Young Pine and Frank Many Fingers from the Blood Reserve to Sydney, Australia, where they represented Canada at an international rodeo. Dad took the All-Around cowboy honours in Australia.

Mindy Shingoose (Saulteaux, Cody Band, Saskatchewan)

Mindy Shingoose is a former outrider who now lives in Calgary and drives chuckwagon for the Calgary Stampede. He also trains horses for the Stampede and for private clients. This interview was conducted at the Calgary Stampede stables in July 1995.

These days I drive the Grand Entry chuckwagon for the Calgary Stampede here in the rodeo. I'm Saulteaux Indian from the Cody Band, but grew up in Yorkton, Saskatchewan. We always had horses back home when I was a kid, I grew up around them. In 1966, when I was fourteen years old, we sold some chuckwagon horses to a competitor. I accompanied that man to the Calgary Stampede and was hired as an outrider. [There are four outriders to each wagon team. The leader man holds the lead horses as they stand at the barrels. When the horn blows, two men throw tent poles into the back of the chuckwagon and the fourth, throws in a stove. They follow the chuckwagon driver around the figure 8, circle the track, and finish within 38 metres or 125 feet of their wagon to receive full points.] I competed at Calgary as an outrider for a lot of years, twenty-three years actually. I drove chuckwagons for myself and other people. After I quit chuckwagon racing, the Stampede Board hired me to drive a chuckwagon in their Grand Entry. I live in Calgary, so I was fortunate enough to get the job. I really appreciate working with the Calgary Stampede and being involved in such a manner. I am also a chuckwagon judge in the evening. Calgary Stampede is a pretty good deal for me.

Actually my family had been involved with horses all their lives. My dad had some racehorses and we always had a lot of ponies and work horses around. We did the farm work with horses. We'd cut and put up hay and it was mainly a horse operation. In later years we sent what you call 'bush horses' to log farms in Ontario and Quebec. Yeah, we were fortunate enough to be around the horses all the time. To us, horses were not a mystery. It's different, you know, there's no cowboys in our part of the world – Yorkton, Saskatchewan – but we always had the horse mainstay.

So what inspired me to turn towards the cowboy lifestyle? I came to the Calgary Stampede and I don't think I closed my eyes for the six days I was here. I was pretty inspired. When I was a kid, I remember always wanting to be a cowboy. I remember putting on my first pair of boots and so on and so forth you know. Yeah, I wanted to be a cowboy. So sometimes I guess your dreams come true for awhile. Saulteaux is an Ojibwa dialect and we were farmers not prairie people, so I think the horse is a new thing to us. However, a lot of us get along quite well with them. A lot of my relatives race horses and have horses, not as rodeo competitors but as horse people, horsemen, I guess you would say.

Because I live here in Calgary, I find a lot of people come to me with their horse problems. They have a problem with their horse and I try to help the situation out, to make for a better horse and a happier rider. I see all kinds of horses coming in, so I spend quite a bit of time fixing, training, and breaking.

When I was young I had won the All American Futurity which is the world's richest quarter horse race. After that I went to Texas to ride racehorses. Then I spent quite a bit of time around the chuckwagon people. I travelled with classes and I learnt from everybody. You know a lot of old-timers, like old horse trainers and horse people that I met up and down the road, took the time when they saw that I was interested and helped me a lot. And that's the way I am now. Like, if someone needs help with a horse I'm willing to help. I think there's enough horses around for everybody so people and horses can live in harmony. So yeah, I try to help out.

Working at Calgary Stampede is pretty exciting. It's a funny feeling, I've competed for so many years, through a lot of hardships and you know it's a job that I hope I can keep for quite sometime. I cherish the job, I'm proud to be able to do a good enough job for the Calgary Stampede. Yeah, I feel pretty good about it. As far as the actual race goes, from what I remember of my competition days, I figure chuckwagon racing isn't for everybody. All your decisions are made in 100ths of a second and any stalling in your decisions could be costly, resulting in injury to yourself and injury to your animals, not to mention the difference between winning and losing. So you've got to be sharp to drive a chuckwagon. It's dangerous for sure, and like I say, a split second decision could make or break you. When I was young, I thought I knew everything, they [horses] showed me I didn't. Made some foolish mistakes when I was young as far as the chuckwagons go. I made some serious mistakes by not putting the right horse in the right spot and I've tipped over several times, got hurt severely. I never won the Calgary Stampede, though. For the most part, though, I worked for the other people, I only owned my own chuckwagon outfit for a year, the rest of the time I was driving for other people. I believe I drove for sixteen different chuckwagon outfits, so actually I drove a lot of different horses. I shod horses, I outrode, I drove the trucks, I helped break 'em in the spring – it was just a job to me.

I didn't have my own farm at that time, like I say I was young and knew it all. So yeah, it's tough. I went to an All-Indian function [rodeo] at my home town at Yorkton, Saskatchewan, and I won the North American Indian Championship at that. Outriding, I've won everything there was to win. I've helped outride for a lot of the winning outfits at the different functions. Chuckwagon racing was good to me, though.

There were different guys who made different handshake deals with different drivers as to how much they got paid. Lots of times my situation was, if I wanted to outride for someone, they give me $25 if I was there, and I don't cause a penalty. But if I caused a penalty for being late, or for hitting a barrel, or for interference, or so on and so forth, I'd have nothing. So you perform to your utmost ability. And there were many races! In 1971 there were forty-four chuckwagons here and there were eleven races a night, and I was in everyone of those races! Actually, I think, when I was at my prime, as far as an outrider, I don't think I missed a race for seven years. I went to every race. I rode a lot!!

As I mentioned, when I came to Calgary, I came as an outrider. There was not one Native chuckwagon involved; however, there's a bunch now. In recent years there have been some Native chuckwagon drivers that I remember from stories and reading. Those who come to mind are Gordon Crowchild and his brothers, Rufus Goodstriker, and a chuckwagon outfit driven by Johnny Swane and his brothers. I guess these were the people of most consequence in the early days. Now Johnny Swane's an old ex-outrider, and he's quite a gentleman. So yeah, it was tough to get involved, I don't know if there were that many Native drivers in the early days, but, yeah, there's quite a few of them now, and top competitors as a matter of fact. There's Ray Mitsuing,

Edgar Baptist, Maynard Metchewasis, Stan Waddell, Brian Laboucane, oh gosh, I'd have to go back into the program, but, yeah, there are a lot of Native drivers now.

I'm involved in several different ways here at the Stampede. I'm a chuck-wagon judge for the races at night and one of the announcers. During my first year of judging, three years ago, a radio interview said of me, 'Yeah, Mindy should do quite well as a chuckwagon outrider judge as he's created most of those penalties himself.' A little bit of jest, but it's quite a feeling being up there in The-Eye-In-The-Sky [announcer's booth at the Calgary Stampede]. I like to think I respect the business and know what it takes to do the job.

The judging system here at Calgary is we have three judges on the ground. There are people judging the stretch runs and there's an infield judge and there's a head judge who's with us in The-Eye-In-The-Sky, and there's a chuckwagon judge for each barrel area. I'm an outrider judge for one of the barrel areas. So there's eight judges that see what's going on, there's four timers and there's two racing judges down on the ground and in the field.

Todd Buffalo (Nehiyaw or Cree, Samson Reserve, Hobbema, Alberta)

Todd has been a working and rodeo cowboy most of his life. This interview took place at the Louis Bull Rodeo, in Hobbema, Alberta, in August 1992. Today, Todd continues to promote Indian rodeos and produces rodeos at his ranch on the Samson Reserve in Hobbema.

I've been living here for thirty-seven years. Been a cowboy most of my life. Been involved with every aspect of rodeo that there is possible. Now-a-days I'm into more of the stock contracting side of rodeo and more on the production end of rodeo rather than the contest end of rodeo.

My wife, Sandy, and my three boys and daughter all participate in the sport of rodeo. I've had my kick at the cat and now it is their turn. Our family's involvement in rodeo goes way back. As a kid I rode steers, and back then, there really wasn't that much going on as far as rodeos go in Hobbema. If you went to two or three rodeos a year then, that was a lot back then. We never really had the opportunities they have now days here in Hobbema.

When I turned fifteen years old, I got on my first saddlebronc and that is where it stuck, 'cause I was a saddle bronc rider for many years. I rode professional, and in Indian rodeos for many of those years. But you know, there was always a downfall in being an Indian cowboy. I went to amateur rodeos and they used to shout at me and stuff. So I stuck with Indian rodeos and pro-rodeos. I always seemed to get a fair shot there.

Over the years I entered different events and I guess the only event that I never really liked was the bareback bronc riding. It was too hard on my body, as I was only 128 pounds when I started riding bucking horses. So you match 1,400 pounds of bareback horse with 128 pounds and a young Indian boy, there is not very much comparison there. But I've rode calves, steer wrestled, team roped, and even rode bulls for a while. But out of all the events I've worked in, saddlebronc riding was probably my best event. That is the one that I really crave to do.

I met my wife through supporting [organizing] a rodeo. She was a barrel racer; she still is today. She is also a talented horse trainer. My oldest boy is seventeen years old; his name is Toby. He really doesn't partake too much in the rodeo, but he just loves to go around and take pictures, and run the video machine. My second boy, Shawn, is fifteen years old now. He ropes steers and in 1989 made it to the Canadian Finals Rodeo [in Edmonton, Alberta] in bareback riding. He won in the IRC [Indian Rodeo Cowboys] in '91. So he has had a pretty good career as a horse and steer rider. Now he is playing basketball and trying to decide whether he wants to pursue his career as a rodeo cowboy. My daughter, she has been horseback riding ever since she could walk. In fact she is about thirteen years old now. She made it to the big one in Albuquerque, New Mexico, to the World Indian Finals [National Indian Finals] in Ladies Barrel Racing. She made us feel very proud of the achievements she has made. She won a couple big ones – major titles, in the IRCA Championships in one year. But barrel racing is probable the toughest of all rodeo events, and good barrel horses are far and few between. My youngest son was ten last fall. He bought his Canadian rodeo card, as well as his Indian card, and he is riding steers now. He was very fortunate to win a Junior All-Around title at the Hobbema Youth Rodeo a couple of weeks ago at the Buffalo Ranch. It was his first trophy saddle. He's doing well for himself; he's got a good start. We will take him to whatever rodeo possible.

Going back to my career as rodeo cowboy, I've been involved in the front end of the various associations. I am the past president of the IRCA, working with the IFR, which is the International Finals Rodeo Commission. They put the rodeo on in Albuquerque, New Mexico, which gives out the World Championship awards. As president of the IRCA, I learned a lot through working with people like Fred Gladstone, Jim Gladstone [from the Blood Reserve in Southern Alberta], and people like that. That helped me in the production end of producing rodeos here in Hobbema.

You realize that Hobbema is noted as the Rodeo Capital of Canada, 'cause at one time we used to average thirty-five rodeos a year, ranging anywhere from youth rodeos, high school low-budget rodeos, girls' rodeos, to professional Indian rodeos. Any kind of rodeo that you could think of, we produced them in Hobbema. But it took a lot of commitment by several individuals, which made all that possible. I mentioned earlier that we never really had the opportunity when we [Native people] first started out rodeoing. But we had the desire, which is probably the big difference. Young cowboys like Denis Sampson from Hobbema have made a mark in rodeo. People like Bert Ward, Dwayne Johnson, Benji Buffalo, the late Howard Buffalo, and Charlie Roasting [all from Hobbema], to name a few, used to work their hearts out producing rodeos for our young kids.

I also mentioned earlier that I used to get the shaft from the amateur associations. I don't know, it must be human nature, but it seems that us Indian cowboys seem to get the wrong end of the stick sometimes. But it is because of these people that we have been able to make our stand in rodeo. Professional rodeo cowboys like Benji Buffalo from Samson Reserve made a big mark in the CPRA [Canadian Professional Rodeo Association] and PRCA [Professional Rodeo Cowboys Association]. Larry Bull, from Louis Bull Reserve, proved himself in professional rodeo, representing and making the Indian Nations very proud. If you get cowboys competing at rodeos such as the Calgary Stampede, it makes all Indian Nations mighty proud.

Part of our heritage, and part of our ability as athletes, is to be able to compete one-on-one with the animals that was set on earth here by the Creator. He had a purpose for him, and we are probably closer to the animals, bucking horse and the bulls, roping cattle and everything [man and animal] involved in the rodeo than any of the other cowboys are. But that always makes me feel good too. To think about the rodeo in that way. We have a respect for the animal, which makes me feel mighty good.

There are different areas of my rodeo career that if I had a chance to change it, I would. Any young cowboy or cowgirl that is coming up now, I would strongly emphasize to take caution. The colour, the glory, the glamour involved in rodeo is not all wine and roses. I used to knock back that beer, drink that whisky, and that was probably my downfall. That is not what rodeo is all about. Alcohol and drugs will damn sure set you back. So I recommend to any kids out there to stay away from that stuff 'cause it will cut your career in half. I have seen a lot of people out there that could have gone a lot farther in their careers if they didn't drink. It's nice to be in the limelight and experience the glamour of the rodeo, but there are better things out there than drinking beer and whisky.

Once you're a cowboy, you have to first of all be proud that you are a cowboy, but most of all you must be proud that you are an Indian cowboy. I mentioned earlier that there is a certain thing there between the Indian cowboys and the livestock. We have a bond, a closeness with the livestock, 'cause of the Indian way of life. Horses have been part of our way of life right from day one. The same with the buffalo and cattle. It all ties in together. As Indian cowboys, we seem to be a lot closer to that end, than generally the cowboy population.

I see myself as a third-generation cowboy. My late father, Howard Buffalo, was a great promoter and his late father was in turn a great working cowboy. His name was Francis Buffalo. Now I've never seen him myself, but I heard stories about him, riding bucking horses. When I was a kid there was always something in me that made me want to have the desire to ride a bucking horse and become a rodeo cowboy. My late father, Howard, being a rodeo promoter, is probably where I got the influence of wanting to become a bucking horse rider.

Now as I got into my bronc-ridding career, people who were very instrumental in my life were people like Matt Holland who is a big time World Champion. Cowboys that I idolized, growing up as a young kid, riding bucking horses, were people like John Holman, a professional rodeo cowboy from Wyoming. But I idolized that man because to me, he was the ideal image of a rodeo cowboy. It was the way he rode bucking horses, the way he used to shake his cowboy hat, just stuff like that made me want to be a rodeo cowboy.

As I got into the timed events, I guess the people that I have to be grateful for [are] people like Jimmy Gladstone. He taught me so much! Not just roping calves, or bulldogging steers, but about being a rodeo cowboy, about going down the road, trying to win the rodeos. He taught me how to do things right – going to and from rodeos, and how to conduct yourself. Jimmy Gladstone won a World Championship in professional rodeo, and he was an Indian!

The late Bobby Gottfriedson, there is another example of an Indian achieving a level of excellence in the sport of rodeo. Now he was probably one of the best bronc riders that ever lived. He won rodeos such as the Calgary Stampede, Pendleton Round-up and he made it to the National Finals Rodeo.

It is not just anybody that goes to these kinds of rodeos. They have to earn their right to be there.Native cowboys that have achieved something in the sport of rodeo, persons such as J. Harwood, a Blackfeet Indian cowboy, who is one of the best rodeo announcers anywhere. He has announced at the National Finals, the Calgary Stamped Pendleton Round-up, Denver, Fort Worth; the kind of rodeos that a lot of people only dream about being at.

There are a lot of top hands out there that have achieved professional status. My point of view is that if you are going to be a professional cowboy, then you got to be competing with the best of the professional cowboys. The late Levi Blackwater summed it all up when he said, 'To be the best, you have got to beat the best!' That is what he emphasized, 'Beat them!' You've got to be able to do the same kind of thing with all the top cowboys, people like Roy

Cooper. You have to be able to ride the same kind of bucking horses, rope the same cattle as them, and beat them! Everybody has got the ability to do it.

I guess another thing that makes a big difference today is the calibre of live-stock that we have. Our [Native] calf ropers are riding the best horses in the country, our barrel racers are riding the best horses in the country, and a lot of these cowgirls and cowboys, they can go to any man's rodeo. They have the ability and they have proven it time and time again. We have cowboys who are now starting up in the stock contracting business. But it is going to be a long process 'cause there is something there that doesn't come easy. I guess being a rodeo cowboy don't come easy. Good luck and good horses are hard to find! You've got to be able to promote yourself to the rest of the country, whether it is an Indian rodeo, a white rodeo, amateur rodeos, it don't matter. You've got to be able to go out there and promote yourself and produce these kinds of rodeos that people want to see.

Well, there are a lot of cowboys out there that can only afford to go on weekend rodeos because of their jobs and family commitments. It's a tough life, and doesn't pay all that great. I guess the benefits are that you see a lot of country; you can be at one end of the country one day and clear across the country the next day. You meet a lot of people, but rodeo careers are very short. There are a lot of champions out there that can make a big impact, but in a couple of years they're gone. Then there are cowboys out there, people like Peter Bruised Head who cowboyed all his life and does rodeos for a living. He is getting senior in his career, but, I tell you, when he was young and working all the events, he was a tough guy. He did about every event in rodeo. Man, I'll tell you, they did it right! You have one-event specialists who work one event and concentrate strictly on one event. Then there are other people who were able to work all the events in rodeo. It takes a certain ability to be an All-Around cowboy. Being able to ride a bucking horse and then pick up a rope and then rope a calf – that's quite something! All the ones I know have been good ones [All-Arounds].

I guess in conclusion, rodeo is a tough sport. As Indian cowboys, we have to strive a little harder in order to survive in this sport. We have never really had anything easy. We have to go through the same school of hard knocks in order to achieve what we have achieved. Now it is starting to fall into place, with our own Indian stock contractors, our own Indian announcers, and everything else in rodeo. Now we have the ability to do it ourselves, and it makes me feel good. Our stock is just as good as anybody else who is producing rodeos. Our cowboys are just as good as anybody going down the road. The one thing about Indian cowboys, as I mentioned before, is that they are mighty proud to be cowboys, but most of all they are proud to be Indian cowboys.

Final Thoughts

The life of the Indian cowboy or cowgirl is not all that different from that of a non-Indian. The rules of the game are the same. Many Aboriginal cowboys compete alongside non-Aboriginal cowboys. The emotions felt in winning and losing an event or a major competition are the same. The rules of the game are also the same because Indian rodeo associations follow the same rules established by the professional rodeo associations.

There are differences, to be sure, between Aboriginal and non-Aboriginal rodeos. One is the discrimination Aboriginal peoples have experienced when participating in non-Indian rodeos, although many will tell you that there is discrimination at all levels of rodeo, including the Indian rodeos. Another difference, and, according to Aboriginal people, the major one is the relationship that Indian cowboys have with the animals they are competing with and against.

For those who have attended an all-Indian rodeo, but do not understand the language being spoken by an elder who might have been asked to say an opening prayer, you have missed an important component of the event. In many instances, especially in Cree country, the person praying is acknowledging that those gathered for competition are entering into a competition with 'sacred beings.' The animals are recognized for their strength and superior abilities. They might be asked to have pity on the human beings who are entering into a competition with them. An elder might pray that neither man nor animal will be hurt, because both are entering into a friendly competition. Finally, the prayer might end with a petition that everyone will make it home safely.

There is no judgment being offered here – that Indian rodeos are better than non-Indian rodeos, or that non-Indians do not have respect for the animals involved in rodeos. The point is that Indian rodeos are simply different. Mike Bruised Head, a Kainai cowboy from Stand Off, Alberta, puts the matter forcefully when he talks about the special relationship between the Blackfoot and their horses, a relationship that was almost lost after the advent of the residential school:

> In the old days you respected your horses – you relied on them with your life. They took you to war, on the hunt, on horse raids, on scouting expeditions and you expected your horse to bring you home. You knew the songs and medicines for your horse to take you into battle and the medicines and songs to cure your horse when it was ill or injured. We were equal with our horses before the residential school. The residential school experience taught us that horses were simply beasts of burden whose purpose was to help us break the land

and pull heavy equipment. Our horses were being crossbred with foreign breeds. They were no longer our pets and our friends. They were no longer sacred.[5]

Notes

1 © May 2002. Morgan Baillargeon. Used with permission of the author.
2 In Plains Cree mythology, there are stories that speak of sacred encounters that took place thousands of years ago between the Cree and miniature horses. These horses shared sacred songs, medicines, and dances that were used in Cree curing ceremonies. Merle Kenny related some of these stories to the Plains Advisory Committee for the exhibition *Legends of Our Times: Native Ranching and Rodeo Life on the Plains and Plateau* in Hull, Quebec, at the Canadian Museum of Civilization, in November 1994.
3 With the exception of the Cree in east-central British Columbia, most Aboriginal people in British Columbia were not Treaty Indians.
4 In many Canadian provinces, there still are Aboriginal people who are not Metis or mixed-blood and whose family never signed a treaty. For some reason, these people were not eligible to take part in All-Indian rodeos. In order to be a member of the association, one had to produce a treaty card.
5 Morgan Baillargeon and Leslie Tepper, *Legends of Our Times: Native Cowboy Life* (Vancouver: University of British Columbia Press 1988) 22. Author's interview with Mike Bruised Head, 1997.

Bibliography

Baillargeon, Morgan, and Leslie Tepper. 1998. *Legends of Our Times: Native Cowboy Life*. Vancouver: University of British Columbia Press.
Bly, Caen. 1993. Interview with Morgan Baillargeon, Stand Off, Alta.
Buffalo, Todd. 1993. Interview with Morgan Baillargeon. Louis Bull Reserve, Hobbema, Alta. Hull: Canadian Museum of Civilization. Audio archives CMC V95–0339.
Currie, Cecil. 1995. Interview with Morgan Baillargeon. Montana Reserve, Hobbema, Alta (June).
Foster, John, Dick Harrison, and I.S. MacLaren, ed. 1992. *Buffalo*. Edmonton: University of Alberta Press.
Goodstriker, Ruphus. 1993. Interview with Morgan Baillargeon. Stand Off, Alta.
Howard, James Kinsley. 1994. *Strange Empire*. St Paul: Minnesota Historical Society. First printing 1970.
Iverson, Peter, and Linda MacCannell (photography). 1999. *Riders of the West: Portraits from Indian Rodeos*. Seattle: University of Washington Press.
Lefthand, Ann. 1993. Interview with Morgan Baillargeon. Calgary, Alta. Hull: Canadian Museum of Civilization. Audio archives CMC V95–0309.

Shingoose, Mindy. 1995. Interview with Morgan Baillargeon. Calgary, Alta. Hull: Canadian Museum of Civilization. Audio Archives CMC V95–0302.

Slatta, Richard W. 1990. *Cowboys of the Americas*. New Haven, Lonn.: Yale University Press.

Standing Alone, Pete. 1992. Interview with Morgan Baillargeon. Stand Off, Alta.

Tylor, Ron. 1976. *The Cowboy*. New York: Ridge Press.

Ward, Fay E. 1952. *The Cowboy at Work: All About His Job and How He Does It*. Norman: University of Oklahoma Press.

Profile of Thomas Charles Longboat (1887–1949)

Onondaga, Olympic Long-Distance Runner

Tom Longboat achieved international fame as a long-distance runner during the early part of the twentieth century. Although he faced criticism as well as outright racism for his unorthodox running style, he persevered to become one of the greatest athletes in Canadian history.

Thomas Charles Longboat was born on 4 July 1887 at Ohsweken on the Six Nations Reserve in Ontario. He was raised on a small farm by his mother after she was widowed when he was five years old.[1] At twelve, he was sent to residential school but ran away in less than a year. While in his teens and working as a farm labourer, he began to run competively.[2]

In 1906 he was encouraged to enter the Hamilton Bay race by the prominent Mohawk runner Bill Davis. Despite heavy odds against him, the then unknown nineteen-year-old Longboat won the twenty-mile race.[3] Over the next several years, his reputation as a runner grew as he continued to win local races. By the time he entered the 1907 Boston Marathon, Longboat was the odds-on favourite. He won that event in record time and his course record remained unbroken until the marathon course was made easier.[4]

Controversy surrounded Longboat in the days leading up to the 1908 Olympics. Although he was favoured in the marathon, Longboat's amateur status was brought into question by the shady practices of his manager, Tom Flanagan. Eventually, Longboat was allowed to compete but the controversy did not stop there. After he collapsed late in the race, allegations were made about him being drugged by bettors hoping to cash in on his win.[5] These allegations were never proven.

A brief public interest in long-distance running in the years leading up to the First World War[6] brought Longboat notoriety. He became an international celebrity and travelled extensively throughout North America and Europe to compete in match races. At the height of his professional success, he won the 1909 'World's Professional Marathon Championship.'[7] He retired in 1913 after interest in professional running matches had begun to wane.

Thomas Charles Longboat. Courtesy of Canadian Press.

In 1916 Longboat enlisted in the army. As a dispatch runner in France, he delivered messages from one post to another[8] and was once erroneously listed as killed in action. He later married Martha Silversmith and the couple had four children. They lived in Toronto and later retired to the Six Nations Reserve where he died on 9 January 1949 at the age of sixty-one.[9]

Today, his legacy lives on, with an athletic award, a street in Toronto, a school in Scarborough, and a running club in Toronto, the Longboat Roadrunners, all named in his honour.[10] The Tom Longboat Award is given annually to an outstanding Aboriginal athlete in Canada by the Canadian Sports Council.

ROLAND SIMON

Notes

1 Bruce Kidd, *Tom Longboat* (Don Mills, Ont.: Fitzhenry and Whiteside 1980), 11.
2 Ibid., 12.
3 Charles Enman, 'Tom Longboat, Canadian Marathon Runner.' www.sirius.ca/running/tom-longboat.html.
4 Ibid.
5 Ibid.
6 Kidd, 'Tom Longboat,' *Canadian Encyclopedia: 2000 World Edition* (Toronto: McClelland and Stewart 2000).
7 Ibid.
8 Brenda Zeman, 'Runner of Messages: Tom Longboat.' In Zeman (with David Williams, ed.), *To Run with Longboat: Twelve Stories of Indian Athletes in Canada* (Edmonton: GMS2 Ventures 1988), 13.
9 Ibid., 13.
10 Ibid., 16.

PART EIGHT

MILITARY

Aboriginal Contributions to Canadian Culture and Identity in Wartime: English Canada's Image of the 'Indian' and the Fall of France, 1940[1]

R. SCOTT SHEFFIELD[2]

When Canada declared war on Germany in September 1939, it had little existing military power to call on. As well, its economy had remained stagnant in the wake of the Great Depression. Yet, over the next six years, more than a million Canadian men and women would put on military uniforms. The economic potential of this vast country would be mobilized and realized in a total war effort. As they had during the Great War, Aboriginal peoples in all parts of Canada also took up the struggle against the tyranny and evil embodied by the Nazi regime and later against Italy and Japan as well.[3] According to official figures, over 3,000 Status Indians enlisted voluntarily in the Canadian armed forces, with perhaps several thousand more Status Indians, non-Status Indians, and Metis joining them as volunteers or conscripts.[4] These Aboriginal servicemen and women would eventually serve in every branch of the military and in every theatre where Canadian forces were engaged. On the home front, Aboriginal families and communities did their part by working in burgeoning wartime industries or through the traditional economic pursuits of fishing, lumbering, and farming. They purchased war certificates and Victory Bonds and gave generously to patriotic and humanitarian causes such as the International Red Cross. Canada's Aboriginal population gave as much as it could of its blood, sweat, and treasure to the cause, something significant in and of itself.

The actions of Aboriginal peoples and communities during the war made an impact on English Canada's cultural confidence and identity in disproportion to their statistical size compared to Canada's population as a whole. In many ways, Aboriginal support for the national crusade developed a symbolic resonance among English Canadians. It helped the dominant society cope with adversity during the war's early years, played a role in defining Canada and what the country was fighting for, and provided an instrument to help motivate and mobilize other Canadians to keep going. In the war years, unlike today, Canadians could think about the 'Indian,' or not, with little reference to Aboriginal peoples' sense of self. Thus, for the most part, this 'contribution,' if that is the right word, to the dominant society's ability and willingness to fight was involuntary and beyond the control of Aboriginal people themselves. It revolved around the ways that the dominant society interpreted Aboriginal actions and the uses to which they put their image of the 'Indian.'

As a case in point, it is worth examining the image of the 'Indian' as it was publicly discussed in the English-Canadian print media during the war's darkest days – the fall of France in the spring of 1940. One might well ask what the defeat of France had to do with the image of the 'Indian' in English Canada because, at first glance, it seems hard to imagine two historical processes more removed from each other. However, France's defeat shattered Canadians' complacent optimism and thrust the country into the uncomfortable prominence of being Britain's senior ally. The process of a nation coming to terms with the onset of total war was abundantly evident in the country's newspapers during that traumatic summer. Virtually everything in the Canadian experience had now to be viewed through new lenses. The 'Indian,' like some old suit dragged out of the cultural closet and dusted off, was scrutinized by journalists and editors from Vancouver to Halifax.[5]

The 'Indian,' as the term is used here, was a construct of English-Canadian society. A relatively well developed historiography of the image of the 'Indian' in the United States has existed since a flurry of monographs first appeared on the subject during the late 1970s and early 1980s.[6] However, the same cannot be said for Canada, which has only a few scattered works on this theme.[7] This chapter draws on the image of the 'Indian' in American literature, and it has also been informed by the work on the discourse of 'race' and imperialism used by Edward Said in *Orientalism* and, in a Canadian context, by Kay Anderson and James W. St. G. Walker.[8] Their approaches are predicated on the notion that the dominant society constructs its image of the 'other' to meet its own needs and for its own consumption. Accordingly, this image reflects the dominant society's assumptions, desires, conceits, and anxieties rather than any objective reality concerning Indigenous peoples. Analysing the image of the 'Indian,' therefore, is a useful approach for examining the impact of Aboriginal peoples' support for the national war effort.

Before the war, the 'Indian' was a common if irregular visitor to the pages of Canadian newspapers. The discourse evident by the 1930s had developed over centuries and had hardened into a relatively static, although still flexible, series of visual images, emotions, and stereotypes. What emerged was a contradictory dual image of Aboriginal peoples. The 'Indian' generally appeared in a positive, yet tragic light, cast as the vanishing 'noble savage.'

Inevitably, the 'Indian' was the subject of the 'colourful' and amusing human-interest story, rather than 'hard' journalism. Along with this benign historical 'Indian,' Canadian newspapers revealed profoundly ambivalent images when they portrayed contemporary Aboriginal people in a negative, often demeaning, manner as 'drunken criminals.' This dichotomy of the 'Public Indian' as both 'good historical Indian'/'bad contemporary Indian' survived into the Second World War.[9]

From the outbreak of hostilities in September 1939 until the German victories between April and June 1940, Canadians remained optimistic about the eventual victory of the Allies. Initially, the war had little impact on the way the 'Indian' was portrayed in English-Canadian newspapers. Given the dramatic international and domestic news competing for limited space, one might expect that 'Indian' stories would have been pushed from the newspapers. However, articles on 'Indian' subjects still appeared with the same frequency as they had before war. By and large, the dichotomous 'Public Indian' remained intact.

Throughout the early phase of the Second World War, English-Canadian writers began to draw links between the current conflict and the 'Public Indian' in a number of different ways. Infrequent and initially tentative, these stories tended to appear in the language and imagery that had marked 'Indian' stories before the war. Even stories that talked about the enlistment of Aboriginal men in the armed forces or about Aboriginal support of the war effort tended to emphasize the 'Public Indian's' colourful nature or historical context.

A prime example of the colourful 'noble savage' in the context of the war was the comments of one Alberta chief about the loyalty of Aboriginal peoples and his predictions for the coming war. Chief Walking Eagle assured Canadians that his young men would enlist because 'every Indian in Canada will fight for King George.'[10] He feared only that they would be too late join the fight, because 'Chamberlain is mad at Hitler now, and he'll soon fix him. Before they talked too much, but now the English heap angry and they'll sure get busy. Pretty soon Chamberlain blow Hitler to hot place.' The quaint pigeon-English and claims of loyalty to the king harkened back to the historical 'Indians' of stories, who always spoke in a broken idiom and were pathologically loyal to the British crown. In this story, the 'Indian' was delivering messages that Canadians wanted to hear. Chief Walking Eagle's sincerity and seriousness was lost in the condescending amusement his statements likely generated. Yet the pleasing tone and the story's wide distribution demonstrated English Canadians' genuine appreciation for his comments. The war had done nothing to simplify the ambiguities that surrounded the 'Public Indian.'

Whereas using the 'noble savage' or presenting the 'Public Indian' as colourful could be accomplished within the confines of the existing dualistic discourse, accounts of young Aboriginal men enlisting or communities making patriotic gestures in support of the Red Cross and the war presented more difficulties. Thus, in a story in the *Saskatoon Star-Phoenix* about the enlistment of young Cree from a reserve in central Saskatchewan, the journalist emphasized the historical context:

> Chief Mistawasis, one of the Indian Leaders who signed Treaty No. 6 at Carleton in 1876, rests peacefully today in the Indians' happy hunting ground. As a young man a bitter enemy of the whites, Chief Mistawasis lived to be a friend of the British, and today he can sleep undisturbed, serene in the knowledge that his descendants not only adhere to the terms of the treaty which he signed with the Great White Queen, but his sons and grandsons ... are still true Indians, true to their bargain and true to their beliefs. ('Eighteen Mistawasis Indians Join Infantry,' 1939)

Yet this interpretation could not capture the immediacy of the event, nor fully explain its meaning to the reader. Something had to change within the public discourse before such information could be truly comprehensible for English Canadians. The same article hinted that the parameters of the 'Public Indian' were fraying under the pressure. It went on to describe in unabashedly positive terms the high enlistment rates of the Mistawasis Cree and the leading figure in encouraging them to volunteer, Chief Joe Dreaver. The respectful tone in a contemporary 'Indian' story was virtually unheard before the conflict, but the patriotic tale of the Mistawasis Band would not have made sense otherwise. Nonetheless, this article was a rarity during the early stages of the war because the traditional images continued to dominate. The quiet months of the Phoney War created no imperative to force a re-evaluation.[11] This all changed in May and June 1940.

It would be almost impossible to overstate the impact that the defeat of France had on English Canadians. Until that stage, they had felt confident that the combination of the British navy and the French army on their Maginot Line would be up to the job of beating Hitler's legions. No one had illusions about the war being short, but neither had the possibility of losing entered peoples' minds. The sheer rapidity and decisiveness of the German Wehrmacht's victories over Denmark, Norway, Holland, Belgium, and France in the spring of 1940 destroyed such complacency. Suddenly the empire's major ally was gone, an invasion of Britain loomed, and the spectre of defeat hung in the air. Winston Churchill spoke of moving the Royal

Navy to Canada and continuing to fight from there should Britain fall. Canadians, in that spring and summer, were forced to come to grips with a total war – a war for survival.

By June 1940, the propagandists' most positive spin on the events taking place in France could not disguise a disaster in the offing. Newspapers stepped up publication of editorials and stories designed to encourage Canadians not to despair and to rally around the flag. On the home front, press coverage of 'Indian' stories remained relatively high in most Canadian papers throughout the summer but peaked during and after France's capitulation on 22 June. This was remarkable considering the extent and dire nature of the news from around the world that was competing for limited newspaper space with 'Indian' stories. Increasingly, the 'Public Indian' began to be linked to the war in various ways. In the *Winnipeg Free Press* and the *Brantford Expositor*, such stories became the norm, largely displacing other 'Indian' stories through the summer. These stories were all marked by a single defining characteristic: each applauded and attested to Aboriginal support for the war effort. Almost every paper consulted carried at least one such piece reassuring Canadians that 'Indians' believed in the national crusade and were doing their bit for the cause. The summer of 1940 brought about the proliferation of a positive and contemporary image, the 'Indian-at-war,' and ensconced it alongside other images of the 'Public Indian' in the Canadian imagination.

The initial concern to Canadians was the loyalty of Aboriginal peoples. Inflated reports of the activities of Nazi agents, subversives, and saboteurs poured out of Europe in the wake of the German conquests. An overwrought press and the Royal Canadian Mounted Police (RCMP) told Canadians that even their own country had been infiltrated by potentially thousands of these 'dangerous agents in the guise of German immigrants, refugees, German Canadian citizens, even discontented Eskimos or Indians, and who knew what else' (Keyserlingk 1988, 60). The result was a highly charged environment where every segment of Canada's polyglot society was suspect, including 'discontented Indians.' The Canadian Press (CP) wire service first raised the alarm with a story about concerns in the United States that 'foreign-fostered groups and domestic anti-Semitic organizations were trying to stir up dissention [sic] among the Indians by stressing grievances against the government' ('Nazis Seeking to Rouse Indians,' 1940, 3).[12] The CP wire story also carried Canadian reaction to the news, which amounted to assurances from the Department of Indian Affairs that 'there is no reason to believe that any Indians in Canada have Nazi inclinations.'

A more articulate appraisal of Aboriginal loyalty appeared a month later in the *Calgary Herald*, which carried a full column editorial under the simple title, 'Indians Are Loyal' (1940, 4). The editor claimed that there was 'no more loyal element in Canada's mixed population than the Indians,' and referred to historical alliances with the Six Nations and to the mystic loyalty to the crown among 'Indians' in remote regions. However, the most convincing demonstration was the fact that Aboriginal men had served in the Great War: 'over four thousand,' according to government sources, and 'it is expected that the Indian contingent this time will be at least as large.' These claims were lent greater significance because the point was made that 'all Indian participation in the war must be voluntary,' as it had been in the last war.[13] Nevertheless, this belief tapped into the potent symbolism of voluntary military service and sacrifice that underscored these positive and contemporary manifestations of the 'Public Indian.'

However, news about the actions and sacrifices of Aboriginal people themselves laid to rest English Canadian anxieties about their loyalty ('Indian Generous to War Causes' 1940, 17). On the same day that news of France's imminent collapse broke in the papers, the *Saskatoon Star-Phoenix* carried a prominent story under the headline, 'Indians Display Loyalty in Gift of Treaty Money' (1940, 4).[14] It referred to a number of bands from the Battleford Agency who had refused to accept their treaty payments for that year or request government assistance, so that the money might go to aid their 'Glorious King and Queen' in the war. Moreover, these First Nations had found what other money they could to offer for the war effort. In light of such gestures, questioning the loyalty of Aboriginal peoples appeared absurd, and concerns were allayed.

Whereas the papers had been both feeding and assuaging Canadians' fears in the initial shock of that spring, they now began working to shore up civilian morale and prepare the country for the sacrifices ahead. In this changing context, the 'Public Indian' discourse was also transformed. The positive, present-day 'Indian' filled several new roles to meet the differing needs of English Canada as it adjusted to total war. The focus on the 'Indian' now shifted from loyalty to positive demonstrations of Aboriginal patriotism and sacrifice ('Stonies at Ceremonial Sun Dance Pray for Victory for Britain' 1940, 1–2). These reports proved advantageous in reassuring, encouraging, and even shaming Canadians into greater exertions for the war effort.

The humanitarian spirit of the 'Indian' received notice in stories about their generous support of the Red Cross ('Aid from Indians: Residents of Manitoba Do Bit in Filling Red Cross Coffers' 1940, 3). Even the *Vancouver Sun*, which seemed scrupulously to avoid printing positive 'Indian' images or stories linking Aboriginal peoples to the war, printed a heart-warming story about work done by Aboriginal children for the Red Cross ('Indian

Children Assist Red Cross' 1940, 16). The story noted that the pupils of the Coqualeetza Residential School had 'expressed a wish to do war work some time ago, and said that they could knit and sew.' This is another element of the new positive, contemporary 'Indian': a sense of agency. The 'noble savage' and the negative contemporary image of the 'Indian' often appeared as passive; however, in this piece the journalist was careful to say that the children had taken the initiative.

Even more noteworthy, demonstrations of Aboriginal enthusiasm for the war effort were frequently and enthusiastically reported ('Men of Tough Northern Breed with Grey and Simcoe Foresters at Camp Borden,' 1940, 5).[15] A series of stories kept the 'Indian' in the public eye in Saskatchewan throughout the summer, beginning with the northern First Nations' decision to refuse relief and donate treaty money to the war effort, reported on 17 June. Two days later, the *Star-Phoenix* printed another dramatic announcement, declaring that 'the Indians of the Mistawasis Reserve are patriotic to say the least,' because they had donated $2,080 to purchase an ambulance for work overseas ('Indians Donate $2,080 to Purchase Ambulance' 1940, 11).[16] This was followed on 2 July by a story about a Metis declaration of support; on 5 July by a story about Chief Dreaver's call for an all-Indian battalion; and on 25 July by another story about the donation of $1,000 by the Fishing Lake Band.[17] In all these cases, the actions of the First Nations were interpreted as patriotism of the highest order and a great example for Canadians. Arguably, such claims reflected Canadian desires more than the real attitudes of the First Nations themselves.

This is not to say that Aboriginal peoples were not demonstrating genuine loyalty and patriotism.[18] A desire to end the tyranny of Hitler's Nazi regime certainly spurred many Aboriginal enlistments and other contributions to the war effort. However, the reasons for young Aboriginal men enlisting were as numerous and diverse as they were for any other young man in Canada: for some it was patriotism; for others the prospect of a steady pay cheque and three square meals a day; some wished to escape an unhappy home life; and others craved the adventure of travelling overseas. But, as often as not, young men enlisted because their buddies did and it was the thing to do. Added to all these motives was the desire, in those Aboriginal communities that still had warrior traditions, for young men to attain their rights of manhood, as had their fathers and uncles in the Great War and their ancestors in previous centuries.[19] Clearly, Aboriginal peoples supported the war, but their reasons for doing so were more complex than the dominant society's discourse acknowledged.

The examples of the 'Indian' aiding the nation not only encouraged Canadians to make greater sacrifices, but, because of the underlying perception of 'Indian' inferiority, also served to push them. This dual purpose can be seen in stories about the gestures made in support of the war effort. For instance, the *Halifax Chronicle* noted that the residents of the Thunderchild Reserve in Saskatchewan, who had donated $101 to the national war effort, were 'never in the best of circumstances financially' ('Three Cheers for the Cree' 1940, 8). The emphasis on the difficult straits of the 'Indians' is noteworthy because it amplified the depth of the sacrifice they were making and set the bar that much higher for the rest of the population to try to meet. It also served to quiet those Canadians unwilling to do their bit because they had just emerged from the Depression's hard times. But, most important, it shamed those supposedly superior 'white' Canadians who had not done as much as had the 'lowly Indian.'

The summer of 1940, with all its trials and strains, brought Aboriginal peoples to the attention of Canadians in a fashion that forced a re-evaluation of long-standing beliefs about the 'Indian.' The public discourse could not explain Aboriginal support for the war effort using the images then available; a new image was needed. This new construct, the 'Indian-at-war,' differed from its predecessors in that it was a sympathetic, flattering figure that existed in the present. Infused with an enviable spirit of sacrifice, unswerving loyalty, and fervent patriotism, this dynamic 'Indian' was as distorted an image as other popular conceptualizations of Aboriginal people. They were no more super-patriots willing to martyr themselves mindlessly for English Canada's cause than they were drunken criminals or archaically noble, but somewhere in the middle of these constructed extremes.

More important than the advent of a new 'Public Indian' image were the reasons for its emergence and the mechanisms that fostered or forced change. Clearly, the reporting of statements made by Aboriginal people and their demonstrations of loyalty and support for the war effort had an effect on the way English Canadians perceived and spoke about them. Such activities, far beyond the collective assumptions and stereotypes that composed the 'Public Indian,' thus forced the dominant society to acknowledge the loyalty and contribution of Aboriginal peoples. Part of the mechanism transforming the 'Public Indian' discourse was the very fact that Aboriginal peoples were willing to lend their youth, labour, and scarce financial resources to the national war effort.

However, on their own, Aboriginal actions could not have forced the creation of a new image because English Canadians could simply have ignored these actions. Aboriginal men and women performed patriotic deeds, but it was the dominant society that assigned significance and meaning to them. That these deeds were not ignored confirms that Aboriginal actions mattered to English Canadians, that they fulfilled some emotional or intellectual need. The dramatic changes in the international situation played havoc with the emotions and morale of Canadians through the war's first year. A definite correlation appeared between events affecting the dominant society and the transformations of the 'Public Indian.' This response from the dominant society to external stimuli was the primary element of the mechanism driving change in the discourse. The actions of Aboriginal people were circulated and publicized because English Canadians wanted, perhaps needed, to know about Aboriginal actions and because they provided some comfort in anxious times.

Had the significance of the 'Public Indian' discourse to English Canadians ended there, the relative prominence of Indian stories in the media would have declined in the following weeks. This did not happen because the 'Indian-at-war' met other emotional needs of the dominant society in its adjustment to total war. First, English Canadians appreciated information that the 'Indian' supported the war effort because it meant that others were with them in the fight. Aboriginal peoples were not the sole targets of this uncertainty, the level of commitment exhibited by French Canadians, other ethnic minorities, and states and peoples around the world also mattered greatly. This anxiety came to a head with the defeat of France, when Canada was left feeling rather naked as Britain's primary support. When thrust into the front rank, it was natural for English Canadians to take a look behind to ensure that they were not stepping forward alone.

In addition, the 'Indian-at-war' served the needs of the dominant society during the first year of the war by helping Canadians to feel better about themselves, their society, and their government. English Canadians assumed that Aboriginal peoples' enthusiastic support for the war effort was a product of the benevolent administration provided by their government over the years. More significantly, however, Aboriginal enlistment and contributions of money seemed to validate and confirm Canada's identity as a kind and just society. The 'Indian-at-war' symbolized all that was different between 'us' and the Nazi regime. It thus functioned as an icon for the nation's moral crusade.

Finally, the 'Indian' was a useful propaganda tool in the efforts to foster national morale and encourage full participation in a total war effort. This role for the 'Indian-at-war' was becoming obvious that summer and would become increasingly so by 1941. In this capacity, the 'Public Indian' proved remarkably flexible, providing both an example to inspire and encourage and a whip to shame and push recalcitrant Canadians to do their part. The distorted 'Indian-at-war' icon provided an ideal of patriotism and self-sacrifice for the rest of Canada to match. However, beneath the surface of the positive characteristics were the negative stereotypes that pressured Canadians to equal the efforts of Aboriginal peoples or suffer humiliation at being bested by the 'lowly Indian.' Certainly, the media used and represented the 'Indian' in this fashion as part of their attempts to foster the nation's fighting spirit and forestall despair during the summer of 1940. This should not be overlooked as a reason for the proliferation and relative prominence of 'Indian' stories even as the world seemed to be crumbling. Thus, Aboriginal activities became part of the forces that galvanized and prepared the country for the long and difficult road ahead.

Canada's Aboriginal peoples contributed generously to the national war effort during the Second World War, as they had a generation earlier. However, their assistance to the dominant society went far beyond the human, the material, and the monetary. In the war's darkest days, when France fell and Britain's defeat appeared imminent, the example of Aboriginal sacrifice and patriotism combined with the flexible utility of the 'Public Indian' discourse helped English Canadians find the cultural and moral fortitude to face total war. Aboriginal support was not the determining factor in this – Canada would not have lost the war without the help of the 'Indian' – but it was one of many intellectual-cultural tools that English Canadians employed to help them cope. The actions and example of Aboriginal support mattered, more than they knew, to the dominant society.

Notes

1 The term 'Indian' in single quotations will refer to the constructed image of Aboriginal people prevalent in English-Canadian society, unless alluding to a thing such as Canadian Indian policy, Status Indians, and the Department of Indian Affairs. Although the focus of the paper is on the dominant society's notions of the 'Indian,' in practice, English Canadians did not always draw distinctions between Status Indians, Non-Status Indians and Metis. Certainly, there were different cultural notions about 'half-breeds' and Inuit, but those cannot be addressed in this paper, given the space constraints.

2 The research for this article was conducted with the aid of an Ontario Graduate Scholarship, an SSHRC Doctoral Fellowship, and a Department of National Defence Military and Strategic Studies Doctoral Fellowship.

3 Officially, more than 4,000 Status Indians served in the Canadian Expeditionary Force during the First World War.

4 The precise figures will never be known. Indian Affairs kept incomplete records and claimed a total of 3,090 Status Indian volunteers, but it did not maintain an account of those Status Indians who were conscripted under the National War Services Act (1940) or of Non-Status Indians, Metis, and Inuit. Beyond those

who actually enlisted were many more Aboriginal men who tried but were rejected because of poor health, inadequate education, or racial barriers. There remains a potent myth, however, that Aboriginal military participation was higher per capita than among other segments of Canadian society. This was not the case. Even assuming that the official number of 3,090 Status Indian service personnel could be doubled to around 6,000 (purely speculative), that still only amounted to 5 per cent of the Status Indian population of about 120,000. Canada as a whole put 1.1 million men and women in uniform during the Second World War, from a population of approximately 11 million, or 10 per cent.

5   The following analysis of English Canada's 'Public Indian' is drawn from a wide range of newspapers from across the country. These include prominent urban dailies: the *Globe and Mail* (by the late 1930s), the *Winnipeg Free Press*, the *Halifax Chronicle*, the *Calgary Herald*, the *Saskatoon Star-Phoenix*, and the *Vancouver Sun*. All six boasted a readership that extended beyond their municipal boundaries. The papers of four smaller communities were also examined: two dailies, the *Prince Albert Daily Herald* and the *Brantford Expositor*; and two weeklies, the *Kamloops Sentinel* and the *Cardston News*. In addition to the community-based papers, the university journals of Toronto, Queen's, and Dalhousie universities, the conservative weekly magazine *Saturday Night*, the popular weekly *Maclean's*, and the left-leaning literary monthly *Canadian Forum* round out the sources consulted.

6   Two of the best early works were Robert F. Berkhofer, Jr, *The White Man's Indian: Images of the American Indian from Columbus to the Present* (New York: Random House 1978); and Brian W. Dippie, *The Vanishing American: White Attitudes and U.S. Indian Policy* (Middleton, Conn.: Weslyan University Press 1982).

7   The best is Elizabeth Vibert's *Trader's Tales: Narratives of Cultural Encounters in the Columbia Plateau, 1797–1846* (Norman: University of Oklahoma Press 1997). Other works include: Daniel Francis, *The Imaginary Indian: The Image of the Indian in Canadian Popular Culture* (Vancouver: Arsenal Pulp Press 1995); Ronald Graham Haycock, *The Canadian Indian as a Subject and a Concept in a Sampling of the Popular National Magazines Read in Canada, 1900–1970* (Waterloo, Ont.: Waterloo Lutheran University 1971); Sarah Carter, 'The Missionaries' Indian: The Publications of John McDougall, John MacLean and Egerton Ryerson Young,' *Prairie Forum* 9, no.1: 27–44; and Peter Geller, '"Hudson's Bay Company Indians": Images of Native People and the Red River Pageant, 1920,' in Elizabeth S. Bird, ed., *Dressing in Feathers: The Construction of the Indian in American Popular Culture* (Boulder, Colo.: Westview Press 1996), 65–77.

8   Edward Said, *Orientalism* (New York: Vintage Books 1994); Kay Anderson, *Vancouver's Chinatown: Racial Discourse in Canada, 1875–1980* (Montreal and Kingston: McGill-Queen's University Press 1991); and James W. St. G. Walker, *'Race,' Rights and the Law in the Supreme Court of Canada: Historical Case Studies* (Waterloo, Ont., and Toronto: Wilfrid Laurier University Press/Osgoode Society for Canadian Legal History 1997).

9 For more information on the 'Public Indian' discourse during the 1930s, see R. Scott Sheffield, 'Winning the War, Winning the Peace: The Image of the "Indian" in English-Canada, 1939–1948,' PhD thesis, (Wilfrid Laurier University, 2000), chapter 1.

10 'Hitler Fated for Hot Place Now British Angry,' *Prince Albert Daily Herald*, 15 Sept. 1939, 8. The story eventually reached the Atlantic coast when the *Halifax Chronicle* reprinted the article from the *Stratford Beacon-Herald*; 'An Indian Chief,' *Halifax Chronicle*, 11 Oct. 1939, 4.

11 The Phoney War, or Sitzkrieg as the Germans called it, was the term given to the winter of 1939–40, between the fall of Poland and the German Blitzkrieg attacks in the spring of 1940. During these months, the German, British, and French armed forces gathered their strength for the coming contest and glared across the frontier at each other, but fought no battles.

12 The story was also carried in 'Reports of "Fifth Column" Operation among U.S. Indians,' *Brantford Expositor*, 5 June 1940, 12; and in a different format in 'Hitler Includes American Indian,' *Saskatoon Star-Phoenix*, 7 June 1940, 7. There was in fact a concerted, if ill-informed and poorly executed, German propaganda campaign aimed at Native Americans during the late 1930s and into 1940. American-based pro-Nazi and anti-Semitic groups also worked diligently to woo Natives to their cause, from the mid-1930s onward, with slightly more success. Such efforts had largely fizzled out by fall 1940 under concerted pressure from the U.S. Indian Affairs Bureau and the Federal Bureau of Investigation. See Kenneth William Townsend, *World War II and the American Indian* (Albuquerque: University of New Mexico Press 2000), chapter 2; also, Jeré Bishop Franco, *Crossing the Pond: The Native American Effort in World War II* (Denton: University of North Texas Press 1999), chapter 1. There is no evidence that a similar attempt was ever made in Canada.

13 This assumption turned out to be unfounded. Not only had Aboriginal men been liable for conscription for non-combatant duties during the Great War, but they would also be conscripted for both 'home defence' and overseas active service during the Second World War. Only about one-sixth of the Indian population was exempted from overseas service owing to explicit verbal treaty promises that had been made during the negotiation of Treaties 3, 6, 8, and 11, between 1876 and 1921. These treaty areas covered a large portion of the prairies as well as parts of northwestern Ontario, northeastern British Columbia, and the Yukon and Northwest Territories.

14 An abbreviated version of the story also appeared in the *Winnipeg Free Press*, 'Indian Aid: Give Treaty Money to Help Win War,' 17 June 1940, 10; and a few weeks later, via the *Windsor Star*, in the *Halifax Chronicle*, 'Three Cheers for the Crees,' 3 July 1940, 8.

15 This was a brief photo essay but the largest picture was of 'Private Jack Kahbejee, Chippewa Indian from Southampton district, [who] laughs broadly as he starts to fill his palliasse with straw.'

16 A similar story about several Alberta Cree communities who gave an ambu-
    lance to the Royal Canadian Army Medical Corps ran on the front page in
    Brantford a week later: 'Cree Indians Give R.C.A.M.C. Ambulance,' *Brantford
    Expositor*, 25 June 1940, 1.
17 'Metis Pledge Their Support,' *Saskatoon Star-Phoenix*, 2 July 1940, 3; 'All-Indian
    Battalion Suggested,' *Saskatoon Star-Phoenix*, 5 July 1940, 4; 'Indian Band
    Donates $1,000 to War Effort,' *Saskatoon Star-Phoenix* 25 July 1940, 4. Chief
    Dreaver's call for an 'All-Indian' unit was carried as well in the *Prince Albert
    Daily Herald* and in the *Winnipeg Free Press*: 'Indians May Form Battalion,' *Prince
    Albert Daily Herald*, 5 July 1940, 3; 'All-Indian Battalion,' *Winnipeg Free Press*,
    5 July 1940, 7.
18 This subject remains poorly documented by historians or anthropologists in
    Canada. However, a sense of the diversity of motivation and response can be
    gleaned from R. Scott Sheffield, '"...in the same manner as other people": Gov-
    ernment Policy and the Military Service of Canada's First Nations People, 1939–
    1945,' MA thesis, University of Victoria, 1995; Janice Summerby, *Native Soldiers,
    Foreign Battlefields* (Ottawa: Ministry of Supply and Services Canada 1993);
    James L. Dempsey, 'Alberta Indians and the Second World War,' in Ken Tingley,
    ed., *For King and Country: Alberta and the Second World War* (Edmonton: Provin-
    cial Museum of Alberta 1995), 39–52; Fred Gaffen, *Forgotten Soldier* (Penticton,
    B.C.: Theytus Books 1985); and Janet F. Davison, We Shall Remember Them:
    Canadian Indians and World War II, MA Thesis, Trent University, 1992.
19 It is not clear the extent to which this influenced young Aboriginal men to
    enlist. James Dempsey attributes prairie First Nations enlistments primarily to
    the continuing survival of a warrior ethos during the First World War; however,
    he never provides evidence directly supporting this claim. See, James L. Demp-
    sey, *Warriors of the King: Prairie Indians in World I* (Regina, Sask.: Canadian Plains
    Research Centre 1999).

Bibliography

'Aid from Indians: Residents of Manitoba Do Bit in Filling Red Cross Coffers.' 1940.
    Winnipeg Free Press (7 Aug.): 3.
'Eighteen Mistawasis Indians Join Infantry.' 1939. *Saskatoon Star-Phoenix* (14 Oct.):
    3.
'Indian Children Assist Red Cross.' 1940. *Vancouver Sun* (6 July): 16.
'Indian Generous to War Causes.' 1940. *Saturday Night* (10 Aug.): 17.
'Indians Are Loyal.' 1940. *Calgary Herald* (4 July): 4.
'Indians Display Loyalty in Gift of Treaty Money.' 1940. *Saskatoon Star-Phoenix*
    (17 June): 4.
'Indians Donate $2,080 to Purchase Ambulance.' 1940. *Saskatoon Star-Phoenix*
    (19 Sept.): 11.
Keyserlingk, Robert H. 1988. 'Breaking the Nazi Pact: Canadian Government Atti-

tudes towards German Canadians, 1939–1945.' In Norman Hilmer et al., ed., *On Guard for Thee: War, Ethnicity, and the Canadian State, 1939–1945*. Ottawa: Canadian Committee for the History of the Second World War, 53–69.

'Men of Tough Northern Breed with Grey and Simcoe Foresters at Camp Borden.' 1940. *Globe and Mail* (1 July): 5.

'Nazis Seeking to Rouse Indians.' 1940. *Winnipeg Free Press* (5 June): 3.

'Stonies at Ceremonial Sun Dance Pray for Victory for Britain.' 1940. *Calgary Herald* (20 June): 1–2.

'Three Cheers for the Cree.' 1940. *Halifax Chronicle* (3 July): 8.

Profile of Thomas George Prince (1915–77)

Ojibwa, Soldier

Thomas George Prince, and other Indian soldiers like him, served their country at a time when they were exempt from military service. If not for his persistence, Prince's exemplary military service might have never happened. Originally, he was turned down by the Canadian military simply because he was an Indian.[1]

Prince was born to Harry and Elizabeth Prince in a canvas tent in Petersfield, Manitoba, in October 1915.[2] In 1920 his family moved to Scanterbury, Manitoba, on the Brokenhead Indian Reserve, about eighty kilometres north of Winnipeg. Prince's military service spanned nine years beginning in June 1940 and continuing until after the end of the Second World War. Starting as a sapper in his first tour of duty, he moved quickly up the ranks.[3] He was honourably discharged with the rank of sergeant on 20 August 1945 – approximately two months after the war ended.[4] He later re-enlisted as a sergeant in the Korean War and served from August 1950 until September 1954.[5]

During his military career, Prince served in five units and regiments: the 1st Corps Field Park Company of the Royal Canadian Engineers; the 1st Canadian Parachute Battalion; the 1st Canadian Special Service Battalion; the 2nd Battalion of Princess Patricia's Canadian Light Infantry; and the 3rd Battalion of Princess Patricia's Canadian Light Infantry.[6] For his extraordinary service, Prince received many medals and decorations, including the 1939–1945 Star, the Italy Star, the France and Germany Star, the Defence Medal, the Canadian Volunteer Service Medal with Clasp, the War Medal, the Korean Medal, the United Nations' Service Medal, the Military Medal, and the Silver Star from the United States Army.[7] After his death, his military medals went missing. When they turned up at auction in 1997, they were purchased by his family for $75,000.[8]

Tommy Prince is honoured in various military museums around the country. For example, his portrait and medals can be found in a place of

Thomas (Tommy) George Prince. Courtesy of Canadian Press/*Winnipeg Free Press*.

honour on the Kapyong barracks wall in Winnipeg, Manitoba.[9] He is also featured at the Military Museum at the Rutherford Mall in Nanaimo, British Columbia. His contributions were recognized by a First Nations community when the 2nd Battalion on the Brokenhead Indian Reserve gave him a special salute and citation in August 1975.[10] A year later, the Manitoba Indian Brotherhood honoured him with their Certificate of Merit for his pioneer work in fighting for Indian rights.[11]

On 25 November 1977, after a life of triumph and difficulties, Thomas Prince died at Deer Lodge Veterans' Hospital in Winnipeg, Manitoba, with his daughters, Beverly and Beryl, at his side.[12] More than five hundred people attended his funeral, including Manitoba's lieutenant governor, Francis Laurence Jobin, and representatives from the French, Italian, and American consulates. Members of the Brokenhead Reserve drummed and chanted the lament, 'Death of a Warrior.'[13]

JENNIFER ARAGON

Notes

1 'Sgt. Tommy Prince: The Most Decorated Canadian Aboriginal Veteran' (2002), 2. www.ourworld. compuserve. comhomepages/aboriginal/prince1/html.
2 Lloyd Dohla, 'Thomas Prince: Canada's Forgotten Aboriginal War Hero,' *The Drum* (summer 2001): 1.
3 A sapper is a low-ranking private in the Royal Canadian Engineers. This military group builds bridges, roads, and runways. D. Bruce Sealy and Peter Van de Vyvere, *Manitobans in Profile: Thomas George Prince* (Winnipeg: Peguis Publishing 1980), 3.
4 Ibid., 26.
5 Ibid., 50.
6 Ibid.
7 Ibid.
8 Dohla, 'Thomas Prince,' 1.
9 Sealy and Van de Vyvere, *Manitobans in Profile*, 49.
10 Ibid., 47.
11 Ibid., 48.
12 Dohla, 'Thomas Prince,' 8.
13 Ibid.

PART NINE

OVERVIEW

Multiple Points of Light: Grounds for Optimism among First Nations in Canada

J. RICK PONTING AND CORA J. VOYAGEUR

Today, as you are my witness, the Nisga'a canoe returns to the Nass River. It has a cargo – a cargo of hope and reconciliation.

– Dr Joseph Gosnell, Nisga'a Nation,
at the signing of the Nisga'a Treaty, 4 August 1998

This chapter identifies positive developments for First Nations in Canada in the three decades since the federal government's 1969 landmark *White Paper* on Indian policy.[1] Our underlying purpose is to counter stereotypes and to offer encouragement about the state of affairs in Canadian First Nations communities for students, community practitioners, educators, and the public at large. We hope to offer an alternative vision to despair, pessimism, fatalistic resignation, 'compassion fatigue,' and the self-fulfilling prophecies that can arise from them. Our emphasis is squarely on positive developments for First Nations, although many of the points made are also applicable to the Metis and Inuit. We shall focus on grounds for optimism in four areas: self-government, organizational capacity, structures of opportunity, and resistance to oppression.

Despite accounts of resistance (Haig-Brown 1988), what might be called a 'deficit paradigm' – a focus on the sufferings, conflicts, and other problems of First Nations and on their status as victims – has been prominent in much social-science treatment of First Nations. Examples include the work of Paul Driben and Robert S. Trudeau,[2] Anastasia M. Shkilnyk,[3] and Daniel Francis,[4] as well as Menno Boldt's[5] thesis of cultural crisis and abdication of leadership. Even the reports of the Royal Commission on Aboriginal Peoples (RCAP) are imbued with a vocabulary of crisis, such as in the special report on suicide (RCAP 1995).

The emphasis on the deficit paradigm is probably due to various factors. These may include the vast disparities between the socio-economic realities (for example, poverty and racism) experienced by much of the First Nations population and the egalitarian ideals (such as Pierre Trudeau's 'just society') of the larger Canadian population. The persistence of some stereotypes of First Nations individuals, and the claims of victimization made by First Nations political leaders, are also relevant here. Further contributing factors would likely be the dominance of small-l liberalism in the Supreme Court of Canada and in certain mass media, and the slowness of Indian and Northern Affairs Canada (INAC) to relinquish its colonial approach to the administration of First Nations.

Although many of the changes this chapter identifies are evidence of a loosening colonial grip, we shall resist the temptation to cast this piece as an essay on decolonization. Simply stated, the changes in the sociological situation of First Nations during the last third of the twentieth century and the opening years of the twenty-first century are so diverse as to defy a single organizing theme. Even our focus on self-government, organizational capacity, resistance, and structures of opportunity omits dozens of other noteworthy positive changes.

Admittedly, any holistic attempt to portray the prospects of First Nations would have to take into account a litany of problems and obstacles such as the colonial and paternalistic Indian Act, underfunding, scant political will among non-Native politicians, racism among some non-Natives, the quality and type of education delivered, escapist behaviour and other effects of residential schools, geographic isolation, rampant unemployment, and generalized community distrust. In our view, such problems and obstacles have received ample attention in the literature.

In our experience in university classrooms, positive elements of the situation of First Nations individuals and collectivities are too readily overshadowed by such negative aspects as those above. Often the result is that unduly pessimistic impressions come to prevail among First Nations individuals and non-Natives alike, which raises the spectre of hopelessness and perpetuation of the worst aspects of the status quo. We seek to combat that here. Hence, we eschew any attempt to achieve 'balance' in our coverage.

As noted, the list of points cited below as grounds for optimism is not exhaustive. Rather, it is a starting point that, one might hope, will look strikingly modest a generation from now.

Two of our focal interests, 'organizational capacity' and 'structures of opportunity,' require some explanation. 'Organizational capacity' is a broad term, used here to refer not merely to the ability of a population to create organizations but also to the ability of those organizations to thrive – that is, the degree to which an organization is structured, resourced, staffed, and led so as to maximize both the attainment of its goals and the healthy functioning of organizational units and their members.[6] Sociologists emphasize the importance of ethnic groups building such organizational capacity (Kallen 1982). Indeed, J. Rick Ponting advocated almost a decade ago that one of the fundamental goals of Indian policy should be to build up the organizational capacity of First Nations (Ponting 1991, 437). Similarly, the RCAP assessed capacity building as being as important for the success of Aboriginal governments as legitimacy, power, and resources (RCAP 1996a, 326–352). Finally, as used here, the term 'structures of opportunity' refers not only to the chance of enjoying a favourable quality of life but also to the relative ease or difficulty in experiencing upward social or economic mobility and in obtaining gratifying employment with adequate remuneration and chances of advancement.

A word about value biases is in order. Terms such as 'optimism,' 'encouraging,' 'positive,' 'progress,' and their opposites, are necessarily subjective. Their use in this article is based on a bias that positively values the opening of opportunity structures for First Nations individuals, the increased empowerment and self-determination of First Nations individuals and collectivities, the elimination of sociological and social psychological dysfunction, and the enhancement of mutual respect between First Nation individuals and individuals from the larger society.

Demographic Context

The substantial changes in First Nations' organizational capacity have been possible in part because the First Nations population is no longer in a state of demographic crisis. Fundamental demographic transformations have already occurred or are under way in the First Nation population.[7] The infant-mortality rate, that brutally succinct indicator of Third World status, has plunged from its earlier scandalously high levels to the point where it has now almost converged with that of the larger Canadian population. Similarly, life-expectancy levels of First Nations individuals have increased greatly, such that the gap of about eleven years in 1975 vis-à-vis the larger Canadian society had narrowed to about seven years for males and about five years for females by 2001 (Statistics Canada 2003b). At a base level, this in itself is an indication of expanding opportunity. The First Nation population has undergone the so-called 'demographic transition' from high fertility and mortality rates to low fertility and mortality rates, albeit not as low as those of the larger Canadian population.[8] The First Nations baby boom is slowing. With fewer children, First Nations women are now able to take greater advantage of opening structures of opportunity.

The First Nations population has grown dramatically, because of such factors as the baby boom, Bill C-31,[9] and improvements in health care and standard of living. Moderate growth projections call for it to reach almost 900,000 by the year 2015.[10] The disappearance of the First Nations population, an implicit goal of the 1969 White Paper, is simply not going to happen. Indeed, the First Nations population has amassed some political and economic 'clout' by virtue of its numbers in some political constituencies and local economies. Furthermore, the population increase is giving rise to certain economies of scale (for example, in service delivery), is creating more viable home markets for First Nation entrepreneurs, and is even making it possible for serious consideration to be given to the 'community of interest' model (RCAP 1996b, 584–7) of self-government in various off-reserve communities.

The First Nations population pyramid is undergoing a pronounced transformation to the rectangular (Ponting 1997, 88–91). This means that the youth-dependency ratio – the ratio of persons under age fifteen to the population aged fifteen to sixty-four – is declining dramatically (from 1.04 in 1966 to .49 in 1995 and a projected .39 in the year 2015). This can contribute significantly to an improved standard of living for First Nations families. For instance, whereas the broad base of the First Nations population pyramid of an earlier era depressed female labour-force participation rates, we can expect this participation to increase as the population pyramid becomes rectangular.

Migration data reveal a small-scale reversal of the earlier population drain from the reserves (Clatworthy 1995, 64). Although over 40 per cent of the First Nations population lives off-reserve, there is now a small net inflow of Registered Indian migrants to the reserves from the large cities, from the small cities, and from the rural off-reserve areas, respectively. As with population growth based on natural increase, this is heartening from several standpoints related to the notion of 'critical mass,' or minimum population size needed to sustain certain organizations and activities. In-migration is good news for on-reserve entrepreneurs, and it also offers an economy of scale in the per capita cost of services delivered by First Nations governments on-reserve. Moreover, it contributes to an increase in the institutional completeness of on-reserve communities. In-migration is also welcome news from a human-capital perspective, because it helps support cultural preservation, especially language retention. Data from Statistics Canada's 2001 Aboriginal Population Survey (APS) showed that one-quarter of Aboriginal people could conduct a conversation in an Aboriginal language (Statistics Canada 2003).

Migration data compiled by Stewart Clatworthy also contradict any stereotype of First Nations individuals as highly transient (Clatworthy 1995,

76). According to the 2001 APS, in the twelve months before the 15 May 2001 Census, 22 per cent of Aboriginal people had moved, compared with only 14 per cent of their non-Aboriginal counterparts (Statistics Canada 2003b). There is, therefore, much more continuity in the social environment of First Nations individuals, families, and organizations than many casual observers might have assumed. The data reveal that only the off-reserve population can be considered to be in a high state of flux.

Human-Capital Development and Healing

Human-capital theory holds that deficiencies in the skills and aptitudes required by advanced industrial and post-industrial economies contribute in a major way to the high rates of unemployment among First Nations individuals. In terms of our focal themes, deficiencies in human capital constrict the opportunities available to First Nations individuals and limit the organizational capacity of First Nations governments and other First Nations organizations in civil society. However, as we shall see shortly, various indicators demonstrate that there have been enormous gains in human capital in the First Nations population. The significance of that data is that we are now seeing the emergence of a class of First Nations workers who possess the analytical and other skills needed by government and by other organizations which operate in the complex, contemporary world. The pool of human capital is deepening and First Nations individuals are becoming better equipped to take advantage of job opportunities that arise on or off-reserve.

With a majority (61 per cent in the 2001–2 academic year) of First Nations elementary and secondary students now enrolled in band-operated schools (DIAND 2002), the hiring of qualified First Nations individuals as teachers, and the incorporation of elders into the formal education of the children, school drop-out/push-out rates have declined dramatically. The percentage of on-reserve students remaining in school until Grade 12 (or 13) and graduating was 31 per cent for the 2000–1 academic year (DIAND 2002, 42). Also, the participation rate of First Nations individuals in post-secondary institutions has increased, narrowing the gap between First Nations and the larger Canadian population. For the population aged seventeen to thirty-four, the post-secondary participation rate for First Nations individuals in 1999 was 6.5 per cent, while for the total Canadian population the rate was 11.5 per cent (DIAND 2002, 46). First Nations university students now commonly express their desire to complete their programs of study to help their communities and their people. Now that a generation of First Nations individuals has surmounted the post-secondary wall and is available as role models to First Nations youths, those youths are more likely than before to regard university and other post-secondary institutions as a viable option. The 'intimidation factor' has diminished considerably.

Among other heartening educational attainment data is the fact that the 2001 Census identified 28,845 First Nations individuals holding at least one university degree.[11] Degree holders from the non-enumerated reserves would be in addition to that. In 2001 alone, approximately 3,700 First Nations individuals graduated from post-secondary institutions, including about 1,400 with baccalaureate degrees and about 200 with post-baccalaureate degrees (DIAND 2002, 49). In the ten years from 1991 to 2001, the number of Registered Indians (and Inuit) enrolled in all post-secondary institutions increased from 21,442 to 25,825, or 20 per cent (DIAND 2002, 45). The distribution of First Nations students across post-secondary disciplines is also improving, in that there is proportionately less clustering in social work and education and more representation across a wide variety of fields. These trends augur well for the future, regardless of whether the graduates of these programs find employment in on-reserve communities or enter the off-reserve economy where their involvement will challenge prevailing stereotypes.

Healing initiatives are also vital to the development of human capital in First Nations communities. Even when opportunities become available, those First Nations individuals in need of healing might be unable to take lasting advantage of them without healing programs. The recommendations of the RCAP[12] reflected the acute need for healing initiatives and provided empowering examples of communities (for example, Alkali Lake, Hollow Water, Uashat mak Mani-Utenam) that have developed successful models of collective and individual healing. It is also significant that the federal government, acting in response to the royal commission, made $350 million available for healing initiatives.[13] While small in comparison, the $1.25-million Reconciliation, Solidarity, and Communion Fund established by the Roman Catholic Church (CBC Radio News, 16 June 1998) in 1998, and a similar sized Healing and Reconciliation Fund of the Anglican Church,[14] are signs that the churches are coming to recognize that words are not enough in addressing the violation of Native children in residential schools.

An encouraging development in the healing process is the acknowledgment of abuse by both individuals and representative organizations and their commitment to monitor the progress of various healing initiatives. The courageous disclosures of individuals have given others the strength to break the silence surrounding abuse in residential schools, in families, and elsewhere. While the federal government's statement of regret for the residential-school abuses falls far short of the apology some sought, it can provide, for some residential-school abuse victims, external validation and recognition of the pain they endured. Further empowerment, healing, validation, and vindication will come for many from their decision to pursue their abusers in the courts, as thousands of individuals have done.

No single approach to healing will be sufficient or appropriate for all First Nations individuals who suffered abuse related to the residential schools. Nevertheless, many First Nations individuals and communities are returning to traditional healing practices involving the elders, healing circles, smudging, sweat lodges, the medicine wheel, and so on. This is a positive development, for it offers individuals a spiritual connection to their cultural roots and to an extensive, holistically integrated world-view and system of meanings.

'Women's issues' – primarily issues of childcare, community programming, and family violence – are also beginning to be addressed. Childcare facilities are being built on many reserves, allowing women to attend school or work. Programs that assist women and families are appearing in communities. For example, distance-learning programs help Aboriginal people gain educational credentials without having to leave home. Programs such as Aboriginal Headstart assist Aboriginal children with school readiness (Voyageur 1995). Further, family violence – a once taboo topic – is now the subject of frequent and well-attended conferences.

Whether healing be in response to the injuries inflicted by family violence, residential schools, racism, poor parenting, or something else, it can often increase an individual's self-esteem, personal pride, and/or cultural pride. These, too, are important gains in human capital, as is the role modelling that people in the healing process can provide to others. In addition, as healing progresses, wounded individuals no longer feel that they must hide their problems and suffer internally.

Human capital is augmented by infrastructure improvements made on-reserve. For instance, electrification is now nearly universal on-reserve, three-quarters of the population has flush toilets, and housing conditions have improved markedly, even though a housing shortage still exists (Ponting 1997, 97). These infrastructure improvements have a positive impact on the health of reserve residents, particularly by decreasing the likelihood of the spread of communicable diseases.

Human capital is also augmented by cultural revitalization. Notwithstanding claims made in some quarters[15] of a cultural crisis among First Nations, a compelling case can also be made that a veritable cultural renaissance swept over First Nations communities in the last third of the twentieth century (Ponting 1997, 138–41). The various dimensions of that renaissance include concerted efforts at language preservation and language training; repatriation of artifacts from museums[16]; the flourishing of First Nations artists and authors; renewed respect for the elders (Meili 1991); reclamation of traditional songs, dances, stories, and drumming; deep spiritual development and rediscovery; and control over an increasing number of media outlets. Clearly, First Nations people are reclaiming their voice. First Nations governments and other First Nations organizations can offer more meaning to their staff and clientele by being more firmly grounded in cultural traditions.

In concluding this section on healing and human capital development, we must stress how important it is to maintain perspective on conditions in First Nations communities, on- and off-reserve. Let us remember that, even among those persons subjected to the trauma and hardships of residential schools, family violence, and so on, some have derived strength and not vulnerability from the experience. Furthermore, as a student once remarked about the government's and churches' efforts at cultural genocide, 'they left a spark of the fire and we have built upon that.'

Economic and Employment Development

First Nations communities and individuals are making significant progress in throwing off the yoke of colonialism by safeguarding some aspects of the traditional economy and by participating in the economy of the larger society. The so-called 'Kamloops Amendment' (Bill C-115) to the Indian Act in 1988 is a legislative change that facilitates participation of non-Indian actors in on-reserve economic development. This in turn expands employment opportunities for on-reserve members.[17] The statute provides for the leasehold surrender of designated reserve land to non-Natives for economic development under conditions more reasonable than those the Indian Act previously allowed. The leasehold interest can now be seized pursuant to section 89 (1.1) of the Indian Act and can thus be used as collateral for a loan or mortgage. The Kamloops Amendment also allows for bands to tax non-Native businesses on designated lands, with obvious consequent advantage to band governments.

The creation of First Nations banking institutions is another positive development. The oil-rich Hobbema bands in Alberta created Peace Hills Trust Company, and the Saskatchewan Indian Equity Foundation and the Toronto Dominion Bank formed the First Nations Bank of Canada as a partnership. These First Nations-controlled institutions increase the likelihood that capital will circulate in First Nations hands, rather than leaving First Nation communities without providing any ripple-effect benefits. In theory, the emergence of such financial institutions also increases the likelihood that First Nations organizations will have access to the financial resources they need to expand. Unfortunately, many of these lending institutions are too new for any systematic empirical data to be available to substantiate this assertion.

The mainstream banks have finally discovered that First Nations individuals and corporations have money. This increases the availability of capital in First Nations communities. Banks' increased involvement in First Nations communities and institutions includes Aboriginal banking departments, advertising in Aboriginal newspapers and periodicals, financial support for such institutions as the Banff School of Management's Aboriginal Leadership Program, and funding for some First Nations ventures that would not have been funded in the past. One result is that the First Nations community is becoming less marginalized vis-à-vis the mainstream economy.

Land-claim settlements also support the creation of economic development opportunities. For instance, the 1975 James Bay and Northern Quebec Agreement provided not only a guaranteed income for persons engaged in the traditional trapping economy but also the capital that led to the creation of such modern corporate entities as Air Creebec. Similarly, in British Columbia, the Nisga'a Treaty provided for a $10-million government contribution to a fisheries conservation trust and an $11.5-million contribution to enable the Nisga'a central government to increase its capacity, in the form of licences and/or vessels, to participate in the west coast commercial fishery.

First Nations organizations are now managing the bulk (85 per cent) of the $4.8-billion annual budget of the Indian and Inuit affairs program of INAC. The administration of those funds, even when constrained by INAC's policies and procedures, provides valuable experience for First Nations organizations. In contrast to stereotypes that First Nations people cannot manage money, only about one-fifth of band administrations received a failing audit, according to the Assembly of First Nations (AFN).

Among the First Nations, professional careers and entrepreneurship, including women's, are burgeoning.[18] Aboriginal Business Canada reports that there were over 20,000 Aboriginal-owned businesses (including Metis and Inuit owners). Similarly, Aboriginal professionals and players in various sectors of the economy are organizing to identify and pursue common interests through professional and industry associations like the Council for the Advancement of Native Development Officers, the Indigenous Bar Association of Canada, the Calgary Aboriginal Professionals Association, the Indian and Inuit Nurses Association of Canada, the Native Investment and Trade Association, and the National Aboriginal Forestry Association, to name just a few. Such professional associations offer benefits (for example, networking and professional-development workshops) that members are likely to bring to the organizations in which they work, which enhances their organizational capacity.

Collectively owned economic ventures are also flourishing in various First Nations communities. One spectacular example is Casino Rama, which is owned by the Mnjikaning First Nation near Orillia, Ontario. It has become a major player in the off-reserve economy of the district. Other examples of collectively owned First Nations enterprises abound, especially in the tourism/recreation industry. Indeed, cultural tourism and eco-tourism hold considerable promise for expanding opportunities for enterprising First Nations who can tap the eager western European and Japanese markets.

Another employment development initiative that offers hope for expanding opportunity structures is employment equity. While Cora J. Voyageur's analysis of federal data collected pursuant to the Employment Equity Act and the Contract Compliance Program shows that this initiative is no panacea and has major shortcomings, the picture is by no means entirely gloomy (Voyageur 1997). For instance, employment of Aboriginal people under the program grew substantially (a 78 per cent increase over the initial 3,862 employees in 1987) during the first nine years of implementation of these initiatives. Moreover, Aboriginal people were less likely than the other target groups to be laid off during the economic recession. Furthermore, over the nine reporting years, both Aboriginal men and Aboriginal women experienced a slight proportionate increase in the so-called 'good jobs' – those in the managerial, professional, supervisory, semi-professional/technical, and foreman/forewoman categories. In 1995 over one-fifth of the Aboriginal full-time labour force in the firms covered by the federal Employment Equity Act consisted of females in 'good jobs' and almost one-quarter of males had 'good jobs' (Voyageur 1997, 121–2). The job category exhibiting the greatest growth over the nine years for Aboriginal females was managerial occupations.

Some First Nations have locational advantages that have yielded economic opportunities. For example, windfall revenues from natural resources have accrued to a small number of First Nations who have used those revenues to diversify the local economy, upgrade physical infrastructure, improve social and educational services, fund political initiatives, and so on. Some others, such as the Mohawk of Kahnawake near Montreal and the Tsuu T'ina Nation adjacent to Calgary, are situated close to the large markets of major urban areas and have taken advantage of related retail, real estate, or recreational opportunities.

Trust and Responsibility

If trust is the cement of society, the assuming of responsibility can be considered the essence of organizational life. A refrain that winds through political discourse, from reports by First Nations researchers such as Madeleine Dion Stout[19] to retrospectives by First Nations leaders,[20] is the need for First Nations people to strengthen and 'buy into' an ethic of personal responsibility – to reject the colonial mindset of the paternalistic Indian Act regime. The recognition of that need, and the willingness to reject the security of dependency and take risks for individual and community development, are much more in evidence today than even twenty years ago. Instances of direct relevance to our focal themes include self-government initiatives (for example, the Manitoba agreement to have First Nations take over the responsibilities of INAC), individuals' decisions to pursue advanced education even when criticized within their own community for doing so, and individuals' challenges to local First Nations politicians whom they believe to be corrupt.

Strater Crowfoot, of the Siksika Nation in Alberta, is an example of a First Nations leader who has challenged nepotism and colonial modes of thinking within First Nations communities:

> We need a paradigm shift in our thinking, away from the cynical, defensive, dependent, entitlement mindset that has been inculcated in us under the colonial *Indian Act* regime, and toward a more trusting, assertively proactive, persevering, visionary, affirming, meritocratic, and inclusive orientation ...
>
> If First Nations do not experience a drastic shift in leadership and followership ... our very future as First Nations will be jeopardized ... (Crawford 1997, 323)

This strikes to the heart of our concern with organizational capacity, opportunity, and self-government, because nepotistic regimes deny opportunity to qualified individuals whose skills could help boost the organizational capacity of First Nations government organizations.

Crowfoot raises the issue of trust in his call for a paradigm shift in First Nations thinking. Trust is also a form of social capital that facilitates risk taking and combats the cynicism Crowfoot attacks. Whether it be in individuals or institutions, trust is a fundamental building block in any community. There are many reasons why some First Nations communities have experienced a generalized sense of distrust. These include the example of the larger society, the residential-school experience, the federal government's betrayal of the spirit of the treaties, strategies of favoritism and of 'divide and conquer' pursued by Indian agents, nepotism and abuse of power by some First Nations politicians, dysfunctional families, rumour, gossip, and conditions of scarcity.

Are there grounds for predicting that the stock of trust within First Nations communities will increase? The very fact that some of the causal factors in the previous paragraph are eroding is grounds for optimism. In addition, in self-government negotiations, the Canadian government's emphasis on transparency and accountability to the grass-roots First Nations population may yield fruit in the form of enhanced levels of trust within those communities. Increased trust is already in evidence in the operations of various organizational entities in First Nations governments and in civil society, such as tribal councils formed by multiple bands, justice committees and sentencing circles within First Nations communities, and Aboriginal professional and trade associations. The increased acceptance of First Nations businesses and professionals within First Nations communities is another sign of growing trust. Particularly important is the increased respect elders are receiving in many First Nations communities where many people are now often seeking their wisdom. Rooted in the history of their people since time immemorial, elders' wisdom is likely to prescribe behaviour and mindsets that enhance community integration and trust building.

The role of women in First Nation communities also provides solid ground for optimism. In many (for example, the Lubicon Cree studied by Rosemary Brown[21]), and perhaps most First Nations communities, it is the women who have been pivotal to the community's survival through a dark era of clashing cultural and economic systems in which the men were stripped of some of their most important roles. Those communities' prospects for healing, survival, and development largely depend on the women. Across Canada, the late twentieth century, and the first years of the twenty first, witnessed a reassertion of agency on the part of First Nations women, as they organized to resist violence and paternalism and to address their and their families' needs more assertively by taking on responsibility at the family and community levels, and beyond, to the national and even the international arena. Joanne Fiske (1990) provides one such case study. Women are now taking an overtly active political role and many have pursued elected political office at the local level and elsewhere (for example, women elected as chief or councillor, the candidacies of Delia Opekekiw and Wendy Grant John for the leadership of the AFN) (Voyageur 2000). Now 15 per cent of the chiefs are women, whereas a half-century ago there was only one – Elsie Knott of Curve Lake, Ontario, who was elected in 1952 (Voyageur 2000).

Politics and Policy

Various First Nations individuals have been elected as members of Parliament (for example, Ethel Blondin-Andrew, Elijah Harper, Willie Littlechild, Jeannie Marie Jewel, Nellie Cournoyea) or appointed as senators (Len Marchand and the late Walter Twinn). Such individuals are able to inject Aboriginal perspectives into caucus debate and bring back to their people insights into the functioning of the larger polity.

Some major policy and legislative victories can be credited to First Nations. Among these, perhaps most relevant to our themes of self-government, organizational capacity, and creation of opportunity are the comprehensive land-claims policy and settlements and their implementing legislation. While these certainly fall far short of First Nations leaders' demands, they have been a major stimulus for self-government and have yielded major benefits for First Nations and, in the case of Nunavut, for other Aboriginal people. Take, for instance, the 1998 Nisga'a Treaty. Among many other positive features, it provides an estimated $196 million (in 1999 dollars) in compensation;[22] recognizes Nisga'a ownership of all mineral resources on or under Nisga'a lands, recognizes Nisga'a entitlement to a guaranteed share of the harvest of salmon and other marine and wildlife species; guarantees a specified volume of flow from the Nass River for Nisga'a uses; recognizes Nisga'a legal jurisdiction over Nisga'a children, repatriates various Nisga'a artifacts from the provincial and federal museums; and protects certain Nisga'a sites under the provincial Heritage and Conservation Act. Highly significant also is the considerable political will demonstrated by the then premier of British Columbia, Glen Clark, in proceeding with the treaty, despite considerable vocal opposition from many high-profile non-Natives in British Columbia.[23] Similarly, in the face of the Reform Party's concerted attack in the House of Commons (it introduced over 450 amendments), the federal government of Jean Chrétien remained resolute in its determination to pass the enabling legislation for the treaty.

A legislative accomplishment on a much more modest scale is the Sechelt self-government model. It attracted considerable interest from First Nations leaders, despite being roundly denounced by many First Nations politicians at its inception. No model of self-government is appropriate to all First Nations, but the Sechelt people found this model acceptable as a means of freeing themselves from some of the constraints of the Indian Act.

Another policy victory by First Nations can be found in the various programs and structural changes that the federal government introduced to accommodate Aboriginal peoples. Just a few, among dozens of examples demonstrating the expansion of opportunity structures, are the creation of an Aboriginal fishery on the Fraser River and the precedence given to it over the non-Native commercial fishery; the Options for Youth Program; the creation of 'Studio 1' (Aboriginal projects) within the National Film Board; the Public Service Commission's National Indigenous Development Program to improve the representation of Indigenous people at middle and senior levels in the federal public service; the adoption of a preference system for Aboriginal suppliers in purchasing by DIAND and other federal departments (the Procurement Strategy for Aboriginal Business); sentencing circles in the criminal justice system (LaPrairie 1992); and the inclusion of Aboriginal peoples as a designated group in the 1986 Employment Equity Act, and the related Contract Compliance Program. The recognition and affirmation of Aboriginal and treaty rights in the Constitution Act, 1982 might be one of the most important of these structural changes, especially if the view prevails that this was tacit recognition of an inherent right to self-government. None of these changes is beyond serious and just criticism from Aboriginal perspectives, but all represent tangible benefits that Aboriginal peoples did not enjoy prior to the 1969 White Paper. Moreover, they all provide a 'foot in the door' for the wider opening of structures of opportunity for First Nations and other Aboriginal peoples. To the extent that some of these programs and policies seek to combat systemic discrimination, they are particularly important reasons for optimism.

Other policy accomplishments for First Nations are found in the realm of devolution of administrative powers from the federal government to First Nations. Noteworthy examples include the 'Indian Control of Indian Education' policy, launched in 1974; the 1994 agreement to dismantle the Manitoba operations of INAC and turn the department's responsibilities over to the Manitoba First Nations governments (Fontaine et al. 1994); and the 1998 Nova Scotia tripartite education agreement which made the federal, provincial, and First Nations governments equal partners in the education of First Nation students in Nova Scotia (CBC Radio News, 19 June 1998).

Some policy victories have been won at the provincial level. Particularly important examples include the change in various provinces' child-welfare policies so that, when First Nations children must be apprehended, concerted efforts are made to place them in their own community or with other Native foster/adoptive parents, rather than in culturally alien non-Native homes. In addition, some provincial legislation requires that First Nations be notified if First Nations children are apprehended.

The historical period under examination reveals that, in their relations with the larger society, First Nations are enmeshed in power relationships that are in a state of flux; that is, the empowerment and disempowerment of First Nations are phenomena that can ebb and flow. First Nations encounter much change, some victories, and some setbacks. However, one important implication of that state of flux is that few defeats are irreversible. Another implication is that as First Nations' power becomes institutionalized – as a web of others with vested interests in new First Nations power arrangements develops around First Nations interests in a symbiotic relationship – it will be less precarious (Ponting 1997, 146). With that more solid power base will come an enhanced ability to influence the politics and legislation of the larger society so as to take better account of First Nations' interests.

Supreme Court of Canada Decisions

At the time of the 1969 White Paper, the prevailing attitude in the federal government of Pierre Trudeau was a Social Darwinian 'survival of the fittest' culture. Neither the human rights of First Nations individuals nor collective Aboriginal rights were recognized and the White Paper sought to terminate the treaties. The leaders of Canadian society, as embodied in the Supreme Court of Canada and the federal cabinet, have come a long, long way since then. This section chronicles some landmark court decisions handed down during the decades under examination. These include Supreme Court of Canada rulings and the entrenchment of Aboriginal and treaty rights in the Constitution Act, 1982. It should be noted, too, that there have been numerous lower-court decisions that have gone in the First Nations' favour and many of these will ultimately be tested before the Supreme Court.

In 1970 the Supreme Court handed down its decision in the landmark *Drybones* case (*R. v. Drybones* 1970). That decision recognized that individual Indians have the same human rights as other Canadians. More specifically, the court found that the section (then section 94[b]) of the Indian Act that made it an offence for Indians to be intoxicated was a violation of the Canadian Bill of Rights.[24] The legislation denied Indians the 'equality before the law' guaranteed by the Bill of Rights since the offence applied only to Indians and not to other persons. The need for constitutional protection of Indians' rights was demonstrated in 1974, when Jeannette Corbiere Lavell and Yvonne Bedard[25] lost their Supreme Court cases in which they used the Bill of Rights to challenge sex discrimination in the membership provisions of the Indian Act.[26] In pursuing the same legal issue, Sandra Lovelace eventually won her case before a United Nations tribunal, which was an important contributing factor to the recognition of the rights of Aboriginal women in section 35(4) of the amended Constitution Act, 1982.

The Supreme Court's decision in the *Calder* (also known as the Nishga or Nisga'a) case in 1973 was instrumental in making the federal government recognize Aboriginal rights. A court of Trudeau's intellectual peers ruled that Aboriginal rights do exist, even though the Nisga'a lost the case on an unrelated technicality – they had neglected to obtain the crown's permission to sue the crown (*Calder v. Attorney-General of British Columbia* 1973). This decision forced Trudeau to deal with First Nations' Aboriginal rights claims and the federal government established the federal land-claims policy. A quarter-century later, in 1998, the Nisga'a signed a modern-day treaty, which settled their land claim. The treaty was ratified by the House of Commons in April 2000.

The 1984 *Guerin* (Musqueam) decision was another victory for First Nations, for it upheld the federal government's fiduciary (trustee-like) obligation to look out for the best interests of First Nations when dealing with their property (*Guerin v. The Queen* 1984). This proved to be a significant incentive for INAC to curtail its involvement in the day-to-day administration of the affairs of individual First Nations. A corresponding expansion of activities by First Nations governments to take back more control ensued.

Before the end of the century, the Supreme Court's unanimous decision in another British Columbia case, that of *Delgamuukw* (Gitxsan-Wet'suwet'en) in 1997, proclaimed that, in the absence of treaties, Aboriginal title to the land is unextinguished and the First Nations are entitled to use such ancestral lands almost entirely as they wish. Furthermore, in what must be seen as a cultural victory for First Nations peoples, the court also ruled in the *Delgamuukw* case that the lower courts must take into account Aboriginal oral histories (*Delgamuukw v. British Columbia* 1997). The *Delgamuukw* decision has been a powerful lever for First Nations in land-claims negotiations since it was issued.

Earlier Supreme Court decisions on the *Nowegijick*,[27] *Simon*,[28] *Sparrow*,[29] and *Sioui*[30] cases had expounded on, and given an expansive interpretation to, the recognition of 'existing Aboriginal and treaty rights' in the Constitution Act, 1982. The court ruled not only that the treaties must be interpreted in a flexible manner that takes into account changes in technology and practice, but also that courts must construe the treaties in a liberal manner, with ambiguities resolved in favour of First Nations people, for the honour of the crown is at stake. The same principles were invoked in the ruling in the 1999 decision in the Donald Marshall, Jr case, where the court upheld the Mi'kmaq Treaties of 1760–1 and said that Mi'kmaq and Maliseet fishers could fish out of season, without a licence, and with nets that violate federal fisheries regulations (*R. v. Marshall* 1999). The *Sioui* decision stipulated that the treaties cannot be unilaterally altered or extinguished by either side, while the *Sparrow* decision required governments to justify any legislation that has an adverse impact upon Aboriginal rights protected under section 35 of the Constitution Act, 1982.

Another Supreme Court decision pertains to justice in criminal trials. In the 1998 *Williams* case, the court ruled that prospective jurors may be questioned about their racial views, to root out those whose prejudices could destroy the fairness of a criminal trial (*R. v. Williams* 1998).

Much legitimation and recognition of First Nations' grievances, rights, perspectives, and so on, have come from the court decisions and government policies identified above. The fact that First Nations are prepared to bear the enormous expense to bring a case to the Supreme Court of Canada speaks volumes of their determination to protect their inherent rights.

Resistance

The resistance that First Nations people have shown to various aspects of colonization down through the generations has received little emphasis in media coverage of Aboriginal affairs but somewhat more attention from historians and feminist academics in general. For instance, J.R. Miller treats students' and parents' resistance to residential schools in considerable detail (Miller 1996, 343–74). The last third of the twentieth century saw considerable resistance in a variety of forms and venues. These included sit-ins, hunger strikes, international lobbying, court injunctions and suits, defiance of court orders, boycotts, blockades, stunting, armed confrontation, and unilateral assertions of sovereignty. Places like Anichinabe Park (Kenora, Ontario), Gustafsen Lake (British Columbia), Ipperwash (Ontario), Restigouche (New Brunswick), Old Man River Dam (Alberta), Esgeno opotit, (Burnt Church), and, of course, Oka, Kanesatake, and Kahnawake (Quebec), have become symbols of First Nations resistance to colonialism, as have individuals and groups such as the Warrior Society, the American Indian Movement, Elijah Harper, the James Bay Cree, and the Lubicon Cree. Through varied forms of resistance, First Nations have demonstrated the truth of the sociological maxim (Parkin 1979) that there is a two-way flow of power in relations of subordination-dominance.

First Nations resistance has constrained the federal government's exercise of its power in tangible ways (such as the lessons learned through Oka) and has empowered First Nations in the process. The radicalization, actual and potential, of some First Nations youth is part and parcel of this constraining effect. International embarrassment and domestic coercion have been two of the tactics successfully used to create, in the minds of non-Native politicians, the political will for genuine change. Yet, the fact that such tactics have mustered political will can be seen as a source of optimism for First Nations people, for First Nations retain the resources to exercise coercive or internationally embarrassing tactics.

Resistance to actual or perceived corruption in local governance has emerged at the grass-roots level of various First Nations. Examples include the Stoney Tribe, Ermineskin,[31] Alexander,[32] Tsuu T'ina,[33] and Beaver Lake[34] First Nations in Alberta and the Poundmaker Nation[35] in Saskatchewan, whose administrations have experienced protests from Nation members seeking greater financial accountability among elected leaders. In response, the AFN established a working relationship with the Certified General Accountants Association of Canada to improve accounting standards and develop a related code of ethics for First Nations' local financial management (Alberts 1998, A8).

Resistance to paternalism and family violence has also emerged more visibly in recent years. One important forum was the RCAP, where various intervenors came forward not only to critique the colonial roots of some family violence but also to tell their stories and urge the commissioners to attack the pro-male bias demonstrated by many chiefs and councils on matters of domestic abuse (Dion Stout 1997, 284–6). With the organized support of their First Nations sisters, First Nations women have also begun to resist publicly a related pressure from some First Nations men: some First Nations women have been pressured to remain silent on issues of family violence so that they do not undermine the drive towards self-government. In place of silence, organizations such as the Native Women's Association of Canada have demanded tighter accountability provisions for chiefs and councils under self-government, such as bringing First Nations governments squarely under the jurisdiction of the Canadian Charter of Rights and Freedoms. The royal commission endorsed their demand, as does the government of Canada.

Resistance is also facilitated by increased access to information technology and by the growing number of websites controlled by First Nations individuals and organizations. Such sites are being used to critique federal policy proposals (such as the AFN's trenchant critique of INAC's proposed Indian Act revisions in 1996) and generally to give voice to First Nations perspectives (for example, during episodes of intense conflict such as the stand-off at Gustafsen Lake, B.C.). In a very real sense, information is power. Mark Crawford and Kekula Crawford point out that swiftly evolving information and communication technologies and networking infrastructures are already playing an expanding role in supporting the self-determination of peoples and emergent nations (Crawford and Crawford

1995). Thus, it is significant that Industry Canada, an arm of the federal government, has launched the Aboriginal Community Access Project to link 400 First Nations schools to the 'Information Highway.' The marriage of computers and telecommunications technology offers an important resource in combating the disempowering effects of the geographic dispersion of First Nations in Canada.

First Nations and other Aboriginal peoples are also creating an Aboriginal voice in academia, the mass media, and other spheres.[36] In the realm of history,[37] literature (Louise Halfe, Molly Chisaakay, Jeannette Armstrong, Thomas King), feminism (Janice Acoose/Misko-Kìsikàwihkwè,[38] Joyce Green, Kim Anderson), entertainment, and other fields (the National Aboriginal Achievement Awards), Aboriginal peoples are now being heard directly, rather than through non-Native intermediaries, as was common in the late 1960s.

Self-Government

We have already mentioned various ramifications for self-government that will flow from other social changes, such as constitutional changes and changes in the human capital of the First Nations population. That ground will not be covered again here. Instead, let us first consider the terms of the discourse surrounding self-government because the discourse shapes the debate over policy options.

Three terms in public discourse on First Nations matters are particularly important. They are: 'First Nation,' 'inherent right to self-government,' and 'nation-to-nation' relationship. Some observers might add 'third order of government' as a fourth such term. Their importance stems from two factors: they facilitate or augment the claims to legitimacy that First Nations make for certain institutional power-sharing arrangements, and they define First Nations in collectivistic rather than individualistic terms.

The 1969 White Paper enunciated what was essentially a termination policy couched in a discourse of equality, sameness, and individual rights. It called for the individuation of the First Nations population, rather than for the strengthening of the collectivity. While the Constitution Act, 1982 recognized and affirmed Aboriginal rights, the 1983 Penner Report (Penner 1983) was instrumental in laying the groundwork for putting 'meat' on the constitutional 'bones' in ways that would involve meaningful power sharing. Indeed, the Penner Report and the 1985 Coolican Report (Coolican 1985) were crucial in impressing upon non-Native politicians the message that workable solutions to problems in relations between Aboriginal peoples and the larger Canadian society must involve meaningful power sharing. Furthermore, in contrast to the framers of the White Paper, but in a tradition established by the Berger Commission on the Mackenzie Valley Pipeline and later adopted wholeheartedly by the RCAP, the authors of the Penner Report engaged in meaningful consultation with First Nations. From those consultations came a framing of issues that gave an enormous boost to the legitimacy of First Nations claims and aspirations. The Penner committee not only institutionalized the term 'First Nation' but also endorsed a wide range of powers for First Nations governments and signalled that they should be treated as a 'third order' of government in Canadian federalism.

The constitutional negotiations of the 1980s were intended to elaborate and define Aboriginal rights in the constitution. The debate came to focus on section 35 of the Constitution Act, 1982, which, Aboriginal leaders argued, referred implicitly to an Aboriginal right to self-government. Most first ministers strenuously resisted the Aboriginal leaders' key demand – constitutional entrenchment of an 'inherent,' as opposed to a delegated or contingent, right to self-government. Instead, the first ministers insisted on definition of self-government before constitutional entrenchment. Just a few years later, after First Nations peoples flexed some political muscle, with Elijah Harper scuttling the Meech Lake Accord and the Mohawk Warriors holding the Canadian army at bay at Oka, the 1992 Charlottetown Accord recognized Aboriginal peoples' inherent right to (undefined) self-government and offered many more gains. The federal government subsequently adopted a policy that claimed to recognize the inherent right to self-government.

The Aboriginal provisions of the Charlottetown Accord were diametrically opposed to the entire thrust of the 1969 White Paper. That the first ministers agreed to such provisions is substantial progress, even though the accord was defeated in a national referendum. The RCAP went even further than the Charlottetown Accord on many dimensions. For instance, the commission called for an expanded land base for both Metis and First Nations and offered the legal opinion[39] that section 35 of the Constitution Act, 1982 encompasses an inherent right to self-government, even to the point of separate criminal codes. The commission also endorsed the notion of Aboriginal governments as a 'third order of government' (as opposed to 'mere' municipalities) in Canadian federalism and recommended that the federal and provincial governments enter into a 'nation-to-nation' relationship with Aboriginal governments under new or renovated treaties. Thus, as politico-judicial discourse has evolved over the decades, the goal posts in the debate have continued to move farther away from those who seek to block meaningful Aboriginal self-government and neutralize First Nations' treaty rights. A pattern of gradualism has been established whereby governments' initial resistance to First Nations leaders' claims gives way to token recognition, which is followed by enhanced legitimacy through judicial and parliamentary recognition, after which come more meaningful (albeit seemingly begrudging) concessions that open the door to substantial reforms by the most assertive First Nations.[40] In that final point there is a further basis for optimism; that is, there is manoeuvring room for the unilateral assertion of sovereignty by determined First Nations, as the Mohawk of Kahnawake have demonstrated. The establishment of Nunavut in 1999 can be viewed in a similar light as a portent of things to come for some First Nations.

In concluding this discussion of gains in the self-government realm, two important matters should not be overlooked. The first, on the symbolic plane, is that with gains in First Nations governments' powers, First Nations individuals come to see themselves reflected in the symbolic output of the (First Nations) state. In this regard, Raymond Breton[41] points out that individuals who cannot recognize themselves in the symbolic output of the state are more likely to become alienated and to withdraw legitimacy from the state. As First Nations governments take up jurisdiction and attend not merely to the instrumental but also to the symbolic aspects of exercising that jurisdiction, the legitimacy-based loyalty of First Nation individuals to First Nations governments is likely to grow. The second matter is on the organizational plane. Simply put, the end of the twentieth century and the opening of the twenty-first witnessed a much greater organizational density among First Nations than was the case at the time of the 1969 White Paper. This reflects not only the development of human capital but also an expanded resource base. At the time of the White Paper, the AFN and its predecessor, the National Indian Brotherhood, did not even exist, and local band councils were often dismissed by their constituents as INAC puppets. Intermediate-level associations, other than provincial political organizations, were rare. Now there is a dense network of national, provincial, tribal-level, and local organizations pursuing political, economic, and cultural goals. While band councils are still highly constrained by DIAND, they have much more autonomy than before and are much better equipped to challenge the department than ever before.

Conclusion

What are we to make of the preceding inventory of social changes? Because of space limitations, we will confine our remarks here to just one of our focal interests – organizational capacity – that both academics and practitioners have identified as being of vital importance.

We believe that the time has come for social-scientific inquiry to move from the deficit/victimization/conflict paradigm to address instead the ways in which organizational capacity can be bolstered. More particularly, we believe that agencies that fund research in First Nations communities should give priority to projects that tackle organizational and community development issues over research rooted in the deficit paradigm. Apart from labour-force training, such as in the realms of policy analysis and the collection and analysis of statistical data, what can social science contribute to the development of organizational capacity by First Nations organizations? From an organizational-capacity perspective, the optimal organization, deployment, and management of the First Nations labour force is a research matter of considerable importance. Some examples of research questions that social science could tackle in the service of First Nations organizational development are:

- How can norms of professionalism be reconciled with Aboriginal cultural imperatives?[42] In particular, how can nepotism be countered with the least political cost?
- What features of First Nations governments have high levels of legitimacy with constituents and how do those features differ from those of non-Native governments?
- What organizational forms (for example, matrix versus hierarchical versus some adaptation of the circle) are best suited to First Nations needs and cultures?
- What models of collaboration and decentralized organization are most appropriate for delivery of services to an off-reserve diaspora?
- What incentives are most effective for skilled First Nations workers and how can the turnover rate for skilled personnel be optimized?
- How do First Nations community members react to changes occurring within their community organizations, such as educated individuals taking up positions in the community?
- What 'public relations' strategies are most effective in minimizing non-Native communities' resistance as First Nations augment their organizational capacity and achieve a shift in the local power balance in their favour?

Not just any qualified researcher can gain community entrée to research these questions and not just any knowledgeable expert can effectively disseminate the research findings. This takes us back to the labour-force training issue. A cadre of trained Native researchers is required to address these research questions. We submit that one of the most important policy issues to arise from the preceding pages is whether universities and funding agencies will take up this challenge to produce a group of applied social-science researchers. One government agency, Statistics Canada, has already answered the call through special statistical-training sessions for public servants in Nunavut and Aboriginal agencies and organizations elsewhere. It is vital that other institutions follow suit, for many of the gains cited throughout this article can be solidified and magnified with proper organizational-development strategies. In other words, when First Nations win political and legal victories that transfer authority and resources to First Nations governments, and those governments then hire skilled First Nations individuals, little has been gained if those government organizations are at such an early stage of organizational development that they have a low organizational capacity. Indeed, in such a situation, the full potential for change is most unlikely to be realized and cynicism and disillusionment could set in.

Our survey of positive changes in the situation of First Nations over the last few decades has been highly selective, of necessity. What we have found has been quite heartening in many respects and has provided a counterweight to those who would focus exclusively on the deficit paradigm. Of course, much remains to be done on these and other fronts, as well as in consolidating the gains achieved to date. Many of the changes have been primarily facilitative in nature (for example, the dependency ratio declining in First Nations communities; the Supreme Court changing one or another of the 'rules of the game'). One can look forward in another third of a century to conducting such a cataloguing of social change in these four focal areas and finding how these opportunities were actually exploited.

The transformation of the First Nations sociological landscape in Canada has been profound and can be seen as indicative of a new era in First Nations affairs. That new era does not yet qualify as the 'paradigm shift' for which Sally M. Weaver (1991) called, but it does contain the seeds for an optimism that, we contend, is definitely warranted. Countervailing forces are formidable and may prevail in some places. However, in many ways, the prospects for First Nations are much brighter at the dawn of the twenty-first century than they were thirty years earlier. Multiple points of light are illuminating the community. First Nations have moved from a position of marginality to one where First Nations interests often must be taken into account by decision makers and others in the larger Canadian society. First Nation interests are not only becoming vested in the Canadian state (Breton 1989) but are also infusing civil society in Canada. While First Nations concerns and interests are far from occupying a central position in Canadian society, their marginalization has diminished substantially and opportunity structures have opened for individuals to an extent unimaginable even thirty years ago.

In closing, we reiterate that First Nations people have made many contributions to life in Canada. Their determination and resolve forced economic, political, and social injustices to the fore. First Nations initiatives have led to changes in Canadian society that benefit all citizens. In the social realm, First Nations exposed the racism and unfair treatment they experienced and held a mirror to Canada's face. The reflection was not always what Canadians wanted to see nor was it what they wanted others to see. It was tarnished with the racism embedded in government policy and legislation.

We are optimistic that Aboriginal peoples are emerging from the margins of Canadian society. They are participating in ways unimagined fifty years ago. For example, they are voting in elections – something that was forbidden to them until 1960. They are obtaining educational credentials at an unprecedented rate. With these credentials come employment, purchasing power, and respect in mainstream society. Entrepreneurship is thriving in the Aboriginal community as more than 20,000 Aboriginally owned businesses in Canada have created 49,000 new jobs (Aboriginal Business Canada 2000). Further, the emerging Aboriginal tourism industry already has revenues of $270 million dollars annually (Aboriginal Tourism Team Canada 2002).

In the social realm, the *Drybones* case illustrated to the Canadian people the potential for individual rights to take precedence over government legislation. However, the *Lavell* case made the Canadian government realize that the Bill of Rights was not strong enough to protect Canadian individuals' rights. This led the Trudeau government to enact the Charter of Rights and Freedoms as part of the Constitution Act, 1982 – the highest law of the land. Bill C-31, with its ban on gender discrimination, brought the Indian Act into compliance with the Charter of Rights and Freedoms. The Charter had thereby been strengthened by the tireless efforts of Indian women, most notably the group called Indian Rights for Indian Women, which fought for sixteen years to have the Indian Act changed.

Canadians can learn much about empowerment from First Nations, especially the James Bay Cree, with regard to effective strategic and tactical operations abroad. The James Bay Cree have been highly successful at creating and capitalizing on leverage. Canadians can also learn much about local group empowerment from First Nations. First Nations have shown that dogged determination in the pursuit of a just cause can, in the long run, yield substantial gains in local self-determination.

In the political realm, Aboriginal peoples have ensured grass-roots participation in constitutional reform. A First Nations man, Elijah Harper, stopped the executive-style politics surrounding the drafting of the Meech Lake Accord. His efforts ensured that the subsequent constitutional amendment – the Charlottetown Accord – included grass-roots participation in the form of a referendum.

First Nations in Canada have every right to feel optimistic about the future. They have made much progress since the Trudeau government's failed attempt at assimilation in the 1969 White Paper. Political and legal authorities have recognized that First Nations' rights, cultures, and claims are supported by Canadian law. Increasing numbers in employment, higher education, and business give First Nations people opportunities for a higher standard of living in this land of plenty. Their economic, social, and political contributions have made this country better for everyone. Now, perhaps, they can share in the prosperity.

Notes

1 Readers unfamiliar with the 1969 White Paper can find an excellent account of its development in Sally M. Weaver, *Making Canadian Indian Policy: The Hidden Agenda, 1968–1970* (Toronto: University of Toronto Press 1981). Suffice it to say that the White Paper was highly assimilationist in orientation and provoked a major, successful political mobilization of resistance by First Nations leaders across the country. See Roger Gibbins, 'Historical Overview and Background,' in J. Rick Ponting, ed., *First Nations in Canada: Perspectives on Opportunity, Empowerment, and Self-Determination* (Whitby, Ont.: McGraw-Hill Ryerson 1997), especially 19–34.

2 Paul Driben and Robert S. Trudeau, *When Freedom Is Lost: The Dark Side of the Relationship between Government and the Fort Hope Band* (Toronto: University of Toronto Press 1983).

3 Anastasia M. Shkilnyk, *A Poison Stronger Than Love: The Destruction of an Ojibwa Community* (New Haven, Conn.: Yale University Press 1985).

4 Daniel Francis, *The Imaginary Indian* (Vancouver, B.C.: Arsenal Pulp Press 1992).

5 Menno Boldt, *Surviving as Indians* (Toronto: University of Toronto Press 1993).

6 Thus, an organization with a highly developed organizational capacity has the ability to perform environmental scanning and adjust to salient changes in that environment; recognize and respond to the human needs (including spiritual needs) and potential of staff members; effectively manage the flow of information within the organization; maintain its legitimacy and trustworthiness in the eyes of its clientele; formulate and adjust its goals and its strategies for achieving those goals; and procure needed input resources.

7 See James Waldram, D. Ann Herring, and T. Kue Young, *Aboriginal Health in*

Canada: Historical, Cultural, and Epidemiological Perspectives (Toronto: University of Toronto Press 1995), 67; Francois Nault et al., *Population Projections of Registered Indians, 1991–2015* (Ottawa: Statistics Canada 1993); and S. Loh, *Projections of Population with Aboriginal Ancestry: Canada Provinces/Regions and Territories, 1991–2016* (Ottawa: Minister of Industry 1995).

8 See Andrew J. Siggner, 'The Socio-Demographic Conditions of Registered Indians,' in J. Rick Ponting, ed., *Arduous Journey* (Toronto: McClelland and Stewart 1986), 57–83; and Statistics Canada, *The Daily*, 98-01-13.

9 Bill C-31 eliminated the provisions of the Indian Act that stated that only Indian women, and not Indian men, lost their Indian status when they married a non-Indian. For a discussion of the bill and its impact, see the Royal Commission on Aboriginal Peoples, *Report of the Royal Commission on Aboriginal Peoples, Vol. 4: Perspectives and Realities* (Ottawa: Minister of Supply and Services Canada 1996), 33–53.

10 Nault et al., *Population Projections*. It now appears that this projection is too conservative.

11 Special tabulation, Statistics Canada, courtesy of Andy Siggner.

12 See, for example, Royal Commission on Aboriginal Peoples, *Choosing Life: Special Report on Suicide among Aboriginal People* (Ottawa: Minister of Supply and Services Canada 1995), 93; Royal Commission on Aboriginal Peoples, *Report of the Royal Commission on Aboriginal Peoples, Vol. 5: Renewal: A Twenty-Year Commitment* (Ottawa: Minister of Supply and Services Canada 1996), 212; and Royal Commission on Aboriginal Peoples, *Bridging The Cultural Divide: A Report on Aboriginal People and Criminal Justice in Canada* (Ottawa: Minister of Supply and Services Canada 1996), 315.

13 For detailed information on this fund, see the DIAND website at www.inac.gc.ca..

14 See www.anglican.ca/ministry/rs/healing for a list of grants made by this Anglican fund since its inception in 1992.

15 See, for example, Boldt, *Surviving as Indians*, 176.

16 See Catherine E. Bell, 'Limitations, Legislation, and Domestic Repatriation,' *UBC Law Review* (Special Issue, 1995): 149–63.

17 The 'Kamloops Amendment' clarified the fundamental difference between designated lands, surrenders, and absolute surrenders. It allows bands the opportunity to lease their lands to non-Natives for commercial, industrial, or residential development while retaining band jurisdiction over these lands.

18 See Wanda A. Wuttunee, *In Business for Ourselves: Northern Entrepreneurs* (Calgary, Alta.: Arctic Institute of North America 1992); and Peter D. Elias, *Northern Aboriginal Communities: Economics and Development* (North York, Ont.: Captus Press 1995).

19 Madeleine Dion Stout, 'Stopping Family Violence: Aboriginal Communities Enspirited,' in Ponting, ed., *First Nations in Canada*, 273–98.

20 Patricia Monture-Angus, *Journeying Forward: Dreaming First Nations' Indepen-*

dence (Halifax: Fernwood), 36, and Strater Crowfoot, 'Leadership in First Nation Communities: A Chief's Perspectives on the Colonial Millstone,' in Ponting, ed., *First Nations in Canada*, especially 299–325.

21 Rosemary Brown, 'Exploitation of the Oil and Gas Frontier: Impact on Lubicon Lake Cree Women,' in Christine Miller and Patricia Chuchryk, ed., *Women of the First Nations: Power, Wisdom and Strength* (Winnipeg: University of Manitoba Press 1996), 151–65.

22 The compensation formula is extremely complex and contains contingency factors which make it impossible to offer a firm figure here. The inflated figures offered in media reports at the time of the initialling of the treaty probably included other benefits, whereas the reference in our text is only to the compensation component of the settlement.

23 The British Columbia government had refused to negotiate unextinguished Aboriginal title for a century.

24 As a mere statute, the Bill of Rights could not override other statutes.

25 *Attorney-General of Canada v. Lavell; Isaac v. Bedard* (1973), 38 D.L.R. (3d) 481.

26 As indicated in n.9, those provisions resulted in only women losing Indian status for marrying a non-Indian.

27 *Nowegijick v. The Queen*, [1983] 1 S.C.R., 29.

28 *Simon v. The Queen*, [1985] 2 S.C.R., 387.

29 *R. v. Sparrow.* [1990] 1 S.C.R., 1075.

30 *R. v. Sioui* [1990] 1 S.C.R.,1025.

31 See Kim Lunman, 'Ermineskin: RCMP to Probe Hobbema Finances,' Calgary Herald, 20 March 1998, A8.

32 See Canadian Press, 'Residents of Reserve Seek Probe,' Calgary Herald, 29 March 1998, A4.

33 See Mark Lowey, 'Aboriginal Affairs: Police Probe Use of Reserve Funds,' Calgary Herald, 9 Jan. 1998, B1.

34 See Kim Lunman, 'Tribal Fund Abuse Inquiry Sought,' Calgary Herald, 7 Feb. 1998, A4.

35 See Kim Lunman, 'Native Affairs: Chiefs Rapped for Wage Secrecy,' Calgary Herald, 9 March 1998, A1.

36 For example, Jeanne Perreault and Sylvia Vance, ed., *Writing the Circle: Native Women of Western Canada* (Edmonton: NeWest Press 1990); and Miller and Chuchryk, *Women of the First Nations*.

37 For example, see Olive P. Dickason, *Canada's First Nations: A History of Founding Peoples from Earliest Times*, 2nd ed. (Toronto: Oxford University Press 1997); and Treaty 7 Elders et al., *The True Spirit and Original Intent of Treaty 7* (Montreal and Kingston: McGill-Queen's University Press 1996).

38 Janice Acoose (misko-Kìsikàwihkwè), *Iskwewak Kah' Ki Yaw Ni Wahkomakanak/ Neither Indian Princesses nor Easy Squaws* (Toronto: Women's Press 1995).

39 Note that the co-chair of the royal commission, the Honourable René Dussault, was a justice of the Quebec Court of Appeal and another commissioner, the

Honourable Bertha Wilson, was a former justice of the Supreme Court of Canada. Accordingly, the legal opinions expressed by the Commission cannot be taken lightly.

40 See Ponting, ed., *First Nations in Canada*, 360, for a schematic model of First Nations' fluctuating sovereignty.

41 See Raymond Breton, 'The Production and Allocation of Symbolic Resources: An Analysis of the Linguistic and Ethnocultural Fields in Canada,' *Canadian Review of Sociology and Anthropology* 21, no. 2: 123–44.

42 See Royal Commission on Aboriginal Peoples, *Vol. 2*, 338.

Bibliography

Aboriginal Business Canada. 2000. *Aboriginal Entrepreneurs in Canada: Progress and Prospects*. Ottawa: Aboriginal Business Canada. Catalogue No. 1206–260X.

Aboriginal Tourism Team Canada. 2002. www.attc.ca/tourism.htm.

Alberts, Sheldon. 1998. 'Band Finances: AFN Signs Accountability Agreement.' Calgary Herald (31 March): A8.

Breton, Raymond. 1989. 'The Vesting of Ethnic Interests in State Institutions.' In James S. Frideres, ed., *Multiculturalism and Intergroup Relations*. Westport, Conn.: Greenwood Press.

Calder v. Attorney-General of British Columbia, 34 D.L.R. (3d) 145, (1973).

CBC Radio News, 98-06-16.

CBC Radio News, 98-06-19.

Clatworthy, Stewart. 1995. *The Migration and Mobility Patterns of Canada's Aboriginal Population*. Winnipeg: Four Directions Consulting Group.

Coolican, Murray. 1985. *Living Treaties, Lasting Agreements: Report of the Task Force to Review Comprehensive Land Claims Policy*. Ottawa: Department of Indian Affairs and Northern Development.

Crawford, Mark, and Kekula Crawford. 1995. 'Self-Determination in the Information Age.' [Cited 3 May]. Available from the Hawaii Nation website: www.info.isoc.org/HMP/PAPER/230/html/paper.html.

Delgamuukw v. British Columbia, 3 S.C.R., 1010, (1997).

Department of Indian Affairs and Northern Development. 2002. *Basic Departmental Data, 2002*. Ottawa: Departmental Statistics Section, Information Quality and Research Directorate, Information Management Branch, DIAND. Catalogue No. R12–7/2002E

Dion Stout, Madeleine. 1997. 'Stopping Family Violence: Aboriginal Communities Enspirited.' In J. Rick Ponting, ed., *First Nations in Canada*. Whitby, Ont.: McGraw-Hill Ryerson.

Fiske, Joanne. 1990. 'Native Women in Reserve Politics: Strategies and Struggles.' In Roxana Ng, Gillian Walker, and Jacob Muller, ed. *Community Organization and the Canadian State*. Toronto: Garamond Press.

Fontaine, Phil, et al. 1994. 'The Dismantling of the Department of Indian Affairs and Northern Development: The Restoration of First Nations Governments in Manitoba: Framework Agreement, Workplan, Memorandum of Understanding' (7 Dec).

Guerin v. The Queen, 2 S.C.R., 335, (1984).

Haig-Brown, Celia. 1988. *Resistance and Renewal: Surviving the Indian Residential School*. Vancouver, B.C.: Arsenal Pulp Press.

Kallen, Evelyn. 1982. *Ethnicity and Human Rights in Canada*. Toronto: Gage.

LaPrairie, Carol. 1992. 'The Role of Sentencing in the Over-Representation of Aboriginal People in Correctional Institutions.' In Robert A. Silverman and Marianne O. Nielsen, ed., *Aboriginal People and Canadian Criminal Justice*. Markham, Ont.: Butterworths.

Meili, Dianne. 1991. *Those Who Know: Profiles of Alberta's Native Elders*. Edmonton: NeWest Press.

Miller, J.R. 1996. *Shingwauk's Vision: A History of Native Residential Schools*. Toronto: University of Toronto Press.

Parkin, Frank. 1979. *Marxism and Class Theory: A Bourgeois Critique*. London: Tavistock.

Penner, Keith, et al. 1983. 'Minutes of Proceedings and Evidence.' *Report of the Special Committee on Indian Self-Government in Canada 40*. Ottawa: House of Commons Standing Committee on Indian Affairs and Northern Development (12 Oct.), 20.

Ponting, J. Rick. 1991. 'An Indian Policy for Canada in the Twenty-first Century.' In C.H.W. Remie and J.-M. Lacroix, ed., *Canada on the Threshold of the 21st Century* Amsterdam: John Benjamins.

– 1997. *First Nations in Canada: Perspectives on Opportunity, Empowerment, and Self-Determination*. Whitby, Ont.: McGraw-Hill Ryerson.

R. v. Drybones, S.C.R. 282, (1970).

R. v. Marshall, S.C.R. 26014, (1999). Decision rendered 17 Sept. 1999.

R. v. Williams. Decision rendered 4 June 1998.

Royal Commission on Aboriginal Peoples. 1995. *Choosing Life: Special Report on Suicide among Aboriginal People*. Ottawa: Minister of Supply and Services Canada.

– 1996a. *Report of the Royal Commission on Aboriginal Peoples, Vol. 2: Restructuring the Relationship*. Ottawa: Minister of Supply and Services Canada.

– 1996b. *Report of the Royal Commission on Aboriginal Peoples, Vol. 4: Perspectives and Realities*. Ottawa: Minister of Supply and Services Canada.

Statistics Canada. 2003a. *Aboriginal Peoples Survey 2001 – Initial Findings: Wellbeing of the Non-reserve Aboriginal Population*. Cat. # 89-589-XIE. Ottawa: Minister of Industry, Science, and Technology.

– 2003b. 'Census of Population: Immigration, Birth Place, Birth Place of Parents, Citizenship, Ethnic Origin, for Visible Minorities and Aboriginal People.' *The Daily*. Ottawa: Minister of Industry, Science and Technology (31 Jan.).

Voyageur, Cora J. 1995. *Aboriginal Head Start Initiative Environmental Scan: Alberta*. Edmonton: Health Canada.

– 1997. 'Employment Equity and Aboriginal People in Canada.' PhD thesis, Department of Sociology, University of Alberta.
– 2000. 'First Nations Women in the Traditional Leadership Role.' Paper presented to a joint session of the annual meetings of the Canadian Indigenous/Native Studies Association and the Canadian Sociology and Anthropology Association, Edmonton, Alberta (29 May).
Weaver, Sally M. 1991. 'A New Paradigm in Canadian Indian Policy for the 1990s.' *Canadian Ethnic Studies* 22, no. 3: 8–18.

Profile of Larry Philip ('Phil') Fontaine (1944–)

Anishinabe, Consultant, Political Leader

Throughout his political career, Larry Philip Fontaine has devoted himself to helping Aboriginal peoples reclaim their traditional culture and identity. He has bucked the pressure of social conformity to bring unpleasant views to public attention and make a difference for Aboriginal peoples in Canada.

Larry Philip Fontaine was born to Jean Baptiste (J.B.) and Agnes Fontaine on 20 September 1944 on the Fort Alexander Reserve in Manitoba.[1] He is a member of the Sagkeeng Anishinabe Nation.[2] He began his education at a residential school operated by the Oblates of Mary Immaculate on the Fort Alexander Reserve.[3] He later attended high school in Winnipeg and graduated from Powerview Collegiate Institute in 1961.[4] He obtained a bachelor's degree in political studies from the University of Manitoba in 1981.[5]

Fontaine's political career began with his involvement in the Manitoba First Nations movement, which led to the formation of the Manitoba Indian Brotherhood in 1968. He remained with this organization until 1972.[6] He served as chief of the Sagkeeng First Nation from 1972 to 1976. During his tenure, the community obtained one of the first locally controlled First Nations school programs, a Child and Family Services Agency, and an Alcohol Treatment Centre.[7] Provincially, he served in various positions in the Assembly of Manitoba Chiefs and was elected as grand chief of that organization for three consecutive terms from 1989 to 1997.[8] During this time he played a key role in the demise of the Meech Lake Accord.[9]

In 1997 Fontaine moved from provincial politics to the national stage when he was elected national leader of the Assembly of First Nations (AFN). As elected leader for the more than six hundred First Nations in Canada, he advocated self-sufficiency, self-rule, self-government, and the unification of the Assembly of First Nations.[10] He also assisted Minister of Indian Affairs and Northern Development Jane Stewart in re-examining 440 specific recommendations regarding Aboriginal standards of health, housing and edu-

Larry Philip 'Phil' Fontaine. Courtesy of Canadian Press. Photographer: Fred Chartrand.

cation in the report of the Royal Commission on Aboriginal Peoples. Stewart presented *An Agenda for Actions with First Nations* in January 1998 – a plan that responded to the unique needs and circumstances of Aboriginal peoples and aimed for a government-to-government working relationship between the federal government and First Nations governments.[11]

The government also unveiled its *Statement of Reconciliation*, expressing profound regret over the past damages done to the Native population and apologizing to victims of sexual and physical abuse in the residential-school system. At the same time, it announced a $350-million fund to promote community-based healing.[12]

As national chief, Fontaine was expected to mend fences with the federal government and lead First Nations people into a mutually respectful relationship with Ottawa politicians.[13] However, his approach to working partnerships with the federal and provincial governments was viewed as 'too cozy' by some constituents. The style that helped him to defeat former AFN national chief Ovide Mercredi would become his undoing at the 2000 election when Matthew Coon Come unseated him.[14] Coon Come criticized Fontaine's comfortable relationship with the federal government.

From 2001 to 2003, Fontaine served as chief commissioner of the Indian Claims Commission, which investigates land claims and acts as mediator between the government and First Nations. He was re-elected as grand chief of the AFN at the annual general assembly in Edmonton, Alberta, in July 2003. In 1996 he received a National Aboriginal Achievement Award for his many years of community service and his contributions to the betterment of Manitoba's Aboriginal peoples.[15]

SOPHIE BONNEAU

Notes

1 Catherine Clay, 'Phil Fontaine.' In Sharon Malinowski, ed., *Notable North Americans* (New York: Gale Research 1995), 149.
2 Ibid.
3 Ibid.
4 Ibid.
5 www.pma.edmonton.ab.ca/events/releases/980813b.htm.
6 'Phil Fontaine.' In Elizabeth Lumley, ed., *Who's Who in Canada* (Toronto: University of Toronto Press 2000), 426.
7 Clay, 'Phil Fontaine,' 150.
8 Lumley, ed., *Who's Who in Canada*, 426.
9 Ibid.

10 Joanne C. Rosnau, 'Backgrounder: Profile of Phil Fontaine,' News Release (Edmonton: Provincial Museum of Alberta, 13 Aug. 1998). www.google.c/search?q=cache:urRW...ab.ca/events/releases/980813b.htm+&hl=.

11 Lynn Boyer, 'Jane Stewart and Phil Fontaine Outline Framework for Partnership between First Nations and Government of Canada,' Press Release (Winnipeg: Department of Indian Affairs and Northern Development 1998). www.ainc-inac.gc.ca/nr/prs/j-a1998/jan15.html.

12 Ibid.

13 Marco Kane, 'Working with the System Didn't Work for Him,' *First Nations Drum* (fall 2000). www.firstnationsdrum.com/fall2000/pol_Fontaine.htm.

14 Ibid.

15 www.ainc-inac.gc.ca/ks/english/3109_e.tml.